Media:

Communication & Production

Advanced

LONGMAN

Introduction

This book will support you in your work towards the Advanced Level GNVQ in Media: Communication & Production.

It is divided into eight units, each of which covers one of the eight mandatory units of your GNVQ.

Each unit is made up of sections which cover the requirements of the elements, through a combination of information and activities with real-life case studies, examples of current media practice, and assignments. The units also contain practical guidance on the wide range of skills you will find useful for successful work on Media: Communication & Production.

The activities are self-contained tasks which are designed for you to test your knowledge and understanding, take part in a rôle play or group discussion or carry out further investigation.

The assignments are larger research-type activities for investigation which clearly match the assessment requirements, and provide opportunities for collecting work for assessment.

You will find the glossary of terms used in the mandatory units for Intermediate and Advanced Media: Communication & Production GNVQ after the study units at the back of the book. In addition, there is a glossary at the end of each unit for media-related terms used in that unit. These glossaries contain brief explanations of these key terms. You will find both of these glossaries invaluable for quick reference and revision. Terms that are in the glossary are in a **bold** typeface the first time they appear in the text in that unit.

There are two core texts in the Longman Media: Communication & Production series – one for Intermediate Level, and one for Advanced Level GNVQ.

Investigating the content of media products

G N V Q

Contents

LONGMAN

Introduction

Increasingly, the media are becoming central to the way we live; to how we are informed, educated and entertained and to the way we perceive, understand and experience every aspect of our world. In the past, people learnt about their world through personal contact but we have grown up with, and been socialised to a large extent by, mass media content. Radio, television, cinema, newspapers and magazines are all part of our daily lives. However, we are not taught how to interpret the information provided. As the media are so influential it is essential that we train ourselves to examine media content critically and analytically. We will then be thinking, questioning audiences, actively participating in a multimedia world, and in future we may become informed and original media producers.

This unit will help you to develop the critical skills for carrying out this analysis of the media, in terms of style, structure, content, author intent and possible interpretation. The unit discusses issues that will be relevant to the other units of your course. The first section of this unit deals with the variety of mass media content available. You will be analysing the construction and language of media products, looking at them as texts, that is, texts that are 'read' by audiences, and can be understood as the products of authors and ultimately of cultures and societies. You will consider media content as a form of communication, examining content structure, the component parts of a text, the codes, conventions and languages used and the relationships between texts in different media such as newspapers and radio.

You will become familiar with four main critical areas as you complete the unit. The concepts and tools that you should acquire are organised under the four headings of *media texts*, *representation*, *genre* and *narrative structures*. Each of these areas corresponds to elements in the Advanced Level Unit 1, and is constructed around the key terms central to our understanding of media products. You will develop a thorough knowledge and understanding of media content. This will enable you to analyse the content of a variety of media products that you encounter during this qualification, both as media producers and as media audiences. You will then be able to relate your own work to that of media professionals both past and present. You will be able to apply the insights and skills gained here to your own subsequent work in the production units.

1 Analysing media texts

What are media texts?

A media text can be seen as the product of an individual or group of people working for a commercial or private organisation or as individual citizens. They produce products for an **audience** which may be an individual or a group (large or small, local, national or international). In a world of multimedia and widening access media texts are no longer the sole preserve of companies or large organisations. Indeed, increasing amounts of media texts are produced by individuals or small groups such as charities, retail outlets, employers as well as schools and colleges involved in media courses.

The text itself can comprise audio, visual, print or graphic material. These can be used singly or combined in any appropriate medium. The medium is the means by which information is transferred from a producer to an audience. The mass media include television, film, radio, books, newspapers and magazines. A text can range in size from a short column in a newspaper to a series of films such as the James Bond series.

Texts and meaning

These two areas are described as the **signifying systems** and are discussed in more detail later in the section.

Meaning is produced through the *elements* of media texts. These are the significant parts of the entire text and can be divided into two areas.

- *The technical elements*: sound, lighting, editing, colour, camera movement, framing, cropping, drawing/illustrations.
- *The symbolic elements*: performance, setting, costume, style, music, font.

All these elements combine to create the meaning of the text. It is through the audience recognising the meaning of these significant elements that the media text becomes a shared language, so that communication is achieved.

The elements of media texts

The arrangement and relationship of the significant elements in media texts are crucial to the communication process. On the following pages there is an examination of the key elements of print, audio and moving image. It is important to remember that the producers of these products have specific intentions. The elements that we are examining have been used selectively to create meaning and transmit it to an audience.

The activity that follows will ask you to recognise these elements and apply them to specific texts, so be sure that you clearly understand the relationships involved within particular media.

Key elements of print
Visual – newspapers, magazines, leaflets and books.

Element	Description	Use in products	Examples	Problems
Words and numbers	Essential part of overall format.	Means of conveying information.	All communication media with written contents.	Intrinsic complexity of language, can act as barrier to universal understanding.
Font or type-face and size	The look of the printed matter that you are reading.	To convey a feeling or an identification through the particular use of styles.	Newspaper banners or headlines, book titles.	Too much variation in font and in size can confuse and even disorientate the reader.
Heading or masthead	The words at the top of the front page. In large bold letters, using a particular font as a trademark.	Instantly identifies products and differentiates between them.	Magazine and newspaper names, book titles and company names on published information.	Similarity in design of mastheads can lead to difficulty in distinguishing between products.
Columns	Size and shape, positioning on page. Emphasis within column and graphics included in column.	Construct page and delineate information in readable format. To create emphasis on lead stories.	Front page stories might take all the columns. Stories on inside pages may require fewer columns.	The column layout of adjacent stories may cause confusion for the reader.
Colour	The words in printed matter are usually in black. Other elements can be in colour.	Draws attention, adds emphasis, and appeals to audience. Also adds realism to material.	Advertisements, banners, photos, maps, illustrations, some words and backgrounds.	Appeal of colour can dominate the senses, and thus divert the reader's attention.
Photographs, cartoons and illustrations	The visual image accompanying stories.	To catch the readers, eye. To illustrate and bring to life stories. To add realism.	Book covers, magazine and newspaper articles. Advertisements. Photo stories.	Detract from the written word. Can become a substitute for the written word.
Captions	Words associated with visual image providing information.	'Anchors' visual image to story.	Newspapers, magazine, and book photographs and illustrations.	They direct the opinion of the reader to a preferred interpretation of the visual image.

The way that all these elements are arranged in a newspaper is called the **layout**. The layout is important to the way that all the elements relate to each other.

Key elements of audio
Audio – radio (talk and music).

Element	Description	Use in products	Examples	Problems
Words	Particular sounds that form and are recognisable as spoken words.	To construct information in structured form.	News, interviews, drama, phone-ins, links quizzes and announcements.	The meaning of words can be misinterpreted and misunderstood.
Music	Tone, rhythm and pitch created by voices and instruments.	Forms content of programmes, frames programmes and is part of drama.	Songs, instrumentals, background music, mood music in drama.	Musical choice can be subjective and personal.
Sounds	Ambient noise/wild sounds. Sound effects. Silence can also be important.	To give the audience a sense of place, or to indicate some action or generate tension.	Background noise from street or room. Sound effects of gunfire or horse's hooves.	Can detract from and interrupt flow of programme or item.

Element	Description	Use in products	Examples	Problems
Voice	Tone, accent, speed, and emotion in delivery. The mode of address to the listener.	Gives the audience information about the person and type of programme.	The reading of the news or the football results, is different from the DJ, comic or actor.	Monotone delivery can be tedious and will soon lose an audience.
Texts or Scripts	Organisation of words and music. Timing and structure. Level or complexity of content.	To organise running order. To maintain timing of programme.	Documentaries plays or dramas. News, sports and most other radio shows.	Scripts have to be written and delivered as if they are not being read.
Jingles	Short music or voice-over track.	Framing or boundary mechanisms. To introduce sections or features.	Station identification. Introduce news, traffic or weather, quizzes, or special features.	Can disrupt flow of programmes, and detract from content.
Dialogue	Conversations and discussions within programmes.	To inform and to entertain in a familiar manner.	Current affairs programmes. Chat shows and phone-ins.	Unscripted nature, can cause problems with timing and control over content.

Key elements of moving image
Audio/Visual – television, film and video.

Element	Description	Use in products	Examples	Problems
Photography	The means of recording an image through the capturing of light.	To visually relay an image, conveying particular meanings through various styles.	Dark and light. Studio and location. Realist, experimental/ surrealist.	Power of the image can dominate the medium at the cost of all other techniques.
Sound	Vocal, instrumental, synthetic and other noises on soundtrack.	To convey narrative, realism, atmosphere, and dramatic mood and emphasis.	Speech, dialogue, music, sound effects. Both on screen and off screen.	Speech has to be clear to be understood. Does not reproduce sound as the ear hears it.
Lighting	The illumination by artificial or natural sources of people, objects and scenes.	To improve the quality of the image, and to achieve dramatic and and artistic effects.	High-key, low-key. Set light, actor light, back light, fill light, and limbo lighting.	The temptation to overlight can make even outdoor shots look unnatural.
Framing	Composition of images within a shot.	To arrange in terms of significance the various component parts of a shot.	Placing of objects or subjects in centre of foreground, in doorway, or by window.	The inclusion of too much information within the frame can confuse viewer.
Camera angles	The placement of the camera in relation to subject or object.	To affect the viewers response to the image. Adds two-dimentionality.	Eye level shot. Low-angle, high-angle, oblique angle, and Dutch angle.	Too many angle shots within a scene will lessen seamless nature, unless this is desired.
Shots	The basic unit of film; from edit to edit. Might include camera movement and focus.	The duration of a shot gives a sense of time. Types of shot add variety.	Establishing shot, long shot, medium shot, close-up. Tracking shot, crane shot, pan and tilt.	The long shot and long take dominate film. The medium shot and short take dominate TV.
Colour	The hue, tone or tint of the image. Brightness or saturation.	For realism, or expression. Conveys atmosphere, under-scores theme.	Warm colours, yellow and orange; cold, blue and green. Sepia to depict the past.	Film on the whole reproduces colours in the real world better than video.

It is useful at this point to consider the relationship between media producer and audience in terms of an encoder and a decoder. That is, the media text is encoded or given a specific meaning by the producer, the meaning is then decoded or deciphered by the audience. The interesting thing about this relationship (of which you will learn more at the end of this section and in Study Unit 6), is that the audience does not always decode the meaning of the text in the same way that it was encoded.

Activity

Using the tables as a guide, write two reports, one on a print/ graphics medium and one on an audio-visual medium, explaining how their elements operate in the particular medium and how they differ between media. Consider these in the light of the non-fiction and fiction products of each medium you have chosen.

Anchorage

The term *anchorage* means the way in which the organisation of elements in a text can determine the meaning of the text. For instance, a caption under a photograph serves to underline or reinforce the meaning of the image. An image can be ambiguous in its meaning but written text directs interpretation towards the meaning intended by the producer. This intended meaning is 'anchored' in the audience's minds.

Activity

Think about the relationship between the captions and images below, and consider how their juxtaposition produces meaning, and how altering their arrangement changes the meaning of the pictures.

Fig. 1.1

'long to reign over us'

'military power takes control'

'workout to build more muscle'

'naughty but nice'

'your greatest fantasy realised'

Anchorage is a concept that can also be usefully applied to headline and sub-headline, or two related images. Close-ups in moving image production can anchor meaning by eliminating alternatives. Focusing on a particular object or person may determine a scene's meaning.

Roland Barthes (1977) is particularly concerned with the way in which anchorage narrows the choice of meaning for the reader. For him anchorage 'is the most frequent function of the linguistic message' and often occurs in press photography and advertising. Here meanings are *fixed* by the juxtaposition of images and captions. They are *ideological*, in that they restrict the meaning of the image, directing them to interpret the image in ways which are socially or culturally pre-determined. For example, an advertisement for cars showing glamorous-looking people driving the advertised brand anchors the relationship between 'success' and car ownership. This is part of western cultural ideology; in other cultures the same images might be interpreted differently, perhaps as indicating decadence or corruption.

Ideology is the body of ideas, often political and/or economic, which determines a person or society's outlook and interpretation of the world around them.

Analysing meaning

The concepts associated with **semiotics** and **semiology** are very influential ways of understanding and analysing media texts and other cultural products of society. These concepts will enable us to discover how meanings in texts are conveyed to, and understood by, audiences.

Semiology is the study of signs and signals; the theory of sign-systems in language is called semiotics.

Linguistics is the scientific study of language.

The basis of semiotics is in linguistics. For semioticians, all forms of communication are kinds of language. In the same way that language is made up of vocabulary, grammar and syntax, all forms of communication have component parts with rules and conventions covering their use. In this sense then, the study of language includes not only written and spoken language but all sounds and images used to communicate.

The semiotic model is a *structural* one concerned with relationships. It has three main areas: first, the sign; second, the codes into which signs are organised, and thirdly the culture in which these signs and codes operate. Semiotic models concentrate on the text of the message. Semiotic insights have led to an interest in the rôle of the audience, who are actively interpreting the message according to their own attitudes and experience.

One of the best ways of understanding the development of these concepts is to look at the approaches of their originators.

The work of Saussure and Peirce

Ferdinand de Saussure first analysed the life of signs within society in his book *Course in General Linguistics*, published in 1916. The term semiotics was coined by Charles S. Peirce who, although working at the same time as Saussure, only became widely known from the 1930s onwards. For both of them the sign is the key component, that is, the smallest unit of meaning.

It was not until the 1960s that the work of Saussure and Peirce began to be developed and applied to different sign systems, and especially to the mass media.

The sign has three main characteristics.
- It must have a physical form, like these words, or a photograph.
- It stands for, or refers to, something other than itself.
- There is a shared agreement within a culture or society that it is a sign.

Structural models used in semiological analysis

Saussure's model

Fig. 1.2
A drawing of an oak tree

Fig. 1.3
A photograph of an oak tree

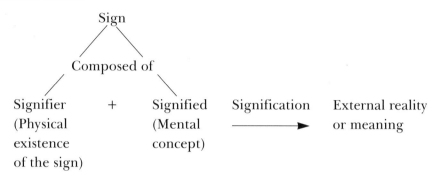

An example of this might be a tree. The signifier can be the word TREE, a drawing or a photograph.

The signified is the image of a t-r-e-e that you now have in your mind. This may be different from the oak tree pictured; depending on your own cultural background you may see a pine, or an acacia tree.

Signification is the relationship between what is in your mind and the real t-r-e-e that you may see out of the window.

How signs work

Saussure's model focuses on how signs convey their meaning and how they relate to each other. For Saussure, the sign is a physical object which is made up of two parts.

1 The signifier or sound-image: i.e., the physical object or material form of the sign's image as we perceive it. This might be a printed word, the sound of a voice, or an image. The signifier is influenced strongly by culture.

2 The signified or concept: that is, the mental idea to which the sign refers. This concept need not have a direct relationship to the signifier but will have been shaped and agreed by people of the same culture. For example, in Britain a bouquet of red roses (the *signifier*) sent by a man to a woman *signifies* that he loves her. There is no direct relationship between roses as objects and love (the signified) as a concept.

The process of signification is the relationship between the sign and external reality. As we shall see, in Peirce's model there is a direct relationship between the sign and this external reality or object as he called it. For Saussure this relationship is less important than those between the signifier and signified.

Peirce's model

Peirce places great emphasis on the sign's relationship to the consumer. In this model the *interpretant* is the mental concept produced in the audience's mind upon seeing the sign, which is then interpreted in terms of each person's experiences. The object in this model is simply what the sign refers to. If you think about a t-r-e-e again, then the sign is the word

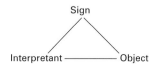

TREE, or a picture, or a photograph, or the sound of a voice saying TREE. The object is the real t-r-e-e itself, and the interpretant is your mental picture of a tree, your concept of t-r-e-e-ness. The three factors in Peirce's model can only be understood in relation to each other.

The uses of signs

It is important to remember that many signs do not have significations, simply because they refer to things that do not actually exist, be they mythical creatures or science fiction inventions. The unicorn or griffin are good examples of this, as indeed are starships, and time travel. In sentence construction conjunctions such as 'and' may be seen as signs, but they do not refer to an external reality.

Signs can also be arbitrary, for instance, using 'red' to express the idea 'danger', or 'stop' in a traffic light code. In a political context, red could mean the Labour Party. Within one society or culture there is agreement about the meaning of such codes or signs.

Social convention: something which is generally accepted or understood within a society, from long usage.

Activity

Below are a series of signs. Identify the types of sign that they are, and consider the physical form that they take (on the page and in reality), and the things that they refer to. Also think about how the signs are used and by whom.

Structuralism and semiotics

The basis of structuralism is an analysis of the systems, structures and relationships within a given culture or society. Structuralists are particularly interested in the governing rules of society that inform and order the way the world appears to us.

Structuralist analysis owes a debt to the nineteenth century work of Karl Marx and Sigmund Freud with their interest in the 'deep structures' of society. For Marx it was economics that governed society, for Freud it was the unconscious or the subconscious.

Fig 1.4

Denotation and connotation

Under the structuralist banner, two French theorists influenced the development of semiotic analysis. The first was an anthropologist, Claude Lévi-Strauss, who studied tribal societies and saw how they developed a series of mythologies about themselves, which served to secure unity among the tribe. The second theorist, Roland Barthes, developed the ideas of Saussure beyond the linguistic. Barthes recognised two orders of signification, **denotation** and **connotation**, which work on two levels, an 'obvious' *denotive level* and a hidden or 'deep' *connotive level*. Put simply, denotation is the literal meaning of something, what it actually is; red, for instance, on the denotive level, is simply a colour. Connotation on the other hand, is the level of meaning; red can mean (connote) danger, it can mean stop, or it can indicate a political party.

The signifier 'car' signifies a vehicle: the signifier may look like a Rolls Royce or a Skoda, that is immaterial, the signification produced is of a c-a-r, a vehicle – nothing more, nothing less.

A low angle shot of a person can connote power and strength. Different types of faces carry different connotations, indeed, the 'look' of people is the basis of stereotype, as we shall see in the next element. The tone of a person's voice can also connote different meanings even when saying the same sentence.

- Denotation is the level at which Saussure worked. This *order of signification* as Barthes calls it, is the obvious, literal or depicted level, it is what can be said to be given by the medium before the audience interprets it. At this point what is given (according to Barthes) is neutral, objective and value-free.
- Connotation is a second order of signification, and is defined historically, culturally and ideologically. This is the more subjective level, where interpretations are made either associated with the given text, or with personal emotive and cultural values and assumptions. On this level the signifier c-a-r type Rolls Royce contains powerful meanings in that it can signify wealth, power, prestige, etc.

Activity

Take a look at the car adverts reproduced here. Consider the connoted meanings that emerge from the images used.

It is worthwhile considering at length the relationship between denotation and connotation. Everything we look at can have connotations; each connotation can provoke and reveal further connotations.

Fig 1.5
Advertisements for two cars

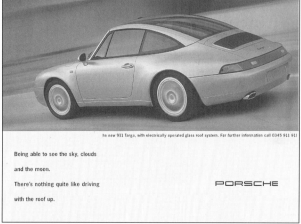

Myths in modern societies

Myth is another second order of signification – a 'deeper' order than denotation. Myths are a culture's way of thinking about and collectively understanding the world. They might be about ideas of what is British, what it is to be a woman or a man, about the idyllic countryside or about other nationalities, for instance. Myths are agreed cultural products that have over time become taken for granted and appear natural and inevitable.

Ideology

The two second orders of signification, connotation and myth, can ultimately be combined into a third order of signification: ideology. *Ideology* here refers to systems of beliefs held by a society that show themselves through signs or codes. These systems are part of how a society organises itself, and the concepts used to perpetuate the status quo.

Ideology in the media does not take the form of obvious or direct statements, its messages and meanings lie in the very structure of media products, the way they speak to us and their narrative form.

Semiotic analysis enables us to consider the rules and 'deep' structures of meanings that lie behind the surface (or denotive) level of communication. We can examine these structures in relation to our cultural setting, in order to illuminate the relationships between media products and society.

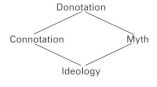

Activity

Assemble a number of advertisements drawn from television, commercial radio or magazines, and examine the levels of denotation, connotation, myth and ideology. Consider how they work to persuade you to buy the product or products. In particular consider what myths or ideologies they are appealing to.

There are a number of broad guidelines which are useful to this sort of advertising analysis.

- Denotation – what are the actual images used (or referred to in radio)? Are they of cars, people, specific objects? These can simply be identified at this level, as they form the core of the advertisement.
- Connotation – what are the meanings being developed? Do they revolve around wealth, prestige or sexuality? Or with specific gender rôles such as mother, father? This is the level at which advertisements work, by connoting value and meaning to objects and tasks.
- Myth – what culturally agreed ideas are the advertisements referring to? These might be about nationality, the countryside, healthy eating or gender. Myths will be the same wherever they occur in advertisements.
- Ideologies – what are the specific ideas that are developed or confirmed by the advertisement? These may be sexist, racist, nationalistic, or purely capitalist. Ideologies can be discerned in all adverts, since to

some degree they are part of capitalism and are thus often used to sell you something. For this purpose they generally confirm the social arrangement of society.

Media codes and conventions

Single signs can communicate but often signs rely upon their relationships to each other to communicate a given meaning. They often communicate best when organised into signifying systems called codes. A code results from linking the *expression plane* (i.e. sound, gesture, image, etc.), with the *plane of content* (meanings, ideas, thoughts, concepts, etc.). In traffic lights, a simple code results from the linking of the expression plane: red light, amber light, green light, with the content plane: stop, get ready, go. The discrete portions of the expression/content plane together form the sign: signifier – green light, signified – go.

Looking at particular **media codes** will enable you to discover the way in which technical styles operate and relate to wider cultural codes. First, you will consider how media codes and **conventions** are constructed. Codes and conventions generate 'deep' or *connotive* meanings, ones that are not apparent. Codes and conventions relate to specific historic periods and cultures, they make use of ideas, icons or images, different people or social variables (such as age, gender, race, class). A shared knowledge of these cultural codes is essential for the message to be understood.

Media codes govern the creation of media content and the relationship between the elements of media products. They only work if the audience recognise them and their significance. The process of being *socialised* into the media means that we all know most of the media codes.

Much popular media production follows codes or formulas, for example, the horror film or the television situation comedy. Newspapers also have codes such as the rules that define the structure of headlines or of the whole paper with its stories, articles, photographs, etc. Deciphering codes is a very useful way of examining technical and symbolic construction. For instance, in moving image construction, the point-of-view shot allows us to see the world from the hero's perspective, combined with camera movement, set construction and the placing of actors which all have the effect of getting us to empathise with the central character. In newspaper writing, the use of semi-colloquial English in newspapers such as the *Sun* or the *Star* combined with articles and photographs of a sexual nature are all designed to appeal to working class male readers. Magazines like MIZZ are constructed and coded for adolescent female consumption.

Socialisation is the process by which a child becomes aware of society and his/her rôle within it.

Conventions

Media conventions, or the established ways of doing things, often appear as common sense because they are so familiar. Conventions such as the placing of the masthead of a paper at the top of the front page, appear

Fig 1.6
Poster advertising the
film *Goldeneye*

It is at the level of the interplay
of elements, codes and
conventions that the media
producer creates original and
exciting material that stimulates
the audience.

functional since it is a convention of western reading that we start at the top left and read across the page. TV news readers sit at a desk and address the camera which views them from a mid-shot: this is a convention.

Codes and conventions are often discussed together, and have overlaps in the construction and analysis of media products. A knowledge of how codes and conventions work will be essential to an analysis of genre products, covered in Section 3. For the moment it is important to be able to analyse how the elements or the significant parts of the whole text, discussed above, fit together into codes and conventions. For instance, study the *Goldeneye* poster, and consider how the combination of elements, the style of letters, the arrangement of images, the icon of the star all combine to give coded messages about the film. The *Goldeneye* poster contains many interesting elements. The typeface (and in the original, the colour) of the title looks like gold bars in the shape of letters. The prominent 007 icon is familiar to the audience. The two central female characters are presented to convey excitement, fantasy and seductiveness. The image montage on the left of the poster indicates the content of the film and generates a question as to the key enigma of the film. The body language of Bond, the positioning at the front of the graphics, and the image of Bond himself (in a traditional stance) shows him to be confident and defiant, underlining the absolute nature of the slogan: 'No fears. No limits. No substitutes'. The slogan anchors the meaning of the images, as Bond is also pictured running leaving behind him a trail of destruction. The combined effect of all these elements is to show that the product is exciting, stylish, and sexy; also that we should associate it with other James Bond films that we have seen.

Checklist of codes and conventions

This checklist (continued on the next page) provides a few examples of codes and conventions in order to illustrate their practical use.

Technical
- Microphone – a reporter holding a microphone talking to camera is one of the *codes* of news or 'live' broadcasting.
- Camera lens – the zoom lens has become standard for the recording of sporting events. The variable focal length allows a moving object to be followed whilst remaining in focus. The *convention* that the ball is always followed in ball games is now achievable with the zoom lens.
- Filters – the use of a sepia filter is often a *code* for the past or old film footage.
- Lights – illuminating a set or location can draw particular elements to the audience's attention. Electronic News Gathering (ENG) lights throw a very bright light straight at the subject; this is now a *convention* of live news coverage.
- Paper – *conventions* of paper include the use of glossy paper for magazines. The glossy paper is a *code* for the quality of the product.
- Computer software – the instructions to the user are encoded in *icons* which are drawn to a large extent from the print medium, and derive their meaning from the same source.

Audio-visual style
- Use of music – it is a *convention* to have a signature tune to introduce all programmes. Orchestral string music is used as a *code* for romance.
- Lighting – there are *conventions* for the use of lighting. High-key lighting is a *code* used in studio-based productions such as magazine programmes or quiz shows. Low-key lighting in film noir is a *code* communicating that a hidden world lies behind the shadows, in the background.
- Camera work – light-weight, hand-held cameras, produce a shaky image, which has become a *convention* of war coverage. The shaking image is a *code* for danger.
- Acting – it is a *convention* of drama acting that the actor does not acknowledge the existence of the camera and thus of the audience.

- Drawings have become a *convention* of law court reporting, since cameras are not often allowed in British law courts.

Written style
- Slogan – by *convention* slogans often contain three elements. The *Goldeneye* poster, for instance, contains the slogan 'No limits. No fears. No substitutes'.
- Copy – by *convention* news copy is written in a shortened style of English. It is now a *code* that this 'news-speak' is important and new information.
- Typeface – different typefaces may serve as codes for different times or places, such as 𝔬𝔩𝔡 𝔈𝔫𝔤𝔩𝔞𝔫𝔡, **Victorian Britain** or even **Hollywood**.
- Use of graphics – the *convention* of a cartoon in a newspaper is that it is a humorous look at a topical subject.

Cultural
- Historical periods – kaftans or The Beatles are historical codes for the 1960s, castles for the medieval period, cowboys for the old west.
- Iconography – icons such as the Statue of Liberty or the Golden Gate Bridge are codes for America.
- Politics – the use of the colour blue is a code for the Conservative Party.
- People – Winston Churchill making his famous V sign is a code for Britain's victory in the Second World War.
- Clothing – different youth cultures adopt different styles of dress as identity codes.
- Non-verbal communication – Winston Churchill's V sign may have a completely different coded meaning when made by you or me or an actor in a play.

News-speak emerged in the early years of newspapers, when information was sent by telegraph: the fewer words the reporter used, the cheaper the message.

This checklist can now form part of the forthcoming activity. However, bear in mind that the checklist is only a starting point: you will be able to identify many more codes and conventions.

Activity

Taking the codes and conventions of two separate media, for example television news or radio phone-ins, draw up a list of their uses and meanings in the programmes' context.

Reading and decoding texts

Activity

Select a media text, a newspaper or a news programme for instance, and write down your reaction to it. Do you accept it all as true? Do you disagree with parts of it? Do you think any part of it is unacceptable? Save your thoughts until the end of this section.

Codes and conventions are not always able to communicate their hidden message or meaning. People bring different understandings of codes to media messages. This different understanding may originate in cultural or age differences. For people from the Far East white is the colour of mourning, so they could misread the coded message of a 'white' wedding.

Aberrant decoding

Aberrant decoding is decoding that departs from what the encoders – the makers of the communication – expected.

In such cases the audience is not decoding the message in the same way that it was encoded. Italian semiologist Umberto Eco recognises the possibility of **aberrant decoding** because of what he sees as the wide social gap between producers/encoders and receivers/decoders. This difference may be in terms of class, educational background or ethnicity, for instance.

This approach emphasises the act of 'reading' a text. The meaning within a media text is open to a number of potential interpretations. Media messages are 'polysemic', that is, they are capable of different interpretations depending on the audiences who are 'decoding' each message. Indeed, the audience can be seen as being in a sense as creative as the author, since they both bring to the text their own use of codes to create meaning.

Show a small number of different media texts to a variety of people, gauge their reactions to and understanding of each piece. How did these vary according to the different social variables between the people you chose to talk to?

Social variables include gender, race, age and social class.

The influence of different *social variables* on people's reading of the texts will depend on the type of text that you showed them. If it was a violent text, did different genders or age groups react differently to it?

David Morley's analysis of *Nationwide*

In 1980 David Morley analysed the television magazine programme *Nationwide* to find out how different social groups read media messages. He examined two *Nationwide* programmes and conducted group discussions with 29 sets of people. He found that the reactions of people varied according to age, sex, class and racial makeup and that encoded messages could be decoded in three ways.

- Firstly, the *dominant reading*. This was the reading given by managers, engineers and apprentices. It emphasises the reading in which the dominant values of society as portrayed by the programme were accepted as a true representation of the world.
- Secondly, the *negotiated reading*. Here, people such as teachers and university students accepted some messages contained within the programme but modified or changed their interpretation of some stories, saw some as only being partially true and rejected others as being untrue.
- Thirdly, the *oppositional reading*. Some groups of people opposed the view of the world portrayed, or found it completely irrelevant to their lives.

According to Morley, the degree of opposition to the programmes' content relates directly to the viewers' social situations. The viewers' social circumstances will determine their reaction to media ideology.

Preferred meanings

There is a tension between the ideologically encoded text and the audience's decoding of it. The notion of a preferred reading is important in understanding this conflict. The media 'prefer' or offer a set of meanings, which they 'anchor' in their content. These meanings work ideologically to maintain the status quo, as discussed earlier. For example, a preferred reading of *Goldeneye* would fit easily into the dominant ideology, as it affirms the values of western male-dominated capitalism. A large number of ideologies overlap to create the Bond world; masculinity, femininity, west, east, individualism, technology, capitalism, etc.

However, these meanings cannot be imposed, only preferred. As Morley showed, some members of the audience will pick up this preferred reading and accept it, some will negotiate their own version of it, whilst others will recognise the dominant meanings and oppose them.

Reading a text is a negotiation between the text and the audience. This process means that the reader is an active maker of meanings from the text, not a passive recipient of pre-packaged meanings.

Activity

Now return to your own reading of the media products that you selected in the first activity in this section. Reflecting on this, consider how critically you read the products? Try to identify in yourself the social variables that may have affected the way you read them. With this in mind, and what you have learnt from this section, carry out further readings of a variety of media texts and examine why you decode them in the way you do.

Assignment

You have been asked to produce a short public information campaign on drugs, alcohol, AIDS, or another area of health concern. Using your knowledge of the various media languages and the relationship between text and image, create a campaign that would be carried in at least two different media. You can construct two different campaigns, one for each medium (one print and one audio-visual), or a campaign that cuts across the media. The campaign should have a logo, central images and a catch-phrase or slogan. Write a report about constructing the campaign and pay particular attention to your use of elements and how they work together to produce meaning in the operation of codes. Make extensive notes on each. Remember also to consider the rôle of anchorage, particularly in your use of a logo. Finally, consider within this report how the images, etc. that you use might be 'read' not just by your target audience, but by other people who might come across the campaign.

# Investigating representation

What is representation?

In media studies, the term representation refers to the way that people are portrayed in the media. That is, how are real people, situations, organisations and even objects re-presented to us via the mass media? Representation is one of the most important areas of consideration for media producers: it is at the heart of story-telling. However, representation is also central to your work as media analysts. How do the media present social concerns, how do they represent society to itself and what do they communicate to members of society?

A great deal of the information that we have about the world comes to us secondhand through the media. Audiences do not simply use the media as a form of recreation, they also learn from it, or have their attitudes and opinions reinforced or challenged. The media provide us with an endless stream of images and ideas about ourselves and other people. Representation occurs in both non-fiction and fiction products, although it is most often associated with drama productions.

There are many ways of categorising both the people and issues represented by the media, and the types of representation.

- People: gender, race, age, sexuality, class.
- Social groups: disabled, religious, family, occupational, class/power, rich/poor, terrorists/freedom fighters.
- Societies and cultures: nations, regions, continents, developed countries/developing countries.
- Ideas: religious (Christian, Muslim, Hindu, Buddhist), philosophical (capitalist, socialist, fundamentalist), political (Republican, Labour).
- Social issues: crime, health, unemployment, community care, education.
- Events: elections, riots, royal weddings, strikes, wars, sports.

As audiences and media producers you must constantly be aware of the idea of 'normality' that the media are portraying. As indicated in Section 1, the media are not neutral windows on the world, they actively construct their messages and products. To think in terms of representation forces us to question the '*mediation of reality*' provided for us by the mass media.

'Mediation' is the act of passing on information from source to receiver. The way this is done will influence how the message is understood. The same information could be mediated in different ways to give different 'readings'.

Activity

Take a sample of a day's newspapers and after removing all the photographs and their captions, consider the various images of society that emerge by grouping the pictures together under the above categories. Use the headings and subheadings to show the

flow of ideas. What picture of the world emerges as you group them together and how accurate do you think it is? You might also separate the views of the different national and local papers. Do they each give different representations of the world?

The influence of media representations

The concept of representation has to be thought of in terms of reality being re-presented to the audience through the media. Images and depictions of individuals, groups, places, ideas and objects are all constructions, they are not neutral but are the result of the decisions made, and the construction processes employed, by the media. These are crucially influenced by society and culture. Attitudes formed by society are shared by producers and audiences alike. In order to communicate their meaning, media producers use familiar representations, assuming knowledge and recognition by the audience. In this way certain representations are perpetuated and indeed reinforced.

Analysing representations

The study of representation draws upon the concepts used in media analysis and applies them to specific examples drawn from media texts. Representations are signs with their own connoted (see Section 1) or second level 'deep' meanings, often working on the levels of myth and ideology. The representation can be seen as the *concrete* form of the *abstract concept* of ideology. The representation of women in advertisements is a good example of this. An advertiser who wishes to sell a 'can of something' to the perceived target audience of 'housewives' wants women to recognise themselves and their rôle in the family and also in society. Thus women are encouraged not only to buy the product, which is portrayed as being good for the family, but also to identify with the representation of a 'good mother'. The advertiser is promising not only the product but also a certain representation of womanhood and motherhood; this representation has an ideological basis.

   Representations evolve and change over time. Indeed it is the job of a good and inventive media producer to challenge the accepted norms of representation and try to redefine them. *Basic Instinct* (1992) is a recent film that attempts to challenge stereotypical images of women. In particular, the central character's sexual aggressiveness is counter to the representation of women in many media products as a sexual object, to be won by the lead man as well as by the audience. *Basic Instinct* can be read as positioning a woman as the subject of the story rather than the object.

The image of a male youth as 'mugger' has been developed by the actions of state institutions (police, probation service, politicians, social services, etc.), and is perpetuated and reinforced by television drama and news reports. These images influence both the way other people behave towards young men and the self-image held by these youths.

Concrete and abstract are oppositional terms. Concrete means actual, solid, real whereas abstract means a mental concept.

It is worthwhile to remember that media content and images do not have a uniform effect on the audience. As you saw in the last section, audience reading or decoding can vary from one audience member to another.

Activity

In a small group, each of you will draw a picture or take a photograph of first, yourself, then of how you see each other member of the group in turn. Then as a group examine how each of you has been represented by yourself and by the others. Examine the extent to which these representations conflict with your own image of yourself and others.

How issues are represented

The representation of issues in the media raises many considerations that particularly concern media *producers*, such as legal and ethical questions. The analysis of representation includes a consideration of the social and political implications of media portrayals.

Media 'laws'

It is useful here to separate legal considerations affecting media production into two areas.

Firstly, there are those laws of the land, which directly or indirectly impinge on production practices. These are mainly laws covering overt bias against social groups or organisations in British media products.

- The Broadcasting Act (1990) states that the Independent Television Commission (ITC) should do all that it can to ensure that nothing is included in programmes which offends against good taste or decency, or is likely to encourage or incite crime, or lead to public disorder, or be offensive to public feeling.
- The Race Relations Act (1976) makes it an offence to publish threatening, abusive or insulting material against ethnic and racial groups or to discriminate in the work place. The Sex Discrimination Act (1986) makes it illegal to discriminate on the grounds of sex.
- Fairness in the representation of political parties in the run up to general elections, and coverage of political party conferences, is ensured by the Representation of the People Act (1983).
- The law of libel, or defamation, is concerned with protecting the reputation of the individual from unjustified attack.
- The Obscene Publications Act (1959 & 1964) forbids the publication of material likely to deprave and corrupt. An article is said to be obscene if 'ordinary people would be shocked or disgusted by the material'.
- The Public Order Act of 1986 makes it an offence to publish threatening, abusive or insulting material relating to race, nationality, citizenship, ethnic or national origins.

Secondly, there are voluntary codes of practice drawn up by bodies representing the media themselves. These are guidelines designed to ensure that the organisations' employees stay well within the law, thus avoiding legal action. For example, the broadcasters' rule that 'due impartiality' be shown in news and current affairs programming.

'Impartiality' means that broadcasters do not take sides on political or social issues. This is often disputed!

Below is a copy of part of the Independent Television Commission Programme Code, which illustrates some of the concerns over representation and the law.

Section 1.1 General Requirements
Section 6(1) (a) of the Broadcasting Act 1990 requires that the ITC does all it can to secure that every licensed service includes nothing in its programmes which offends against good taste or decency or is likely to encourage or incite to crime or lead to disorder or be offensive to public feeling...

Section 1,4 Bad Taste in Humour
1.4 (i) Jokes about personal disability
The roots of laughter are often found in deviation from the normal and familiar. But there is a danger of offence in the use of humour based on physical and mental disability. Even where no malice is present such jokes can all too easily, and plausibly, appear to be exploitation or humiliation for the purposes of entertainment. This not only hurts those most directly concerned; it can and does repel many viewers. The use of such jokes in broadcast programmes needs to be considered with great care on every occasion...
1.4 (ii) Racial jokes
There is a danger of offence also in jokes based on different racial characteristics. Producers need to be sensitive to the possible effect of such jokes upon the racial minority concerned, as well as to changes in public attitudes to what is and what is not acceptable. Even though it might be unlikely that matters intended as a joke would constitute an offence under the provisions of Section 22 of the Public Order Act 1986, they may nonetheless offend against good taste or decency or be offensive to public feeling.
1.4 (iii) Other minorities
Similar considerations apply to the treatment of other, less obvious and vulnerable, minorities including older people, homosexuals, and minority religious faiths or language groups.

Section 1.12 People with Disabilities
Careless or insensitive references cause distress both to the individual and his or her family. Any unnecessary reference to disability should be avoided, and patronising expressions such as 'crippled with', 'victim', 'handicapped' should, where possible, be replaced by more neutral forms such as 'he/she is disabled' or 'uses (not 'confined to') a wheelchair'.

Guidelines from the ITC Programme Code

Activity

Taking one medium, research and report on as many of the relevant laws and guidelines that you can find, which might affect representation in that medium. Give particular consideration to non-fiction representation. There are many sources of this kind of information: there are books on law and copies of Acts in most libraries. The Broadcasting Act (1990) is particularly useful. For institutions, get hold of a copy of the ITC rules, or the BBC Charter. You might also talk to people in the media as to how laws affect them on a day-to-day basis. Remember that your work should cover all representational issues, as discussed in this section.

Media ethics

Concerned media producers must take into account ethical considerations. Representations can be positive or negative, portrayals can supply good or bad rôle models. However, in the search for 'realism' in film or television drama, many assumptions are made about the nature of society and portrayals are constructed that are based on stereotypes or indeed are the

The problem of tokenism is the other side of the coin here, in that there is a temptation to include ethnic minorities, young people, women and the disabled, just to fit in with the legal requirements discussed above, or simply to be seen to be 'politically correct'.

result of some current moral panic.

Ethical considerations about freedom of speech are central to many discussions. How ethical is it for example, to aid and allow the use of media by terrorist groups, political extremists, or sexual deviants, as a platform to represent their views? Other ethical considerations concern the extent of media intrusion in the representation of sensitive topics such as abortion, AIDS or of the private lives of public figures, e.g. the royal family.

Social and political considerations

Social and political concerns include the effects of media representations on the audience. An example of this drawn from various media products is the construction of the idea of beauty. This affects all people and how we see ourselves, in the widest sense, re-presented in the media. In newspapers, magazines, films, and television perceptions of beauty are established, reinforced and encouraged.

The ideal of female beauty is portrayed as Pamela Anderson from *Baywatch*, or the 'supermodels' from fashion magazines. Male beauty is projected as the muscle-bound Gladiators.

At the centre of this concern is what can be called the *manipulation* of the final image. A great deal of effort and money goes into constructing a particular representation and visual definition of beauty. We have to consider the possible effect of such 'perfect' images on the rest of the population. This is important when considering the vulnerability of young people. It is often argued that anorexia, feelings of inadequacy and self-loathing are caused by the ideals of beauty promoted by the media.

Xenophobia (that is, fear of other cultures), *homophobia* (that is, fear of homosexuals), sexism and racism might be encouraged by the nature of some representations. Members of the affected social groups may then feel alienated from society. Also of concern is the way that sexual representations are exploited by the media, to sell newspapers, for instance.

Representations, in our relatively free media, of the activities of repressive regimes may have unforeseen political and economic effects on the nation. An offended foreign government might decide to take diplomatic or economic action such as a boycott of British products. In a global market one country's media products become available for all to see. The nature of representations that the media produce affect the way we perceive others, and are perceived by them in return.

There are then many aspects to consider when dealing with issues of representation in the media. These range from legal concerns for fairness, and the social impact of certain kinds of representation, to possible effects both nationally and internationally of our media content.

The representation of issues

When you analyse how issues are represented it is important to take into account three levels of understanding. First, you must gain an understanding of the author's or producer's intent, who the target audience is and the nature of the medium used. The second level is that of the content. What are the issues and how are they represented, what sort of information is being given and what is the relationship of the representation to reality? Finally you must consider the audience. Who are the audience (not just the intended audience), what are their expectations, and what are the potential effects of the representation on them?

Representations of issues in the media are constantly in flux. The following model will allow you to analyse changing representations. The example below uses this model to examine very generally the representation of women in advertising.

Model for issue analysis: advertising and gender

Production

- *Author/producer intent* What is the intent of the author? Is it to inform, to educate and/or to entertain? Advertisers hope their work will persuade the consumer to buy the product. Firstly, something persuasive must be communicated to the consumer; secondly, the consumer should yield to the persuasion, and finally act on the new information or attitude.
- *Who are the target audience?* What social groups are the media products aimed at? The composition of these groups will often determine the nature of the representation. Target audiences' media habits are important when deciding where to advertise.
- *The nature of media* Television and film as audio/visual media can convey a wide range of information about many products. Radio is a good conveyor of verbal information and catch-phrases. Magazines, newspapers, and hoardings are all useful for conveying powerful, stunning images as well as information that can be re-referred to. Television can show how products work and how a situation can change over time.

Content

- *What are the issues?* That is, who or what is being represented and who is being appealed to: men, women, teenagers, children, or social groups?
- *How are they represented?* What are the various types of representation used? What are the representations of women? Are they of mothers, 'sex-objects', daughters, sisters, single women, secretaries, housewives, etc. With what products are they associated?
- *What information is given* about the content of the media product, or in relation to the portrayal of society? In advertising, the information is usually associated with the product itself, and what it will do for us.
- *The relationship of representation to reality* Any critique of a media product inevitably begins with an evaluation of how realistic it is. Advertising with its own created symbolic universe and signifying power should be evaluated carefully. The need to convey messages rapidly relies on the use of verbal and visual 'shorthand'.

Audience

- *Who are the audience?* This will depend to a large extent on the nature of the media content. Some genres are gendered, such as soap operas, women's magazines or sports pages. Many advertisements are also gendered; the majority of domestic products are targeted at women. The majority of car and DIY advertisements are targeted at men.

You should be wary of 'media talk' of *target audiences*: the audience for any product can possibly include everybody, and everybody will decode the message in some fashion. Thus some advertisements may be 'targeted' at women, but men will also see them, and their content may reinforce the ideology of a woman's place being in the home.

- *Audience wants and expectations* Two approaches are interesting and useful here: *uses and gratifications*, and *Maslow's hierarchy of needs* (discussed in detail in a later Study Unit), specifically with reference to advertising. You will learn more about the uses and gratifications approach in Study Unit 6 Section 2: it is an approach concerned with the audience's motivation for consuming media products. McQuail *et al* (1972) identify four sorts of gratification from media products, *diversion* – or escapism; *personal relationships*, that is for company or as a talking point with other people; *personal identity* – to locate and identify ourselves in relation to others we see in the media; *surveillance*, or using the media as a source of information. Maslow's emphasis on an individual's needs is important because much advertising is designed to persuade people that they have a *need* for a certain product or service that they do not yet recognise. Advertisers often have to overcome resistance from consumers.

- *Potential effects on audiences* Media products vary from the information-based, to those associated with the construction of the image of a whole society. Advertisements give information about products but also construct images of society – images which may be inaccurate but which may influence the way people see their rôles in society.

Activity

Using the above model, analyse an issue of your choice, drawing out as many of the relevant points as you can. Choose only those elements which are applicable to your chosen issue. You may not be able to gain all the information you require. Author intent or audience expectations are often difficult to acquire information on. In such cases an informed guess or estimate, based on the media content you have in front of you and your knowledge of media studies approaches, may prove fruitful.

Access to the media

This situation is changing: even Hollywood now has a growing number of women directors, technicians and studio executives. Employment access for women and cultural minorities is often seen as the key to changing the content and direction of media products.

It can be argued that representations are the way they are because of the domination of the power structure of the media by white, upper- and middle-class males.

One way to bring about change in representations is to increase regional coverage and general access to media facilities. It is often felt in the United Kingdom that too many of the media are based in London. Widening access for individuals through such things as video boxes, community access television (on cable), and local newspapers is seen as a way to broaden the representation of views in the media. There is undoubtedly an imbalance between the access to the media of powerful groups such as MPs, political parties or large multinational industries, and smaller interest groups such as people objecting to a by-pass or new housing estate. Large organisations spend a great deal of time and money on how they are represented by the media, employing PR companies to influence the **agenda setting** rôle of the media.

Activity

Write a brief report on your examination of the multicultural broadcasting policy of either the BBC or ITC. Contact various organisations involved in multicultural broadcasting, examine the legal requirements, and look at the programming itself.

Stereotyping

Examples of stereotypes are: that Scotsman are mean with money; women from Essex are all blondes called Tracy; Conservatives are upper class.

Stereotypes are oversimplified representations of people, institutions, styles or even events.

Stereotypes are widespread, we all use them in our relationships with people throughout our lives as part of our basic need to categorise people into 'types'. We start with the simplest divisions such as male or female, and add layers of complexity according to elements such as dress, accent, size, shape, skin colour, etc. These categories are not fixed, they are open to reinterpretation in the light of experience. Stereotypes are shorthand and often clichéd interpretations, grouping together a number of people under a recognisable banner, such as 'football hooligans'. They can be associated with racial or other prejudices.

A cliché is an overused, hackneyed expression; it is a verbal stereotype.

The representation of people as stereotypes

Media narratives rely heavily on representations. Stereotypes provide the media with shorthand images for constructing stories which must be told quickly, as in advertisements. Stereotypes provide recognisable short-cuts and instant cues. Indeed, in the next section on **genre** you will see how they are almost indispensable. They are used most often and overtly in comedy, such as newspaper cartoons or situation comedy on television. Because they are assumptions by their nature, they often appear as neutral and are taken for granted, occurring almost unnoticed in much media output. Stereotypes occur outside the media but the latter have a key rôle in generating, relaying and reinforcing them. Very rarely does any person or thing conform to a stereotype. However, stereotypes must contain 'a grain of truth' to remain viable as tools for media representation.

Labelling

A related media rôle to stereotyping is *labelling*. The difference between them is that official organisations such as the police, social services, and the legal system all contribute to label construction. The media have the power to label a person or group in particular ways, often by associating them with some form of deviant act. This power is particularly strong where the audience have no firsthand experience of a particular type of person and are thus dependent on the media for information. There is a lot of evidence about the rôle of the media in labelling people as deviant, be they drug addicts, homosexuals or youth sub-cultures.

Another question concerning stereotypes and labels, as with general representations, is to what extent they are accepted as 'real' and seen, by children especially, as rôle models. This brings us back to the discussion on the media and socialisation. For instance, are the limited images of women as mother, wife and sex-object accepted by young girls and women as their future roles, or are alternatives suggested by media content?

Howard Becker (1963), in his classic study, demonstrated the rôle of the media in the labelling process and in shaping new images of deviancy.

Deviancy is any form of behaviour which differs from what is considered 'normal' by the majority of people.

Activity

With the above in mind, carry out some content analysis. Draw up a list (or coding schedule) of the rôles filled by women in the media. Make it as exhaustive as you can. Then in an evening's viewing simply make a mark against each type of portrayal. At the end of your sample period count up and place in order which portrayals dominate television content.

When considering stereotypes, as with representation generally, we must consider the nature of the portrayal. Although portrayals can be negative, simplistic and misleading, some are positive and accurate, whilst many are very complex. In particular, the stereotypes of professionals, such as doctors, teachers and lawyers are very positive towards their subjects.

Although this section has concentrated on the subjects that are actually portrayed, it is also worthwhile considering the representation which is constructed when a subject is *absent* from the media. For example, many 'extreme' views concerned with political, religious or sexual matters are not expressed in the media. By their absence these issues are *marginalised* and may then be seen as unimportant.

Marginalised topics or people are those largely ignored by most of society – they are confined to 'the margins' of society.

Assignment

Using this discussion of the elements of representation as your guide, carry out two case studies comparing the portrayal of gender in film and in magazines or newspapers over the last four decades. Assess how stereotypical images of gender have developed and been challenged or reinforced. Use as much material as you like but possibly a sample of two films and two magazines/newspapers from each decade if you are working alone, or four if you are working in groups.

3

Analysing media genres
Identifying genres

The term genre derives from the French word meaning 'type' or 'kind'. It is used for grouping and classifying media products. In genre analysis we are especially concerned with how similar products within a genre are constructed and relate to each other. That is, what elements they have in common, and then how audiences recognise and respond to them.

Genres occur in all media; they are forms of narrative not media in themselves. Thus, the western is a genre, which occurs across all media; film, television, radio, books, magazines, comics, etc.

News is also a genre, but it does not occur in all media. For instance, we no longer have newsreels, so news does not appear in the cinema. It does, however, dominate television, newspapers and radio.

Activity

The tables that follow show the leading genres in the modern mass media. In the first table, indicate in the appropriate box (with a tick, a cross, or a question mark), where each genre (identified on the left) is found in each of the five media listed.

In the second table identify some titles for each genre, drawn from across the media, and then write down a description in short list form of the elements that they have in common, i.e. those characteristics that make them part of the same genre. Think about all the elements (discussed in Section 1) of media texts that produce meaning, not just the visual ones.

When you have completed this table, keep it for reference and as part of your work for assessment for this unit.

In this section you will gain an insight into tools and concepts which will help you classify and identify genres with more certainty. You may then wish to return to table 1 and reconsider whether some of the genres can fairly be described as such. You may also wish to enter the argument as to whether film noir is a genre or not.

Activity table 1

	Film	TV	Radio	Newspaper & Magazines	Books
Western					
Sci-Fi					
Thriller					
Comedy					
Horror					
War					
Crime					
Gangster					
Musical					
News					
Current Affairs					
Documentary					
Quiz Shows					
Sit-coms					
Talk Shows					
Soap Operas					
Romance					
Satire					
Pop Music					
Rock Music					
Classical Music					
Country Music					
Jazz					
Blues					
Tabloid					
Broad sheet					
Agony aunt					
Leader column					
The novel					
Short stories					
Tragedy					
Action					
Adventure					
Breakfast show					

Activity table 2

Genre	Titles	Common Elements
The Western		
Soap Operas		
Comedy		
Science Fiction		
Horror		
Musical		
Romance		
News		

Mise-en-scène as we shall discuss later is a crucial feature of genre identification. It is French, meaning 'putting into a scene'. It is through *mise-en-scène* that all the elements, discussed in the early part of this unit, work together to create meaning. *Mise-en-scène* might be all the elements arranged on the front page of a tabloid newspaper, as well as all the elements arranged in a scene from a television drama or a film.

As your work on table 1 has shown, there is room for debate as to whether certain things are genres or not. Are tabloid papers genres, or simply styles of newspapers? Are pop music, country music, jazz, etc., genres of music? You may have noted that **film noir** has not been included in the list. This is because it is often thought of as a style rather than a genre. Also, film noir can be seen as part of other genres such as crime and the thriller. It is only its look or *mise-en-scène* that distinguishes it, not its content.

Table 2 is useful in that it helps us to identify and consider what common factors are central to our identification of particular genres as well as the range of products available in any one genre.

Actors and directors can become associated with particular film genres: John Wayne and John Ford with westerns or Arnold Schwarzenegger with action/adventure, Christopher Lee and Wes Craven with horror, Alfred Hitchcock with thrillers. Writers become associated with particular kinds of novels: J. T. Edson with westerns, Stephen King with horror. Companies become associated with certain genres: Mills and Boon with romance novels, BBC Radio 3 with classical music, and Hammer with horror films.

The study of genre is largely based on description and classification. Analysis begins with an exploration of the largest categories of genre, such as fiction and non-fiction, moves through various popular genres such as soap operas or horror films and finally considers the smallest divisions of what are called sub-genres, such as the road movie. The road movie is seen as a sub-genre of the western, because it contains a number of significant elements which are found in westerns. For instance, the motor bike takes the place of the horse in the story of *Easy Rider* (1969).

What is the nature of genre?

When considering what the nature of genre is, it is crucial to observe that genres are not an imitation or representation of the real world, but of other media products. Thus, news may be about world events, but its format is constructed along particular lines which are similar across media. Genre works through, and depends on, **intertextuality**. We recognise news in any medium because of its structure, its mode of delivery and its language. All genres are constructed around a central core element or series of elements. The generic core of news is the listing and reporting of events. That is the essence or central point around which the news genre revolves. The generic core of a western is often the landscape of the 'old west'.

Audiences' understanding of a genre will be dependent on their experience of it elsewhere, their familiarity with it, and their recognition of its elements such as people, objects or story lines. In this way they are able to make sense of what they are seeing.

The history of genre

Genres themselves have developed over many years. The first kinds of genre were probably the two kinds of ancient Greek drama, tragedy and comedy. In the nineteenth and twentieth centuries dividing media products into genres became a useful marketing tool. A romantic book or western film can easily be sold to specific target audiences. Media producers use the notion of genre when deciding which products to finance, and then publicise those products via genre ideas and images, in order to appeal to the target audience. The key relationships in the production of twentieth century genres are those between the genre, the media producers and the audience. This is a triangular relationship:

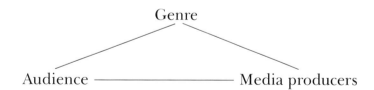

By drawing upon a pre-defined set of tools and conventions, both producers and audiences categorise media products into particular genres making communication between the encoder and the decoder easier.

Genre allows media products to be packaged and targeted at an audience who can then select products according to their previous experience of genres. Audience preferences affect the genres available in any period. For instance, very few musicals are made in the 1990s compared with the 1930s and 1940s. There are increasing numbers of soap operas and tabloid newspapers. As media critics you must be sceptical of the industry and ask yourself the crucial question: do the audience get what they want in terms of genres, or simply make do with what they get?

Intertextuality is the way in which one text relates to others and is understood through its relationships to those other texts.

We all call upon and use our 'generic memories' in such situations. Generic cores, codes and conventions such as headlines in news, or jingles on radio, or thunder and lightning in horror films, will determine the audience's expectations of the specific genre. For example, audiences expect to be scared by horror films, informed by a documentary or emotionally moved by a love story.

Genre is so important to the media industries that they have developed and constructed themselves along generic lines. Newspaper organisations, for instance, have always been divided into news, features, sport and advertising departments. The BBC has drama, current affairs, light entertainment departments, etc.

Take a look at the BARB weekly viewing figures for the week ending 8 September 1996. How many of the top ten programmes for each channel are genre products? Compare these figures with more recent figures. How similar are the figures you have found, and what does this say about the popularity of types of genres?

BBC 1 — MILLIONS VIEWING (Including Timeshift)

Programme	Total	1st Showing	2nd Showing
1 EASTENDERS (THU/SUN)	17.18	13.69	3.49
2 EASTENDERS (TUE/SUN)	16.10	13.53	2.57
3 EASTENDERS (MON/SUN)	15.67	13.93	1.74
4 X CARS (MON 2030)	11.77		
5 NATIONAL LOTTERY LVE (SAT 1951)	10.81		
6 NEIGHBOURS (MON 1342/1739)	10.59	3.55	7.04
7 NEIGHBOURS (TUE 1343/1737)	10.43	3.22	7.21
8 NEIGHBOURS (WED 1341/1737)	10.36	3.25	7.10
9 NEIGHBOURS (THU 1342/1737)	9.93	2.99	6.94
10 NEIGHBOURS (FRI 1341/1738)	9.83	2.82	7.00
11 DANGERFIELD (FRI 2134)	9.35		
12 999 LIFESAVERS (TUE 2001)	8.43		
13 CRIMEWATCH UK (TUE 2203)	8.22		
14 BEST/N.HOUSE|PARTY (SAT 2008)	8.05		
15 THE HELLO GIRLS (THU 2031)	7.94		
16 BACK TO THE WILD (THU 2000)	7.73		
17 NINE O'CLOCK NEWS (FRI 2100)	7.60		
18 J DAVIDSON'S/GAME (SAT 1807)	7.44		
19 HARPUR AND ILES (SAT 2108)	7.40		
20 GREAT ANTIQUES HUNT (SUN 1835)	7.24		
21 ONLY FOOLS/HORSES (WED 2000)	7.16		
22 WATCHDOG (THU 1901)	7.07		
23 BIG BREAK TRICK/SPCL (TUE 2031)	7.00		
24 NINE O'CLOCK NEWS (MON 2100)	6.85		
25 DAD'S ARMY (SAT 1737)	6.77		
26 PARKINSON/INTERVIEWS (FRI 2224)	6.39		
27 DUE SOUTH (SAT 1905)	6.34		
28 SIX O'CLOCK NEWS (MON 1800)	6.33		
29 NEWS AND WEATHER (SUN 1735)	6.31		
30 SIX O'CLOCK NEWS (TUE 1800)	6.25		

ITV — MILLIONS VIEWING (Including Timeshift)

Programme	Total	1st Showing	2nd Showing
1 CORONATION STREET (MON/WED)	16.53	15.64	0.90
2 CORONATION STREET (WED/FRI)	16.36	14.85	1.51
3 HEARTBEAT (SUN 1930)	14.22		
4 YOU'VE BEEN FRAMED (SUN 2032)	13.08		
5 CORONATION STREET (FRI 1929)	12.90		
6 LONDON'S BURNING (SUN 2103)	12.72		
7 THE BILL (FRI 2002)	12.00		
8 EMMERDALE (TUE/THU)	11.50	10.65	0.85
9 EMMERDALE (THU 1859)	10.67		
10 SOLDIER SOLDIER (TUE 2101)	10.55		
11 THE BILL (THU 1959)	10.42		
12 HOME AND AWAY (MON 1325/1801)	10.28	3.47	6.81
13 HOME AND AWAY (FRI 1326/1801)	10.05	2.96	7.09
14 HOME AND AWAY (WED 1326/1801)	10.04	3.19	6.85
15 HOME AND AWAY (THU 1325/1800)	9.93	2.90	7.03
16 HOME AND AWAY (TUE 1326/1800)	9.75	3.03	6.71
17 MURDER SQUAD (THU 2101)	9.60		
18 THE BILL (TUE 1959)	9.50		
19 FREDDIE STARR SHOW (THU 2031)	8.74		
20 HOME ALONE (WED 2005)	8.73		
21 TARRANT ON T.V (SUN 2204)	8.07		
22 WHEEL OF FORTUNE (WED 1902)	8.04		
23 NOWHERE TO RUN (MON 2101)	8.02		
24 FAMILY FORTUNES (SAT 2017)	8.00		
25 LAST BOY SCOUT (SAT 2105)	7.92		
26 STRANGE BUT TRUE (FRI 2033)	7.92		
27 BRUCE'S PRICE/RIGHT (MON 1859)	7.74		
28 NEWS AT TEN (MON 2200)	7.68		
29 LUCKY NUMBERS (FRI 1859)	7.63		
30 NEWS AT TEN (THU 2202)	6.57		

BBC 2 — MILLIONS VIEWING (Including Timeshift)

Programme	Total	1st Showing	2nd Showing
1 GRAND PRIX (SUN 1300)	5.10		
2 GREAT RAILWAY JRNEYS (WED 2130)	5.01		
3 CHANGING ROOMS (WED 2100)	4.20		
4 TRAVEL SHOW (THU 2059)	4.15		
5 DARK SECRET (THU 2129)	3.77		
6 TOP GEAR (THU 2029)	3.73		
7 BOTTOM (FRI 2102)	3.66		
8 GARDENERS' WORLD (FRI 2031)	3.54		
9 STEPTOE AND SON (TUE 2101)	3.30		
10 FRED DIBNAH STORY (WED 2030)	3.23		
11 TRACKS (TUE 2030)	3.14		
12 STAR TREK NXT GENRTN (WED 1800)	3.00		
13 SYKES (MON 2101)	2.73		
14 HANCOCK (THU 2159)	2.70		
15 GHURKHAS (TUE 2131)	2.65		
16 FARNBOROUGH'96 (WED 2000)	2.64		
17 BEND OF THE RIVER (SUN 2150)	2.54		
18 ROOM 101 (MON 2200)	2.53		
19 READY, STEADY, COOK (FRI 1631)	2.52		
20 SUNDAY GRANDSTAND (SUN 1201)	2.48		
21 READY, STEADY, COOK (THU 1631)	2.43		
21 READY, STEADY, COOK (WED 1631)	2.43		
23 NATURAL WORLD (MON 2011)	2.39		
24 READY, STEADY, COOK (TUE 1631)	2.26		
25 PULP VIDEO (FRI 2132)	2.22		
26 NEED FOR SPEED (SUN 2102)	2.13		
27 DEEP SPACE 9 (THU 1801)	2.11		
28 ESTHER (FRI 1700)	2.10		
29 HEARTBREAK HIGH (TUE 1825)	2.07		
30 TODAY'S THE DAY (FRI 1601)	1.98		

CHANNEL 4 — MILLIONS VIEWING (Including Timeshift)

Programme	Total	1st Showing	2nd Showing
1 BROOKSIDE (FRI/SAT)	6.39	3.87	2.53
2 BROOKSIDE (TUE/SAT)	5.96	4.31	1.65
3 BROOKSIDE (WED/SAT)	5.51	3.40	2.11
4 FRIENDS (FRI 2131)	5.07		
5 CUTTING EDGE (MON 2102)	3.62		
6 COUNTDOWN (MON 1631)	3.22		
7 WHOSE LINE/ANYWAY (FRI 2231)	3.16		
8 COUNTDOWN (TUE 1629)	3.11		
9 COUNTDOWN (WED 1630)	2.96		
10 CYBILL (FRI 2102)	2.93		
11 COUNTDOWN (FRI 1630)	2.83		
11 COUNTDOWN (THU 1630)	2.83		
13 BLUE STEEL (SUN 2200)	2.79		
14 POLITICIAN'S WIFE (TUE 2103)	2.73		
15 FATHER TED (SAT 2155)	2.47		
16 RICKI LAKE SHOW (WED 1700)	2.35		
17 GARDEN PARTY (FRI 2001)	2.30		
18 LITTLE MAN TATE (THU 2204)	2.27		
19 RICKI LAKE SHOW (THU 1701)	2.26		
20 SHORT STORIES (WED 2033)	2.14		
20 MONTEL WILLIAMS SHOW (MON 1701)	2.14		
22 EQUINOX (SUN 1901)	2.10		
23 RICKI LAKE SHOW (TUE 1700)	2.04		
24 AMERICAN GOTHIC (WED 2203)	2.01		
25 TRUE STORIES (TUE 2218)	1.98		
26 E.R (SAT 2100)	1.83		
27 LITTLE KILLERS (MON 2001)	1.79		
28 ROSEANNE (FRI 1827)	1.78		
29 BABYLON 5 (SUN 1807)	1.64		
30 AVENGERS (TUE 1801)	1.48		

The formal characteristics of genre

Genres rely on the audience's knowledge and experience of them so that a process of understanding or intertextual 'reading' can take place. Genres actually work, and are recognised through their *formal characteristics*. These are essentially *codes* and *conventions*; they include *stylistic characteristics* (camera work, lighting, sound effects, speech, writing style, music, graphics, etc.), *iconography*, *mise-en-scène*, and **narrative structure**.

Iconography means the symbols used in a medium, and their meaning.

Stylistic characteristics

Formal characteristics alter between media. For film and television, stylistic characteristics such as camera work, lighting, sound and editing are vital parts of the codes and conventions by which we recognise each

Fig 1.7
A still for *Dracula has risen from the grave*

Fig 1.8
Still from *Bram Stoker's Dracula*

Fig. 1.9
A still from the TV series, *The X-Files*

genre. In television news for instance, the opening mid shot of the news reader is a crucial visual code, which, alone, tells us that this is a news programme giving information that is important and 'true'. High-key lighting, minimal editing of news reader, and lack of background music are important to the 'look' or 'feel' of the genre of television news.

In audio and radio work, stylistic characteristics of sound, speech and music are central to distinguishing between different genres such as breakfast show and news. Both genres rely on dialogue but the style of dialogue in a breakfast show is upbeat, jolly and entertaining while in a news programme it is serious, detached and delivered in a way that emphasises that the information given is important.

In the print medium, language, typography, photography and graphics help to distinguish between the two main newspaper genres of tabloid paper and broadsheet. Both purport to bring us news and information, one in an 'entertaining' fashion, and one in a more serious fashion. Tabloids use much more colour and much less text than the broadsheets and these factors convey their different approaches to the news. Mastheads are used as icons of the genres the papers belong to.

Iconography

Iconography is very important in recognising genres. An icon is one of the three keys types of *sign*, and is something which resembles the object for which it stands but which has a meaning beyond its physical form. A Stetson hat is an icon for the western genre, for instance. A horse in a western is an icon for power, masculinity, control, and survival.

Once an object (or person) is recognised as an icon, it will have the same meaning in all media products in which it appears. An icon provides a form of shorthand for both the producer and the audience, it saves them having to laboriously fill in the background to each person, image or object. If you look at the images from horror genre films in Figures 1.7 and 1.8 (*Dracula Has Risen from the Grave* (1968) and *Bram Stoker's Dracula* (1992)) even though they are from different decades, your knowledge of genres will immediately tell you much about the central figures and the objects around them. You will have particular associations with these images and expectations of what the films would be like. The same can be said for the icons contained in the still from the television series the *X-Files* (Figure 1.9). Mulder, for instance, wears a recognisable 'detective' style of coat, an icon worn by many different detectives in many other stories.

Iconography is much more associated with the visual media than with audio, although a voice can have iconic value, especially a well-known one such as Chris Evans, John Humphreys or Jimmy Young.

Fig 1.10
A selection of film posters

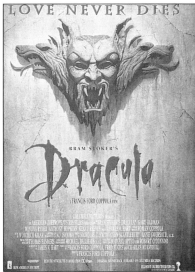
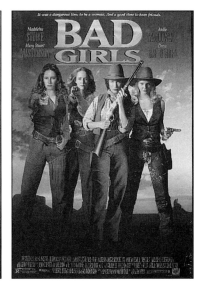

Activity

Examine closely the three film posters reproduced. Describe the ways in which the icons used inform the audiences, through genre recognition, about the type of film each is.

Mise-en-scène

Mise-en-scène in moving image production includes everything within the frame: location, image, set-design, costume, and the kind of characters (for example, dominant/frightening), lighting, the camera's position and the angle of view. All these elements generate mood, atmosphere, and the feeling of a genre. *Mise-en-scène* gives us crucial visual clues to the genre concerned. In the two stills taken from Dracula films the iconographical image of Dracula himself tells us much about him. There are also associated props, a victim, a coffin and a cape. Period costume is also central to the *mise-en-scène*, as is the castle vault, with its large solid-looking stones, and the shadows cast by barred window and chains. The *mise-en-scène* created through this iconography provides visual cues which nudge our memories of the genre and give us specific expectations for these films.

   Mise-en-scène in print and audio genres can be described as the look or feel of a product. The *mise-en-scène* of tabloid newspapers involves the combination of all their stylistic elements: size, masthead, typeface, colour, photographs, etc. In radio *mise-en-scène* would involve voice, accent, speed of delivery, type of music, amount of talk, comic or serious content.

Narrative structure

Narrative structure is a key formal characteristic of genre; fictional genre products, in particular, have typical and recognisable stories. Narrative form (or narrative structure) means all the elements used in developing a story. For example in westerns, the list of elements may look like this:

- conventional central characters – cowboy, sheriff, Indian, cavalry officer
- conventional representations or stereotypes – cantankerous old man, saloon girl, innocent child, savage Indian
- conventional locations – the plains, the western town, the Indian camp
- conventional settings – inside the saloon, the covered wagon, the jail, the tepee.

Activity

Continue this list for objects, costumes, dialogue, music and plots found in the western.

The sorts of plots you have remembered will probably include some of the following elements: gunfighter comes to town; gunfighter causes trouble; sheriff challenges gunfighter; sheriff wins gunfight; peace restored to town.

Any story-based genre, such as soap operas or sci-fi films, comics or novels can be analysed like this. You may be surprised if you also attempt to apply it to non-fiction genre products!

Modelling the plot

The last convention, the plot, is one found in all genres and can be identified as the 'classic realist' Hollywood text. This refers to the fact that all Hollywood films have a beginning, a middle and an end. This narrative structure is particularly strong in genre products, providing as it does another recognisable trait of particular genres. The diagram below left illustrates how this works. On the right, we now apply this to the earlier example of a western gunfighter story.

Beginning	HERO VILLAIN PROBLEM

Beginning	Sheriff Gunfighter Trouble in town

Middle	QUEST AND/OR BATTLE

Middle	Sheriff advises gunfighter to leave Gunfighter refuses Gunfight

End	VICTORY PEACE CHANGED SITUATION

End	Sheriff wins Peace is restored Sheriff and or town have developed in some way

This model can be applied to any fictional genre product. Despite obvious differences in genre products, genres as diverse as westerns, musicals and horror share this common structure of the 'classic realist' Hollywood text.

However, each genre has its own particular elements, patterns and processes to which all the above formal characteristics contribute. These include themes, sub-plots, non-central characters, additional locations, musical signatures and particular use of language.

Genre as a formula

The combination of narrative elements and formal characteristics creates the formula upon which each genre is based. Genres are often described as formula products because they adhere to a set of rules (a formula) that the genre must follow in order to be identified.

By varying the formal characteristics of a genre, new stories and themes can emerge. Thus the use of formulas need not restrict the development of a genre product. For the imaginative media producer formulas provide the framework or map upon which he or she can plan their own route, knowing that their audience have an idea of the road being taken but can be constantly surprised by unexpected twists.

Activity

Take a sample of four genre products, for example a tabloid newspaper, five minutes from a breakfast show on radio or television, a photo story in a magazine, a blues record, or five minutes from a horror film. Examine how their formal characteristics enable us to identify them. You should consider their *mise-en-scène*, their chief icons, narrative structures, codes and conventions, and generic cores.

Analysing themes in genre

Formal characteristics help us to see how genre products are constructed and provide us with clues for classifying them. In Section 1 we discussed Lévi-Strauss' and Barthes' idea that myths are a way in which societies think about themselves. A genre can be seen as a kind of myth. Themes within genres reveal social and cultural concerns within society.

There are three general categories of thematic concerns: firstly, metaphysical themes such as life and humanity; secondly, social themes such as crime, science, or politics; thirdly, ideological themes such as gender, race and sexuality. Looking at these thematic concerns in genre products reveals the similarity of themes that run through a number of products within the same genre. An ideological theme of tabloid newspapers is that young women are sex objects, a social theme that runs through all gangster products is that crime doesn't pay.

All genres are products of society and speak to that society. Stories set in the past or the future still refer to the values and concerns of the present, though this is more obvious in contemporary stories.

Metaphysical themes

The hospital drama genre is contemporary in its setting and uses *metaphysical themes*. Metaphysical themes are those ideas in society which are general and abstract. That is, ideas about 'life, the universe and everything'; ideas about humanity, and what it is to be civilised, are all metaphysical. Some of the most influential metaphysical ideas emerge through religion and what religious belief means to the individual. In the past people turned to the church for explanations of the world. More recently, people have turned to science for these explanations. It could be argued that medical science is a new faith and the hospital has replaced the church for healing and 'redemption'. The hospital drama tackles many social issues because it includes many kinds of people and problems.

In hospital dramas such as *Casualty* and *ER*, the plots may make use of metaphysical concepts, for example, a cleansing of the body, a renewal of mind and spirit; the idea of healing the body and redeeming the mind. Many patients have problems beyond their physical illness. The process of curing and contact with medical staff leads them into a greater exploration of their problems. Through this, the programmes explore social issues such as abusive relationships, drug addiction or family breakdown.

Activity

Consider the central characters in a hospital drama. Follow their progress through the narrative, focusing on the metaphysical ideas that emerge. For example, is the concept of faith, which we associate with religious belief, portrayed in the process of the story telling? Is faith in the individual or society renewed through the interaction of characters? Does life for the characters become worthwhile and meaningful again? Do the characters present the audience with a sense of hope?

Social themes

The majority of genre products are contemporary in their focus. Soap operas in particular deal with social themes, including sexuality, racism, crime or drug addiction. Soap operas enact symbolically and mythically the problems and contradictions of our society.

The way that themes are dealt with in the soap opera genre is important here, not individual story lines.

TV police genres such as *The Bill*, *Cracker*, or *Heartbeat* reassure us about the institution of the police and about how our society deals with crime.

Myths are a means by which society symbolically comes to terms with its problems and contradictions, and maintains its self image.

Binary oppositions

Another way of considering the portrayal of social themes in genre products is provided by Lévi-Strauss's notion of binary oppositions. Binary oppositions create their meanings through a series of opposites established within a text. These include binary opposites such as good–bad, hero–villain, cowboy–Indian, doctor–patient. A genre story may contain many of these oppositions, as they are central to the way we understand what is happening.

Ideological themes

Ideological themes in genre are concerned with the use of myths, meanings and values in society. They are best understood by analysing representations in genre media products. Do genres rely too heavily on rigid stereotypes as part of their shorthand style of story telling? To what extent are genres re-representing existing social relations? That is, does the use of recurrent themes, attitudes, situations and characters reveal the ideologies prevalent in society or does it simply reinforce the status quo?

Ideological themes in the romance genre revolve around traditional concepts of sexuality, love, marriage and gender rôles. In the recommended structure of romantic novels the man is usually older than the woman, rich and/or powerful. The romance starts slowly or even quite antagonistically, but develops and blossoms in an exotic location. Marriage is the essential happy ending. Echoes of this genre appear in everything from fairy-tales to magazine and newspaper stories, and even coffee adverts. Romance-based photo-stories in teenage magazines serve to emphasise the search for 'the' partner to their audience. This promotes the ideology that everybody should get married and 'settle down'.

Ideological themes can be found in even the most apparently neutral programmes. Animals in wildlife documentaries for instance, are nearly always given human attributes: animal behaviour is compared to human behaviour and social organisation. This is called anthropomorphising and is a process that contains many ideological lessons. Male and female child-rearing rôles are often emphasised, as are battles over territory. In this way, the same human activities are ideologically underpinned, in that they are seen to be part of the 'natural' world.

Ideologies of nationalism play a key rôle in many genres, particularly war films, spy films and westerns. Film and television products, in particular, display these ideologies to both a national and an international audience. Thus, in the case of American genre films, what are the American ideologies that we in Britain and the rest of the world are receiving?

Activity

With this in mind, from your viewing of a war film, an action/ adventure film or a spy film, construct lists of national attributes of the various countries involved: people, places, objects, opinions, technologies, etc. When the lists are complete, compare and contrast the positive and negative images of each country. Do the positive images favour one country or another? To what extent do you consider them to be ideological?

Analysing the functions of genre

Winona Ryder, who plays Mina in *Bram Stoker's Dracula*, says, 'I had never seen a Dracula or vampire movie in my life. When I saw the title I thought Urggghhh!-Dracula. Guy with fangs. Runs around biting people.' (*Empire* magazine March 1993). This illustrates the power of genre recognition, in that although Ryder had never seen a vampire film, she was still very much aware of its generic core.

In asking what functions genre serves, we are returning to the triangular relationship mentioned earlier between audience, genre, and media producers. How do audiences recognise genres? Which audience segments do different genres appeal to? What are the financial implications of the various genres for the media producing industries?

Audience recognition

Audience expectations may be activated before they even start to watch, read or listen to a media product: they may have seen advance publicity, read reviews, talked to a friend, or more likely, previously come across a similar genre product which they enjoyed.

Audience recognition, with its use of generic memory discussed earlier, determines how audiences react to and approach genre products. They can make assumptions about the product through their knowledge of the particular genre. These assumptions can be triggered by the formal characteristics of genre as well as by the five main elements of any genre product: stories, set-pieces, visual sign-posts, audio sign-posts, and people or personalities.

- *Stories* – boy meets girl; scientist experiments with human being.
- *Set-pieces* – girl goes down into dark cellar and finds light doesn't work; chat show host sits down on chair next to an empty sofa.
- *Visual sign-posts* – Indian wearing war paint; picture of bingo scratch cards on front of tabloid newspaper.
- *Audio sign-posts* – bugle blowing charge; music based on the sound of a telex machine; creaking floor board.
- *People or personalities* – John Wayne; Bob Monkhouse; Trevor McDonald.

The predictability of these elements is so strong that each one will remind you of your knowledge of that genre – you recognise it immediately and remember a wide range of information about the genre.

Audience pleasure and entertainment

A key function of genre and its formulaic construction is audience pleasure and entertainment. In going through the list of elements above you gained a sense of pleasure in recognising the familiar – like 'old friends'. Further pleasure is gained by guessing the next event. This is how genres work and is part of their popular appeal. If we now suggest a number of developments to each of the above situations then you will gain further pleasure if your prediction was proved right, or be surprised at a new dimension added, or frustrated at a cliché confirmed or a ridiculous turn of events taken.

- *Stories* – boy and girl don't like each other and never meet again; scientist experiments with human being, but the experiments go wrong, it attacks people and is eventually destroyed.

- *Set-pieces* – girl goes down into dark cellar and is terrified by something down there; chat show host is joined by celebrity on sofa.
- *Visual sign-posts* – Indian wearing war paint rides into a ravine to attack a cavalry patrol; the scratch cards have to be set alight to reveal prize.
- *Audio sign-posts* – bugle blowing charge turns out not be the US cavalry but an Indian trick to get you to leave your post (Ulzana's Raid 1972); music based on telex machine introduces television news; creaking floorboard is mended by the knocking in of a nail with hammer.
- *People and personalities* – John Wayne is visiting the children's ward of hospital, he appears wearing full western regalia, the cheer lifts the roof; Bob Monkhouse interviews the Prime Minister; Trevor McDonald says nothing on the news, or tells us there is no news today.

In each of these elements your generic memory and expectations have been confirmed or denied, or you have been set up for the next generic development. Whatever the situation, you have tried to make sense of it, and sought explanations either in other genres, such as comedy, or in similar situations we have come across in the same genre. Each exposure to a genre adds to your generic knowledge.

Activity

Using the two images in Figures 1.7 and 1.8, use your generic memory to construct what you consider were the events leading up to the scenes shown and those that might have followed. There is not a wrong or a right answer to this, it is the process of using your generic memory in conjunction with all the formal characteristics (stylistic, *mise-en-scène*, iconographic, narrative) and your recognition that is important.

Segmentation

Segmentation is a marketing term. It means that audiences can be divided into parts, called segments, who are interested in different products. Thus the whole audience for newspapers has several segments of people interested in different kinds of paper.

In analysing how genres function in the mass media, the notion of audience segmentation is important. Segmentation helps us to analyse the ways in which media output is both categorised by genre, and marketed at particular audiences. Much of the new cable and satellite output is broadcast on thematic or generic channels such as the Children's Channel, sports channels, the Discovery Channel (documentaries).

An analysis of television or radio listings or even a scan of magazines and newspapers will indicate the target audience for each genre product. The titles and images on the front of women's magazines or car magazines are designed for a particular audience segment. Soap operas are scheduled in the late afternoon and early evening to capture children, young people and housewives.

Genres are also gendered: males are supposed to watch war films and westerns, females are supposed to watch soap operas and quiz shows.

There are also women's and men's sections of newspapers. Advertisers insist on this division (another form of segmentation), since they want to advertise on pages directed at specific audiences for their products.

Genres are often aimed at specific target audiences. Situation comedies are largely family-based, featuring a cross section of society in order to have wide appeal. Different types of music are sold to different audience age groups. Tabloid and broadsheet newspapers are sold to different socio-economic groups. Target audiences for genre products are not only divided by traditional social variables such as age, gender and class, they are also segmented by interests or attitudes. Newspapers are directed at people with different political affiliations. Specialist magazines cover a wide range of interests from trainspotting to naturism.

The financial function of genre

Genre can be seen as a way of delivering an audience to the media industry. Because the audience has expectations of a product genre, born from their experience, they will buy similar products. The industry has confidence that certain tried and tested formulas will always deliver an audience, or a certain type of audience, such as young people, housewives, car owners, etc. If every media product was a one-off, it would be very difficult to generate audiences, and thus revenue.

Genre development

Genre products are popular, attract large audiences and are a good financial investment. But how do they maintain their popularity? Part of the answer lies in audience recognition and pleasure, part lies in the development of new themes, concerns and the expansion of genres themselves, plus new styles of presentation and new audiences.

Changes in themes and the expansion of genres

Genres develop over time and in different social, political and production contexts. For example, the western genre had adapted and changed over 40 years. The social context of production has changed, with far more women (*Bad Girls* 1994) and black men (*Posse* 1993) being portrayed.

Sub-genres, or films that draw on elements of a larger genre, are another way in which genres develop and diversify. The road movie for instance is a development of the western, casting many of the same themes out on to the open road in a twentieth century context.

Developments in genre include combinations of and associations between genres. In film, for instance you can get comedy westerns (*Blazing Saddles* 1974), musical westerns (*Paint Your Wagon* 1969), and sci-fi westerns (*Outland* 1981). Combinations in television include drama-documentaries or comedy soap operas. Combinations ultimately comment on both the original genres and rely on audiences recognising the combination of the elements, finding it acceptable, and then buying the combined product. Unless new genres sell, they will not continue to be produced.

A model for genre development

Christian Metz, in *Language and Cinema* (1974), explores the development of a genre. His ideas suggest that genres pass through four phases of existence:

- the experimental
- the classic
- the parody
- the deconstruction.

The experimental phase of the western occurred early on with such films as *The Great Train Robbery* (1903) and *The Virginian* (1914). The classic phase occurred once the genre was established and its conventions widely used and recognised and includes films such as *Stagecoach* (1939) and *Red River* (1948). Parody means films that mimic the genre, such as *The Professionals* (1966) or *Blazing Saddles* (1974). Finally, in deconstruction the generic elements of the western call attention to themselves by being placed out of context. *Outland* (1981) does this by re-doing *High Noon* (1952) in space. Post-westerns also deconstruct the genre, by placing the western hero in a contemporary and usually urban American setting, *Midnight Cowboy* (1969) and *Coogans Bluff* (1968) both do this.

Activity

Devise a parody or a deconstruction for a genre of your choice. You may create either a storyboard or a short script. These genres can be from any medium of your choice, film, television, music, radio, newspapers or magazines.

New styles of presentation and new audiences

The development of technical innovations is crucial here: for example, video games (many of which are based on genre products, especially sci-fi); cable and satellite; the video recorder and pay cable channels have all aided the development and spread of genres nationally and internationally.

Genres originating in western culture, such as sci-fi, have been exported around the world while non-western genres such as Kung-Fu and Indian Masala films are now easily obtained in the west.

As you have seen in this section, genre is the most powerful way of classifying and understanding media products, it cuts across boundaries between media and across international borders as well as social groupings. New technologies provide new genres and new target audiences, whilst older genres constantly develop and even combine. Genre products are very dynamic and lie at the heart of media production.

Finally, it is worthwhile considering some criticisms of the notion of genre itself. There are four main ones which can be summarised as follows.

- *Circularity:* the problem is that to establish a genre, you have to isolate its content and you can only do so if you have a pre-existing set of criteria.
- *Linearity:* the generalised nature of descriptions may prove too static to allow generic developments and diversity.
- *Labelling:* are the generic systems too large? We have to sub-divide into sub-genres or post-genres. The crime genre is sub-divided into police drama, private eye, thriller, film noir, etc., and some of these may now be genres in their own right.
- *Repetition:* is genre merely repeating the same worn out formulas to an audience lacking a variety of non-generic products to choose from?

In the assignment for this section that follows, it may be worthwhile bearing these criticisms in mind as you consider a number of genres. Do you think these criticisms are valid?

Assignment

Write a report tracing the formal characteristics, thematic concerns, functions and development of three genres of your choice. Pay particular attention to how your examples appear in different media. One or two of your examples may be your favourite genres but also try to examine a genre with which you are not familiar. A good starting place for identifying genres of interest are the two activity tables at the beginning of this section. Sources of information on particular genres can be found in specific books on the western, film noir, gangster film or soap opera, but also in some of the general film encyclopaedias. An important part of this activity is gathering examples of genre products and analysing them. This section can be used heading by heading to do this, as can the various activities. Below is a checklist of the main areas considered which will help provide a framework for your reports.

Checklist for generic analysis

- **Grouping and classifying**
  Examples from across media
  Common elements
- **Formal characteristics**
  Stylistic
  Iconographic
  Mise-en-scène
  Narrative structure

- **Themes**
  Metaphysical
  Social
  Ideological
- **Functions**
  Audience recognition
  Entertainment
  Segmentation
  Financial

- **Genre development**
  Changes in themes/concerns
  Expansion
  New styles
  New audiences
- **Criticisms**
  Circularity
  Linearity
  Labelling
  Repetition

Investigating narrative structures

Introduction to narratives

Narratives are basically stories which can be found across all media. They may be told by any means: verbally, in writing, in pictures, in photographs, or in music. In the nineteenth century, as more and more people read popular novels and penny newspapers, the mass media expanded. The content and structures of stories moved from the oral and face-to-face traditions to more permanent formats. With the advent of electronic technologies in the twentieth century, the same structures of story telling were delivered to previously undreamed of numbers of people, through film, radio, television and mass circulation print-based media. The larger the audiences these media had to reach, the more similar and familiar these stories and structures had to be.

The world comes to us in the form of stories. They may be the stories we tell each other when asked, 'what did you do over the weekend?' They may be memories related by parents or grandparents, or they may even be the way that we relate to each other as societies, nationally or internationally. In a news media context a story is generally regarded as the recounting of a factual incident, be it a wedding, a political conference or a war. Story-telling is a central form of communication and it is through the **mass media** that we experience the majority of narratives.

The construction of narratives

A narrative is built by the media producer using a variety of styles and patterns depending on the type of medium. In most media products, unlike literature, there is not necessarily a narrator but there is still a story with a beginning, middle and end. Narratives, whether fiction or non-fiction, are everywhere in media products, cutting across national and cultural boundaries.

The analysis of narrative structures

Two approaches

There are two basic approaches to the analysis of narrative structures. First we can look at how the narrative develops from beginning to end, at how one event follows another. This is called the **syntagmatic approach** and we will look at this through the **formalist** work of Vladimir Propp. Secondly, we can consider the narrative as a unit or whole, looking at the patterns that exist within it. This allows us to examine the underlying structures behind narratives. This is known as the **paradigmatic approach** and is associated with Lévi-Strauss. An example of this is that 'soaps' can be seen to reflect the dominant view of the family.

Narrative – the plot and the narration

The simplest function of a narrative is to tell a story. Narratives are made up of the plot, or the substance of the story, and narration, or the way the story is related. The plot may be boy, Jack, meets girl, Jill, romance ensues, followed by marriage or separation. In this kind of fiction material the audience can often guess what will happen so the pleasure derives from following the process of the story through to its end. The narration, on the other hand, may be the way that the story is told – either in the third person (Jill fell in love with Jack') or in the first person ('My name is Jill and I have fallen in love with Jack').

In non-fiction material, there is often no discernible end to the narrative. For instance, in ongoing news stories, we are aware of the characters, we have knowledge of past events and the news item simply feeds us more information on the story.

Types of narrative structures

In media products, there are many forms of narrative structures. Listed below are those we experience most often (you will be able to identify possibly more than one structure in each narrative).

- *Open structures*. Here the structure is limited to a small number of central characters whom we follow through a number of events for the duration of the story, which may continue through several episodes over a number of days or weeks. Crucially there need not be a resolution to the narrative. These occur most often in television narratives, such as series.
- *Closed structures*. These are mostly associated with films, television or radio plays, short stories in magazines or even sports events. The story may revolve around one central character and ends with the particular film, play, story or game.
- *Single strand*. Narratives often follow and revolve around the adventures of a single central character, such as Dirty Harry, Superman, or Ripley in the *Alien* films.
- *Multi-strand*. Here, several characters form the focus of the narrative. This is particularly apparent in soap operas including television series such as 'ER'.
- *Linear*. In this form of narrative structure, events progress often in chronological order, one following another.
- *Non-linear*. Events here do not necessarily follow each other, stories are often told in flashback, *Citizen Kane* (1941) for instance, or some of the classic film noirs *Mildred Pierce* (1945) or *Double Indemnity* (1944).

- *Investigative narrative*. This is very much tied to genre products (see Section 3). In an investigative narrative the structure of the plot is based on the investigation of a crime. It might concern a mystery which is being solved, an event which is being explained, or a quest being pursued rather than an actual crime. The *X-Files* is a good example of this.
- *Realist*. This describes the dominant form of narrative, and refers to the fact that the world presented within the narrative structure should appear plausible and coherent.
- *Anti-realist*. This might also be described as alternative or counter narrative and will be examined later. The text attempts to challenge the readers' expectations and make them aware of the narrative.
- *Non-narrative*. There are very few real media products that do not contain narratives. However, abstracts, clips or trailers, being representations of full products, could be seen as being non-narrative although these may have fragments of narrative within them.

Activity

Using the above list identify or reveal the types of narrative structures in at least six different media products. The most interesting results often emerge from applying these structures to non-fiction products. For instance, consider advertisements and news items; look at examples in print, on television and on radio.

Modes of address

The way we speak to each other, the body language we use and the context of that communication all affect the way messages are understood. In media products, there is no personal contact, the communication has to take place solely through the text. In the construction of narrative, the media producer constructs the story with reference to the perceived addressee (the audience), as well as with reference to him/herself, and his/her own sense of identity. An article in *Women's Journal* will be targeted at a particular audience (middle class, possibly working women) and will fit in with the ethos of the magazine.

Ethos: the 'character' of a medium, the values it promotes or is associated with.

There are basically four modes of address in media products which can be seen to *position* the audience. These can be labelled **voyeur** or **observer**, **empathiser**, **direct addressee**, and **inclusive addressee**.

- The majority of media products position the audience member as a voyeur or observer, simply being asked to watch or listen to what is happening.
- In imaginatively entering into the feelings of the central character, the audience is drawn into the plot. The audience empathises with the central character and understands the plight and position of this person.
- In the direct address, the audience are recognised by the media producers, and are addressed as listeners, readers or viewers. This might involve inviting some form of response such as in a quiz, or asking them

to agree with an opinion, an editorial in a newspaper or a news item on television.

- The mode of address called **inclusion** is used most often by those media producers intent on opposing or disrupting traditional narrative structures. Thus alternative styles are used to disrupt the product, to actively frustrate and alienate the audience, getting them to recognise the media product as an artificial construction, not reality. A good example of this is Dennis Potter's *Lipstick on my collar*.

Activity

Give examples of the four modes of address using either fiction or non-fiction material.

Components of narrative structures

Narrative structures all have component parts. For example, in classical Greek theatre a play was usually organised into acts, the standard being three acts. The act is a structural unit or component of the drama, usually containing more than one scene, which develops the plot. The three acts are divided into the first as the set-up, the second for the confrontation, and the third for the resolution.

The simplest model for revealing such component parts is that used in the previous section to illustrate the genre convention of plot. It is reproduced here so that you can begin to understand these components.

	HERO	
Beginning	VILLAIN	*Opening*
	PROBLEM	

	QUEST	
Middle	AND/OR	*Conflict*
	BATTLE	

	VICTORY	
End	PEACE	*Resolution*
	CHANGED SITUATION	

The most obvious components are the beginning, the middle, and the end. This can also be described as **opening**, **conflict** and **resolution** (or **closure**). Within each of these boxes you can see how a chain of events develops to produce the overall narrative. You can also see how the audience moves through a narrative, starting with the introduction to the main characters, moving through the various components of action (the quest and/or battle), to the finale.

Activity

Using this simple model, apply its framework (as we did with the gunfighter story in the last section) to five or six fiction narratives, in three or four different media. Also, apply it to non-fiction narratives, such as news programmes or documentaries.

Other components in the narrative structure

Cause and effect, enigma

Such narratives as described above can be seen as a chain of events or a cause and effect relationship. That is, that the hero or heroine and the villain meet, a problem emerges, there is a battle and a victory. One event has caused or led to another. This may follow a chain-like or linear pattern as described above, or a non-linear fashion using flashback to find the cause or identify the **protagonists**. The key to the action may well be a central question, problem or **enigma** such as the shark in the film *Jaws* (1975). In a teenage photo montage story, love might be the enigma, or in a murder mystery the crime is the enigma to be solved.

Openings, closures and oppositions

The **opening** and **closure**, or resolution, are particularly important. The opening sets the scene for conflict and establishes the central characters and *mise-en-scène*. It can also establish the genre and the style of narration. The closure resolves the central enigma of the narrative, answering all the questions posed at the start as well as those which emerged as the narrative progressed. There are no loose ends; loose ends or unfinished narratives cause much frustration amongst audiences, particularly where fictional products are concerned. One of the primary pleasures of audiences is to have all conflicts resolved. The end of the product must relate to the climax of the narrative, the high point of the action. For example, in a western the climax may be a gunfight where the villain is finally killed; the closure, where peace and happiness are restored, is a consequence of this climax.

Oppositions will be revealed by the analysis of narratives. They are a central component of all media narratives, the key to understanding the world. We know and understand what one thing is because of our knowledge of its opposite. We know what hot is because we know what cold feels like. We can understand what black is because we know what white is. In narratives, we know what the villain is like because we understand what the hero is like. These are examples of binary oppositions: two things are being opposed to each other.

Varieties of binary oppositions might be:

Good	v	Evil
Male	v	Female
Humanity	v	Technology
Nature	v	Industrialisation
East	v	West
Labour	v	Conservative
Dark	v	Light
Dirt	v	Cleanliness
Rational	v	Irrational

Activity

Taking two current narrative products, one fiction and one non-fiction, make a list of as many binary oppositions as you can identify.

Equilibrium

When a story opens there is extensive *exposition* with characters and scene being set and delineated. Then some problem or dilemma is raised which needs to be resolved. After several complications the problem or dilemma is finally resolved as the story comes to a conclusion (closure) with a newly found **equilibrium**. An example of this can clearly be seen in the western in which, generally, the scene is set, a stranger comes into town leading to a series of events which are resolved at the climax of the narrative, and a new state of order or equilibrium concludes or 'closes' the narrative.

Todorov (1977) has identified the movement from the opening to the closing of a narrative, as being a movement from one state of equilibrium to another. This process is called narrative transitivity, which draws our attention to the dynamic movement in a text from equilibrium to disequilibrium then to the establishment of a new equilibrium. Todorov's formula is best visualised like this:-

Equilibrium = plenitude ->

Opposing force ->

Disruption/disequilibrium ->

Unifying/equalising force ->

Quest ->

[opposing V equalising force] ->

Disequilibrium/disrupting forces ->

New equilibrium = plenitude

Ideology in narrative can be examined via Todorov's formula, by considering not only the fact that the status quo has been re-established, but also how the new equilibrium has been reached. Is this achieved through officially sanctioned, and thus legitimate violence? Is it through marriage? Or perhaps through the subjugation of some minority group? Or women returning to their 'rightful' place?

Todorov's formula when applied to narrative points up several key aspects of structure. Firstly, there is a clear linear cause – effect relationship within the narrative. Secondly, there is a positive narrative closure, the mission is accomplished, the world is saved, or at least is returned to its normal condition. Thirdly, there are positive character rôles, and these rôles fit the cause and effect chain of events. Narrative transitivity is also of interest in that it refers to the way in which the audience moves through the narrative, witnessing the various stages of the story.

Characters, functions and motivations

Characters are central components of all narratives. Fairy-tales are useful to analyse because they contain stock characters and structural ingredients. In Vladimir Propp's (1975) work on Russian fairy-tales, first published in 1928, he isolated structures common to all fairy-tales. After studying one hundred and fifteen fairy-tales Propp was able to identify seven main character 'Rôles', as he called them:

1 the Villain
2 the Donor (or provider)
3 the Helper
4 the Princess (or sought for person) and her father
5 the Dispatcher
6 the Hero
7 the False Hero.

Turner's book *Film as Social Practice* is very lucid and excellent on *Star Wars*.

1 the Villain – Darth Vader
2 the Donor – Ben (Obi-Wan) Kenobi
3 the Helper – Han Solo
4 the Princess – Princess Leah
5 the Dispatcher – R2 D2
6 the Hero – Luke Skywalker
7 the False Hero – Darth Vader.

Some of these rôles may well be filled by the same character, they may also be filled by more than one character. The most often cited example of this is *Star Wars*. This is because it makes an interesting point of comparison between the tradition of the fairy-tale and the classic moving image product.

The **function** is the act of a character who has a rôle to play. The rôle is only so defined because the action of the character has a particular significance. The hero is a hero because he has defeated the villain and his action has heroic significance.

Motivation is an important component of narrative structures since no action of a character appears without a reason and that reason is tied to the development of the plot. This is also the case for objects and events. If you see an extreme close up of a gun, then you will have expectations that someone is about to be shot. It may be a ruse, but a director cannot pull that trick very often, since audience expectations are such that each element or event should have a narrative function.

Principle demands of narrative structure

Narrative structure in moving image production, as well as other narrative-based media products, is particularly dominated by the features of the classic realist text, or the Hollywood narrative style. The main features of this are:

- narratives are dominated by verisimilitude, that is that they should be believable
- there should be a single diegesis, that is, one main storyline, although there may be a limited number of sub-plots
- the chain of events should follow a logical sequence, and have an inner logic
- the chain of events should be governed by the actions of central characters
- the audience should empathise with central characters (drawn in by close ups and POVs, as well as the use of the star system)

- the focus is on individuals rather than on the societal or collective level

- the pattern of enigma and resolution, where all questions established during the narrative are answered

- the technical and symbolic elements in media texts are subordinated to the construction of the narrative, and the need to drive it along. Editing is the most obvious process whereby the components of narrative are organised and structured. Seamless or continuity editing ties together the acts, the scenes and the shots. That is, the construction elements of a narrative.

How time is represented

Of particular importance for moving image products is the temporal or time world which is created. Filmic time is distinguished from physical time, or story time. Physical time is the real time that it takes to watch a film or television programme, this might be 90 minutes or 30 minutes. Story (narrative) time is the time of the events covered; in *Citizen Kane*, for instance, the time the events span is about 50 years, although the film lasts 119 minutes. Story time or dramatic time is the fictional duration in which the events take place. Dramatic time within the narrative is important in that it emphasises only that which is narratively important: thus, we can see the events of a person's lifetime or 100 years in the time it takes to view the film or programme.

Very few film products run in real time, Alfred Hitchcock's *Rope* (1948) and the final hour of Fred Zinnemann's *High Noon* (1952) being exceptions. Some television products do however run in real time, quiz shows for instance, and 'live' sports coverage.

Dramatic time uses a number of devices to 'concertina' or compress time. Flashback and flashforward are good examples of swift movement across time. Another strategy is parallel action or development, where two sets of events or actions are intercut so as to be seen to be taking place at the same time; this often leads to a common dénouement. Editing is obviously the most important moving image technology for achieving control over the temporal world, however, slow motion and fast motion are other techniques that enable film to narrate outside real time.

Activity

You have been asked to write the opening scene for a moving image or radio play, in which one of the characters will eventually be murdered. As we have seen, narratives usually develop around the conflict between two people. Using the above components of narrative as well as your knowledge of narrative and character development, write a short script or sketch a storyboard which will introduce the central characters, their motivations and their actions.

Alternative narrative structures

CONVENTIONAL NARRATIVE	ALTERNATIVE NARRATIVE
Narrative transitivity Chain of events, cause and effect, central enigma.	**Narrative Intransitivity** Gaps, interruptions, episodic, digression, break up of narrative.
Identification Empathy & emotional involvement.	**Estrangement** Direct address, multiple divided characters.
Transparency Window on the world, seamless editing.	**Foregrounding** Making the technical overt and explicit.
Single Diegesis Homogenous world.	**Multiple Diegesis** Heterogeneous world.
Closure Self-contained, resolution of central enigma.	**Aperture** Open-ended, overspill, intertextuality.
Pleasure Entertaining, satisfying & confirming	**Unpleasure** Dissatisfaction, provocation & alienation.
Fiction Actors wearing costume, doing a performance.	**Reality** Real life, non-professional actors, breaking up representation.

Alternative narrative structures as mentioned earlier in this section, have to be examined as a counter to, or as a reaction to, dominant narrative styles. That is, the components of narrative as discussed above are applied in a non-standard way in order to achieve different effects on the audience than would be expected from a standard narrative.

Hollywood narrative film set out to soothe and please its audience. It worked to meet their expectations and reinforce their ideologies. Alternative narratives in all media products set out not only to challenge the codes and conventions of production but also to challenge the audience. Instead of the audience being in the passive position of spectator, observer, empathiser and voyeur, they become active, critical and even alienated from the product. This can be attempted by altering the mode of address, perhaps by directly addressing the audience during a stage production.

Activity

Write a report as to how you might reconstruct a familiar fairy-tale in terms of an alternative content and form. You can do this in any medium you wish. Try to clearly illustrate the traditional conventions that you are attempting to challenge.

Modernism and postmodernism in narrative

In 1953 Virginia Woolf stated 'They've changed everything now... we used to think there was a beginning and a middle and an end'. Modernist writers in literature wanted to get away from traditional realist fiction and create a new or alternative type:

- focusing on the mind, or private narratives of individual characters
- abandoning the chronological convention
- often concentrating on single events such as the day in the life of a character
- they were interested in the form of their art, which became reflexive, that is, referring back to itself.

However, postmodernism of the 1980s and 1990s has developed the notions of narrative, alternative narrative and non-narrative, emphasising:

- hyper reality – media reality becomes more important than actual reality
- fragmentation – transgressing barriers, media products swap formats and style

- discontinuity – narratives are mixed, and genres are mixed, the audience can attend to them in a pick-and-mix fashion
- pessimism – nothing is new, there are only recycled themes
- hypersignification – multiple intertextual and semiological references, calls upon visually a sophisticated audience to have a wide knowledge of media products and styles
- relativism – rejection of moral codes and values; barriers between high and low culture disappear
- erosion – time and place become similar, as signs and symbols from across history and cultures get mixed and lose their initial value
- 'Macdonaldisation' – the growth of multinational corporations inevitably means that narratives will become more and more similar, as they strive to appeal to the widest possible multicultural audience.

New narrative forms

It is important to recognise the development of new technologies in the growth of new types of narrative. Two examples of these are video and computer games. Interactive technology allows the audience to work within a framework and develop their own particular version of the narrative.

Multimedia is increasingly important in the development of narrative styles, combining computer graphics, animation, music, film and video all in one product. The British director, Peter Greenaway, has used multimedia packages to stunning effect in such films as *Prospero's Books* (1991). The effect of multimedia narratives are that they develop story-telling away from the domination of language towards a visual and sign-based form of communication.

New technologies such as satellite and digital communication shrink our perception the world, creating two possibilities for narratives. The first is that they will draw upon many different cultures for their meaning and style. Secondly, narratives will become more and more universalised and similar, probably dominated by the Hollywood style and appealing to the 'lowest common denominator' of audience interest.

Analysing the structure of alternative narratives will encourage you to question the rôle of the media in society. What are the media for? Whose interests do they serve? What are they saying?

Narrative structures and audiences

The creation of meaning

Who creates the meaning in media products – the author who produces the text, or the audience?

There are three different types of reading.

1 In the *preferred reading*, the audience is directed towards a particular, usually ideological, meaning. This can be done through realism, pleasure, genre or representation. Images can be anchored by captions.

Headlines often refer us to dominant values simply by their outrage at the abnormal or unacceptable.

2 In *negotiated reading*, the audience member may or may not recognise the meaning, either accepting, questioning or rejecting it. This is often the case with the reporting of news: you may not accept the need for a strike, you may be swayed by the arguments or by your own experience and opinions.

3 In *oppositional reading*, the reader does not recognise the dominant meaning in the narrative and falls back on their own experience and opinions to construct a different reading.

Therefore the struggle for meaning is fought between the media producers, who build preferred readings into the text, and the audience who produce a range of negotiated or oppositional readings.

Assignment

Examine three media texts. One should be print-based, such as a newspaper or magazine; the other two should be time-based, such as a radio or television programme. One of the texts should be from a series, and one should be produced by the student. One of these texts should have alternative narrative structures. This could be a multimedia package. Produce a narrative analysis of each.

You should use two separate approaches in your analysis, depending on the type of media text you are using. These will be *either* how the narrative develops from beginning to end (the syntagmatic approach) *or* the patterns within the narrative (the paradigmatic approach).

Remember to include an explanation of the use of components within the narrative structure and an analysis of the relationship between the narrative structures and audiences.

Summary

In this unit you have been asked to critically assess, to analyse, to interpret and to interrogate things in the media that many of us simply take for granted and allow to flow over us. The act of stopping this flow dead has to some extent involved you in learning a very different language and taking up a new stance to media products. The aim of this has been to provide you with the tools to become not only thinking, informed and original media producers but also critical audiences.

The unit has aimed to draw your attention to the main areas of analysis in the textual study of the media: textual analysis and construction, representation, genre analysis and narrative. There have been two overarching concerns: the first has been with the creation of meaning within the text, and the second with the creation of meaning for the audience. We have found in most cases that these particular tools of analysis have had a very successful general application to the investigation of most forms of media products.

Bibliography

Barthes, R. (1977) *Image-Music-Text* Fontana Paperbacks

Barthes, R. (1957) *Mythologies* Paladin

Becker, H. (1963) *The Outsiders: Studies in the Sociology of Deviancy* US: Free Press

McQuail, D., Blumler, J. G., and Brown, J. (1972) 'The Television Audience: A Revised Perspective'. In: D. McQuail *Sociology of Mass Communication* Penguin

Monaco, J. (1981) *How to Read A Film* Oxford University Press.

Propp, V. (1975) *The Morphology of the Folk Tale* University of Texas Press

Solomon, S. J. (1976) *Beyond Formula: American Film Genres* Harcourt Brace Jovanovich

Turner, G. (1993) *Film As Social Practice* (second edition) Routledge

Glossary

agenda setting is the process by which the media are able to define those issues that are important in society at any one time, and also the terms of reference of any debate. Allied to agenda-setting, is **agenda-building**: this is the process by which powerful industrial and governmental bodies are able to determine through their manipulation of the news-gathering process the content of the agenda that is set by the media

alternative narrative structures non-standard application of the components of a narrative or new narrative forms

auteur theory is concerned with the rôle of the director as the artist in the film making process. Their rôle as the sole creator of meaning in the text has been challenged by genre theory, which says that the audience read a text in relation to other similar texts they have encountered

connotation the hidden or deeper level meaning of a word or sign. The colour 'red' connotes 'danger' or 'stop', according to its context

cropping is a term for the deliberate selection of a segment or portion of a still photograph in order to emphasise and direct the readers' attention

denotation the literal meaning of a word of sign. The word 'red' denotes a colour

direct addressee a media consumer who is apparently 'spoken to' directly by the media producers, for example when asked to write in with opinions

empathiser a consumer of a media product who enters into the feelings of the central character

enigma the central question or problem in a narrative

equilibrium the order which is established at the beginning and end of some narratives

film noir films of the 1940s and 1950s in America that were seen to have a particularly bleak attitude to society, this was reflected in the use of black and white film, with an emphasis on low-key lighting

formalism limits its attention to the signifier. That is formalist approaches are concerned with the structure of film without reference to the audience, to social context, or to any extra filmic reality

function the act of a character who has a rôle to play

inclusion a mode of address which is used to alienate the audience

inclusive addressee a media consumer whose normal mode of understanding narrative structure is disputed deliberately by the media producer by the use of narrative style which emphasise the artificial, 'constructed' quality of the media product

intertextuality occurs where texts refer to other texts and can only be fully understood if the audience recognises and understands these cross-references

linear process models of communication concentrate on the passage of a message from one point to another. That is from source to receiver

mass media channels of communication which reach a very large audience, such as television, film, newspapers, radio

mise-en-scène the composition of a scene in terms of background, props, costumes and actors

modes of address there are four modes of address in a narrative – voyeur or observer, empathiser, direct and inclusive addressee

motivation the reason why a character appears in a narrative: used to awaken the audience's expectations early in an action

onomatopoeia are words that sound like the object or action that they mean. For instance, cuckoo for the bird of that name, burp for belching

opening and **closure** the beginning and end of a narrative

oppositions two things which are exact opposites. They are central in the analysis of narrative. To know that something is good, one must know what bad means.

paradigmatic approach an approach to the analysis of narrative structures – how narrative is a unit and has patterns within it

protagonist the word comes from the Greek for 'first actor'. It is a more useful word than 'hero' as the central character of a narrative might be a villain. A protagonist may be male or female

semiology the study of signs and sign systems. **Semiotics** deals with the theory of signs as used in language

signifying systems the technical and symbolic elements making up a text

syntagmatic approach an approach to the analysis of narrative structures – how narrative develops from beginning to end

voyeur (or **observer**) someone who passively watches or listens to a media communication

Planning and research for media production

G
N
V
Q

Contents

Introduction

The start of the process in producing any media product is the idea. This might be your own idea as the producer, or an idea or commission from a client.

The next stages involve careful research and planning to establsih whether the idea can be developed, how this will be carried out, and the resources that will be required to do this.

In this study unit you will have the opportunity to develop these skills for a range of different media: print, audio and moving image.

In the first section, you look at the different sources of information available, and identify research methods and techniques that will be useful when you are preparing a media production. You will combine this information into a production research handbook, which you will be able to refer to when you go on to produce your media products in the following units.

The second section looks at developing ideas for a range of print products, and identifies some of the issues to consider when you are planning print products.

Audio products are created through a different series of processes, and in the third section you will be examining these in detail, and focusing particularly on both commercials and news features.

Finally, in the fourth section you will be developing ideas and undertaking research for moving image products.

The research and the planning that you carry out in this unit will be valuable information to help you in developing future products. These products might result from ideas you have researched during this unit, or you might decide to develop new ideas in the light of your experience.

1 Research methods

In this section you will investigate methods of research. You will identify sources of useful information, research methods and techniques that you need when you are preparing a media production. In addition you will examine how legal, ethical and representational issues need to be considered before you can begin any project. You will also identify the basic methods of audience research techniques.

As you work through this section you will discover that research sources are not restricted to books and libraries, but include the information that people can tell you themselves. Before any media production can begin, there is a great deal of information that has to be obtained, gathered together, analysed and presented so that it is available to everyone working on the production who might need it.

Assignment

All the information you collect on these topics will enable you to build up a class production research handbook. You will be able to use this as a resource for all your future research work in media studies. The research handbook will contain information on procedure, useful addresses and contacts and sample research methods. You may find that the best way to keep your handbook is in the form of a ring binder, so that it can be updated. It is important that you update it when information changes or you have additional relevant information to add.

In addition to the handbook, you should have an assignment portfolio, in which you write down your own contributions to the handbook, together with your notes on classroom activities and discussions and any individual work that you have carried out while working on this section. Your work on the compilation of this handbook and your assignment portfolio will form the evidence indicators for this section of the study unit.

Content research

'Yes – oh dear – yes. The novel tells a story,' wrote E M Forster, the author of such novels as *A Room with a View* and *Howard's End*, which have also been adapted for the cinema. But how do film-makers find their stories? And how do directors and producers of non-fiction find ideas for their productions?

Activity

Write down what you think may have been the sources for the feature films listed below. For example, the source for the film *Black Beauty* was the well-known children's book by Anna Sewell.

- *The Flintstones*
- *Sense and Sensibility*
- *Tommy*
- *Braveheart*
- *Apollo 13*
- *Othello*

For the famous Swedish director, Ingmar Bergman, the idea for a film can spring from almost any source:
'Often [film making] begins with an image... Or it may be that a few words are exchanged; two people who suddenly say something to each other in a completely personal tone of voice ... I can't even see their faces but I am forced to listen to them...'

From Harry Geduld (ed.), *Film Makers on Film Making*, Indiana University Press, 1967

Fig. 2.1
Research methods carried out by Red Flannel, a women's film and video workshop

In writing down these sources, you will have become aware that scripts for feature films are based on a variety of original texts or may also come from real life. The ideas for films – and other media productions – can come from a wide variety of sources. For example, the German film director Margaretha von Trotta has written that her inspiration for a film was a picture of a woman who looked so sad that she aroused the director's curiosity. She therefore read everything she could about the woman, including her published letters and finally made a film about her.

Ideas for media productions can be found in many places. However, if you are about to begin a media production, you need not only the original idea, but as much information as possible about the subject. Good scriptwriters immerse themselves in the subject and use both primary and secondary research sources.

HOW WE MADE THE FILM

The core of the film rests on the interviews we did with women in the Valleys. We met many of them through the screening groups we had set up in the Valleys. Out of these groups there also emerged a core of women who were interested in working with us on the film and acting as consultants. They formed a production company which saw the film through to its final stages. As well as the contacts made from the screening groups we also visited Old People's homes in the Valleys.

We then found a lot of our archive material from the BFI, the BBC film library, St Fagans, the Miner's library, Swansea and local libraries and museums. We also spoke to women historians like Dee Beddoe and Angela John and spent a lot of time talking to as many women as we could find, as well as employing a Welsh speaking feminist historian who found a lot of interesting material in the Welsh language.

'Mam' was very much a Red Flannel joint effort, all members of Red Flannel worked on its research and we had regular meetings where all our information was brought together and knocked into shape.

By the end of the research period we had a pretty thorough understanding of women's role in the developing history of the Valleys, but we wanted women themselves to tell the story, through their own memories and experiences.

From the very many women we spoke to during the research period we finally chose our film interviewees. We chose on the basis of firstly personality, women who could speak articulately and engagingly about the past. Secondly we needed a good age range so that the film could cover a long period in time. Lastly, it was important that their personal stories reflected what was the common experience.

The script was developed through the following process:
- Screening and discussions on questions raised under 'background'
- Formation of production group
- Sound interviews
- Archive research: feature films, documentary, stills
- Background reading: historical, sociological, economic, literature
- Choosing material for dramatisation and documentary development
- Creating basic structure of film
- Drama improvisations
- Shaping of documentary material into cohesive sequences
- Final scripting

The production group carried on working with us during the editing of the film, so that our decisions could be informed by their opinions.

Red Flannel feel that because of the long term involvement of Valleys women during the making of 'Mam' via screenings, discussions and within the production group, that the final result is a truer representation of their lives, than a film made under normal mainstream constraints would allow.

The difference between primary data and secondary data is shown below.

Primary	Secondary
Raw data that you have collected, but not adapted in any form. This can be from:	Data that has been adapted and published in some form. It may include:
• observation • questionnaires • researchers' notes • press releases • short stories • novels • existing films and television productions • stories people tell you.	• reference books • articles • broadcast material • videos • photographs • electronically retrieved material, i.e. from the Internet.

Activity

You have been commissioned to make a television programme about the English Civil War (1642–8). This can be either factual or fiction, whichever you prefer. In groups, make a list of the possible sources you would want to consult in preparing the production. Do not forget that these preparations should also include the information you will need on the subject to give to costume designers, location scouts, property buyers, etc. Make sure that you include primary and secondary sources.

In your lists you will certainly have included history books on the subject and you may also have included novels set during the Civil War as well as existing films and television programmes set during this period. You may also have expanded the lists to include paintings of Oliver Cromwell and Charles I in the National Portrait Gallery and pictures of buildings which were destroyed during the Civil War.

In compiling your lists you will probably have considered that secondary sources provide the easiest and quickest ways of obtaining information. However, primary sources often provide crucial details that are not included in secondary sources.

Activity

In groups, list methods of primary research and the kind of media production where they would be most valuable. For example, if you were making a programme on the effects on children of violence in the media, you would need to interview both children and parents and possibly also teachers. You might use audiotaped interviews and/or questionnaires.

Your lists may have included personal and telephone interviews. You may also have suggested photographs and notes made from personal observations.

Activity

As a class, discuss your lists and prepare a final list for your handbook. Include not only sources such as novels, short stories, notes, but actual locations, such as the names of your local library, film and television archives. If you are planning a production on a certain topic, you may wish to add the names and addresses of specialists on these topics whom you can consult. For example, if you are doing a project on safety on the roads, your contacts would include the local branches of the AA and RoSPA (Royal Society for the Prevention of Accidents). If you are doing a historical project, your history teacher may be a useful source of information or may be able to suggest other sources.

Sources for film and television archives can be found in two guides published annually: *The BFI Film and Television Handbook* (published by the British Film Institute) and *The Media Guide* (published by the Guardian/Fourth Estate). These guides will be needed throughout this section and will subsequently be referred to as *The BFI Handbook* and *The Media Guide*.

Audience research

In order to market a media product, you need to be aware of the audience for that product. You will study media audiences and how they are researched in more detail in Study Unit 6 and marketing techniques in Study Unit 7. In your research handbook, therefore, you should simply note down the basic methods of audience research.

After you have studied Study Units 6 and 7, you may wish to return to your handbook and insert additional information to make it a more comprehensive guide to research.

Media researchers need to know as much as possible about their audiences and they have a number of ways of categorising them:

- *Demographics*. This characterises the population in terms of age, sex, occupation, location, education, ethnicity and socioeconomic class. The most common form of social grade classifications have been standardised as social grades A, B, C1, etc., as shown in the following table.

Social grade	Social status	Head of household's occupation
A	Upper middle class	Higher managerial, administrative or professional
B	Middle class	Intermediate managerial, administrative or professional
C1	Lower middle class	Supervisory or clerical, and junior managerial, administrative or professional
C2	Skilled working class	Skilled manual workers
D	Working class	Semi- and unskilled manual workers
E	Those at lowest subsistence levels	State pensioners or widows (no other earner), casual or lowest grade workers

- *Geodemographics*. This form of analysis was developed because of dissatisfaction with the A–E classifications, which did not give researchers enough detailed information. Several geodemographics systems have been set up in the UK. Almost all of them use data from the Census of Population and many of them are also closely linked to the postcode system. The most common system is ACORN, which classifies the population according to types of housing and neighbourhood. ACORN also classifies according to **lifestyles**.

The ACORN Family Group Classification by housing

ACORN groups	1990 population	(%)	Household (%)
A Agricultural areas	1836	3.4	3.3
B Modern family housing higher incomes	9546	17.5	16.2
C Older housing of intermediate status	9752	17.9	18.8
D Older terraced housing	2281	4.2	4.4
E Council estates – I	7169	13.2	12.6
F Council estates – II	4789	8.8	9.6
G Council estates – III	3812	7.0	6.5
H Mixed inner metropolitan areas	2079	3.8	3.4
I High-status non-family areas	2238	4.1	4.7
J Affluent suburban housing	8623	15.8	15.9
K Better-off retirement areas	2068	3.8	4.6
L Unclassified	294	0.5	0.0

CACI

- *Lifestyles*. In addition to the basic demographic definitions, there are 24 ACORN Lifestyle groups and 81 ACORN Lifestyle types, which link neighbourhood and lifestyle. This linking of geographic area with demographics accounts for the origin of the term *geodemographics*.

ACORN Classification by lifestyles

Household composition	Age structure
Singles Adults living on their own, usually without young children	*Younger* Youngest – adults most often between 18 and 24
Couples Two adults, almost certainly married, with or without young children	Maturing – adults most often between 25 and 44
Family Two adults, almost certainly married with at least one other relation in residence, either child or other adult	*Older* Established – adults most often between 45 and 64
Homesharers Multiple adults living together but not couples or family	Retired – adults most often over 65

- Other systems used for classification apart from ACORN are the MOSAIC, which is a similar system but also includes a credit rating, and 'Sagacity' classifications.
- Geodemographics define people according to broad categories, but many researchers find them inadequate and want more specific segmentation. This has been produced by Target Group Index (TGI), operated by the British Market Research Bureau (BMRB). TGI describes in detail specific groups of consumers and their media exposure. Thanks to the work on TGI carried out by the (then) Arts Council of Great Britain, it also includes details of consumption and attendance at all forms of arts activity. This employs ACORN neighbourhood types within selected samples, using random wards, parishes and streets. All those sampled are given a self-completion questionnaire which covers a wide range of consumer and media practices.

Quantitative and qualitative research

The purpose of audience research is to interrogate audiences and discover which categories they belong to. There are two basic categories of audience research: *quantitative* and *qualitative*. Quantitative research calculates quantity; it is basically 'number crunching' – how many attended, bought, listened, watched etc. Quantitative research answers the questions: 'Who?' 'When?' 'How many?'. It cannot answer 'Why?'. For that, you need qualitative research. There are a variety of methods of research for both categories. For quantitative research, these are ways of measuring audiences, while for qualitative research, they are ways of interrogating audiences. The most thorough research projects combine both categories.

Many methods used in qualitative research are described as *psychographic*. These are methods which are drawn from psychology and which endeavour to probe an audience's subconscious reactions to products. These methods have been developed because for many reasons people may not tell the truth in straightforward research. They may say what they think the interviewer wants to hear or what they feel they should say or, if they are part of a group discussion or **focus group**, they may echo what other members of the group have said. In psychographic research methods there are no 'right or wrong' answers and the researchers can therefore form a more accurate picture of what the interviewee really thinks about a subject.

Activity

Below are listed most of the major methods of audience research. Do you consider them to be quantitative, qualitative or both? List them accordingly.

- Questionnaires
- Diaries (e.g. recording media consumption)
- **Electronic recording devices** (e.g. fixed to TV sets)

As you will see in Study Unit 7, *lifestyle* is also a term used by marketeers to define the consumer in general terms of aspirations, tastes and spending habits.

Psychographic research methods are discussed in detail in Study Unit 6.

'The essence of qualitative research is that it is diagnostic; it seeks to discover what may account for certain types of behaviour... It seeks deeper understanding of factors, sometimes [unconscious], which influence buying [and watching and listening] decisions. It is impressionistic rather than conclusive; it probes rather than counts. It observes and reflects on the complexity of human activities in satisfying many needs. Intrinsically it is subjective.'
Peter Chisnall, *Marketing Research*, McGraw-Hill, 1992

- Interviews
- Readership surveys
- Audience observation (e.g. at special film previews)
- Panel discussion groups/focus groups
- Measuring box office attendance.

You may have decided that some of these research methods are clearly quantitative, some are clearly qualitative and some have both quantitative and qualitative features. Different media require different methods of research, particularly of measurement, for example, electronic measuring devices for TV and box office receipts for cinema. However, when it comes to qualitative approaches, there are methods which can be used for a variety of different media.

These can be described under the headings of *closed experiments* and *field studies*. Closed experiments are the media studies equivalent of carrying out research under laboratory conditions. They may include panel viewings or readings. The research is carried out in a manner which is controlled by the researcher and can be duplicated elsewhere. In field studies the opposite is true. The researcher merely observes what happens in the real world and such behaviour may differ from place to place depending on individual audience behaviour.

Activity

Work in groups to investigate the audience research methods listed above. Divide them among the class, so that each group investigates one method.

In professional market research there are complex ways of determining the numbers involved in surveys. All *you* need to do is to survey a large enough number of people to get a valid result i.e. two people are not enough.

- Write a short outline of how the research is carried out; note how many people may need to be included in the research to ensure that the results are valid.
- Consider which forms of media are best suited to each method and what uses are made of its results.

The resulting information should be put into your research handbook.

Content considerations

Activity

Read through the (fictional) text on the next page. In groups discuss why the various mistakes and disasters occurred and what should have been done in advance to avoid them.

'Well, I can't say it was my favourite shoot. We had one disaster after another and, by the end, the crew thought that the locals had put a curse on the whole production. We were two days into shooting the main love scenes when we were told that everything had to stop because apparently the scriptwriter had based his screenplay on a short story that he'd heard on the radio and, so he says, forgotten about. It took the producer a few days to sort that out, pay the original writer, promise credits, that sort of thing. Then because of the delay, when we started to film again, we didn't realise that our police permits to film on the highway had expired and so they had to be renewed. Then there was that bit in the paper about how our director had insulted a young black cameraman who had wanted to work on the production and the producer had to find a new director because of the court case. Of course that wasn't the only court case – we were sued by the owner of one of the gardens, because he said we had filmed it over the wall without his permission and the producer was also in trouble because he insisted on our filming until late one evening and forgot that the children involved in the scene had already worked up to the limit of hours allowed on any one day. Other problems were the usual kind of thing. Drives that had to be resurfaced because of all the damage caused by our lorries, damage to people's property. Irritating really when you know that for the next few years they will do nothing but tell everyone how exciting it was to have their village used as a film set. But that's the way it goes...'

Section 2 in Study Unit 8 looks at the regulations which cover the media in detail, but for the purpose of your research handbook, you should be aware of the legal, ethical and representational considerations that you would have to consider before developing a media production.

In your discussions you will have noted that the film company ignored many basic considerations such as copyright and following ethical codes of practice. The production also broke laws relating to race relations, the Highways Act, privacy and the use of children in films.

Activity

In groups, research the legal considerations that you have to address regarding media productions and make a list of them – *The Media Guide* will be a good starting point. Some of the considerations relate to the laws that everyone has to observe, such as those dealing with copyright, libel, driving, etc., while others cover representational issues such as gender, age and race. Add to your list the names and addresses of the relevant organisations dealing with these issues, for example, the Equal Opportunities Commission and the Race Relations Board.

In your research you may have found that many of the organisations which you listed have information sheets outlining their work which you can write to them for. Wherever possible, add these to your handbook.

In addition to legal restrictions, there are ethical considerations which are covered by codes of practice and prevent media producers from falling into the traps listed in the disastrous scenario above. Obviously if you use an experienced producer, he or she will already be familiar with these codes of practice and will know what restrictions there are and how you can obtain the various permissions you need. But if you were a foreign producer coming to make a production in Britain for the first time, it might not be so easy to find that information.

Activity

Imagine you are a production manager about to make a film with a foreign producer which requires location work in various parts of Britain. His office has asked you to prepare a summary covering any restrictions, noting any relevant codes of practice and listing permissions that have to be applied for. In groups, discuss where you would find this information and how you would research it.

In your discussion you may have considered that the primary source of asking experienced production managers was the easiest way to obtain all the information. Using a directory of media bodies (such as *The Media Guide*), you may have also considered that unions, such as BECTU (Broadcasting Entertainment Cinematograph and Theatre Union) and trade associations, such as the Directors Guild of Great Britain and PACT (Producers Alliance for Cinema and TV), are also good research sources.

BECTU was formed in 1991 by the merger of the ACTT and BETA.

Activity

Look at the topics covered in the code of practice for the print industry. Make a list of codes of practice for other forms of the media and contact the appropriate organisations for copies. These should be kept in your research handbook.

It is not only audiovisual productions that have codes of practice. Newspapers and magazines are covered by the code of practice which is enforced by the Press Complaints Commission. Study Unit 8 looks at these codes of practice in more detail.

1	Accuracy	10	Intrusion into grief or shock
2	Opportunity to reply	11	Innocent relatives and friends
3	Comment, conjecture and fact	12	Interviewing or photographing children
4	Privacy	13	Children in sex cases
5	Listening Devices	14	Victims of crime
6	Hospitals	15	Discrimination
7	Misrepresentation	16	Financial journalism
8	Harassment	17	Confidential sources
9	Payments for articles	18	The public interest

Headings of the Press Complaints Commision Code of Practice

Sources of production research

The producer of any media production is in charge of an army of specialists, each of whom has to be responsible for his or her own area of activity.

Fig. 2. 2
Structure of film unit

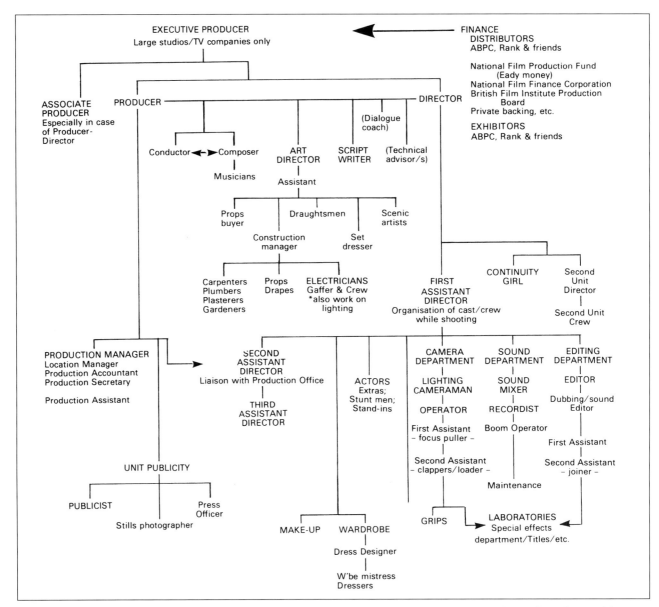

O'Sullivan, Dutton and Rayner, *Studying the Media*, Edward Arnold, 1994

Location

It is often said that the more expensive the production, the more **locations** are used. As a rough guide this is generally fairly accurate. Finding locations, getting permission to shoot there, changing the look of locations to suit the needs and period of a production and then, finally, transporting cast and crew to locations – all of these activities are extremely expensive.

British Film Commission, 70 Baker Street, London W1M 1DJ. Tel: 0171-224 5000

You will probably find it useful to find out the name and address and director of your nearest Film Commission and include this in your handbook (source: *The BFI Handbook*).

Fig. 2. 3
Advertisement for a US Film Commission office

'Going to large houses, historical houses, is very expensive, you are paying a thousand pounds a day these days. They are either National Trust or the owners are members of the Historical Houses Association and they have a scale of rates you have to pay. We went to one house and all we did was an exterior of the house and the moat that went round it and it was £750, just to shoot the exterior, which is quite expensive. But if you are going for period shows, there is not a lot you can do about it, you have to pay the money. The actual **OB** [**outside broadcast**] itself is very expensive. Once you are on the road it is exceedingly difficult to control what is being spent...'

From 'Case study: the production of *Vanity Fair*' in R. Giddings, K. Selby and C. Wensley, *Screening the Novel*, Macmillan, 1990

In a film or television production the most common method of location hunting is first to go to the British Film Commission and find the address of the nearest Commission office covering the area where the production is considering basing its shoot. There are 13 regional Film Commissions in Great Britain – they are relatively new in Britain, but have existed in the USA for many years. Their function is to persuade film and television companies to film in their area because of the financial benefits – for example, to hotels, restaurants, shops, etc. – of having a production there.

A Film Commission office will offer the film company a library of possible locations, assist in getting permissions and help with any other local problems, such as dealing with the local police and fire brigade.

Activity

Imagine that your class is the Film Commission office for your area. Working in groups, put together a location library and a list of useful contacts. You should include:

- the name of the place you are suggesting as a possible location
- the address of the place – you should also note its position on a map of the area
- notes regarding provision of basic services such as electricity, water, etc.
- special features – whether it has a twelfth-century ruined castle or a large modern shopping mall, for example
- contact names and telephone numbers of people you would need to contact for permission, such as the owner, local office of the National Trust, etc. (if telephone numbers are not easily obtainable, just include the address with a note that the number is ex-directory)
- notes on possible genre for which the location would be suitable – for example, thriller, historical drama, contemporary drama
- photographs (in the case of a house which is open to the public, you may be able to include postcards showing interior views).

Be imaginative. Do not just include the large country houses in your area, but also add empty factories which could be used in a thriller or a police drama, and views of countryside completely free of pylons and electric cables, which could belong to any period.

You may also wish to make a wall display of some of this material with pins on a map noting the locations and arrows pointing to photographs, descriptions, etc.

Activity

Divide the areas of activity listed on the next page around the class, with groups each taking responsibility for researching sources of information on different topics.

For many of these research subjects your first source of reference material will be the annual guides. In addition to *The Media Guide* and *The BFI Handbook*, the most useful guides are *The Knowledge*, *Benn Business Information Services* and the *Broadcast Production Guide*. These last two yearbooks are extremely expensive and you will probably only be able to consult them at libraries.

Yellow Pages includes useful information.

- Transport
- Permissions
- Risk assessment
- Talent
- Props
- Music
- Sound effects.

Transport

A large film or television production may need to film in planes as well as ships, trains, buses and cars. Transport covers both transporting the crew and equipment and being responsible for finding transport needed for filming. Information about the former can be found in film directories such as *The BFI Handbook*, under 'Production Services'. For the latter, however, you will need to use a variety of sources to make your lists. The local tourist office is a good place to start. It will give you information about local tourist features such as small-gauge steam trains, vintage car collections, etc. You should also add names and telephone numbers of local bus and taxi companies, and other transport offices.

Fig 2.4
An example of the kind of services offered to the film industry

Permissions

You are by now aware that any shoot – even your own – means getting a number of permissions. These include location permissions and permissions from the police to shoot in the street.

There are also the permissions you need for using copyright material. This includes both written and sound material – even a few lines of poetry or the noise of fire engines taken from a sound-effects record are protected by copyright. The following organisations are good places to begin your research and both will be able to provide you with information sheets for the handbook: the Mechanical-Copyright Protection Society (MCPS) and the Performing Rights Society (PRS). MCPS issues licences for the recording of its members' copyright material in television, film and video production. The PRS collect fees for the use of music in broadcast and live performances. It is a non-profit-making organisation, which exists to support composers. For use of printed copyright material you have to contact the publisher whose name and address are shown on the publication data page.

If you use excerpts from films or photographs from archives, then the archive will tell you who owns the copyright and whom you should apply to for permission to use it.

If you film anyone and want to use that footage in a film, television or video production, then you will need the individual's written permission. In the case of shooting anyone under the age of 18, you will also need permission from a parent.

Risk assessment

This information should take the form of checklists. Make lists under different headings to cover all eventualities. They should include the names and telephone numbers of local emergency services.

In compiling these checklists, imagine you are shooting in your school/college and think of all the information the lists should contain. This will include:

- fire regulations and fire drill
- first-aid information – where the nearest first-aid box is, for example
- public liability insurance – if you are involving members of the public.

For other locations:

- Protective clothing may be needed if you are working in hazardous conditions – from building sites to mountain walking
- Weather is critical for outdoor shooting and can be a hazard in difficult terrain, so include the number of your local Meteorological Office.

You might ask a representative of your local authority Health and Safety Office to come and talk about these issues or to send information for your handbook.

MCPS Elgar House, 41 Streatham High Road, London SW16 1ER

PRS 29–33 Berners Street, London W1P 4AA

For lists of archives, see *The BFI Handbook* and *The Media Guide*

Contact musicians' and actors' unions for guidelines which will give you the accurate wording of these permissions, as well as other permissions that you may need. Add these to your handbook.

If you are near the sea/mountains/rivers, you should also include the telephone number of the coastguard, mountain rescue, river rescue, etc.

You might like to get information from St John Ambulance on what to include in a first-aid box and include this on your list as well.

For the types of protective clothing that you may require, associations for the relevant activities, such as yachting or mountaineering, will be able to give you guidance. Local builders will be able to provide guidelines.

You will find lists of various other specialist emergency organisations in *The Media Guide*, from the Air Accidents Investigation Branch to the Underwater Search Unit and Victim Support.

Talent

This word is being used in its widest sense to include anyone who will be needed to take part in your production. It relates to anyone you wish to interview for print products, as well as those you include in audiovisual productions. In addition to those who will be acting in productions or taking the rôle of interviewers, there are those whose experience you might wish to include. For example, if you were making a production about the problems of families living in bed and breakfast accommodation, then you would need to include members of several such families, as well as 'experts' in the field.

In professional productions there are casting agencies who exist to persuade directors and producers to employ their members. For your handbook make lists of sources of talent, such as specialists in the field of your media production – you may wish to add to this when you start work on an actual production.

Include sources such as national organisations like the Film Artistes' Association (which handles extras) and other agencies, for example, The Spotlight, the casting directory for film and television, which exists as a CD-Rom as well as in book form, and Crews Employments, a free service to the film and television industry, which has a computer database of freelance union members. You might also include a new interactive casting service, launched in April 1996, Interactive Casting Universal, which offers producers the opportunity to view information on their desktop computers.

Also make lists of local sources of talent including local amateur dramatic companies, theatre and dance schools, etc. Use your local library as a source for this information.

Props

The most important information for the designer of any production which he or she will need to pass on to the property buyer is the budget for the props and the date by which they are needed.

Research sources for props should include other organisations which use props, such as local amateur dramatic companies plus local auction houses and antique shops. Use primary sources – for example, other film-makers – for their lists of props and add these to your lists.

Music

The reflex action for most people researching music for the first time is to turn to recordings, such as CDs and cassettes, either from record libraries or from their own collections. Professional film-makers will use specially commissioned music as well as music from recorded-music libraries. Therefore it will be useful to include the major libraries in your research material.

The address of Crews Employments can be found in *The BFI Handbook*.

In the world of professional film and television the props budget can be huge. Films may buy or make 'antique' furniture and one American hospital set has spent more on equipment than the actual annual budget for a real British hospital. In your productions things will be very different and the person in charge of props will need to show ingenuity and inventiveness.

'... For *Vanity Fair* there was so much music in the production – characters had to play, they had to sing and they had to dance. All that had to be sorted out before any filming could be done ... I tried to research dance music from the period but in the end I wrote it all myself. It was pastiche music because then you could be guaranteed that it was the right length, that it would fit the action.'
Composer Nigel Hess in 'Case study: the production of *Vanity Fair*' in R. Giddings, K. Selby and C. Wensley, *Screening the Novel*, Macmillan, 1990

Fig. 2. 5
Advertisement for the
Musicians' Union
aimed at professional
film-makers

In 1994 more foreign film and TV makers were
recording their music in the UK than for many
years. Why? Because for quality, expertise and
sheer value for money British musicians are
virtually unbeatable.

If you want any of your specific queries about
Agreements, Contractors, Composers, Musicians etc etc
answered, then contact **Stan Martin**, Assistant General
Secretary responsible for media, **Marilyn Stoddart**,
Media Organiser, or **Don Smith**, Session Organiser.

Dennis Scard
General Secretary
Musicians' Union
60/62 Clapham Road
London SW9 0JJ

Tel: 0171 582 5566
Fax: 0171 582 9805

Music publishers also have
libraries of recorded music of
their own composers. You can
find the names of these in the
British Music Yearbook
(Rhinegold Publishing) in your
local library.

To cut the costs of your media production, you should also think of
alternative sources of music. These can include music played by members
of your school or college and the possibly music commissioned from
students studying music at a nearby university. Include all these research
sources in your handbook and use your music teacher as a primary source
to suggest additional sources.

Sound effects

Whistles, bangs, sirens, trains, birdsong – all these sounds are available on
records for the use of film and audio productions, although they are
subject to copyright and permission must be applied for to use them. For a
small production you will usually find it cheaper to create your own sound
effects. If, however, you do need a special sound effect, you will need to
research this from a sound archive or tape library.

The principal resource for sound effects is the British Library National
Sound Archive. It offers free public listening for researchers, although this
is by appointment only. There are several other commercial sound
libraries and many public libraries have records of sound effects made by
the BBC. The BBC sound effects library itself exists for BBC productions
only.

You will find the lists of sound
libraries in the *British Music
Yearbook*.

2 Planning and researching print items

Just look around you and you will see how much the printed word is used in our society today. And it's not just words which are effective communicators of meaning – visual images such as cartoons, photographs, illustrations and **graphics**, are also included with words to form what we can call print items.

However, if you are to be successful in using print items, you need to plan and carry out effective research. This section considers some ground rules which you need to apply to your print items if people are to fully understand the message you are trying to give them.

What are print items?

The first stage in the planning and researching process for print items is to categorise the types of print items you want to use. There are four main categories:

1 *Text-based* – these are print items which use words to communicate their messages. You can find examples of these in newspaper or magazine articles and stories, textbooks, advertisements, leaflets, posters and brochures.
2 *Image-based* – these are visual texts where words are not used to communicate the messages. Examples include photographs and cartoons; illustrations on advertisements and posters; company logos; graphics on brochures; and drawings – artwork – in books.
3 *Fiction* – these are print items which are based on creative imagination, such as stories in comics; novels or thrillers; children's fairy tales; and cartoon characters.
4 *Non-fiction* – these are print items which are based on factual reality. Examples could be a news story in a newspaper or magazine; facts explained in an encyclopaedia; and graphics or charts showing statistics.

Activity

Produce a list of at least four examples of each of the four categories. If you can, include examples. Keep your notes and examples for your portfolio.

Fig. 2. 6
Example of a fiction print item

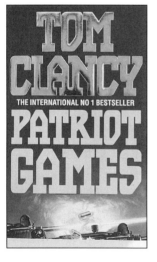

Fig. 2. 7
Example of a non-fiction print item

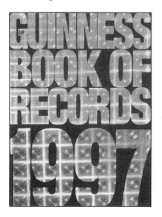

Purpose of print items

Identifying the purpose of the print item assists you in understanding the practice of categorising print items. This, in turn, helps you plan the direction of your print item in terms of your item's message to the readers. Print items need to take account of the overall aims of the final product to which they contribute. The key questions you must ask yourself in terms of purpose are: 'What type of message am I trying to get across to the readers?' 'Am I trying to inform them, educate them, or persuade them?'

Print items can have one, or a combination of four basic purposes.

1 To pass on information. An example of this is a news report in a newspaper or magazine, where certain information concerning an event is being passed on to the readers, such as a report on a parliamentary by-election, or on a more light-hearted scale, your daily horoscope!

2 To educate. Perhaps the best example of this is this book in which you are learning, through the texts, about the media. Other print items could be a series of encyclopaedias, where the content of the text is aimed at improving the reader's knowledge.

3 To entertain. Cartoons and funny stories are two examples of texts which have the purpose of entertaining.

4 To persuade. An example of a print item where the aim is to persuade is an advertisement.

Resources

While good ideas are important when planning and carrying out research for print items, these ideas need to be explored realistically. There is no use putting forward grandiose ideas which have no hope of becoming practical realities. You have to work within your means, and this is especially true in terms of resources. There is no point in researching and planning a project if you do not have the necessary equipment to carry out your research objectives to their natural conclusion – the production of a print item. A planning checklist will help you tackle your project in a practical way. It covers four main areas of resourcing which must be considered:

- *Human resources.* Do you have enough people to successfully complete the research for the print item? The situation you want to avoid is that you have too many tasks to complete, and not enough people to complete them.
- *Financial resources.* Do you have enough in your budget to complete the research? It's important not to run out of money or go over budget.
- *Materials.* Have you enough on-site equipment, such as computers or telephones to complete the research? Have you got transport to locations, and permission for the off-site activities?

- *Time*. Have you allowed yourself enough time to complete the research for the print item so that you meet the agreed deadline?

To understand the practical workings of using this checklist to plan and research, let's look at a scenario in which you are planning an article on the use of drugs by teenagers for your school or college student magazine. This is how you would approach such a print item:

- *Human resources*. We need someone to research the types of drugs which teenagers use; someone to research the effects of these drugs on the mind and body; someone to research the legal consequences of being caught in possession of drugs; someone to research what advice and guidance exists to help young people; someone to research teenagers who would be willing to share their experiences with the student magazine.
- *Financial resources*. How much will it cost to get photos of the various types of drugs; or copy the front covers of advice leaflets on drugs?
- *Materials*. Pens and notebooks to take notes, cameras and film, photocopier, computers with word-processing or desktop publishing software to input reports; access to darkroom facilities for developing prints; library for books and leaflets on medical and legal information.
- *Time*. In library to get information on effects of drugs, both legal and medical; looking for photographic opportunities; talking and interviewing people on their experiences; deadline when the print item has to be ready for production in the magazine.

Design

Design and layout skills are discussed in Study Unit 3.

As well as the content of a print item, you also need to plan its artistic and creative aspects. It is important that the item not only reads well, but must also be visually interesting. For example, if a teenage magazine contained only written text and no photographs, it would look very boring.

To help your product to be visually appealing, you need to plan its presentation.

Presentation

It is important to think carefully about how you can design your print item so that it attracts the eye of the reader. Take once again the example of the article on drugs. The following might be useful:

- a headline for the article
- a graph or other illustration

- a chart showing the number of people who have become HIV positive through drug abuse
- a picture of a graveside funeral service with the headline: 'Drugs kill'
- a photograph of a drug addict.

The target audience

While understanding the purpose and aesthetic criteria of your print item are very important to the planning process, it is also equally important that you constantly bear in mind your target audience – the readers at whom the print item is aimed. You must recognise that your individual print item could form the overall content of a final print product. Knowing your target audience and the print product can assist you in selecting and developing text and images.

In answering the question, 'Who am I producing the print item for?', there is a practical checklist which you can use during the planning and researching stage to identify precisely who will comprise the target audience. The checklist contains the following criteria:

- *Age*. What is the age range? Is the print item for a youthful readership, or an older adult readership? For a younger age group, you would write in a more punchy style, whereas for an older readership, you could use more description and analysis, as well as toning down the writing style.

- *Gender*. Is the print item aimed at a male or female audience? For example, if you were writing about the latest fashions for a male readership, you would want to use language and photographs that would create the image of a fashion-conscious good-looking male.

- *Interests*. Have you clearly identified the main areas of interest as they affect your target audience? Again, the article on the dangers of drug abuse relating to illegal substances would be better placed in a teenage magazine, rather than in a magazine of romantic stories for older people. For example, the April 1996 issue of the dance magazine *M8* included an article on drugs – 'Drugs. *M8* tells politicians to CHILL OUT!'. You would be unlikely to find a similar feature in the *People's Friend* magazine, which is aimed at a much older readership.

Compare the fashion hints in a magazine aimed at young women with fashion tips in a magazine like *Woman*, which is aimed at an older age group.

Fig. 2. 8
M8 has clearly identified its target audience – the cover highlights the features which are likely to be of interest to its readers

Concept as a key feature

Clearly, you need to define the concept of your print item. A concept is an idea or invention to help sell or publicise an item. Summarising the planning process to date, you need to know what the print item's message to the readers is (its purpose); the importance of making an impact with that message (design); who the message is aimed at (target audience). Now, you need to plan ideas for getting that message across – that is, how you plan the effective communication of your message. This communication process is known as 'concept'.

Investigative methods

While the extent of your research depends on the time scale and human and financial resources available, there are a number of methods which you can use to compile information for your print items. These fall broadly into two main categories: primary and secondary methods.

Primary methods

When interviewing, remember to be polite at all times and phrase your questions clearly.

When you are planning or researching a print item, you should ask yourself the question: 'How can I illustrate the written text?' Better still, you should adopt a multi-vocational approach to media skills by learning not only how to write, but also how to take photographs. In terms of research, photographic evidence can often be vital in trying to support the claims made in a text-based print item. In some cases, the photograph alone may be all the proof you need to make your point.

Always remember to make sure you have film in your camera – and that your camera's batteries are fully charged.

These are methods whereby you have *direct* contact with the people or events about which you are gathering information. The methods include:

- personal interview on location – this is where you are face to face with the interviewee asking him or her questions. You can record the answers in a notebook, or on audio cassette tape or video tape.
- interview by telephone – you can compile the information by using a telephone. Remember to write down the answers.
- personal observation – this is where you attend a function or activity and use your eyes and ears as the research tool, not word-of-mouth questions. Your rôle is that of an observer, not an interviewer as in the first two primary methods. To record the information as an observation, you can use a notebook and pen, tape recorder or video camera. Personal observation concerns the skills of watching and listening, not verbal questioning. Remember the rules – look, listen, learn.
- taking still and moving images – it has been suggested that a picture is worth a thousand words in terms of the communication of a message. Just look how conflicts around the world are explained through the use of the photograph. Take, for example, the photograph of masked Protestant paramilitary members in Northern Ireland. You can create an image in the reader's eye using words, but the actual photographic evidence truly emphasises the real situation.

Fig. 2. 9
Protestant extremists
on parade in
Ballymena, Northern
Ireland

- making audio recordings – involves recording the person speaking using
  a tape recorder. This allows you to play back the tape later and write
  down what is being said phrase by phrase, at your own normal writing
  speed. You should also keep the tapes as further evidence to back up
  what you have said in your written text.

Checklist for using tape recorders as an investigation method

- Make sure you have the correct type of tape for the tape recorder.
- Check you have enough tape to complete your research.
- Make sure you put the tape in the tape recorder before you begin
  the recording.
- Check that the tape recorder's batteries are working, or that there
  is an electric socket available at the recording location if you are
  using the mains supply to run your tape recorder.
- Make sure you have a microphone if there is not one built into your
  tape recorder.
- Before recording, check sound levels to ensure you obtain a clearly
  audible recording.
- After recording, immediately play back some sections to ensure
  that your interview can be clearly heard. If the recording is poor,
  you will have to record it again.

- Make sure you write the topic of the recording as well as the date on the cassette tape so that you remember which interview is on which tape. Don't forget to keep the tape in a safe place so that it is easily accessible and is not accidently wiped.
- You can also obtain a telephone microphone to record information gathered over a telephone. In this instance, remember to ask the interviewee's permission.

- questionnaires – these are a series of written questions set out in a particular sequence which is exceptionally useful at obtaining precise information.

Secondary methods

The essential difference between primary and secondary methods is that with the latter there is usually no *direct* contact with people or events to gain the research information, as takes place with interview, photographing or questionnaire testing. With secondary methods, the information could be described as indirect, or secondhand; that is, it has been recorded in another format. These formats can include:

- books, for example, textbooks, reference books, even fictional works such as novels and thrillers
- articles, such as stories published in newspapers and magazines
- archives, which may be contained in museums, libraries, or media organisations cuttings sections, or even broadcasting institutions' film and video archives
- videotapes – a considerable amount of visual material is available on video
- audiotapes – as with the videotapes, you can use the tapes as sources which you can transcribe on to paper
- electronic retrieval – from the Internet and electronic mail (e-mail) you can get information from around the world in a matter of minutes – even seconds, depending on the topic you are researching.

A large amount of film footage is now being transferred on to videotape for reference purposes.

Activity

You should now be in a position to begin the actual planning process of your print items. Using the practical guidance and checklists given in this section, make notes on the primary and secondary sources which you could use to get research material for your print items. Keep these notes in your portfolio.

Representation considerations

These involve making sure that you are not being deliberately or accidentally biased or discriminatory against particular groups in society in the research material you gather for the print items. There are four broad areas of potential bias or discrimination:

Legal and ethical content considerations are covered in Study Unit 3.

- Age
- Gender
- Minority – ensuring that you accurately represent the cultural, historical beliefs and image of ethnic minorities
- Social issues.

Assignment: Part 1

This is the first part of a two-part assignment which will enable you to collect evidence for your portfolio. It focuses particularly on the record of research and identification of the content considerations for three print items – two text-based and one image-based. You must work on this assignment individually. You should note that the print items are not necessarily the entire products, but could be, for example, an article or feature for inclusion in a print product.

1 **Decide which of your print items will be fiction and which will be non-fiction.**

2 **Prepare and implement a written action plan to compile research information for the three print items. You should also keep a brief record of the actual research carried out.**

3 **Make notes on the investigative research methods which you used to compile the information for the print items and state why you chose these methods.**

4 **Make notes identifying the content considerations during the researching of information for the three print items.**

5 **Make notes comparing the research information which you have gathered for your three print items to existing published items in the real world. In this task, you may wish to use some of the published material which you have compiled as part of previous activities.**

Turning research material into print items

Once you have compiled your research information, you will need to present it in the form of print items which are text-based and image-based. Each type of print item has clear features which you need to include.

The production of an entire print product is covered in more depth in Study Unit 3.

Fig. 2. 10
Example of an advertisement from *M8* magazine

Text-based items: the advertisement

When planning an advertisement, five questions need to be answered: who, what, when, where and why?

Activity

Look at the Merlin Productions advertisement, and think about what features cover each of these questions.

Text-based items: the leaflet

As with the planning for an advertisement, the five questions can be used to put together a leaflet. Look at the leaflet highlighting the features of a historical farm. It covers the questions by:

- highlighting the farm museum, gardens, tea house, craft shop, antiques and animals
- listing opening times
- including an address and map showing how to get to the farm
- what there is to see, enjoy and learn.

Fig. 2. 11
Part of a leaflet advertising Brookhall Historical Farm

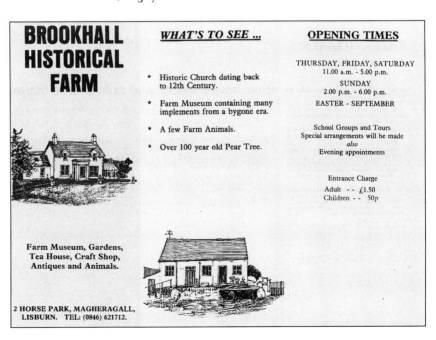

Image-based items

These items rely on the visual impact of their content, and they are broadly identified in three categories:

- Photographs. You can also use text-based captions to assist the understanding of the photograph's content.
- Graphics are usually any drawn illustrative material which is used in page design to highlight important pieces of information. They help the target audience to understand the information contained in the print item, for example, a graph.
- Cartoons. The purpose of cartoons is sometimes simply to amuse the target audience, or at other times to communicate the cartoonist's views on serious issues and newsworthy events.

Comics are entire print products which are composed of cartoons.

Suitability

When producing print items, you need to ensure that they are suitable to be read by the target audience, and that the information contained in them matches the concepts in which they were produced.

Remember your concept checklist – purpose, design, style, content and layout.

To judge suitability, put yourself in the mind of the target audience who will view the print items and ask yourself these questions:

- Is there a possibility that the target audience will fail to understand the message of the print items because there is too much visual impact in them?
- Is there a possibility that the print item could have the opposite effect on the target audience than the one which the writer intended, i.e. a negative reaction?

Assignment: Part 2

You should complete this assignment individually. Using the research material which you compiled for Part 1:

1 **develop three print items, of which two should be text-based and the other image-based, and at least one fiction and one non-fiction**

2 **write notes justifying each item produced in terms of key features and available resources, and comparing your three print items to existing published items**

3 **produce a written report of other print ideas which you originated as part of the overall assignment, and indicate how each idea was evaluated.**

3 Planning and researching audio items

In this section you will examine the processes which go into the creation of audio products by looking at two of the most important present-day genres or styles of product – commercials and news features. You will almost certainly have heard a wide range of commercials and news features on the radio, but remember that these products can also be used in a variety of other situations, such as in-store advertising, when audio messages are targeted at shoppers over a public address system, or promotional tapes distributed by car manufacturers containing a mixture of factual and advertising material which are designed to be played on car cassette players.

The ideas you come up with for your assignment can be carried forward to Study Unit 4, when you may have the opportunity to translate your ideas into actual audio products.

Styles and conventions

In order to develop your ideas, it is first necessary to become familiar with the styles and conventions currently in use, so that you can compare and test your ideas against those of professionals working in the industry.

Activity

In your own time over several days, listen to as many radio stations as you can. Make notes of what you hear, so you can discuss the following questions for each station. Keep notes of your group discussion in your portfolio.

- Who is likely to listen to the station? For example, BBC Radio 4 is likely to be listened to by businesspeople and politicians; and Atlantic 252 by students.
- What is their motivation for listening? For example, Radio 4 would be listened to for information; Atlantic 252 for music.
- What presentation styles does the station use, and how do these relate to the tastes and interests of the likely audience?

You will return to this activity later in the section to examine other key features of each station's style.

Conventions of radio

While every station will strive to create a distinctive style, most will conform to the conventions of radio which have developed over many years. These conventions help us to tell the difference, for example, between a real police officer speaking in a news broadcast and an actor playing the part of a police officer in a comedy show. Much of this differentiation revolves around the use of stereotypes – which may or may not be exaggerated.

For example, a real police officer in a news bulletin can be female or male, may have any accent, and while speaking formally is unlikely to use stereotypical language. However, a police officer in a drama will often be cast as male, probably with a deep voice. In a comedy, this effect may be heightened by including lines of dialogue such as 'Evenin' all' or 'Mind how you go', which are not realistic, but which are ingrained in popular culture as a code which enables us to identify the police character immediately.

The following table – while not comprehensive – may help you to identify some of the common conventions.

Programme element	Language used	Style of delivery	Use of music and sound effects
News	Formal	Sincere	Little use
Discussion	Informal	Sincere	Little use
Feature	Formal	Sincere	Some use
Drama	Conversational, some stereotypes	Sincere	Great use
Comedy	Exaggerated, many stereotypes	Exaggerated	Great use
Commercial	Exaggerated	Varies	Great use

The table can only be a guide, as broadcasters will always seek to come up with new ideas; many features, for example, are delivered in an informal style so as to make them more accessible to a wide audience. Other conventions are fixed, such as the sincere delivery for news, as the vast majority of listeners would consider it inappropriate or offensive to deliver information about death or serious injury in any other way.

Creative promotion and advertising

All radio stations have an enormous appetite for creative material, whether they be speech-based or music-based; very few broadcasters can succeed in an increasingly competitive market by simply recycling old ideas, or the same music, over and over again. Most stations, be they national or local, carry news in some form and all stations carry promotional messages of one sort or another. Independent (commercial) radio stations carry both spot advertising, in the form of commercial breaks within the programmes, and sponsored features of various kinds (weather, traffic, sport or specialist music programmes) where the sponsor's name is linked with the feature by way of credits within programming. BBC radio stations do not carry advertising or sponsorship, but they still carry messages to promote forthcoming programmes or events (such as the 1 FM Roadshow) or to publicise the availability of study packs or support materials for educational programmes.

Activity

1 **Continue with the listening activity you started above, this time looking at promotional material on the various stations – whether it is for advertisers' products, other programmes or something connected with the radio station. Keep a note of at least ten of these messages, and for each try to answer the following questions:**

   - What was the purpose of the message? It could be promoting a forthcoming programme, advertising a special deal on used cars, publicising a DJ appearance, etc.
   - Who was the message aimed at? It could be existing listeners, people thinking of changing their car, people looking for a day out with the family.
   - How was the message put across? It could be a formal announcement of forthcoming programmes; an up-tempo commercial with music and sound effects; or a chatty mention by a presenter in a very informal style.
   - How effective would the message be in reaching those people it was aimed at?

2 **Now consider the news (or news features) you heard while you were listening around the dial. In small groups, for each station, discuss the following:**

   - How much news was there?
   - Was the news specific to the station, presented by a newsreader who is identified as part of the station team, or did it come from an external agency such as Independent Radio News (IRN)?
   - Were there a lot of local places and events mentioned, or did the bulletin concentrate on national and international events?
   - What do your answers tell you about the priority the station gives to broadcasting news, and the resources it devotes to providing a news service?
   - What costs are involved for the broadcaster in providing the service you heard? You should consider aspects such as:
     - Staffing. How many people are involved?
     - Technical. What costs would be involved for telephones, satellite links, radio cars, etc?

A broadcaster may compensate the supplier of a prize by providing publicity for the product, such as a holiday or a car, which may then persuade others to buy that product. In other cases, a broadcaster may offer commercial airtime to the supplier of a prize to the same notional value as the prize itself. This is known as a contra deal.

- Royalties. If music or other copyright material is used, royalties are due to the artists, composers, publishers and owners of any mechanical copyright.
- Prizes. If a broadcaster tries to attract listeners through offering large prizes, what costs are involved?

The BBC meets its costs through the licence fee; Independent Radio through its sale of airtime, in the form of commercials and sponsorship. This doesn't mean that commercial radio is free to the listener – you pay every time you buy a product which has been advertised on the radio.

Developing your ideas

You can now move on to develop your own ideas for audio products. For your assignment, you will need to research and develop two scripts for two different products; one will be a commercial, and one will be a news feature. (One should be predominantly music-based, and one speech-based.) If you concentrate on the same subject for both your products, this will enable you to compare the different styles – genres – used for persuasive messages (in the commercial) and informational messages (in the news feature). The opening of a new supermarket, for example, gives ample opportunity for devising new commercials to promote the facilities on offer, the discounts available, and the advantages of shopping in the new store as opposed to any other outlets in the area. It can also provide scope for a news feature, in that there will almost certainly be conflicting opinions about the development. On the one hand, it may have created new jobs, or a new focus for a run-down community; on the other hand, there may be planning concerns about the location (it could have been built on green belt land, or may generate increased traffic along residential streets) or about the effect on an existing town centre, where small shopkeepers could well be opposed to what they may regard as unfair competition.

Assignment: Part 1

Imagine you are working for a local radio station which serves the community from which the majority of you and your fellow students are drawn. The station is an Independent Local Radio station, relying on advertising and sponsorship for its income, but with a 15-minute news magazine programme broadcast at 5 pm daily, Monday to Friday, in which the emphasis is given to the discussion of controversial local issues. Almost any development in your local area can be considered as a suitable topic for inclusion in this programme. You have been asked to

At its most basic level, news can be defined as anything that happens which is out of the ordinary. This can be good news, such as the opening of a new factory, or tourist attraction, or bad news, such as a major fire or a road accident.

research and develop two scripts – one for a 30-second radio commercial, the other for a news feature of up to three minutes' duration.

Activity

In small groups, draw up a list of six current topics which you think your imaginary local radio station could feature this week. For each subject, suggest the positive messages which could be included in a commercial promoting the subject; then discuss both the positive and negative aspects which could be explored in a balanced news feature.

Case study: Transperience, Bradford, West Yorkshire

Fig. 2. 12

Transperience – a transport-based discovery park in Bradford – provides a good example of the issues raised above. Developers wanted to create a unique visitor attraction based around the theme of transport, which was not a museum. Old buses, trams and trolley-buses were to be an important element of the park, which covers a large area, providing ample scope for 'rides' on preserved vehicles; but these were to be only part of a wider theme which would include an exploration of how and why people travel, various multimedia presentations on transport subjects and a vigorous presentation of the various green issues raised by developments such as the private car. Managers had to face the problem of getting the idea – an attraction that wasn't a museum – over to a public which had never previously experienced such a concept, and which was perhaps expecting a new museum in the traditional sense.

The launch of Transperience therefore prompted the need for two distinct approaches to putting across audio messages:

1 news and feature coverage of the development plans and the opening

Fig. 2.13
A radio news item (left) and an extract from a feature covering the opening of Transperience (right)

Transperience

Crowds are gathering at Low Moor to await the arrival of Coronation Street star Ken Morley.

He'll be there to open Bradford's latest tourist attraction Transperience, which aims to show the history of motoring and transport from the past and into the future.

Live from the scene, Richard Horsman…

Bradford's TRANSPERIENCE discovery park opens this morning… offering families an exciting new way to explore the world of transport. Combining rides on historic vehicles with state-of-the-art displays and video show, the complex occupies a 15-acre site just off the M606 at Low Moor. Director Mike Haynes says there's nowhere quite like it in the world…

TRANSPERIENCE
Dur: 25″
o/c transport issues

2 commercials to 'sell' the new concept to different audiences.

PULSE PRODUCTIONS

Client: Transperience	Duration: 30″
Cart. number: 5444	Writer: LW
Title: Doctor	Exec: TS
Production Time: 4	Cost: £331

Music:
Boy: **Tickets please!**
FVO: I don't know what's up with him, doctor.
Boy: **Ooh – I can't change that for yer mate!**
FVO: They won't have him at school now!
Boy: **Move on down the tram, ladies.**
MVO: All right. What's the matter with you, Johnny?
Boy: **You can't leave these bags here love!**
MVO: I see.
Well, I'm sorry Mrs Bailey but …

FX: *Drone*
MVO: (*deep voice*) Little Johnny – is having a Transperience.
DeepAnncr: Historic vehicle rides meet state of the art interactive technology head on.
FX: *Crash. Explosion. Dynamic.*
Transperience – West Yorkshire's Transport Discovery Park is now open. Junction 2 off the M606 or bus number 268 from Bradford Interchange.

FVO   female voice over

MVO   male voice over

FX   (Sound) effect

DeepAnncr   Deep Announcer

Metro Radio Group

In small groups, discuss what aspects of the development would be of interest to journalists covering the story as a factual development, and to publicists seeking to attract visitors in a persuasive capacity.

Journalists will seek to highlight positive issues, such as the potential for creating new jobs and the development's importance to the region in economic terms; but for balance, they will also highlight the cost to the local taxpayer, through grants and subsidies to the developers and the potential difficulty of launching a new theme park, especially after the well-publicised financial difficulties of attractions such as EuroDisney (since renamed Disneyland Paris). They may also seek to highlight the political implications for an educational attraction, partly paid for by public money, which puts such an emphasis on 'green' issues.

Publicists will highlight different aspects of the scheme. They will seek to play up the fun, 'hands-on' aspects of the visitor experience and will want to stress its potential for a family day out, offering something new and different. They will also seek to get across precise information about admission prices and opening times which are unlikely to find their way into a news feature.

Choosing a topic

In choosing your topic, you must do some detective work to identify subjects which you believe will make good topics for audio treatment. This means reading local newspapers and listening to other local radio stations to decide what is on the current news agenda, and speaking to individuals concerned, either face to face or by telephone. This can provide an ideal opportunity to practise your interviewing skills, and to practise using recording equipment, before you embark on your assignments in Study Unit 4. You will also need to carry out some library research, for example finding out which councillors represent the area you are working in, and which bodies carry the responsibility for planning or transport policy.

Bear in mind that some subjects (like fine art) are difficult to tackle in the radio medium, because the lack of visual images can be a major problem (you can only describe a painting, you can't show it).

Constraints on subject matter

You must also remember the legal constraints on journalists, especially when matters are due to be heard before a court – once a person has been charged with a crime, you must not discuss anything on the air concerning the facts of the case, as your presentation of them could potentially influence a future member of the jury to believe the accused is guilty or innocent before they get into the courtroom. You must also be aware of the laws of libel, which exist to protect an individual's reputation from damage by the publication of false statements.

For a fuller account of the laws of contempt of court and libel, see Study Unit 4.

Other constraints may involve ethical issues – whether publication of a feature is in the public interest. For example, a report on possible side-effects from a drug may protect some patients from harm, but it may also panic others into not taking the drug, where for them the risks could be even greater by not taking it. In covering an issue such as crime against elderly women you must also consider whether you are exploiting the fears of vulnerable individuals, when statistics show that young men are far more likely to be the victims of a violent assault; and you must avoid representing minority groups in a stereotypical way – not all elderly people are frail, for example.

Who to involve

In creating your news feature, you must decide which groups and individuals to approach for comment.

Activity

1 Imagine that a new road is to be constructed to bypass a bottleneck on the busy route near your school or college – to the delight of motorists and local residents plagued by town-centre traffic, but to the dismay of environmentalists who believe it will increase the volume of traffic; a farmer, whose field of cows is divided from his milking shed by the road; and some pupils at a school separated from their playing field by the new road.

   In small groups, rôle play the different interest groups in the scenario. These could include the long-suffering residents of Main Street, the Road Haulage Association, the local Chamber of Trade; Friends of the Earth; parents with children at the school; the farmer, and any others you decide are important. Each group should give a short presentation outlining its case.

   Make notes on each presentation, and then working individually, try to decide which three aspects you would include in your feature to make it balanced.

2 Carry out a similar exercise on paper for each of the topics you are considering for your assignment.

   • Who should you approach to give a balanced account of the issue for your listeners?
   • Can you think of any individuals/groups who would be upset to be left out of your feature?
   • Would their complaint be justified, or is their point of view effectively covered by another speaker?

Proposals and scripts

Having studied the above, you are now ready to work on two proposals for your assignment; one for a 30-second radio commercial, the second for a radio news feature of up to three minutes' duration.

Look at the examples given of script layout in the Transperience case study, and follow the conventions used. Remember most people speak at around three words per second, so a 30-second script for the commercial will require no more than 90 words, less if there is to be any significant use of sound effects or music. When scripting the feature, write out the sort of comment you would expect to hear from the various interest groups – or if you have the opportunity, record a real interview with a spokesperson from the group and transcribe – copy out – the important bits from what they actually say.

Remember, you may want to do another interview on your chosen topic once you get on to Study Unit 4. If that is the case, it's probably not a good idea to interview your subject twice on tape, as they may not have the time to let you do so.

Assignment: Part 2

You must now write out a summary of your decision-making processes, explaining why you chose the topic, why you think it is relevant to your imaginary station's audience, and how you selected (and rejected) possible interviewees. You will need to submit this summary with your scripts.

Compare your scripts

You should now compare your finished scripts with real audio products you have heard on the radio.

Activity

- Transcribe the script of a real radio commercial that you like from a local or national commercial station. In small groups, read out (or act) that commercial. Do the same with your script for the 30-second commercial. How do other students think it matches up to the conventions and the production devices of the real broadcast product?
- Repeat the activity with your feature script, recording off-air and transcribing a feature from a real radio broadcast (you will probably find a BBC local station to be the most appropriate comparison). Again, read out the transcription alongside your version. How do other students (and your tutors) think the two match up?

You are now ready to go on to Study Unit 4 – which will give you the opportunity to put your ideas for audio items into practice.

Planning and researching moving image items

In this section you will look at ways of generating ideas for moving image products. You will consider how to evaluate your ideas to determine whether or not they are practical.

You will also be developing ideas and preparing **treatments**, **proposals** and **scripts**. These are essential for providing evidence for assessment. But first you should understand a little about the market that there is for moving image products.

The market for moving image products

Broadcast television or films are not the only way that a moving image can be shown. There is a huge market for 'Pop' videos that are shown on broadcast television but also in the 'sell through' market – those that are produced on video cassette and sold through retail outlets.

Many companies make '**corporate**' video programmes that show the products or services that the company provides. You may have seen videos playing in your local supermarket. These '**point of sale**' productions are designed to make you stop and watch a demonstration of the product. The use of a moving image and sound is intended to simulate the broadcast television you see at home.

Target audience

The products that you are going to make will be targeted towards an audience. The nature of the audience will determine the language that you use, the material you use in the product and the way that you deliver it. Television programmes have strict controls over what can be shown and when. Certain programme content cannot be shown before 9 pm – the watershed – because it may contain strong language or material unsuitable for young audiences.

Programmes designed to appeal to female audiences tend to be shown during the day; those aimed at male audiences tend to be shown later in the evening. This reinforces the stereotypical view of women looking after children at home and men going out to work. Throughout the planning process you should be aware of issues relating to the portrayal of rôles in society. If you were to portray certain groups of people as stupid or lazy, then you would be perpetuating a myth. You would also be in breach of programme ethics as laid down by the Independent Broadcasting Commission (IBC) and race relations legislation.

Activity

Look at a range of television programmes broadcast throughout the day. If possible, tape some of the programmes. For each of the programmes write down the audience that you think it was aimed at.

Ask yourself who is going to see your programmes. One particular age group, an audience with a particular need or an audience that wants to learn something? You should make your programmes fit the needs of the target audience. You also need to consider the message you want to put across to your audience.

Media messages can be very powerful.

Activity

Once again tape and watch a variety of programmes that deal with a particular image issue (such as pollution, education, local government, drugs, etc.). Is the message they are trying to put across one that favours one side or is the message balanced and impartial?

The BBC and Independent Television companies are required to give a balanced view in their programmes. If one side is allowed to give its reasons for an action, then the opposition must also be given an opportunity. This allows viewers to make up their own minds about an issue. You will need to produce programmes that have a balanced view, and later in this section you will look at issues that are important to the planning and recording process.

Fiction or non-fiction?

For your assignment you will need to produce two treatments and two scripts, one of which is fiction and the other non-fiction. You should be clear in your mind what these two categories are.

Fiction should be products of the creative imagination. They may be:

- stories already published
- original stories written specifically for the programme.

Non-fiction should relate to factual reality. It comprises:

- documentaries, for example, about your town or school
- news programmes
- promotional programmes, for example, a school or college promotion.

Genres

'Film and television genre is created partly through setting, appearance, plot and characterisation but also through the expectations (based on previous experience) of the audience which consumes or 'reads' the particular fiction or non-fiction form.'

Stuart Price, *Media Studies*
Longman, 1993

When programmes share similar characteristics they are said to belong to a particular **genre** or category of programme. Genres translate across both fiction and non-fiction programmes.

When you begin to think of ideas for your moving image products you should consider the words of Stuart Price and take into account not just what you think the programme is about but also what the audience expects from your programme.

Thinking of ideas

It can be difficult to think of ideas without some help! Many authors have sat for days staring at a blank sheet waiting for inspiration. Unfortunately, you will not have the luxury of being able to sit and wait. Time for planning your products has to be weighed against the time available for producing your product. Try the following activity and see if it helps you to produce ideas.

Activity

In the middle of a large sheet of plain paper write down a key word about the programme that you might want to plan. This key word in the case of a promotional programme for your school or college might be the name of the school or college. From this word draw out lines to make a spider diagram. At the end of each line write an idea about the way that the programme might develop. Put down all your ideas however silly they may seem. Examples of key words may be 'Day in the life', 'After hours' or 'Behaviour'. Finally, go through all the ideas you have written down and eliminate the least good ones, which should leave you with some ideas for your programme. Once you have identified an idea, and taking into account the audience, you could then develop ideas about the programme content.

Case study: planning a programme about photography

   The spider diagram was the starting point for the planning of a programme about photography. The idea for the programme came out of a discussion between the producer and a professional photographer. They realised that there were no programmes about the world of professional photography. They sat down and brainstormed some ideas. Later in this section you will look at how this programme was developed through the treatment and proposal stages.

Fig. 2. 14
This spider diagram was the starting point for the planning of a programme about photography

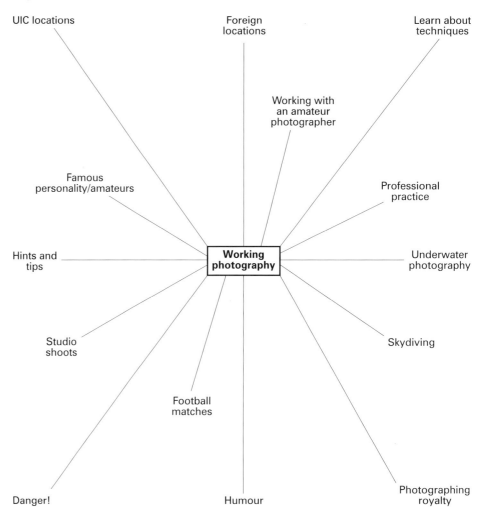

   As you can see from the diagram, there were many ideas which were eventually whittled down to the main features of the programme.

Assignment: Part 1

This is the first part of a three-part assignment. Think of a key word for a programme that you would like to make. This could be a non-fiction or fiction programme. Put this word at the centre of a spider diagram and try to find as many idea strands as you can.

When you begin to analyse the words you have written down, you may well see a pattern of words that start to tell the story. These connections may be the start of the narrative of your story.

The words from the photography spider diagram that work together are:

- professional practice
- working with an amateur photographer
- hints and tips
- humour
- location shoots
- studio shoots
- learning about techniques.

These words started to form the basis of the story that was eventually made into a finished product. This was the first stage in the planning and production process.

Resources

Make sure that your ideas match your resources. For example, it would not be sensible to make a programme about the undersea world if you did not have easy access to the sea and to specialist equipment.

If there is not enough information available to help with your research, then you might not be able to make your programme reliable and honest.

Before the ideas about the photography programme could be finalised, the resources for making the programme had to be considered. The cost of travel, specialist materials and insurance against accidents had to be taken into account. A target audience had to be identified.

In the case of the photography programme the initial ideas had to be modified because of the high cost of using famous personalities. The original concept of filming at foreign locations was also modified in light of available funds for travel. Once all the modifications had been completed, a proposal was made to the client.

Researching the proposal

Before the proposal could be formulated, a considerable amount of research had to be undertaken. First, the audience for the programme had to be identified. The producer contacted all the professional photographic bodies and manufacturers that he could find and asked for information about any current photographic programmes they were involved in. They were also asked to identify the age groups that the programmes should be aimed at and also the content of the programmes. It would be no use making a programme similar to one that is already available and meeting the need of the audience. In the commercial world, a video programme that covers a subject that has already been produced successfully would make no marketing sense.

Researching the needs of amateur photographers was the next step and letters were sent to a cross-section of photographic societies throughout Britain. Views of professional photographers and possible locations providers were sought by bringing together

All of the research data was stored just as your research material should be stored in your portfolio.

a panel of these people to discuss the content of the programme and to identify any potential problems that might arise.

All of this research was undertaken before any firm proposals could be assembled. Modifications to original ideas could be undertaken before a client was approached and valuable time and money spent on proposals and treatments.

Research material for the photography programme was obtained using the following methods:

- writing to professional photography bodies and manufacturers
- telephoning these organisations if materials did not arrive
- watching other photography programmes
- noting down ideas from these programmes
- sending questionnaires to amateur photographic organisations asking for their views on the possible content of a photography programme
- meeting professional photographers and asking for their help in making the programme
- asking amateur photographers to fill in questionnaires about the things they would like to see in the programme
- compiling a report that analysed the research findings.

Remember to keep copies of all the research information that you personally find and the information obtained by your group.

All the information obtained was stored in a production research handbook similar to the one that you started at the beginning of this unit.

Activity

Using the programme idea from the spider diagram activity, plan out how you would undertake research for your idea. List all of the areas that you need to research and then identify how you would obtain the information. This research should also indicate the resources that you will need to undertake the successful completion of the programme.

You should have been able to produce a comprehensive list of research and resource requirements for a fiction or non-fiction programme. Resource issues are discussed in greater depth in Study Unit 5 but for the purposes of this activity you should identify major resource requirements such as a television studio. Remember to keep this information for later use.

Finally, consider the following key points that you should always refer to when planning your programmes:

- *The idea* – can you find sources of information; identify audience; produce initial outline?
- *Practicality* – are resources available; can you find suitable locations or studios?

Later in this section you will have to look at your completed scripts and justify them to a client or group of students. You will need to be aware of these key points when you begin the justification process.

Throughout the research activity it would be useful to practise some of the techniques you will be using in Study Unit 5. When you look at locations, if possible take a camcorder with you to record potential scenes or you could tape record an interview with the person who has requested the work to be undertaken. Do not worry at this stage about professional camera techniques or sound quality, this will be developed later.

You may wish to develop your ideas further in Study Unit 5 when you have to produce two complete moving image products.

- *Feasibility* – will your ideas work; have you enough time to complete them?

If you cannot complete all of these key points, then you will have to reassess your programme.

Assignment: Part 2

1   Compile a research document for the idea that you decided to brainstorm in Part 1 of this assignment. This document should contain a record of all the research you have undertaken with notes detailing the research methods you used and your sources of information. Use the methods of research detailed earlier and refer to the information at the beginning of this section.

2   When you have completed all the work on one item, either fiction or non-fiction, you should then produce a similar package for the alternative product. Go through the stages of brainstorming ideas and research as you did for the first product.

Content considerations

Earlier in this section you looked at the considerations that you need to take into account when planning your moving image product. When planning your programme, you will need to be aware of the factors that may influence the production of the programme.

In the case study of the photography programme there were several things that came up when the programme was first planned. One of the early episodes took place at a fashion show in a top London restaurant. The following were just some of the issues the producer had to address.

Legal
Copyright

- Filming the clothes might infringe the copyright of the designer – someone might watch the programme and copy the design.
- The music being played as the models walk down the catwalk might be someone's copyright – the individual may require payment for using it in the programme.

Discrimination

- Did the programme deal with men and women in the same way?
- Was there evidence of racial discrimination? Were particular groups of people represented in a negative way?

Defamation

Did the programme make any reference to companies or individuals that showed them in an unfair or derogatory way?

Representation issues

Stereotypes

- Were women represented in a stereotypical way? The producer was concerned that the use of female models might suggest that all women can do is to parade on a catwalk. The programme used a female amateur photographer to counter this view.
- Were men represented in a stereotypical way? For example, was the professional photography industry shown as male only? Professional female photographers were included in later episodes.

Ethics

- Did people who were not directly involved in the programme – in this case, the restaurant's customers – object to being filmed?

You will need to address all the above issues in the planning, recording and post-production stage. It's important to analyse them well in advance of the recording stage. When you commence recording, you also need to be aware of these issues if you change your script as you progress. In the post-production stage it is easy to miss out sections of the programme, changing the emphasis and ignoring the issues that you identified in the initial stages.

The proposal

The proposal is the first link in a chain of planning and production. The ideas that you have had, the resources that you have identified as being available and your research can be translated into a document that can easily be considered by a client. Sometimes the person reading the proposal will not be media literate and therefore the wording should be understandable. Using technical terminology may not be helpful.

Initial proposals to broadcast television are notoriously difficult to produce. Most commissioning editors want a proposal that is to the point but which puts across an idea successfully. Many proposals are filed in the waste-paper bin because they do not get to the point. The following example of a proposal (on pages 99 and 100) is for a broadcast programme on the theme of photography. The proposal was sent to a number of commissioning editors who were in the process of commissioning new work. The proposal, if accepted by the commissioning editor, would then be developed into a treatment.

'It is the representation of what has originally been presented. Representation means the way in which ideas, objects, people, groups and life forms are depicted by the mass media'
Stuart Price, *Media Studies*
Longman, 1993

98

Philip M Holmes
Productions
PROPOSAL FOR
Working Title: 'Working Photography'

Introduction
We all know photographers such as Lichfield, Snowdon and Bailey but there is so much more to the world of photography than the public see from these icons of the genre. Their particular style of photography is how many people perceive the world of photography, glamorous and exciting, but is it always so?

Working Photography will, each week, look at a particular style of photography that the public may have seen but never really appreciated. **Each programme will pair a local, working professional photographer with a well-known, local personality, who is also a keen amateur photographer, and they will explore the chosen field of photography together.** The interaction of the professional and the amateur will give the programme an entertaining feel and will also show the chosen field of photography in a new light. **The professional will offer advice on cameras, lenses, composition and technique.**

The programmes will cover a range of specialist photography including working with a wedding photographer, a forensic photographer, a sports photographer, an aerial photographer and a glamour photographer. The amateur will have an interest in a particular field of photography. All of the professional photographers and personalities will be based in the Yorkshire Television area.

Both informative and entertaining, the programme will be for anyone interested in gaining an insight into the world of working photography and obtaining new skills in photography. This includes approximately 2 million camera users in the Yorkshire Television area.

I propose an initial 6-part series of 24 minutes duration.

Form
Each programme will start with a brief introductory profile of the amateur and the professional photographer, this may well be built into an opening sequence. This will be followed by a briefing session in which the details of the day's shoot are outlined, taking place in an appropriate location, possibly the photographer's studio. This session will give an excellent opportunity for a relationship between the two to be built.

During the following 20 minutes we follow the pair as they undertake an assignment that may take them high in the sky to photograph towns and cities, to the scene of a crime to collect photographic evidence, to capture a beautiful bride or spend 90 minutes in the rain behind the touchline.

The programme will finish with a short discussion between the professional and amateur at the location shoot or in the location used for the briefing. Here the two compare notes and photographs, and discuss the tips that the amateur has picked up. These will be emphasised by the professional, **making this an educational experience as well as an exciting programme**.

Presenter
At this stage there is no presenter planned, the opening sequence will give information about the programme and can be backed up by graphic display with relevant details. The rôle of the professional photographer is currently under discussion with the BIPP, the professional photographers' association. They will give support through their membership of professional photographers in the Yorkshire area.

The appointment of local personality amateurs is currently being researched. This area will need further development once outline approval is granted.

Target audience
Photography is a very popular hobby, next only to fishing, in the UK. The public spend over £30 million pounds a year on equipment and in excess of £40 million a year on processing and printing of their films. Most people come into contact with photography on a daily basis but many have no idea about the way that the photograph is obtained. The programme sets out to show people just what goes into making that image in an interesting, and sometimes amusing, way. The interaction between the professional photographer, and the well-known local amateur photographer will provide an entertaining balance between facts and fun. The aim of the programme is to educate and give advice in an informal setting.

This programme would work in the sell-through video market and would be enhanced by a follow-up book available through a local publisher.

Schedule
The series will be shot on tape with approximately 6 weeks' pre-production, 3 weeks' shooting and 5 weeks' post-production. Further development work will need to take place and a researcher will be appointed when appropriate.

Detailed budget proposals are available.

Producer
Philip M Holmes is an experienced professional photographer who has been involved in many photographic areas. He has worked with amateur photographers for many years and is currently researching into the media for a doctoral thesis. Philip M Holmes has been involved in corporate video production both as an independent producer and as producer for a large manufacturing organisation. He has worked in broadcast film and sound and is currently teaching corporate and broadcast television skills.

Production
Working Photography will be produced in collaboration with [*under consideration*] This will give the production a broadcast credibility and will ensure that necessary broadcast principles will be adhered to at all times.

Production costs for the series will be in the region of £75,000.

Treatment

A treatment is a narrative description of the production. Like the proposal, it is intended that the treatment be read by a client who may be entrusting his or her money to you. The treatment should be written as if you were describing what you were seeing while watching a playback of the completed production. You should avoid using moving image terminology, for example, 'dissolve', 'voice over' or 'big close up'. Remember that the person reading your treatment may not be a media professional. The client should be able to read the treatment and proposal easily and understand just what the programme is all about and what it will ultimately look like.

Look at the example of a treatment for one episode of the proposal on 'Working Photography'. This treatment reflects the nature of all the episodes and therefore the commissioning editor can get an idea of them all through just one sample.

Once the treatment has been agreed with your client, you should then begin the process of writing a script.

> Remember that commissioning editors and other clients will not have the time to read through page after page of information. Be succinct in your writing.

TREATMENT FOR
WORKING PHOTOGRAPHY
EPISODE 3

This 24-minute programme will open with a discussion between the professional photographer and a well-known personality. The discussion will take the form of a briefing for the task ahead, in this case taking action photographs at a Premier Division football match. The professional will explain the equipment to be used, the type of film to use and why, and rules and regulations at the ground.

The programme then follows them on their journey to the ground and monitors the interaction between them, the ground officials and the crowd.

The action of the photographers is interspersed with action on the pitch, including sound effects.

The match over, the professional and the celebrity return to base, discuss the work done and wait anxiously for the negatives to be developed.

Discussion between the photographer and celebrity will focus on the results of the work and will take the form of a critique of the celebrity's work compared with the professional's.

The programme will conclude with follow-up material reiterating the equipment uses and the techniques developed in the programme.

Initial research has identified a professional sports photographer and a personality from the world of showbusiness.

Costs for this programme will be approximately £4,000 and production will take two days with three days' post-production at Eyewise Facilities.

Scripts

'You need three things for a good film and they are the script, the script and the script.'

A Hollywood saying

A good script is essential. It is the blueprint by which a production is guided. The script is the culmination of all your planning and research. You will have gathered all your information, found locations, arranged resources and persuaded the client that your programme is worth making. The next step is to develop a script that follows on from your original proposal and treatment.

There are various types of script for different forms of programme.

Fiction scripts

These scripts contain the dialogue being spoken by the actors. They also contain an indication of the action that is taking place and details of the framing that will be recorded by the camera.

Look at the example of a draft fiction script for a programme recorded in a studio using two cameras.

DRAFT SCRIPT FOR 'A QUESTION OF STAFF'

	Camera	Sound
Scene 1: A television studio. Three people seated around a table facing an interviewer.	1 W/A	Music
Mix to:		Music fade out
Interviewer: Hello and welcome to 'A Question of Staff', a new weekly programme where we put teaching staff on the hot spot.	2 C/U	Dialogue Mic 1
On my right, I have John Smith, headteacher at Chislehurst Grammar School and on his left, Brenda Small, a teacher at Grange Hill Comprehensive.	1 W/A	"
My last guest is Brian Jones, one of Her Majesty's Inspectors of Schools.	2 C/U	"
Guests: Hello.	1 W/A	Mic 2,3,4
Interviewer: First to John Smith. John, I understand that your school has a one hundred per cent pass rate at GCSE Rose Pruning. Why is this?	2 C/U	" Mic 1
John Smith: Well, I think it is because we only enter five people for this examination. All of these pupils spend 12 hours a week perfecting their pruning techniques.	1 M C/U	" Mic 2
Interviewer: Brenda, why does your school not enter pupils for this examination?	2 C/U	" Mic 1
Brenda Small: Well, we are situated at the crossroads of three motorways and nothing can grow in our grounds.	1 M C/U	" Mic 3

Note: W/A = wide angle   C/U = close up   M C/U = medium close up   Mic = microphone

You can see from the example that all the information needed for the actors and crew is contained in this document. The camera crew know when their camera is being used and what kind of shot they should use. The actors know which camera to look at at any particular time and the sound recordist knows which microphone needs to be 'live'. Of course, this is only one page of a script that covers many pages and scenes. This was the first draft of the script and it was changed several times before the final version was completed.

Activity

Write down why you think the script went through many changes.

This draft fiction script allowed the actors and crew to practise their words and camera movements. It also allowed the sound operator to experiment with recording all those voices and matching them to the same sound level. The script may well be changed for any number of reasons until a final version is agreed by all the crew.

Non-fiction scripts

These scripts consist of information about location, narration or interviews. They may contain the key questions to be asked in the interview. The main visual elements, for example, framing of shots, details of what to include or not to include in the shot, will be indicated.

Look at the example of a draft script for episode 3 of the 'Working Photography' programme discussed above.

DRAFT SCRIPT FOR
WORKING PHOTOGRAPHY
EPISODE 3
'BEHIND THE GOAL'

Scene 1: Interior photographer's studio.	V/O Today's photographer is Joan Brown and helping him is Jason Smith
Scene 2: Discussion taking place between Joan and Jason	Dialogue
Scene 3: Joan and Jason look at examples of photographs taken at football matches. They discuss techniques to get the best shots	Dialogue
Scene 4: Joan shows Jason the range of cameras they will be using	Dialogue
Scene 5: Joan and Jason leave in car for the football match	Music
Scene 6: Joan and Jason arrive at ground and look at locations	Music/background dialogue Dialogue
Scene 7: Jason meets the managers	
Scene 8: Joan and Jason sitting behind goal in rain	Music 'Raindrops Keep Falling on My Head'
cont.	

In this instance the script went through fewer changes than the script for the fiction product you saw earlier.

There is no hard and fast rule about how to lay out a script. There are script layouts for film and scripts layouts for single- and multiple-camera television productions. For the purposes of this unit, you need to prepare your two scripts in a way that allows you to develop them further in Study Unit 5. This means that a draft script will be the evidence that you have for assessment. Your final draft script may well be dog-eared and tatty by the time you have made adjustments. In this case it would be sensible to keep your amended versions for assessment as well as a neat final copy.

Assignment: Part 3

When you have written the proposal, ask someone who has had no part in the planning of the programme ideas to act as your client. It may be possible to use your teacher for this rôle. Present the proposal to your client and ask for some feedback. Your client may well be able to point out problems that you have not thought of and these could then be incorporated in a new version of your proposal.

1 **Using the ideas that you brainstormed and researched earlier, produce proposals for each programme that you could send to a potential client or commissioning editor.**

2 **Once the proposal has been seen by your client and he or she has agreed that it is a good idea, prepare a treatment. Remember to make the treatment read as though the client is being taken through your programme step by step. Your client should be able to visualise what is happening by the words that you write.**

3 **Using the material you have developed, prepare two scripts, one for a fiction-based product and one for a non-fiction based product. Use the techniques you have looked at and prepare a draft initial version that you can work on and a final neat version.**

Comparing your work with other scripts

When you have completed your scripts you will need some feedback on how your work compares to other material. Why not try to obtain some examples of scripts from well-known programmes? Many of these can be obtained from books on popular programmes such as *Red Dwarf*. By using these scripts and watching the programmes that they refer to, you can begin to see how a script can be translated on to the screen.

If your moving image product is a news programme, then tape a similar format programme and try to analyse the way that the programme has been scripted. It may be possible to ask your local television station to provide a script from a recent programme that you could record. It is certainly the practice at some BBC venues to offer a copy of the programme script to visiting student groups. This can then be analysed alongside the video recording.

You will be able judge from these programmes whether or not your scripts compare with professionally produced programmes. If you consider scripts from other groups of students, then you can compare the way that they have produced their work in comparison to your own. Why not arrange a script reading of your programme for your client or for another group of students? Ask them to comment on the standard of your script against a pre-recorded programme of a similar genre.

You should also ask your client or another student group to assess whether or not you have represented various groups in an unsatisfactory way. They may also be able to advise you on the feasibility of producing your programme in light of the available resources.

All of the information that you obtain from your client or other groups should be recorded in some form and stored in your portfolio.

Summary

In Section 1 you have produced a comprehensive list of research sources and have gained a good understanding of research methods in the media. It is important, however, that you regard your research handbook as a growing resource. You will certainly gain additional knowledge about many other aspects of research and research methods in later study units and you may find it useful to update the handbook so that, by the time you have completed all the units, you have built up a comprehensive set of resource references.

In Section 2 you have looked at the production process for print from selecting your ideas, through the research stage, to developing three print items. You will have had the opportunity to compare the print items which you produced with existing published items; to develop the practical research skills used to compile completed print items; and to research and develop ideas to a copy stage without having to produce a completed print product.

In Section 3 you have examined the processes which go into the creation of audio products by looking at two of the most important present-day genres – commercials and news features.

In Section 4 you have initiated ideas, undertaken research and prepared scripts for two moving image products. You should now have a comprehensive folder of work that indicates your skills in planning and carrying out research for moving image items. The ideas and scripts that you have developed may be useful when you undertake the production of your moving images programmes in Study Unit 5. You may decide to develop new ideas in light of your experiences in this unit. It is however essential that all of the work that you have prepared is stored not only for assessment but to assist you in future programme planning.

Glossary

'corporate' indicates a programme made for a company to promote its goods or services; it could also be a programme for internal communication or training

electronic recording devices the term which covers all electronically controlled ways of measuring audiences, including those fixed to television sets which register when the sets are turned on and which channel is watched

focus group a group discussion in which members have the opportunity to express their views and react to the views of others

graphics usually refers to any drawn illustrative material used in page design

lifestyles a way of categorising consumers according to their habits of consumption

location a place chosen for conducting a recording other than a recording studio, either indoors or outdoors

location scouts those responsible for finding locations for media productions

OB (Outside Broadcast) mobile film/video units used to shoot on location for outdoor events such as sports and news coverage

'point of sale' relates to using a video programme at the point at which the product being promoted is sold, e.g. in a supermarket where a video player and monitor are situated by the goods being demonstrated on the video programme

property buyers those responsible for acquiring props for productions

scripts there are many forms of script in use in the media industry. The ones referred to in this unit are scripts for single- or multi-camera video shoots. They indicate dialogue, sound and camera positions

Producing print products

Contents

Introduction

In this unit you will acquire the skills necessary for the planning and development of print products. You will have the opportunity to demonstrate a clear understanding of the print production and editing processes. You should view this unit as developmental in that it provides you with opportunities for experimentation, innovation and creativity. The print product could take the form of a student or community newspaper or magazine, or even a comic. It could be in the form of a series of posters, leaflets or brochures. Within the actual content of your publication there could be other print products such as cartoons, horoscopes, graphics, illustrations and photographs.

Section 1 introduces the essential characteristics of print products and you will plan the initial content of a specific print product. In Section 2 you will generate materials for this print product according to the industry's codes of practice and conduct and then begin the editing process for the product. In Section 3 you will prepare the edited material for inclusion in your print product according to recognised industrial conventions and guidelines. Section 4 will help you to review and evaluate the completed print product in terms of its effectiveness, impact and quality.

1 Planning the production process

Print products are all around us and, no matter where you go, you will be affected by them. Print began in prehistory when early people first scribbled on the walls of caves. Now we have electronically published newspapers, books, magazines and journals which can have different editions in numerous countries around the globe.

Print can be divided into two categories:
- written text composed of words
- imaged-based texts, such as photographs and cartoons.

There are also two main styles of text:
- fiction, such as novels or stories in newspapers or magazines
- non-fiction, such as brochures, leaflets, factual stories in newspapers or magazines and textbooks for study and reference.

Broadly speaking, we can identify four main purposes for print products: for information, for education, for entertainment and for persuasion. Often these purposes are mixed – for example, advertisements can amuse, but they aim to persuade people to buy a product.

Proposals for print

When proposing a print product, the five questions of who, what, why, when and where are important to ask. In this section you will present a proposal and planning example in relation to magazines which you can find at any newsagent.

Who?

The target audience needs to be clearly identified. Who are the people your print product is aimed at? Who will read the product? This includes a description of:
- the age range of your target audience
- the gender of your target audience
- the interest of your target audience.

What?

Which medium of print will be the most effective in communicating your message? Would you use a newspaper, magazine, book, brochure, leaflet,

For example, the magazine *More!* is aimed at teenage girls, whereas *Woman* is aimed at adult females.

For example, a magazine aimed specifically at a male target audience would be *GQ*, a magazine aimed specifically at a female target audience would be *Marie Claire*, and a magazine aimed at both men and women would be *Hello!*

For example, people interested in keeping fish for their home might read *Practical Fishkeeping*.

advertisement, photograph, cartoon, graph or illustration? For example, to:

- communicate what is happening in a community in terms of news, you could use a weekly newspaper
- communicate information specific to a particular target audience, you could use a magazine
- entertain people with a romantic story you could use a fictional novel, printed as a book, a serial or a photo romance
- highlight the best bargains in a summer sale, you could use an advertisement
- provide information about holidays you could use a brochure
- convey information about a political party or cause leaflets can be used
- explain facts you could use encyclopaedias, news reports in newspapers and magazines.

Will the content be fiction or non-fiction? Fiction print products are generally accepted as being based on the creative imagination, such as novels, light articles or comics. Non-fiction print products are those which are based on factual reality.

Why?

What is the purpose of the product? It could be information, or education, or entertainment or persuasion, or a combination of these purposes.

A print product with information could be a map which tells you which routes to take. Textbooks and encyclopaedias are educational and for reference. A novel, crossword or comic provides entertainment. Persuasion is the aim of a political leaflet or poster urging you to vote for a particular party.

When?

How frequently is the product produced: weekly, daily, monthly or only once? How much time is there to produce the print product, and what can we sensibly achieve within that timescale?

Where?

Where are we going to get the equipment and people to complete the print production process? How much will the operation cost? In terms of the required resources the checklist could read: pens, pencils, notebooks, computers, image setters, printing presses, paper, computer disks, software packages – and people!

Activity

Take two print products and find out for each:

- *who* the target audience are
- *what* styles of print media are used
- *why* the item was produced
- *when* and *where* the item is produced.

Proposals

Proposals for print products usually rely on a 'market' – whether for commercial (for sale) or internal use, for example a handbook for use within a company. This highlights the target audience, and getting the product to them is amongst the first considerations. Proposals are discussed including questions such as:

- What are the requirements or suggestions for this product from the client?
- What ideas can be presented based on the expressed requirements?
- What resources do we have available/do we need?

You may need to allow some time to think out ideas and proposals. When considering ideas for a product, you should keep three questions in mind at all times:

1 What is the purpose of the product: education, information, entertainment or persuasion?
2 What resources are available to successfully produce it?
3 Does the product as described meet the requirements set for it?

Activity

In a small group, brainstorm proposals for products. Then, individually, develop one product further by describing it in terms of target audience, medium, its purpose and how it will be produced. Prepare your arguments using the three questions above.

Outline of content

A 'precis' or an 'executive summary' gives the content of a chapter, article or report in outline. In the same way, an outline is used before a full article, feature or chapter is written. Decisions about the concept, **angle** and the approach are made using such outlines.

The angle and the approach

The angle is the main point stressed in a story. The approach denotes the overall content of the article, and how the points will be developed in the main text. You will also consider the sequence in which the points are made in the story or book. These two areas, the angle and the approach, dictate the precise nature of the content material which will be used in the story that appears on the page.

Production process

As in any task, there are a number of different aspects to consider.

- Who will be responsible for gathering the information, checking it for accuracy and ensuring an appropriate structure for page design and **layout**?
- What is the content of the print item? Will it be fiction or non-fiction?
- Why is the item produced – to inform, educate, entertain, persuade or a combination of any of these?
- When does the information need to be ready?

The following table gives examples of print origination and production rôles.

Explanation of these rôles is given on pages 115–116.

Product	Gathering information	Checking	Designing and layout
Newspaper	reporter researcher	editor copy editor	graphic designer
Advertisement	copywriter	editor client	graphic designer graphic artist
Textbook	expert writer researcher	editor expert reader	graphic designer typographer

Consider the story of a student who escaped from a train disaster in the United States. The story was published in a local weekly newspaper (Figure 3.1).

- *Who*? The reporter is responsible for gathering information and will talk to the student. The reporter will telephone him at his home.
- *What*? The content is a factual story of how a student escapes from a swamp in Alabama, USA.
- *Why*? The item is produced because it affected a local person and is local, hard news.
- *When*? The information needs to be ready by Tuesday when the completed copy goes for sub-editing and layout.
- *Where*? The story is for a news page and will be illustrated by a photograph. It will be typeset and printed as part of the newspaper's production process.

Fig. 3.1
Article from *Down Democrat*, Wednesday 29 September, 1993

Production stages

Each print product goes through different stages, depending on its complexity and the speed with which it has to be produced. Producing a company handbook requires clear approval and signing-off procedures because many different departments are involved as shown below.

Fig. 3.2
Production process for a company handbook

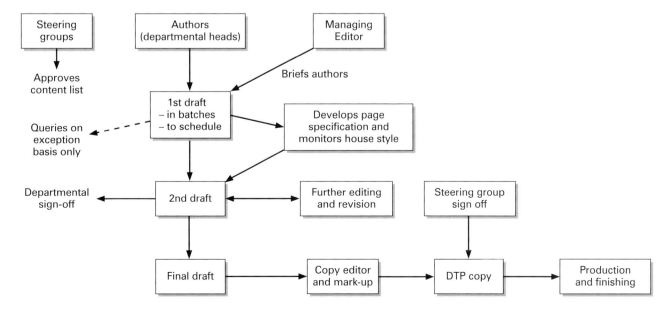

Think about the stages your product would have to go through and draw a flowchart to illustrate this. Then estimate the time each stage would take.

Text and image

The format of the material will be decided by its purpose and by the resources available. It will be text-based or image-based, with photographs, graphics, cartoons or illustrations, or it could be a combination of both.

Text-based formats, also known as writing **styles**, are represented in newspapers, magazines, periodicals, books, leaflets, brochures, posters and advertisement. They are used for:

- *news reports* – stories detailing the main facts in an event with relevant quotes from the people concerned
- *feature* articles – longer stories probing the background to an issue or series of events
- *human interest* stories – articles which focus on people and the issues which directly affect them including quotes from the people concerned
- *editorials* – written text which sets out the newspaper or magazine's viewpoint on a particular issue
- *reviews* – reflective articles in which the writer sets out his/her views
- *columns* – articles in which the writer outlines his/her personal views on issues, topics and people
- *advertisements* – very persuasive form of words encouraging the reader to buy a product or service, for example.

In image-based formats the actual image, rather than the writing, is the most important part. This can be:

- *photographs*: which capture the emotion and atmosphere of an event without using descriptive words
- *graphics*: used to illustrate written text, diagrams or drawings
- *cartoons*: real or imaginary characters drawn often with exaggerated features.

Find print products for each of the categories listed above. Cut out and keep the examples you find.

The key production rôles

Within any planning or production process for print, it is necessary to know who will be doing what. To develop printed items there is usually an editorial team and a production team. The key rôles are:

- *The information gatherer* – the person who collects or writes the information for the print product, i.e. journalist, researcher or expert writer
- *The information checker* – the person who checks the accuracy of the gathered information, i.e. the editor, copy editor and proofreader
- *The information designer* – the person who is responsible for the visual presentation of that information in the print product, i.e. the designer.

The basic production process revolves around these three rôles: gathering, checking and designing. These rôles are the same for all print products from national newspapers to community leaflets. What does change is the number of people involved in the production process: this depends on the size of the print product and the speed with which it is produced. For example, a few of you could produce a leaflet or poster announcing a party, whereas many people are involved in the production of a national newspaper.

A monthly magazine has a large team, responsible for planning, origination and production. On the editorial side this might include:

- *The **editor*** is in overall charge of the publication and decides on the editorial objectives of the magazine. These might concern house style; the types of text-based and image-based material which should be included in the publication; the balance of news and features; the purpose and bias of the product – this can also be referred to as the corporate policy of the publication; the target audience; the content considerations in terms of legal, ethical and representational issues; the resource requirements, i.e. personnel and equipment. The editor will also assess the risk to staff of using the equipment and of covering certain events, such as riots. With the support of the deputy editor and assistant editor, the editor will write the editorial sections of the product.
- *The picture editor* deals with the image-based material, especially photographs, and is responsible for assigning photographers to cover events and for getting those photographs processed in time to meet the production deadlines.
- *The production editor* is in charge of the smooth running of financial and technological resources and production methods. Based on the amount of advertising revenue raised and resource constraints, such as the cost of paper, the production editor advises the editor on pagination (the number and order of pages of the publication) and is also involved in drawing up a production schedule.
- *The chief **sub-editor*** makes decisions about the overall layout of the print product and how the material will be displayed on individual pages, determining the length of articles, use of images, typeface, use of white space, juxtaposition of text and image, number of columns, headlines and overall page concepts.
- *The features editor* has responsibility for feature articles which analyse what has been happening in the news reports and also oversees human interest reports and the reviews.

If the magazine has special sections, there may be a sports editor, a women's editor, a political editor, business editor and an education editor.

115

- *The graphics editor* is responsible for the design of illustrations, graphics and other non-text related material, often together with the graphic artist.
- *The advertising manager* is responsible for the raising of advertising revenue through the sale of advertising space in the product and also oversees specialist advertising features on a range of topics, such as Christmas shopping or holiday breaks. The amount of advertising revenue which a product can generate influences the size of the publication in terms of the pagination as well as the financial resources of the product.

The section of the team who will originate material includes:

- reporters
- photographers
- researchers
- feature writers
- columnists
- regional correspondents
- specialist correspondents.

Feature writers have a similar rôle to reporters, but usually work on a longer timescale.

Visit a newspaper or magazine office or publishing company in your area, or invite a member of staff from one of them to your centre to give a talk on his/her work and the overall planning and production process.

Activity

Select at least five print products, making sure you include fiction and non-fiction products. Look at the content of the product and list the people you think would have been involved in the planning process and origination of these products. Write brief notes on each example, explaining why these people would be involved.

Layout

Planning how the print product will look or be visually displayed is called design and layout. Design is the overall look of the product, and layout is the arranging of the content on the page, following a page specification (see below).

Fig. 3.3
Page specification for a tabloid newspaper

The layout contributes to the clarity of the product's message. When planning design and layout, make your plan as lifesize as possible and think about how you can use your product's appearance to kindle the reader's interest. Use visual material to make it more interesting. For example, the front pages of newspapers at the turn of this century were only text or the printed word and, whilst they contained a lot of information, they were hard to read.

After the design has been approved, the layout artist puts together the plan for the pages. In magazine production, a layout artist is often called a sub-editor. Layout is largely considered page by page: will the content be displayed on a page, or perhaps over two pages, known as a **double-page spread**? Making decisions like this is called 'deciding the **page concept**'. Each page is made up of one or more **columns**, which will determine the length of the article or story. The length can be measured in words or paragraphs. In professional or scientific journals, the final extent is often determined by the length of the contributions.

When deciding about the layout you will have to consider:

- the wording in the headline, or title
- the use of margin space or **gutter**
- the typeface and size used which will influence the space required for a certain number of words
- borders
- the positioning of the text and the images on the page
- white space.

Type

There are many typefaces available in all sizes and thicknesses, with a variety of spacings and leadings. The two main type groups in the Roman alphabet are serif and sans serif (see below). The serif is characterised by letters in which the strokes are of varying thickness with the ends finished off with a decorative flourish or tail which is called the serif. The sans group has letters of mostly even strokes without the decorative flourishes or serifs.

Activity

Describe the layout of one of the printed products from a previous activity. Make written notes identifying the page concepts, typefaces, use of white space, juxtaposition of text and image, number of columns, headlines, gutters and borders.

Assignment: Part 1

Now produce two proposals for print products for an organisation of your choice. One will be an image-based cartoon strip, the other a centre page spread in the local newspaper.

The 'gutter' is the margin between two printed pages. White space is where there is no text of any kind. Also known as air, it stops the pages becoming cluttered, making them easier to read.

Borders are print rules or black lines which are used to put articles in boxes on a printed page. They are also used for display effects in layout, and especially to distinguish one article from another.

Fig. 3.4

sans serif typeface
sans serif typeface
sans serif
typeface

Serif typeface
serif typeface
serif typeface
serif typeface
serif typeface

1 In a small group assume the rôles of an editorial team and allocate the tasks in the origination and production process for the two print products.

2 Now plan both products and argue in favour of them with your colleagues. Explain the purpose, target audience, content and layout. Describe their resource requirements. Write up your proposal as a group.

3 Identify potential material for written text and for visual items for the two print products. Decide which written texts and visual materials each of you wishes to provide.

4 Prepare outline schedules for the two products and include these in your proposal reports.

Legal considerations

Everyone working in printing and publishing should be aware of legal constraints. The four main areas covered by laws are defamation, copyright, discrimination, and national security.

Defamation

A libel is where a person complains that their character or livelihood has been damaged as a result of something published in print. The originator (journalist) as well as the editor/publisher could be charged under the Defamation Act 1952, and the outcome could be a heavy fine in the form of damages. An example of a libel is stating in print that someone has committed fraud when in fact there is no proof of this.

Copyright

Copyright law controls how much of other people's words, artistry or photographs you can use in your print product. Under the Copyright Designs and Patents Act 1988, copyright protects any literary, dramatic, artistic or musical work, sound recording, film broadcast or typographical arrangement. There is, however, no copyright in facts, news, ideas or information. Copyright exists in the form in which information is expressed and the selection and arrangement of the material. It could be said that anything worth copying is worth protecting and the reproduction of a substantial part of a copyrighted work may constitute an infringement. For example, it could be an infringement if you reproduce substantial passages from a book without the author's permission.

Discrimination

You need to be particularly aware of the Race Relations Act 1976, the Equal Opportunities Acts and the Sex Discrimination Act 1976.

Anti-discrimination legislation makes it an offence to publish writing which is prejudiced against a person because of race, colour, religion, sex, or sexual orientation, or to any physical or mental illness or handicap.

National security

D Notices are written in general terms and describe the broad areas where the government and media members of the committee have agreed that secrets affecting national security lie. However, the committee has no statutory powers and the final decision on whether to publish rests with the editor. Information which is the subject of a D Notice is regarded by the government as secret.

Various Official Secrets Acts detail a range of crimes from spying for a hostile country to revealing sensitive information which could pose a threat to national security. Under the legislation, you could also be charged if you refused to reveal where you obtained certain kinds of sensitive information. Guidance on national security is made available to people working in the media through the Defence Press and Broadcasting Committee. This committee can issue D Notices.

Activity

Look back over the five printed products you collected for the activity on page 116. Make notes identifying which laws you would have to be aware of when planning for the articles which have been published in these printed products.

Ethics in print

Everyone has standards or values by which they live their lives. In many industries, including the media and print production, these values or standards are known as ethics.

When planning a print product, you may be faced with three types of ethical considerations: confidentiality, privacy and offensive material. It has been suggested that there are no binding rules on what is the correct decision to make when faced with an ethical consideration, and that each individual situation must be judged on its own merits and guided by a person's own conscience. This means that one person might agree with an ethical decision, but someone else could disagree with it. Others argue that there should be a set of ground rules.

Confidentiality

When someone tells you something 'in confidence', this is taken to mean that you will not repeat the information. If you are given information for the content of your print product in confidence, it is your duty to keep secret the identity of the person or source who gave you that information.

The decision not to reveal the person's name is known as 'protecting confidentiality'. For example, when reporting about terrorism in Northern Ireland or Great Britain, a member of an illegal organisation could provide the information for the article. Journalists have come under pressure in the past to reveal those sources. Other confidentiality questions which journalists or researchers may have to face include:

- Should you ever lie or be deceptive in the pursuit of material for a print product? For example, would you pretend to be a doctor to gain access to a hospital patient?
- Should you ever edit a direct quotation?
- Should you accept free gifts from people about whom you are compiling information? Should you accept them only on certain conditions? Are there any significantly different ethical issues in being offered a book for review, a free ticket to review a film, play or concert, and a free trip to Barbados for a travel feature article?
- What will be the impact on your values and standards if you receive a lot of awards given by the organisations you are writing about?
- How important is it for you to protect your sources? Would you be prepared to tell lies to protect the identity of that source?
- Can you justify chequebook journalism, i.e. paying sources money for information for your print products?
- If you were a member of a political party or a campaigner for a particular cause, would this interfere with your professionalism and notions of being fair? Could you accurately represent a viewpoint which strongly opposes your own beliefs?
- Would you ever break an **embargo**, which is a deadline before which information which has been made available should not be published? It is a concept based on trust between the media person and the source.

Privacy

Have you ever been told to mind your own business? There are three main areas which are generally frowned upon in terms of intruding into someone's private life to gain information which you intend to print. They are:

1 entering private property without the permission of the lawful occupant
2 placing a surveillance device – or bug – on private property without the consent of the lawful occupant
3 taking a photograph or recording the voice of an individual who is on private property without consent.

Activity

There has been considerable debate concerning articles and photographs about the lives of members of the Royal Family, and music and film superstars. Discuss in a small group whether you

think such people should have a private life as ordinary human beings like you and your fellow students. Or are their private lives 'in the public interest' because of the positions they hold in society?

Other privacy questions to consider are:

- Is it right to tape a conversation and not tell the interviewee or the person you are talking to that it is being recorded?
- Would you contact the parents, other relatives or friends of a school pupil who had just committed suicide?
- What special considerations should you think of when dealing with material concerning the mentally ill?

Offensive material

Many people hold strong views on issues. Expressing those views in print for publication is likely to cause offence. Questions to consider are:

- To what extent should you provide readers of your print product with the right to reply if you have been inaccurate or provocative in your content?
- Should you carry in your print product government misinformation during times of either war or peace?
- Is it possible to provide rules on questions of bad taste and the use of 'shocking' pictures or foul language?
- To what extent does the language you use in your print product indirectly create discrimination against individual people or a group within society?

Activity

Choose two questions from each of the three areas of ethical consideration: confidentiality, privacy and offensive material. Using your own conscience as a guide, write answers to the questions posed. Keep the answers in your portfolio.

The National Union of Journalists
Acorn House
314 Gray's Inn Road
London WC1X 8DP
(tel. 0171 278 7916)

The Press Complaints Commission
1 Salisbury Square
London EC4Y 8AE
(tel. 0171 353 1248)

The Advertising Standards Authority
2 Torrington Place
London WC1E 7HW
(tel. 0171 580 5555)

Codes of practice

A number of media organisations have a code of conduct or a code of practice which can help you decide the correct procedure for an ethical consideration. They are:

- *The National Union of Journalists (NUJ)*, which is the media industry's largest journalistic trade union. It has a 12 point code of conduct.
- *The Press Complaints Commission (PCC)*, which deals solely with complaints against the press, including complaints of unfairness and intrusion into privacy. The Commission has an in-depth code of practice.
- *The Advertising Standards Authority (ASA)* also has a code of advertising practice which governs the content of printed advertisements.

The PCC has been involved with the censuring of journalists who have compiled their own quotations. One of the most famous instances was when a national newspaper invented an interview with the wife of a Falklands war hero killed in battle. The PCC has also criticised journalists who do not keep their notes because if complaints are made against newspapers there is little ground on which to base a defence.

Activity

Talk to someone working with print products in your locality about the ethical considerations which he/she has to face. This could be a reporter on a newspaper or magazine, or someone dealing with advertising. Write notes on your questions and the answers and keep them in your portfolio.

Representation

What gets printed has to meet the demands of the target audience and should not discriminate against any groups in society in any way. Such representation issues fall into four broad categories: age, gender, minority and social issues. These considerations apply equally to fiction as well as non-fiction products and some are covered by law.

Age

You must ensure that your print product is covering the age range of the target audience, and that people from that target audience's age range would be interested in the issues raised in your product. Avoid age discrimination.

Gender

As with age, you must ensure that your product covers issues which the target audience in terms of its gender would be interested in. A teenage magazine aimed at females would not cover issues which are of interest to middle-aged businessmen. Avoid gender discrimination.

Minority

It is important that you take account of the views of minority groups in your print product and avoid making sweeping generalisations. By ignoring minority views, you may be excluding part of your target audience and could accidentally provoke discrimination against that minority. Do not fall foul of anti-discrimination law.

Social issues

Reflect the genuine social issues as they affect your target audience. For example, a magazine aimed at covering the issues which affect an inner city area with poor housing and heavy unemployment would be insensitive if it ran an article on expensive bathrooms and kitchens for a country manor which only the very wealthy could afford. In the same way, you could discriminate against people from one social class by suggesting that people from the working class were less well educated than people from the middle and upper classes.

Assignment: Part 2

You will need to provide outlines for both your print products, with notes on design and layout, and a full production schedule for one of the products, supported by a record of resources. There will also be notes identifying the material and content considerations for each print item.

In a small group:

1 **Using the material lists which you produced for the two print products in the first part of the assignment, provide brief outlines for the two products. These outlines should include notes on the page specification and article concepts for both products.**

2 **Using the information contained in this section as a guideline, make written notes on the potential layouts for both products. These layouts should contain information on length of articles, use of images, typeface, use of white space, juxtaposition of text and image, number of columns, headlines, the gutters and borders.**

On your own:

1 **Select one of the two proposals outlined above and write a production schedule for that print product, taking account of the following factors:**
   - the number of people who will be required to complete the product
   - what the individual rôles of those people will be
   - what resources, including money and technology, will be required to produce the print product
   - how long it will take to produce the product, identifying the particular deadlines for both individual items of content and the overall product
   - identifying and resolving any risks or problems which could inhibit the production process.

Finally:

1 **Write notes listing the individual items of your print product, such as the written text and image-based texts**

2 **Write notes identifying the legal, ethical and representation issues which must be considered when completing each individual item of content in the print product.**

2 Originate and edit print material

Activity

Collect a number of print products (see below) which catch your eye, including a newspaper article, a magazine article, an advertisement, a brochure, a photograph, a leaflet, a cartoon and a double-page spread from a book. Note down why you like the print product and why you think it is effective.

Fig. 3.5
Examples of printed matter

One of the criteria which you may have used to make your selection is simply that it looked nice to you. To be able to make your print product appear more visually appealing, you should consider the following factors.

Size

Newspapers can be divided into two types: **tabloids**, such as the *Sun* and the *Mirror*; and **broadsheets**, such as the *Guardian* and the *Daily Telegraph*. An easy way of distinguishing between the two formats is that a broadsheet page is roughly the size of two tabloid pages. Paperback books largely come in two sizes. Reports and journals are often A4.

Layout

It is not only the size of the newspaper or magazine which is important, but also the way in which the written materials and photographs are

As well as by number of columns and centimetres, print products can be measured by page size, such as A3 (297 x 420 mm), A4 (210 x 297 mm), and A5 (148 x 210 mm). The most commonly used page size for print products such as leaflets or brochures is A4. An A3 page is the equivalent of two A4 pages side by side, and A5 is half the size of an A4 page.

displayed. The content can be measured in columns. For example, in the broadsheet *Guardian* newspaper there are eight columns to a page. If the written text fills one of these columns, it is known as a single column report. If the text goes across two columns, it is known as a **double column** report. Written text and photographs for posters, books, brochures and leaflets are measured in the same way, using similar formats such as column widths. Advertisements are measured in column centimetres, and this style of measurement could also apply to brochures and leaflets.

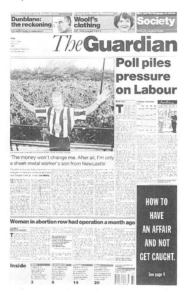

Fig. 3.6
Different column widths of two well-known daily newspapers

Positioning print

Newspapers and magazines are made up of a range of items. There is generally accepted practice about where in newspapers and magazines different items are placed. For example:

- News is to be found at the beginning, with the most important stories on page 1.
- Features tend to follow the news stories and can occupy two or three pages, depending on the topic.
- Human interest reports can be found alongside or accompanying the features, because they focus mainly on people.
- Editorials are usually found in the initial sections of the product.
- Advertisements are placed throughout the product, although there may be specific sections for certain types of advertisements, such as cars, jobs or housing.
- Photographs can be seen throughout the product, but their use depends on the type of report they are illustrating.
- Graphics are located throughout all parts of the product depending on the report or advertisement they are accompanying.
- Sport items are found at the end except in a specific print product devoted entirely to sports, such as a soccer or rugby magazine.

You will already have decided under which heading your material will come. When researching for your printed material you can be guided by the general approach of a product and by where an item is usually placed.

Fig. 3.7
Leading article from a
well-known daily
newspaper

Text design

In addition to arranging text in columns, a number of other decisions have been made to make it visually attractive and accessible to the reader. These include the use of the following:

- *Headline* – a few words at the top of the article, usually in larger print, summarising the contents, for example, 'New judges herald reform'.
- *Sub-head* – a smaller heading below the main headline which provides some explanation about the content of the article. In the case of Figure 3.7, the sub-head is: 'Top legal roles for Bingham and Woolf'.
- *Intro* – the first paragraph, or **introduction**, in the article which acts as a summary of the report or article.
- *Main text* – the remainder of the article which explains the rest of the story in more depth than is outlined in the intro.
- *Grammar* – the article must also read well. Sentences should be kept short and snappy; paragraphs should also be kept short.

A headline or key words could be used with leaflets, posters, brochures and books. With image-based material, it could be the impact of the photograph, cartoon, or graph which attracts the eye. Similarly, image-based texts can often stand alone without the use of words to make their point. In many advertisements which use photographs, the wording which accompanies the image is usually secondary to the impact of that image. When analysing and researching print products, therefore, the essential area to examine is the balance between text and image in the product, focusing especially on the question: what is it which initially attracts the eye to this product?

Activity

Select five different examples of texts from your collection for the previous activity. Using the basic guidelines on the use of headings and design devices, make a written list of any used in the product and explain why you think they have been used.

A photographic or cartoon image can also help the visual appeal of your product. Once you have collected the material for the written text, ask yourself if it would look better if there was a photograph, illustration, graphic, cartoon or some other image to accompany the words. Are graphs needed to illustrate the data?

Researching material

The content of any print product, even a novel, will need research and information gathering. The location of this information, whether from a person or a product, is known as a **source**. There are essentially two types of sources: **primary**, or direct contact sources; and **secondary**, or indirect contact sources.

Primary sources

Primary sources can be divided into two types: first or face-to-face interviews, which involve people; and firsthand information, which can come from products, such as other print material.

Interviews

One of the best ways of researching information for a print product is through the use of interviews. You can use the information which the person gives you as potential content for your print product. There are basically two types of interview: fact-finding and opinion-seeking.

In a fact-finding interview you are trying to get facts from your interviewee, and the questions usually start with these words: who, what, where, when or how. An opinion-seeking interview focuses on someone's views on a subject or event, and the questions usually take the form of: what do you think of…? or, why do you have…?

Secondary sources

These types of sources usually concern material which you can consult, and they fall into five broad categories:

- previously printed material, such as back editions of newspapers and magazines
- audio and video material
- bookprint material such as travelguides, dictionaries and biographies
- reports and minutes
- databases, such as Ceefax, the Oracle, libraries, cuttings files, contacts books, and information stored on computer, micro film or the Internet.

You can get data on public limited companies from Companies House.

Research resources fall into two areas: resources to record information, and resources to obtain information.

Recording information can be done in three main ways:

- handwritten notes using speedwriting or shorthand
- tape recordings using a cassette recorder
- visual means, using a video camera, photographs, or photocopy.

Obtaining information from primary sources involves either telephone calls or visits.

Activity

1 Decide which information sources you will need for the content of your product and how you will record the information.

Health and safety

Working as a researcher or journalist can be dangerous, for example reporting from war or riot zones. Whilst working in print media is not always as directly dangerous as this, there are a number of safety checks which you need to be aware of to ensure that you do not do yourself harm.

- Follow health and safety guidelines when using computers or any other electrical equipment.
- Keep a regular check on your equipment, such as batteries for tape recorders, in case the batteries leak or become corroded.
- When working in an office or design studio, follow health and safety guidelines – for example ensure that there are no trailing wires from your equipment.

Personal safety

If you are going to a location outside the school or office, always remember to tell someone in authority where you are going, who you are going to see, how you are getting there and leave a contact number for yourself at that location. It might be wise to let your office or school know that you have safely reached your destination. Remember, in terms of safety, put yourself *first*. Where a situation is likely to be volatile, it is better not to go on your own.

Content considerations

You saw in the previous section how legal and ethical considerations affect the content of printed materials. Here are some further requirements for content.

Accuracy

Content

No matter what print product you are gathering information for, it is extremely important that all the material you collect is accurate. Mistakes in print can upset others enough to take legal action against you. If you lose such a legal case, it could cost either you or your company a lot of money. To ensure that your material is accurate when producing a print product, record your material in the way described above.

Spelling

If you are unsure about the spelling of a word, take time to look it up. Using a good dictionary is one of the safest ways of ensuring that the information you have collected is spelt correctly. There are dictionaries specifically for writers and editors.

If you are using a wordprocessor for writing your material, you may be able to use a spellcheck system to check the accuracy of your spelling.

Grammar

Spellchecks are for spelling; they cannot spot mistakes in tense, sentence size, paragraph construction or punctuation. Take time to always check your work.

Authenticity

Read over the material you have collected to ensure that any references and quotations are accurately attributed. Remember, it is always best to double check, so if you are unsure contact the person who made the quotation or verify it against the document in which the reference is made.

Correct usage and authenticity procedures, together with the implementation of house style, are checked at copy editing stage.

Editorial objectives

Remember how in the previous section you considered the importance of concept as a key feature when planning for print items? These same basic guidelines are also important when planning and researching for the overall print product, no matter what that product is.

1 Editorial objectives will inform the research for your print product. Some of these were introduced in the first part of this unit. Depending on the size of the print product, the purpose can vary with each item which is included.
2 Design: Is the print product designed to ensure that the purposes are communicated to the target audience?
3 Layout: Have the editorial objectives been met through the visual appeal of the product?
4 Style: Keep the same style throughout your print product. Is it sympathetic, aggressive, business-like? For example, if you are doing an article about a holiday resort for a brochure, you would use written text and images which portray the resort as a great place in which to have a holiday, with many superlative statements.
5 Content: Does the content of the product reflect the editorial objectives? For example, if you are producing a leaflet about a carnival in your home village or district, does it contain all the information which anyone wanting to come to the event would need, such as the starting time, activities, car parking?

Activity

Take the proposals which you initiated for the previous section, and make a list of the editorial objectives for them, with explanations.

Content checklist

Editorial objectives will take into account legal constraints, ethical guidelines and representation approaches as outlined in the first section of this unit. You should apply the following checklist during the originating and editing process, whichever print product you are dealing with.

Legal, ethical and representation checklist

Law
1 Have I written anything which could be considered as a libel?
2 Have I infringed any copyright laws concerning the material in the printed texts I am using?
3 Have I made hurtful comments about anyone on the basis of their race, sex, sexuality or disability?
4 Have I endangered national security as outlined in the Official Secrets Act?
5 Is the material which I intend to publish in the public interest?

Ethics
1 Have I been able to keep the text free of any bias against an individual person, or a group?
2 Have I ensured the confidentiality of a source who has given me material and wishes to remain anonymous?
3 Have I gathered any material which if published could be regarded as being offensive?

Representation
1 Have I gathered any information which I wish to use in my printed product which could be regarded as detrimental to someone on the grounds of their age, gender, disability or ethnic origin?

Activity

In twos, select approximately a dozen examples of print products ranging from newspaper and magazine articles to advertisements, brochures and leaflets.

1 Apply the legal, ethical and representational checklist to each of the selected examples.

2 Write a report on your findings and briefly present your findings in class.

Assignment: Part 1

For this part of your assignment you are asked to research material for a print product. Provide brief notes identifying content constraints on the material you have researched.

1 In a small group, brainstorm ideas for 'real life' events, places or activities in your locality which you could use as a topic for a print product. This could be a newspaper or magazine article, brochure, leaflet, poster, illustration, cartoon or photograph.

2 Now select at least two topics and visit the locations to gather information. Plan how you will collect the information and how you will record it. Keep notes on how you go about this in your portfolio.

3 Using the research material gathered, produce examples of the drafts for your print product.

4 In a brief report, describe any content constraints which you faced and explain how you sought to resolve them. This should include how you observed the correct legal, ethical and representational codes when gathering the material and checking the information.

You might consider presenting one topic in different formats. For example, a community event in your locality could be represented in a newspaper article, a poster, a leaflet, photographs or even a cartoon or graphic design. You may wish to produce two or three types of print product for the same topic. These could be submitted as part of your portfolio of evidence.

Arrange an interview with someone from a local newspaper, community magazine or publishing company with responsibility for coverage of events and activities in the community, for example a local newspaper reporter who covers the councils and courts.

Copy editing

Copy editors will be looking for errors in four key areas:

1 *Spelling*. They will make use of a good standard dictionary or a computer spellcheck on any work they are unsure of.

2 *Typographical errors*. They will ensure that headlines and sub-heads are with the proper intros and main texts; that captions are below or with the appropriate photographs; that illustrations and graphics are with their proper texts, and that advertisements are correctly put together.

3 *Inconsistencies*. They will check the facts of a report or text.

4 *Grammar*. The material must not only read well, but it must also make sense in terms of tenses, sentence and paragraph construction, punctuation, proper use of words, double meanings and innuendo. You must pay particular attention to the last on this list as there is always the danger that your print product could be misrepresented or become a joke through the misuse of a word or phrase.

Activity

Look carefully through a reference book or a guide for copy editors or sub-editors which summarises the work of a copy editor and explains house style, use of punctuation, alliteration, compound nouns, American English and so on. You can use what is appropriate from this to copy edit your own products.

A copy editor's guide is likely to include some or all of the advice on the following page.

- Standardise spelling and use of hyphens.
- Spell out all numbers from one to ten; use numerals for numbers above ten.
- Use short words where you can, for example, use 'now' not 'at this precise moment in time', and 'although' instead of 'in spite of the fact that'.
- Avoid using foreign or unusual words, for example use 'meeting' instead of the French word 'rendezvous'.
- Avoid the excessive use of adverbs and adjectives, for example 'broad daylight' or 'completely untrue'; or clichés, such as 'stunning blonde' or 'brutal murder'; or those which are double adjectives, such as 'deep blue sea' or 'fine sunny day'. An adjective should extend the noun, not prop it up.
- Avoid using excessively long sentences. This does not mean that you should only use sentences of eight words or fewer, but the aim should be clarity and there is less chance of confusing the reader with shorter sentences.
- Be consistent in your use of tense to avoid difficulties in phrasing. The past, present and future tenses will serve the majority of your requirements.
- Do not use jargon, especially government or civil service phrases, or words such as 'downturns' and 'formal approaches'.
- Avoid parentheses, dashes and dots.
- Keep punctuation simple. It should only be used if the meaning of the phrase or sentence is in doubt without it.
- Keep paragraphs short.

Once the material has been copy edited (see below), it is sometimes sent back to the person who originally wrote it for rewriting.

To reduce the word count, see how many adjectives you can take out without losing the meaning.

Example
These are all time-expired clause 4 optants and delay in referral would distort the quarterly submission ratio.

Copy editors will ensure that the texts comply with the recognised legal, ethical and representational codes and conventions. A copy editor also makes sure that house style is followed in use of terminology and spelling.

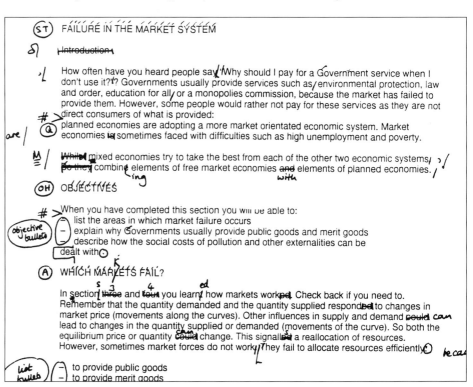

Fig. 3.8
Copy edited material

For large publishing projects, extensive copy editing guidelines will be produced to clarify the copy editor's responsibilities in preparing the text for typesetting and printing. This can include checking that the typescript is complete, raising queries with an author or expert reader, checking glossaries and completing the **mark-up** following a page specification and using the conventional mark-up code.

Activity

In pairs, exchange written reports compiled for one of the activities. Copy edit each other's work, listing any corrections which need to be made and querying any lack of clarity.

Fig. 3.9
Proof correction symbols

Instruction	Textual mark	Marginal mark
Insert in text the matter indicated in margin	ʌ	*New matter followed by* /
Delete	Strike through characters to be deleted	♂
Delete and close up	Strike through characters to be deleted and use close-up sign	♂
Leave as printed	· · · · · under characters to remain	stet
Change to italic	—— under characters to be altered	ital
Change to even small capitals	═══ under characters to be altered	s.c.
Change to capital letters	═══ under characters to be altered	caps
Use capital letters for initial letters and small capitals for rest of words	═══ under initial letters and —— under the rest of the words	c.& s.c.
Change to bold type	∼∼∼ under characters to be altered	bold
Change to lower case	Encircle characters to be altered	l.c.
Change to roman type	Encircle characters to be altered	rom
Wrong fount. Replace by letter of correct fount	Encircle character to be altered	w.f.
Invert type	Encircle character to be altered	9
Change damaged character(s)	Encircle character(s) to be altered	×

Proofreading

This is the skill of reading typeset text against a manuscript which has the copy editor's changes and mark-up on it. This is done before the item is printed to ensure that all mistakes, omissions and inconsistencies in layout are spotted and corrected. **Proofreaders** have a very important part in the editing process. Originators and writers should always carefully read all their work before setting. Once it has been set, a proofreader will read through either **galley** or **page proofs** to check extent and cross references using the standard proofreading symbols for correction (see Figure 3.9), and to ensure that the **desktop publishing** (DTP) operator or typesetter has accurately followed the text and mark-up for design on the manuscript.

Practice makes perfect and the more experience you have of reading other people's work, the more proficient a proofreader you will become.

Assignment: Part 2

Keep the examples of drafts and rewrite as part of your assessment.

This part of the assignment focuses on copy editing and proofreading of text which you have produced.

1 **Take the first draft of the article or report based on the research material from the first part of this assignment and copy edit, then rewrite the draft yourself.**

2 **List the general corrections which need to be made and identify content constraints which need to be resolved. You now have a second draft.**

3 **Give the second draft to a colleague for further copy editing. You should be provided with a list of suggested answers to your corrections.**

4 **Now implement your page design for your text, using DTP. Ask a colleague to proofread the article against the marked-up manuscript.**

3 Sub-edit and lay out print products

Selecting and organising material

You will recall from your previous work that the sub-editor, or sub, is the person who checks and places material for a print product, fits the content into the space on the page, and approves headlines and introductions for each item. By this time, the content of the product has been gathered, written, copy edited, set and proofread.

Teamwork

In print production, teamwork is vital. If we take the newspaper industry as an example of a print product, the process is roughly as follows:

1 The reporter or contributor or columnist writes the story and passes it to a **copy taster**, usually the news editor, who makes initial checks for accuracy and news potential. The news editor will decide whether it is to be included in the paper.
2 If the story passes copy tasting, it moves to the sub-editing department where it is again judged on news value, and checked for grammar, spelling, balance, legality and accuracy.
3 The sub-editor decides on a headline, and a possible page number. Using new technology, sub-editors work directly on the layout at computer terminals. This is known as **on-screen page make-up**, and the sub-editors will use the appropriate DTP or image-setting software. Sub-editors may have to **cut** stories to a given word count or column length.
4 Each complete page is then photographed and sent to the printing plant.

Selection

The first practical task in sub-editing is to select and organise the material which is to be included in the print product. The sub-editor ensures that three principles are adhered to:

1 *Balance* – in spread of items such as news, features, sport, photographs
2 *Balance* – in the content on specific pages, that is the relationship between written stories, photographs and advertisements
3 *Consistency* – in the use of headlines, typefaces and in the overall design of the pages.

The sub-editor in newspaper and magazine production decides the news value of each item for the print product. Not every item submitted is actually included in the final completed print product. The sub-editor will divide the items into written text and images and then organise this material into its various formats, such as news, features, sport and reviews. This all needs to be done within the print room's **deadline**.

A range of practical skills is needed for the work of a sub-editor or copy editor.

- Checking – locations, facts and names; mistakes in spelling and grammar; legal, ethical and representational aspects
- Editing – cutting the written text so that it fits a given space on the page; combining material from a number of sources to make a new story or ensure that an item takes up the required length, rewording all or part of the material to reach the required balance and length, revising the item if necessary as new information is obtained, **deleting** unnecessary words and phrases, making every word count, being tough on the use of adjectives, keeping in long quotations only if they explain the item fully
- Layout – providing any **captions** which are required for photographs or other image-based texts, writing headlines for the stories to fit the space available
- Text variation – brightening the visual impact of the product by using a number of devices to highlight parts of the written text: marking some paragraphs or key phrases in bold or italics; using blobs or black squares; underscoring the lines of type in certain paragraphs; breaking up long passages of type with sub-heads, which are usually one or two words in a larger type size which identify the content of the following paragraphs; using a **by-line**, which is the writer's name, and setting it in a panel, or box, somewhere near the intro or middle of the article.
- **Rejigging** – revising a print item after it has already been edited and designed. This can happen because new facts have emerged or its place in the product has been altered, or you have had second thoughts on matters of legality and representational issues.

In the composing room, specialist sub-editors check the pages on screen, searching for errors. Appropriate command instructions for page layout are inserted so that the item is set in the correct type size and **measure**.

Activity

What kind of errors could a sub-editor spot at this stage?

You may have suggested a mismatch between text and photograph; a clearly unfinished item; columns not following on correctly.

Grammar and syntax

A sub-editor needs to be accurate and confident about use of grammar and syntax. Errors can creep in as a result of condensing material or trying to liven it up. If the meaning is unclear because of a grammatical mistake, there is no harm in checking the item with the writer rather than risk getting the sense wrong in print.

Using technology

A sub-editor will insert the command instructions for DTP or image setters on each item so that it can be put in the right sequence for its spacing in the final product. Each item will have a column and edition location.

Activity

For your own product, lay out and print part of the items which you have written. Apply the sub-editing and copy editing guidelines from Section 2 in this unit and from your editing guide.

Ordering material

The selection and organisation process discussed here concerns the content and layout of an individual page to ensure that it is balanced in its final look. To decide the order of importance of the content of a page, ask: what are the most topical items? interesting items? relevant items for the target audience? likely items to catch the reader's attention?

In newspapers and sometimes in magazines, each location on a page has a particular name:

- Splash – the main story on page 1
- Page lead – the main story on an individual page
- Half lead – the second most important story on a page
- Down page report – other stories on the page, sometimes located below the page lead
- Crawler – a story located at the bottom of a page
- Filler – a short item of one or two paragraphs
- Caption – text which identifies or describes a photograph on a page.

Whilst these are the various types of articles, decisions on inclusion and positioning are based on several criteria, not only for text-based material, but also for image-based material. These are:

- *geography or proximity*. When you are abroad on holiday, you will find little reference to events 'back home' in the newspapers and magazines of the overseas holiday destination. A revolution in a South American state may only get a few paragraphs in the British press. Likewise, the wedding of a prominent local businessman in your area may have a photograph and text describing the wedding, whereas in a national newspaper it would not even be mentioned. Think local and ask: what do my readers want to read?
- *individual or personal*. Selecting your material for editing must also focus on who you are writing about. For example, a minor accident to a pop

star or a member of the Royal Family will make national headline news, whilst the same accident involving a local dentist would only make the local weekly press.

- *special interest*. For example, a local weekly newspaper serving a rural community would include agricultural items, whereas an urban-based community magazine could have a considerable number of items on the problems of inner city housing.

National newspapers have special interest areas and slant their coverage towards this. The *Guardian*, for example, is strong on educational and media matters, the *Daily Telegraph* on overseas news, and the *Financial Times* on technology, energy and the economy.

Activity

Find a local and a national newspaper and a weekly magazine and cut out articles from each which illustrate the criteria of geography, personal and special interest. Explain your choice.

Page layout

Page design should be a balance between checking the key features of the print product, working to agreed guidelines and responding to formats and styles suggested by the contributors. Individual creative design then completes the task.

The page design should:

- accommodate all necessary features: text, images, advertisements or forms and response space
- attract the eye of the reader from the target audience by creating a visually pleasing pattern
- signpost the various items on the page by using type sizes and positioning
- give your print product a visually recognisable appearance and character through consistency in the typeface you choose.

Within the overall page design, the layout of each page will be slightly different depending on the precise content and juxtaposition of elements. The components of a printed page are usually: text, headlines, photographs and advertisements. To help you with the layout of the page, you could use a **page plan** or layout sheet, a rough map which indicates where you want the four components to go on the page. Page specifications, detailing the design and layout elements will usually include the following.

Headline

What about this headline to a report about a riot: 'Police have quizzed ten people after a probe into a cash grab following a ram-raid joyrider drama at local shops ended in a theft spree'.

The main purpose of a headline is to attract the reader's attention to the item. There are some basic rules which the sub-editor should bear in mind when writing or checking headlines whatever the page design:

– no punctuation or quotation marks: they look too messy
– avoid using slang or jargon words (known as journalese)
– use an active verb, especially in factual headlines

– do not use abbreviations

– try to avoid using 'he', 'she', or 'they'; instead, personalise where you can

– try to avoid asking questions of the reader

– avoid using the past tense in items which deal with immediate topics as it dates the items

– avoid place names unless they are of vital importance as elements in themselves.

Varying the typeface

Varying the size and weight of the typeface adds interest to the page. It is generally considered more appropriate for a product with a serif typeface to vary it with a sans face rather than another serif face which would clash. This also applies to type styles, such as **bold** and *italic*. A bold sans face will provide an effective contrast against a lighter face with serifs.

Photographs

The main factors in the editing of photographs will be:

• relevance to the print item

• position of the figures in the photograph in relation to the space available.

It is important that the figures in the photograph do not look out of the page on which they are placed, (i.e. look to the right when positioned on a righthand page) or away from the written text which they are accompanying. Once the photograph has been selected, the next stage in the editing process is to decide how much of it to use. This is known as **cropping** and **scaling**.

For both cropping and scaling a light box is used. The photograph is placed face down on the light box so the detail of the photograph is highlighted. The area which is indicated becomes the image and size which will appear in the final photograph to be printed. If you have no light box, hold the photograph up to a light.

• Cropping: the back of the photograph is marked off with pencil lines to indicate the area which must be used.

• Scaling: working out the size needed for the photograph after it has been cropped to an agreed format. This is done by drawing a diagonal line in pencil from the top right of the cropped area to the bottom left. If the width is known – this could be single column, or double column, for example – the measurement is taken across from the left side of the cropped area until the line intersects the diagonal. To find the depth corresponding to this width, the measurement is taken downwards from the point of intersection to the bottom of the photograph. Figure 3.10 shows how it is done.

Advertisements on the page

Liaison between editors and designers about the shape and design of advertisements needs to take place early on. The layout of the text and photographs has to accommodate the advertisements on the page plan. Space for advertisements is sold by size and often the income from advertising pays for the entire publication. Often advertisements are invited alongside an article on the same topic, for example conservatories or cars.

Fig. 3.10
Scaling a photograph

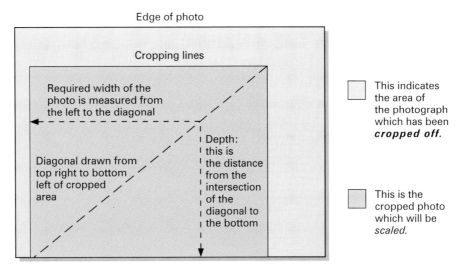

This is how photographs are cropped and scaled, or measured to fit a particular space. This figure outlines how the pencil lines on the back of the photo are drawn.

Technology

With new technology, page layout is usually done directly on the screen using the computer keyboard and mouse.

Activity

What do you think are the advantages of using screen-based page layout?

You might have suggested:

- not having to deal with **hard copy**
- the articles can be checked for length by relating the word count and number of lines given on the screen to the space allocated on the page plan
- fact and word pruning can be carried out as with hard copy, but perhaps on-screen alterations can be made faster
- clean **copy** without any annotations can be printed out
- after each change, the text automatically rearranges itself on screen
- a 'split screen' allows the sub-editor to work on two print items at once.

You may have suggested that rewriting is endlessly possible, until the deadline. Final copy can be sent straight to the printroom.

Compose a page plan

Figure 3.11 from the *Sun* newspaper shows both a page plan and how the page actually appeared in print. When you design your own page plan, make sure you decide about every item in the checklist on the following page.

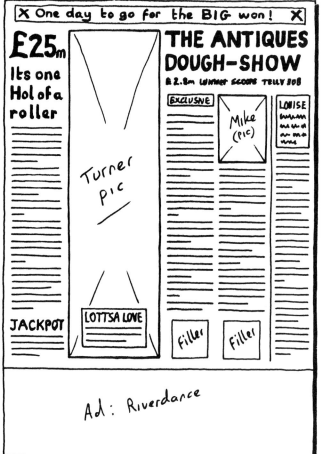

Fig. 3.11
Page plan and final
page layout

Page plan checklist

Fount or font means all the
characters, that is, the letters,
figures, accents and
punctuation marks of any one
typeface in any one size.

You will be able to judge if this
balance has been achieved by
asking a question: has the
message of your product been
effectively communicated
through the use of the text and
images?
Take a look at examples of
pages used in this unit and see
how borders are used as
guides for the eye when you
are reading. There are different
sizes and types of borders.

- the juxtaposition of text and image
- the use of white space, or air
- the number of columns
- the size and wording of headlines
- precise location of captions
- location of gutters and borders
- typefaces being used and use of **fonts**
- story extent
- use of images such as graphics

When using a page plan:
- draw the plan neatly: this will allow you to include more information
- make sure you have a balance of text and image
- allow space for headlines
- make sure the correct photos go with the proper text
- vary the typeface and size of the headlines to provide a visual variety to the page
- allow space for advertisements
- make effective use of the gutter if you are using a double-page spread
- borders are useful for adding to the visual impact of a page.

1 Collect a number of print products which are similar to the ones which you are completing for your assignment. Make sure you include single pages and double-page spreads as well as different ways in which the content is displayed on the pages.

2 Use these real print pages to draw up page plans for your pages, paying particular attention to the points in the checklist box.

3 How would you change the layout? Make brief written notes stating whether you would make any changes to the material on the printed pages. Give your reasons.

Sub-editing

The origination process now moves into sub-editing where the material for the page is placed on the page plan or layout. The sub-editing applies to written text and images. Sub-editors will mostly be dealing with other people's work. You have already seen the approaches used by sub-editors. These can be summarised as follows:

The sub-editing process also applies to images and it includes:

- cropping
- scaling
- sequencing
- blowing up
- graphics.

- adding text to that already written by a reporter or researcher
- deleting text and cutting a story by removing words, phrases, sentences or paragraphs or trimming
- structuring: to ensure that the report makes sense from beginning to end. This is also known as sequencing
- **casting off**, which is calculating the column space a story needs. This can be done by counting the number of words in conjunction with the typeface, size and leading. In the days of 'hot lead' this was done by a typographer
- headlining and re-writing – this refers to writing the:
  - headline (the title of the story)
  - sub-head (the secondary headline)
  - banner (a headline which crosses the top of a page, also known as a streamer)
  - blurb is (a piece of self-promotion composed of written type, but sometimes with illustration, which is used to draw the reader's attention to the contents of other pages in the print product)
  - breaker (a device such as a quotation or single word which is used to break up the text in a page)
  - caption (a line of type identifying or describing a photograph)
  - label (a headline without verbs)
  - catchline (single word in top right-hand corner of every page used to identify the story)
  - cross-heads (small headlines within the body of the text)
  - re-nosing (putting a new intro on a story using different material or a different angle)

- revising (checking and correcting or improving edited material)
  - star-burst (headline or slogan enclosed in a star-shaped outline, used especially in blurbs)
  - strapline (a headline in small type that goes above the main headline, also known as an overline)
  - tag-line (an explanatory line or acknowledgement under the bottom line of a headline).

Size in print

To emphasise a story or photograph on a page, we can make the headline larger or smaller. For example, a page **lead** will have a large headline using large type, and a filler will have a smaller headline. Varying the size of headlines is an important layout technique in making the page more visually attractive. The size of the headline is measured in points, and the higher the point size, the larger the headline. Note that the larger the typesize, or if you use capital letters, the lower your wordcount can be in order to fit the headline within the width of the column or columns.

Activity

Decide on the size and font of type for the headlines and sub-heads of your printed material. Explain why you chose the type and size.

Mark-up

Marking-up means indicating the specific treatment of text, diagrams, headings and margins according to the design specification, using recognised mark-up symbols.

With the introduction of new technology, much copy editing and all sub-editing is done on screen using the typesetting software. In many ways these functions have become more important with electronic editing.

With electronic editing, there is no intermediary to correct a wrong instruction once the story leaves the sub-editor and enters the computer. Practising on hard copy can help to improve your sub-editing, copy editing and mark-up skills.

Although we focus here on newspapers and magazines, the skills are relevant to other printed products. Figure 3.12 shows some of the symbols which are used in marking-up hard copy ready for print.

Fig. 3.12
Marking-up symbols

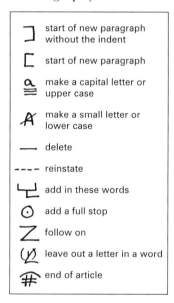

Hard copy is typewritten copy, as opposed to copy entered directly into a computer, which is known as **direct input**.

Activity

1 **As a group, arrange for a copy editor or sub-editor from a newspaper, magazine or book publisher to visit your school and to outline his/her rôle and responsibilities. Ask the sub-editor to bring copies of page plans so that you can compare them with the printed pages.**

2 Produce a simple flowchart of the process of origination, copy edit, mark-up, setting and subbing as it has been explained to you.

3 Exchange a hard copy of text which you have prepared with a fellow student, preferably an un-edited printout. Sub-edit the copy and mark it up ready for printing. Discuss your notes and corrections with the author.

Production schedule

The production schedule details resources needed, i.e. equipment, people and time. Keep the following checklist in mind.

Production checklist

- Do we have the resources to complete the print product? For example, is there access to a camera to take your photographs?
- Do we have the people to complete the print product? For example, do you have people who are skilled in using computers, even if it is only to wordprocess hard copy?
- Will we have the print product completed in time and will these deadlines be met?

If you were producing leaflets and posters to advertise a village sale, your production schedule would be altered if the time and location of the sale was changed. You would have to ensure that these changes were subbed and incorporated into the new leaflet and poster design as well as being produced and distributed in time for the sale. This new material will have to be incorporated or written into your article. This could mean changing the intro or the main text itself or possibly the angle of your article. This amended copy will also have to be proofread to ensure there are no mistakes.

Financial resources for wages and fees are vital, as is the right equipment. Planning the schedule with typesetters, DTP operators and printers is crucial as no-one wants their equipment to stand idle.

You will find that adjustments may have to be made to the production schedule as the process continues.

Assignment

You need to finally edit and lay out your print product. This should be supported by:

- a draft page layout
- a page layout with the material in place
- evidence of sub-edited material.

In a small group:

1 Select the two print products for which you have already produced a production schedule. In this assignment, you are putting that schedule into operation.

2 Allocate the tasks in the production process and describe the responsibilities.

3 Select, organise and edit the material which will be included in your print product. As part of this process, you should spend time discussing possible page layouts.

143

4 Examine the position of photographs.

On your own:

1 Design a draft page layout for the product so that it captures the reader's attention.

2 Produce a page layout with the material in place.

3 Proofread the entire print product using the established codes and conventions; make notes on changes which were made, and any deviations from the production schedule. In this respect, you should identify and resolve any clashes in page elements.

This could be done by cutting out and pasting the material on to the layout, or completing the page using the computer and a DTP software package.

Evidence of copy editing and sub-editing the material could be hard copy which has been corrected, or computer printouts both before and after subbing.

For all of the above individual tasks, make brief notes explaining your decisions and the selection of the material for the layout, as well as noting any changes which you made to the production schedule. These could include reasons why you decided to include new material in your print product, or why you decided to leave out certain material. It could also involve any change in your individual rôle or the rôle of other people in the group.

4 Review and evaluate print products

Success in publishing

For most printed matter success is measured in number of copies sold within the market to which the product is aimed. The market will be different for a specialist geological journal, for example, in comparison to a mass circulation newspaper or magazine. Presenting what the readers want in a product may lead to increased circulation.

In this section you will look at how to evaluate the success of a product by gathering and analysing feedback. We begin by looking at distribution. If you do not get the product to where people can buy it, it will not sell.

Distribution

Distribution refers to both time and place. For example, it would be rather pointless if a Sunday newspaper was not available to buy until Monday, or if your leaflet highlighting an event was distributed the day after the event took place. Ask yourself:

- Which outlets will people go to get our product?
- How will we get the product to those outlets?

Newsprint, magazines, paperback novels, dictionaries and children's books are available from newsagents, supermarkets, bookshops and cornershops. Specialist products such as legal texts and reports or education material will be available through bookshops and by mail order.

A local weekly community newspaper or a regional daily title will be distributed from a number of outlets from where the potential target audience can be reached. These are:

- the newspaper shops or newsagents
- petrol stations with shops
- supermarkets and general grocery shops
- hotels, restaurants, pubs, clubs and leisure centres.

Mail order

This is a home delivery delivered directly to the home or place of business. In practical terms, there are three types of home delivery distribution methods (these are listed on the next page):

1 for newsprint, the newspaper boy or girl: people who do the weekly or daily delivery round to homes in their locality. This is normally organised by newsagents.
2 a distribution or circulation agency which specialises in distributing print products to homes. The newspaper publishers will pay the agency to ensure delivery of the product. This is known as a **mail shot**, or a **leaflet drop** if the information is produced in leaflet format.
3 Royal Mail delivery: many magazines operate a subscription service by which the product is posted directly to the home or office.

Freesheets

The distribution of newspapers directly to homes and offices has led to the creation of a range of **freesheets**. These are newspapers and magazines which are distributed free of charge to the target audience. They are free to the readers and paid for by advertising revenue. Newspapers and magazines which have a cover price also invite advertising and much of the money raised through the actual sale of the products goes towards the cost of distributing the products.

To distribute the product to the sellers, such as newsagents, shops and so on, the product publishers can use one of two methods:

1 own fleet of vans to deliver the product to the shops
2 a distribution agency which delivers the product to the outlets for a fee.

The first method would be favoured by local weekly titles which would use a couple of vans to deliver copies each week. It is also favoured by some high distribution regional daily and regional Sunday titles to deliver copies around the country.

Packaging

As with any product which is distributed, whether by hand delivery, postal service or by van, you need to consider the way the product is packaged for the journey so that it reaches the target audience whole and undamaged. Many products which arrive by post direct from the publishers will be sealed in a plastic covering to keep the product from getting torn, wet or folded wrongly and to prevent leaflets or loose pages inside the product from falling out.

Activity

Select a number of print products which are available in your area. See if you can find out how many different types of outlets, such as shops or home delivery, there are for that product to reach the target audience. Make brief written notes listing the outlets.

Activity

How would you distribute your edited print product to the target audience?

You should have considered:

- Will the print product be distributed within the premises? If so, why? If not, list the outlets where it will be distributed.
- Will the printed product be distributed as a freesheet, or will there be a cover price?
- What packaging precautions have you taken to ensure the printed product reaches the target audience in good condition?

Audience feedback

A publisher has to be able to evaluate the success and quality of a product. To do this, a response from the target audience must be obtained and accurately assessed.

The principal aim of testing audience response is to obtain information about your print product from the potential readers. This information, known as **feedback**, is essential if you are to develop your print product by making improvements, building on what is popular in the product, removing what the target audience does not like, and discovering what pieces of content the target audience want to see in the product. Remember, your product's success depends on its popularity with the target audience.

You need to:

- know why you are evaluating the product
- design measures or criteria by which to evaluate
- develop measuring instruments, such as a questionnaire, interview schedules, a feedback form or simply sales figures
- analyse the data
- decide on changes if necessary.

The best way of getting the target audience's views on a print product is to ask questions, even if it is only a basic 'what do you think of this print product?' The easiest method of gaining answers to these questions is to interview the target audience. There are basically two types of interview techniques which can be used:

- face-to-face street surveys
- telephone polls.

Alternatively you could include questionnaires in the publication.

Look back at Study Unit 2 for more information on interviewing.

Interviews

Interviews can be:

1 *non-directive*: this is where there is no structure or order to the questions and the interviewee can talk about anything.

2 *structured but open-ended*: to avoid the looseness of the informal approach, the interviewer gives pre-set questions in a predetermined order to every interviewee. The main advantages are that responses can be far more easily assessed, no topics are missed or fleetingly covered, and the questions can be used by several interviewers at the same time. The disadvantages are that the answers are less natural, and the wording of the questions can reduce the richness of the answers.

3 *fully structured*: again, the questions are fixed and ordered, but in addition the interviewee can only answer according to a formal system, such as answering 'yes' or 'no'; or responding to a statement by selecting a response ranging from 'strongly agree' to 'strongly disagree'. The advantages are that this type of interview is very quick to complete and provides results which can be easily generalised. The disadvantages are that the information gained can be narrow, and can be distorted by complex words or an inappropriate response choice list.

Questionnaires

With questionnaires, the interviewee does not generally have to provide the answer immediately. Questionnaires are essentially a series of written questions which the target audience can complete in their own time and return to you. This means that questionnaires can be less immediate and less personal than the **vox pop** interviews and can probe situations in more depth. You can ask substantially more questions than in a vox pop interview and the respondent can take more time to think over the answers. Whilst a face-to-face interview in the street could last for a couple of minutes, a questionnaire could take up to 20 minutes depending on the number of questions and the format of answering.

Look back at Study Unit 2 for more detail about questionnaires.

Activity

What do you think the advantages of questionnaires are in comparison with structured interviews:

1 **for the publisher?**

2 **for the respondent?**

Draw up your notes in a small group of three or four.

You may have suggested the following for the respondent:

- *Anonymity*. This can be useful for a member of staff answering a questionnaire about the helpfulness and efficiency of the senior management team.

- *Location*. You can complete the questionnaire in the privacy and quietness of your own home, compared to the hustle and bustle of a busy main street with people maybe eavesdropping on your answers and when you are in a hurry.
- *Time*. You have the advantage of being able to take time to answer the questions fully, thoughtfully and accurately.

The feedback can be compiled and analysed in the knowledge that all respondents have answered the same questions without interference from an interviewer.

Disadvantages of questionnaires are:

- *impersonality*: they lack the personal human touch of a person, hopefully politely, seeking your views on a topic, as with a vox pop
- *confusion*: if the respondent does find difficulty in answering a question, who can he/she turn to for clarification?

The number of items used in a questionnaire needs to be kept manageable in terms of time and the respondent's patience. You do not want a situation where the respondent is spending a lengthy period pondering and worrying about the answers. If this is the case, there is a good chance the respondent will put your questionnaire in the bin.

Sampling

This is the process of deciding on the size and composition of the population whose views will be sought.

In this case, the population represents all the members of the target audience, namely the readership of your print product. But as the population, or target audience, would normally be too big to ask everyone who saw your print product, you have to select a sample to work within. There are a number of sampling methods to achieve this. We will use the example of the college newspaper again to illustrate these methods.

1 *Representative sample*. You could decide to interview everyone in a particular form or class at school or college concerning your print product.
2 *Random sample*. You could go around the canteen at lunchtime asking people at random what they thought of your product.
3 *Stratified sample*. If you want a representative sample of students you might decide to take business studies students, arts students or computer studies students in proportion to their total numbers. If 10 per cent of the college or school population comprises business studies students, then 10 per cent of your sample will be business students. If the sample is going to be 50 students, then five will be chosen from the business studies department.
4 *Quota sample*. This method has been popular among market research companies and opinion pollsters. It consists of obtaining people from

various walks of life according to their occurrence in the general population. In practical terms, if you were interviewing fifth formers about your college newspaper, you would stop when you reached a quota according to their percentage of the overall student population.

5 *Cluster sample*. This means taking a certain geographical area, and the clusters could represent as many students as you wanted to interview from a particular housing estate, street or even village.

6 *Snowball sample*. Here, you select several key people to be interviewed and contact with them may lead on to further important contacts to be interviewed.

7 *Self-selecting sample*. This could be where you simply watch how many people bought the copy of your magazine and noted the number on a chart.

8 *Opportunity sample*. This is where you simply ask other people in your own class for their reactions.

Activity

Use your experience of designing a testing format on a number of existing products as a guide to devise a method of sampling the target audience's response to your own completed and edited print product. Again, write out the questions you will use, making brief notes on the sequence, choice of test – for example, vox pop or written questionnaire – and your reasons for selecting the format of the sampling.

The sample size

One of the most popular excuses used by students when they are asked to evaluate their results is that 'the researcher should have tested more subjects'. What happens if the research failed to show any significant criticisms of the print product? You may well suspect that the survey questions have been weighted against unfair criticism of your product. This could mean that your survey is biased. In general, the larger the sample, the less likely a sampling bias. For example, if you only asked 20 students for a reaction to your product, you could select your 20 best friends at college all of whom you could rely upon to give to favourable comments in their feedback. One disadvantage for large samples is that you cannot always properly organise such samples due to the amount of time.

The questions

What all the methods of testing have in common is that they ask questions. Although the numbers and length of the questions will vary according to the nature of the print product, they all have certain areas of testing in common. Again, these areas can be identified by using the theory of the five Ws:

- *Who?* Does the product fully cater for the target audience in terms of needs?
- *What?* List what you like or dislike about the product.
- *Why?* Is the product a good or bad example compared to similar print products for the target audience?
- *When?* How often do you think the product should be published; are you able to receive a copy of the product on time?
- *Where?* How do you get a copy of the print product? Is it through home delivery or from another outlet? Where would be the most convenient place or outlet for you to obtain a copy of the print product?

Activity

Have a thorough look at the section of draft questionnaire below. These could be the types of questions used to discover if the target audience was satisfied with the print product. Adapt this questionnaire for your own purposes.

Fig. 3.13
Sample questionnaire

QUESTIONNAIRE ON TARGET AUDIENCE'S FEEDBACK ON COLLEGE MAGAZINE

1. Have you see our new college magazine?   YES ☐ NO ☐

2. If you have not seen a copy, has this been because:

    Did not know it existed; ☐
    Not interested in college magazine; ☐
    Could not find a copy of it; ☐
    Heard bad reports about it; ☐
    Other reasons. ☐

Please state these: _____

3. Overall, did you like the magazine?   YES ☐ NO ☐

4. If YES, please state what parts of the content you liked or enjoyed:

  News stories ☐   Letters ☐
  Photographs ☐   Advice column ☐
  Competitions ☐   Cartoons ☐
  Horoscope ☐   Reviews ☐
  Features ☐
  Sports ☐

5. If your answer was NO overall, please state why: _____
_____

6. Was our magazine:

  ..... Easy to read   YES ☐ NO ☐
  ..... Well written   YES ☐ NO ☐
  ..... Well presented   YES ☐ NO ☐
  ..... Had a sequence which was easy to follow   YES ☐ NO ☐

7. What areas of the magazine do we need to improve?

  Leave it as it is   YES ☐ NO ☐
  Make it more widely available to students   YES ☐ NO ☐
  Distribute it to staff and relatives   YES ☐ NO ☐
  Improve the layout to make it more attractive   YES ☐ NO ☐
  Use more photographs   YES ☐ NO ☐
  Have more articles   YES ☐ NO ☐
  Make other improvements   YES ☐ NO ☐

Please state what additional improvements you would like to see: _____
_____

THANK YOU FOR TAKING PART IN THIS QUESTIONNAIRE.

Criteria for evaluation

With assessment, you are aiming at two goals. Firstly, you should identify which plans and ideas were the most useful in setting up the production process and in its smooth running. Secondly, you should reflect on what is useful and what you should do if you were producing further editions of your print products. So the agenda for discussion involves:

1 *fitness for purpose.* How well did the product fulfil its purpose of informing, educating, entertaining and persuading, or any combination of these factors? For example, your product may have been more popular if you had included more entertainment articles.

2 *suitability for target audience*. How well does the product identify and represent the image, needs and demands of the target audience in its content, as well as through the presentation of that content? For example, although you covered music generally in your reviews, you did not include heavy metal albums as there are a considerable number of rock fans at your school.

3 *production methods*. Were the planning and production methods sufficiently well prepared to make the best possible use of the equipment and human resources available? For example, rather than sticking photocopies of pictures onto the pages, more efficient research at the planning stage could have told you that your college contained a scanner.

4 *commercial viability*. Are all the costs being met by the advertising revenue raised and the circulation levels? How much does the cover price help meet the costs of distribution to the target audience? Is the print product running at a financial loss, making profit, or just breaking even? If you had stated that all the cash raised from your magazine was going to charity, would more people have taken out advertising which would have given you more revenue to produce a better product?

5 *product satisfaction*. How well pleased is the target audience with its product? Does the target audience feel it is getting value for money? Again, the feedback from the sampling will inform you as to the content which the target audience would prefer to see in your print product. Team members also need to address these issues:

- How satisfied is the actual production team themselves with the final edited product?
- Have individual members of the production team been able to objectively evaluate the strengths and weaknesses of their own contributions to the final print product?

Feedback on newspapers and magazines

In terms of print products, especially newspapers and magazines, the publishers need quantitative information which will help them accurately answer two questions:

1 How many copies of the product have been sold – this is known as a print product's circulation.
2 How much money has been raised through selling adverts – this is known as advertising revenue.

These two areas are interrelated. If the print product is to be a commercial success, or even be commercially viable, it needs to sell copies and bring in enough revenue to cover the production costs and have some capital spare for future development.

Circulation

This is the actual number of copies of the newspaper or magazine which are sold to the target audience. It should not be confused with the number of copies distributed to the outlets. Newspapers, for example, talk about their **ABC** figures. This is a reference to the Audit Bureau of Circulation which is a recognised body that provides accurate information over a period of time of how many copies have actually been sold. Advertising sales representatives can use this figure when selling advertising space to show how popular their print product is. In terms of free distribution newspapers, they will boast that their circulation figure comprises the number of homes to which copies of the product is delivered. They too have a regulatory body which will authenticate the claims of the freesheet distributions.

Advertising revenue

This figure is essential to the commercial survival of the print product because the cash flow from selling advertising space means that bills can be paid, jobs secured, and expansion plans considered and implemented. Print products need advertising revenue to survive financially in the same way as other manufacturing firms require sales to stay in business. The key amount or figure in this area is the amount of revenue which is left over once the production costs have been paid. In business terms this is profit. It is not good enough for a print product to break even financially. It must make a profit to be able to expand its market. If it is only making enough money to break even, there is the real danger that a competitor could produce a better rival product. Once circulation and advertising revenue raised dip below the 'break even' financial level, the whole area of the product's viability comes into question as losses begin to mount.

Case study

The *Today* newspaper was launched as part of the new technology revolution in print production. But eventually, with falling circulation and slipping advertising revenue, financial losses began to mount. With no prospect of a buyer to bail out the newspaper and write off the debts, the title was forced to close.

Other feedback indicators

As well as obtaining regular circulation and advertising figures, publishers can obtain accurate feedback on the success and quality of their products in other ways, which include:

1 *comments from advertisers themselves*. They can inform the sales staff about the response from the target audience to their advertisements. For example, a shoe shop which advertises a cut-price sale in the local press could judge the impact of buying the advertising space by the number of customers it had in the shop after the advertisement was published. However, if the advertisers get very little response from the target audience, they could conclude that it is not worthwhile taking out more adverts because the target audience is not reading the printed product. Similarly, if the shoe sale is going well, the shop owner could continue with his adverts to attract and remind customers about the sale.

2 *readers' letters*. Members of the target audience can write to the editor of the print product giving their views on the content of the print product. They can either praise or criticise aspects of the content. Depending on the amount of letters on a given topic, the publishers can amend the content accordingly by either leaving out the content, or increasing their coverage of a particular topic.

Analysing the feedback

The easiest method of analysing feedback is to establish the number of 'yes' answers as a percentage of the total number of people surveyed. For example, if 50 students were respondents to the survey in Figure 3.13 and 10 of them indicated a tick at 'No' for Question 1 on whether they had seen the college newspaper, then you would know that 10 out of 50, or 20 per cent of your sample had not seen or read your print product. Your questionnaire will also have established the reason(s) for this.

The first stage of the evaluation is to categorise the feedback answers under a number of criteria headings. This enables you to assess the success of the print product in terms of meeting the demands and needs of the target audience. The second stage is to draw conclusions on how you can produce an even better product which the target audience finds more appealing.

The evaluation guide

Here is the step-by-step guide which you should follow in your evaluation and assessment process for your print products.

1 Collect all feedback information from the target audience.
2 Present all necessary statistics and percentages from the answers to the production team.
3 Include recommendations for changes to be decided on.
4 Draw up an action plan to implement the changes.

Basically, the evaluation criteria fall into the following categories.

1 *Article concepts.* Did the target audience like the approach taken to the content of the print product?
2 *Editing.* How easy did the target audience find it to read the product? Did the layout assist readability and understanding?
3 *Style.* Does the product treat the topic in a sensible and business-like fashion?
4 *Layout.* How does the layout assist the visual impact of the print product?
5 *Professionalism.* Does the print product provide a balanced and professional series of articles?
6 *Editorial objectives.* How successful is the product in communicating the views of the target audience's needs?
7 *Other commercial products.* How popular is our print product when compared to other print products who serve the same target audience?
8 *Audience response.* How many people actually responded to the survey? Overall, is the target audience happy with the print product?
9 *Rôles.* How does this information affect the overall team's rôle in the production process, as well as individual contributors to the production process?

Implementing changes

The changes to make the product more appealing now have to be implemented. Just as you have devised an action plan listing ideas which could improve your print product, so the publishers of real-life print products must also come up with an action plan to improve their products. This action plan should address the following criteria:

- content
- fonts and types
- size
- finances
- resources
- availability
- frequency
- publication day.

Activity

Take a selection of print products and, using the evaluation and assessment lists as guidelines, make written notes detailing why you think the print product is a good or bad example for that particular target audience. For example, you may wish to select one of the latest teenage magazines and assess whether it successfully represents the image, needs and demands of today's teenage population. Keep these written notes for your portfolio.

Case study

In the late 1980s, the Northern Newspaper Group in Northern Ireland launched a new community newspaper in Larne on the northeast coast of Northern Ireland. It was called the *Larne Guardian*. The town already had an existing local weekly title, the *Larne Times*, which had been published for almost a century at the time of the *Guardian's* launch. The *Times* was published on a Thursday and was a tabloid costing more than 30p. Initially the *Guardian* was also published on a Thursday as a broadsheet and also cost around 30p. Eighteen months after its launch, to reflect the needs and demands of the target audience in Larne, the *Guardian*:

- changed its format to a tabloid
- changed its publication date to Wednesday, the local market day
- cut its cover price and advertising rates. The publisher had concluded from market research that the target audience wanted a local newspaper in the format with which they were familiar – a tabloid. By making it available a day earlier and at a cheaper rate, audience would be taken from the *Times*. The survey was carried out by the advertising staff who spoke to

advertisers in the town; the distribution team also spoke to outlets, and the editorial staff spoke to their community contacts. It was carried out over a month-long period, gaining as much feedback as possible within that period.

Activity

Take a series of print products which have a similar target audience, such as teenage girls, football fans, computer buffs. Compare the content and presentation of the products, making written notes on how they differ. Write a report detailing how you would assess and evaluate the suitability of the products to satisfy their target audience. Support your claims with cuttings from the products.

Activity

Arrange to interview the editor or deputy editor of a local magazine or newspaper, or the publisher of leaflets, brochures or posters. Ask how they collect, assess and evaluate the feedback from their target audiences, and what changes have been made to their print products as a result of this feedback. Write up your notes in the form of an essay, and keep them for your portfolio.

The new technology

You are likely to be able to use computers and DTP packages to produce professional print products. The main impact that the new technology, especially computerisation, has had on the print industry is to reduce the time needed for planning and production. There are options for working with hard copy or transferring disks and using facsimiles. Electronic mail gives immediate access to reports and information. It also means fewer people are needed.

The use of facsimile machines, known as fax machines, means that information, such as **press releases**, can be sent immediately rather than waiting almost a day for the postal service. The advance in computer technology means that reporters can carry small portable terminals with them to the scenes of incidents and, using a modem, they can send their reports via the telephone directly into their newspaper's main computer for processing.

Advances in software packages mean that it is easier to plan, design and produce print products, such as news sheets, handbills and leaflets, posters and brochures.

The future

How will your print products be different in the 21st century from the ones which are produced now? Whilst new technology and the rapid development in computers was the central influence on print products during the last quarter of the 20th century, so the Internet, the so-called information superhighway, will probably be the main influence on print production in the 21st century. Just as many homes, schools and businesses have computer terminals, the Internet is a way of linking them all up. You can get information from the Internet by typing in your request and the computer does the searching.

If you subscribe to the Internet you can communicate globally in a matter of minutes – even seconds, depending on the information you are looking for or sending. What does this mean for print products? It might be that the product instead of being printed on paper, is just available on a computer screen – but if you really wanted a copy to read later, you could have it printed out. In terms of newspapers and magazines, it could lead to the development of the 24-hour newspaper or magazine.

The national press can even have their newspapers on the Internet in different languages. This could help the present print products compete with the immediacy of television and radio.

How do you think electronic pages will be different from conventional printed products?

Assignment

In a small group:

1 **Decide on the method of distribution of your product to the target audience. Once you have reached agreement on this, implement the distribution process and make written notes listing your reasons for selecting this method and how it was practically implemented. You should also keep brief written notes on how the print product was packaged for distribution.**

2 **Design a questionnaire to evaluate the print product you have produced in terms of the following assessment criteria:**
   - fitness for purpose
   - suitability for the target audience
   - production methods
   - commercial viability
   - product satisfaction.

3 **Decide how you will choose your sample audience, and how you will gather the feedback.**

On your own:

1 **After the feedback on your print product has been collected, you should write a detailed report which analyses the success and quality of your print product. This report should address the following topics:**
   - article concepts
   - editing
   - layout
   - professionalism
   - editorial objectives
   - other commercial products
   - audience response.

2   Based on your comments in your evaluation report, you should also write notes which assess the effectiveness of the planning and production processes for your print product.

3   Assess your own individual contribution to the planning and production processes for the print product, as well as the team's overall contributions. In making these rôle observations, you should avoid making personal comments about other students' contributions, but should draw conclusions about the importance of particular rôles in the production process.

Summary

Now that you have completed Study Unit 3 you should have:

- gained an understanding of the key elements of various print products and identified how you would research material for them
- demonstrated an understanding of the ethical, legal and representational codes of practice involved in gathering and using information for print products
- developed your practical skills in producing an actual print product using recognised industrial processes, focusing specifically on sub-editing, layout and design
- evaluated the success of your completed publication in terms of product requirements, effectiveness of the various production rôles, and reviewing your readership's responses.

Glossary

ABC the Audit Bureau of Circulation, which provides official figures for newspaper circulation

angle the main point stressed in an article, usually mentioned in the intro

background the part of a news story or feature article containing information to contextualise the main elements

body text the copy which comes after the first paragraph or introduction

broadsheet an A1-size newspaper, such as the *Times*

by-line the name of journalist who has written the article, usually positioned near the beginning of a story

caption text accompanying a photograph or artwork

casting off estimating the final length of copy from the number of words, the size of the typeface and the spaces between letters

catchline usually a single word to identify a story, typed in the top right-hand corner of every page

CD-ROM Compact Disk-Read Only Memory

clippings stories cut from newspapers or magazine

column the vertical section of an article appearing on a page

copy editorial material

copy taster in the newspaper industry, the person who makes the initial checks for accuracy and news potential – usually the news editor

crop how a photograph is cut to appear on a printed page

cross head a small headline placed within the body text of an article

cut removing copy from manuscript, screen or page proof

deadline the time by which copy has to be submitted

delete cutting or removing information from a story

desktop publishing (DTP) producing written material by computer, with illustrations as required

direct input the process by which text goes straight from the editorial screen into typesetting

double column a page layout using two columns on the page

double-page spread a feature article occupying two facing pages

draft a version of written text

editor person in overall charge of the editorial content of the print product

embargo a deadline before which information should not be published

feature a longer article, which carries more background information and descriptive writing

feedback the response to an article, or to the contents of the entire print product

filler a short story which fills in space when a longer story runs short, also known as a 'brief'

font American term for fount, which is a typeface of one particular size and style

freesheet newspapers and magazines which are distributed free of charge, paid for by advertising revenue

galley proofs typeset copy, with copy editing changes made to it, but which has not yet been divided into separate pages

gutter space between pages in a centre spread

hard copy copy which is presented on sheets of paper

hard news a story focusing on the questions: who, what, where, when, why

human interest story one which focuses on the successes, failures, tragedies of people

introduction the opening paragraph of a news report or feature article

justify where a line of text is set to fit given measure

layout arranging the text and images following the page design

lead pronounced 'leed': the main story on a page

mail shot or **leaflet drop** distributing print products directly through individual letterboxes

mark-up indications to a typesetter about treatment of text, diagrams, headings and margins using recognized symbols

measure the width to which a complete line of type is set

off the record statements made, not for publication but for background guidance

on screen page make-up when the layout of text, headlines, introductions, images and advertisements on a page is carried out at a computer terminal

on the record no restrictions on reporting what is said

page concept the decision as to whether the coverage of events will be contained on a single page, or across two pages

page plan layout sheet indicating where text, headlines, photographs and advertisements should go

page proof a typeset page with copy editing changes made to it

press release an announcement made by an organisation or an individual distributed for use by the media

proofreader someone who checks proofs for accuracy, usually against the copy edited manuscript

rejig rearranging the copy

running story a story which runs, or develops, over a number of editions or days

scaling calculating the percentage enlargement or reduction of a photograph after it has been cropped

source where required information is found, whether a person or a product
primary source direct contact sources e.g. face-to-face interviews and firsthand information.
secondary source indirect contact source or material which you can consult, e.g. published printed, audio and visual material, databases

style the special rules within publications relating to spellings, punctuation and abbreviations

sub-editor/sub the person responsible for editing reporters' or writers' copy, writing headlines, captions, and laying out pages

tabloid a newspaper whose pages are A3

vox pop a series of quotes on a particular theme, taken from the Latin phrase, *vox populi*, meaning 'voice of people'

Producing audio products

Contents

LONGMAN

Introduction

In this unit you will examine the different types of audio products with which you are familiar, and the processes which go into their production.

Although radio is by far the dominant audio medium, you should not overlook the many other situations in which audio products can be used effectively. Talking books for the blind, for example, allow people with visual disabilities to enjoy books read aloud; and cassette guides to museums and art galleries allow visitors to hear a recorded commentary on headsets whilst enjoying the exhibition.

There is also a vast industry devoted to the production and marketing of music in various formats, and although it is not the purpose of this unit to explore in detail the specialist techniques involved in the music recording studio, the basic principles of sound recording described here still apply.

Within radio programming, there are two main strands or **genres** – factual programmes (such as news, documentaries and educational series) and non-factual or creative programming – the various forms of radio drama and, increasingly, advertisements or commercials.

This unit will help you to design, record and edit two products for your course assessment: one factual piece – a radio feature of up to three minutes' duration; and one creative piece – a 30-second radio commercial.

The radio commercial can be seen almost as a 'mini-drama' encapsulating a message within a predetermined time limit – generally 30 seconds or one minute. Radio commercials have developed greatly in their level of sophistication in the 20 years or so since independent radio began in the United Kingdom. The first radio ads were often sound tracks taken from television or cinema commercials, or 'shopping lists' of prices taken from newspaper copy and read in an excited and forceful tone by the **voice-over**.

In a group, discuss the following:

* Compare the advertising material you have seen or heard in different media.
* Why is the sound track from a TV commercial unlikely to work effectively on radio?
* What elements of the original message are missing?
* Why is it unlikely that reading a newspaper advertisement on the radio will be effective?
* What can a newspaper reader do which a radio listener cannot?

These early commercials were ineffective because they ignored the attributes of the medium, and instead tried to impose conventions from other media (print and TV) which are inappropriate for radio.

The great strengths of radio, apart from its cheapness and essential simplicity, are its flexibility and the closeness it is possible to achieve with the audience.

Although in the early days of radio (during the 1920s and 1930s) it was quite usual for a family to sit around their radio receiver to enjoy the programmes together, technical advances such as the transistor radio, car radios and personal stereos have meant the medium is now one which individuals generally enjoy alone.

Activity

In a group, think of the times and places when you or people you know listen to the radio.

Examples probably included:

* when my radio alarm clock wakes me in the morning
* in the kitchen whilst I'm having breakfast
* on my personal stereo whilst I'm travelling to school or college
* whilst I'm in the car
* whilst I'm in the bath
* whilst I'm doing my homework
* in my bedroom before I go to sleep at night.

Radio is therefore an intimate medium – individuals enjoy a one-to-one relationship with the people they hear, and this is something which both radio stations and advertisers can exploit to their benefit. On one West Yorkshire radio station during the early 1980s, a presenter had a feature on his programme in which he played a romantic song 'just for you and me together', without ever specifying a named individual. He regularly received letters from delighted listeners, who were amazed that he knew their 'special song', and knew to play it for them at a time when they were especially lonely or depressed. He had created an illusion of a one-to-one relationship when in fact the song was heard by tens of thousands of anonymous listeners.

Radio advertising can make use of this same intimacy, but more importantly it can capitalise on another of radio's great strengths – the ability to fill the listeners' 'theatre of the mind'. When an individual is listening to any radio broadcast, the part of their mind which would hold and interpret the visual images presented by TV or print illustrations must instead create a picture in the imagination solely from the words, music and sound effects used by the broadcaster.

Theatre of the mind gives great creative freedom to writers and producers working in radio. For example, to create the effect of a towering inferno on screen requires an enormous investment in sets and special effects, but to do the same on the radio requires only an appropriate blend of easily obtained 'stock' sound effects such as flames (perhaps multi-tracked to heighten the effect), fire engine sirens, screams and maybe a helicopter flying overhead.

Many radio commercials use theatre of the mind, but they can also work effectively by creating larger-than-life characters – audio cartoons – which leave a strong impression even if the listener is preoccupied.

Douglas Adams, author of *The Hitch-hikers Guide to the Galaxy*, was interviewed about the radio and TV adaptations of his book. He was asked if he preferred the radio or the TV series. His reply is revealing about the attributes of the different media: 'The scenery was better on the radio ... and the sound effects were better in the book.'

1 Planning the production process

In this section you will begin the process of creating the two audio products required for your assessment – the radio commercial and the radio news feature. Preparation for your assignments takes place throughout the section.

Fig. 4.1
Radio production
studio in use

The radio commercial

In producing this audio product you will be working alone on the scripting and editing of your material, but you will need to work with other students to record material for your commercial.

In Study Unit 2, you examined the ways in which the Transperience visitor attraction in West Yorkshire went about answering some important questions. You will also be familiar with commercials you have heard on local and national radio.

Assignment: Part 1

For the purpose of this assignment, you are to take on the rôle of a commercial producer on an independent radio station. You are to write, record and edit a radio commercial for the client you selected in Study Unit 2, Section 3.

Agreeing the brief

The first stage is to agree a production brief for the commercial. This is in effect a contract between you, as the supplier, and your clients, as the purchaser, in which you discuss what they hope to achieve by their advertising campaign, any ideas or requirements they have regarding the content, and the budget they have with which to achieve their aims.

In deciding the brief for your radio commercial, it is important, above all, to answer the following questions:

- WHO am I talking to?
- WHAT do I want them to do?
- WHY should they do it?

Activity

In a small group, discuss some of the radio commercials you have heard recently. Write down a description of three that you like, and three that you don't like. List the content of each one: How long is the commercial? How many voices are used? Is there a jingle, or other music? Has the producer used sound effects? Do the voices sound natural, like real people talking, or are they exaggerated, larger-than-life characters?

Now answer the WHO, WHAT and WHY questions outlined above for each commercial.

Discuss how effectively you think the commercials you have listed answer these questions. You will probably find that you can do so easily for the ones you like, but it will be more difficult for the ones you don't like (unless the ones you don't like are clearly targeted at a specific group, like retired people, with whom you may not share a common interest).

WHO? asks you to define the target audience for the commercial. For some clients, such as the holiday company Club 18–30, the target audience may be explicit. For others, such as local authority leisure centres, the targeting process may be more complex. They may want to attract more parents with toddlers, or perhaps they want more pensioners to use facilities at off-peak times. These target audiences may change over time and between individual advertising campaigns. Be as precise as you can; it is a common mistake to address your message to 'everybody'. This creates the danger of the finished product appealing to nobody.

WHAT? asks you to examine the client's objectives. Effective commercials go beyond simply giving a name and address for the advertiser – they demand a particular response from the listener. The client may wish to encourage more people to visit a car showroom, or telephone for a brochure. The best commercials avoid confusing the listener with choice ('call in today or phone for a brochure') – they specify only one course of action.

WHY? asks you to give a reason for the listener to respond. You must motivate listeners to do what the client wants them to do. Perhaps there is an offer of a free prize draw, or a discount available for a limited period. At a more subtle level, you can bring in elements of quality and prestige – the client offers a superior product, therefore listeners are seen to enjoy more status or taste if they choose the product.

These questions are clearly fundamental to the creative process, as the style of the finished commercial will be determined by the answers.

These techniques are also used very effectively in radio drama, where the intention of the writer is to entertain, or to involve the audience emotionally in a fictional world of his/her creation. It is unlikely that the primary aim within a drama production would be to persuade, in the sense of a commercial persuading a listener to consume a product. The message is likely to be more complex, involving the motivation of characters and the consequences of their actions. Whilst still having to work within overall constraints of time determined by the broadcaster's format (which can range from a few minutes to an hour or more), a fiction writer has much more freedom to develop both character and situation than is possible within the short, rigid constraints of the commercial.

The questions can be interpreted across a wide range of products. For a double glazing company, for example, the answers may appear straightforward – the company wants to reach householders who don't have double glazing.

However, further research can create a commercial which is much more effective. The company wants to reach householders who have been putting off the decision to buy; they want the potential customer to ring a 'call free' telephone number for a quotation; and the customer should do so now because there's a special offer for this week only.

Activity

Discuss the different approaches you would take to:

a) **writing a commercial encouraging fans to attend a match involving your favourite football team**

b) **writing a short drama about the atmosphere in the changing room immediately before a Cup Final involving that same team.**

Researching the brief

To carry out your research, it will be very useful for you to meet your client – a store manager or similar person if you are working in the real world, or a tutor 'rôle playing' the part of the client if you are simulating this exercise within your work group.

It is better to meet the client on his/her premises, if it is possible to do so safely. You should pair up with another student (or form a small group) for this part of the exercise, and your colleague(s) should make notes for you; not only the answers to your direct questions, but also other information which will be useful when creating your commercial. You should ask for copies of any promotional materials (leaflets, brochures, etc.) used by the client, and you should note anything which impresses you about the organisation, for example: Is everybody friendly? Is the showroom or

You must keep the notes from your research meeting for your assessment.

The rate card on the facing page shows how much it cost to place spot advertisements of varying lengths on The Pulse radio station in West Yorkshire in March 1996. Note that it is more expensive to place advertising within popular time segments, such as the breakfast and evening drivetime shows, when more people are listening. It is also more expensive to advertise at the end of the week, when people are planning weekend activities such as shopping trips or days out.

customer area warm and inviting? Is there plenty of car parking? Does the company display letters on the wall from satisfied customers? These are all details which could be useful when it comes to writing your script, especially if your client has many competitors offering similar products at similar prices.

Your programme brief must specify the length of the commercial to be produced. Radio stations operate a tolerance of less than one second over or under length, and exact durations are especially important for those stations operating automated transmission systems, where ads are inserted by computer into predetermined windows which may allow different parts of their transmission area to hear commercial breaks tailored to that area – in this case, it is obviously vital that all the different commercial breaks are exactly the same length, so that the main programme can restart simultaneously across all transmitters.

The brief must also take into account the production and airtime budgets that the advertiser has available, given that each actor (known as a voice-over) in the commercial will require a fee, music must be commissioned or licensed, and sound effects must be sourced, licensed or recorded specially for the production.

One other crucial factor here is the length of the proposed airtime campaign. A simple one-voice commercial with no sound effects or music is the cheapest to produce, and would be appropriate for a hard-hitting message over a single weekend, after which it will be scrapped. A year-long campaign, with the intention of planting the advertisers' name and reputation in the minds of potential customers for when they make a decision to buy at some time in the future requires a more subtle approach, perhaps using several voices or even commissioning a custom-made jingle, which can cost several thousand pounds on top of the airtime bought.

Most commissions will fall somewhere between the two, and the budget to be spent on production must be determined at an early stage.

Assignment: Part 2

You should now write up your programme brief for your assessment. It should include notes of the planning process so far, and should answer the following questions.

- Who is the client?
- What is the purpose of the campaign?
- How long will the commercial be?
- What style have you agreed with the client?
- What did you discover from your research?

Who is the client?

You will need to specify the name of the business and the person you have spoken to when you discussed the requirements for the commercial.

Fig. 4.2
Local rate card

LOCAL RATECARD

97.5 & 102.5 FM

The Pulse of West Yorkshire

Effective 4th March 1996

TIME SEGMENT	60 SECONDS	50 SECONDS	40 SECONDS	30 SECONDS	20 SECONDS	10 SECONDS
0600–0200	86	79	62	48	38	24
0600–1800	103	95	74	58	46	29
0600–1200	125	115	90	70	55	35
1200–1800	86	79	62	48	38	24
1800–0200	53	52	41	29	23	15
0700–0900	156	144	113	88	69	44
1600–1830	107	99	78	60	48	30
THU-SAT ONLY						
0600–0200	95	87	68	53	42	26
SUN-WED ONLY						
0600–0200	54	50	39	30	24	15

TERMS AND CONDITIONS

- General terms and conditions of contract are published and copies are available from the Radio Station.

- Pre-payment – all accounts will be pre-paid unless credit facilities have been arranged.

- Any cancellation must be made in writing to the Sales Director at least TWO WEEKS before transmission date.

- Daytime and T.A.P. Packages are subject to availability and are pre-emptible.

- All prices exclude V.A.T. and Commercial Production.

- To top and tail a commercial break 25% fixing.

1278 MW 1530

What is the purpose of the campaign?

You should write out the answers to the *Who? Why? What?* questions as outlined earlier in the section.

How long will the commercial be?

You must decide a length for your commercial, within the constraints of the client's budget (see the rate card above). For the purpose of this exercise, you will probably choose either 30 seconds, 40 seconds or 1 minute, but remember in the real world many commercials are shorter, and are repeated more often for maximum impact on the listener.

What style have you agreed with the client?

The style you choose will be determined to a large extent by the product, and the mood which the client wants to create in the mind of the listener. For example, a hard, driving music bed (music used as a background) may be appropriate for promoting a nightclub or selling a soft drink, where the client wishes to be associated with youth and energy. Such a style would be inappropriate for selling soft furnishings or garden products, where the client would rather create a feeling of ease and relaxation. Such a mood can be achieved with soft music or countryside sound effects.

Much will depend on the client's preferences – general issues, such as whether the client wants to include music and/or sound effects, and whether the commercial is to be humorous or serious, must be resolved before you can start on the creative process. The client may have other requirements, such as a preference for a male or a female voice-over. In the real world, the client must also operate within the constraints of the budget, although for the purposes of this exercise that need not affect your creative thinking. Write down what ideas and alternatives you have discussed with the client, and what feelings he/she expressed about your ideas.

What did you discover from your research?

Write down a summary of what you found out from your visit to the client – include your impressions of the premises, anything that would make you want to buy there (competitive prices, good range, high quality, convenient location, helpful staff, etc.) and any problems that the client has to overcome (new to the area, lots of competition, hard to find the shop, etc.).

Preparing the script

People initiate ideas for scripts in different ways. There are however standard conventions and abbreviations used for the finished script as shown in the following chart.

Abbreviation	Meaning
ANNO	Announcer – formal-style read, often used to start or finish a commercial which has 'character' voice-overs within it
ATMOS	Atmosphere – used to describe a general effect, such as 'windswept moor' or 'busy office' rather than a specific sound effect such as 'telephone rings'

Abbreviation	Meaning
FVO	Female voice-over
GRAM	Music ('gram' is an abbreviation of gramophone, or record player)
JINGLE	Jingle
JINGLE ENDS or J/E	Jingle comes to an end
MUSIC	Music
MUSIC BED	Music used as a background to a voice-over – often to set a mood, such as 'relaxed music bed' or 'up-tempo music bed'
MUSIC ENDS or M/E	Music comes to an end – usually a natural end, rather than an abrupt stop
MUSIC FADES or M/F	Music level reduces slowly
MVO	Male voice-over
MVO1	First male voice-over (MVO2 = second male voice-over, etc.)
SFX, FX or F/X	Sound effect
VO or V/O	Voice-over (gender not specific)

The words to be said, and directions, are written in upper and lower case characters.

The client's name, a title for the commercial (and/or a reference number) and the intended duration should be written at the top of the script, together with the name of the person who has written it.

Remember when writing the script that, as always in radio, you are writing for the ear rather than for the eye.

This means you must write the words as your character would actually say them, avoiding the conventions of the printed page. For example, you would never go into a café and say, 'Now pay attention, Jo – would you like (a) a cup of coffee, or (b) a cup of tea?'. Instead you would say, 'Hey Jo – tea or coffee?'. To communicate effectively on radio you must write your script using the language people actually use. You must also be careful not to use too many words to convey a simple idea. In natural speech, listeners pick up much more from the way in which something is said, and the context in which language is used, rather than from the words themselves. Something as simple as 'Oh dear' can have various meanings:

MVO:	My dad's poorly.	
FVO:	Oh dear!	*(Sincere; as in 'Oh dear, I am sorry')*
CHILD FVO:	Mummy! I've hurt my knee in the playground!	
ADULT FVO:	Oh dear!	*(Reassuring; as in 'Oh dear, never mind')*
UNITED FAN:	We lost three-nil on Saturday!	
CITY FAN:	Oh dear!	*(Mocking; as in 'Oh dear, but I'm not really sorry')*

Such devices act as verbal shortcuts, conveying a great deal of information about the characters in a very short space of time. A line such as

MVO: 'Cheer up, mate!'

if said in a light-hearted tone, carries a great deal of hidden information:

- The person being spoken to is miserable or depressed.
- The speaker is a friend, or is at least on familiar terms with that person.
- The person being addressed is probably male, 'mate' not being a term frequently used between women, or by a man to a woman.
- The light tone implies that whatever is wrong, it's not too serious.

The danger of writing too much, or 'giving the ear a feast', is that much of the information will be lost as the listener struggles to keep up with the facts; it is also very unlikely to sound natural.

The final test for any radio script is to read it aloud yourself; if it feels wrong when you say it, it's probably badly written.

Activity

Collect together some written advertising material such as newspapers, magazines or leaflets. Try reading them aloud. What problems do you notice? Why does it sound wrong, and what's missing?

Compare the material you've found with the examples of radio scripts included in this section. Notice how the language is different, and the way description is used to compensate for the lack of visual information.

Casting a commercial is clearly a key stage in the process – the voices used must be exactly right to convey the words you have written in the way you intended, as the audience has only the voice to go on when giving a physical shape to the actor within its imagination. Professional voice-over actors can use this to their advantage, and can learn a complete repertoire of voices to use on demand.

Special effects

When choosing special effects you must consider how you are going to obtain the sounds you need. Most commonly used sound effects are easily obtained on cassette tape or CD from music shops for use by home-video enthusiasts (or students). You must however remember that these recordings are copyright material, and may not be broadcast or used for commercial productions outside a home or educational environment without permission, which normally involves paying a fee in proportion to the size of the potential audience.

As an alternative, or if the effect you require is not available on disc, you may wish to record your own sound effects on location at the clients' premises or within your own work or home environment. Experiment with

David Bowie used the technique of speeding up the tape for the voice of the 'Laughing Gnome' in his 1973 hit recording, and in the early days of children's entertainment both 'Pinky and Perky' and 'The Chipmunks' owed their distinctive voices to vari-speed recording.

different ways of making sounds yourself, rather than recording the real situation:

- Dried peas dropped on to a sheet of paper over a padded box make a realistic rain effect.
- A teacup and pencil can be used to create a sound just like an old-fashioned fire bell.
- You can create a realistic echo in a studio by opening the **fader** from the tape machine you are recording on to just a fraction; the **feedback** created, if contained so as not to overwhelm the person speaking, can give the impression of a cave or a cathedral.
- **Vari-speeding** voices can also be very effective: you will need to use a reel-to-reel tape recorder to do this. Running the tape slightly slow will deepen the voice and lengthen the words. Speeding the tape up a little will make the voice higher and faster.

Advertisers wishing to include popular recordings by big-name artists in their commercial should be aware that the costs of using hit songs by famous artists (such as Michael Jackson) can be prohibitive, as the artists and their recording companies are well aware of the attraction of such material to advertisers and its power to influence audiences. Studio time is also expensive, and the more complicated the production, the longer will be required in studio.

In writing your material, remember what you learnt about the theatre of the mind – by clever use of music, voices and sound effects you can transport your listeners anywhere you want within their imagination. If your production is going to be complex, rather than a straight read, you will also need to consider appropriate beginnings and endings – these are called intros (short for introductions) and outros (a made-up word to pair with intro: the last line of a commercial, which finishes it off). Intros and outros are often read by a voice-over as an announcer (a narrator rôle) rather than in character – this would be indicated in the script as ANNO.

Intros can be very explicit, leading the listener straight into a fantasy situation, such as:

ANNO: Meanwhile in Santa's workshop, the elves are very busy making presents for Christmas…

or they can be more cryptic, teasing the listener into a potentially frightening situation:

ANNO: It was a dark and stormy night, and something nasty was about to happen in the old house on the hill…

Alternatively, a character can perform the intro by focusing the listener straight into a situation:

MVO 1: Hello mate… have a pint… is that your new car?

This sets the scene that the characters are friends in a pub… and one of them has a new car which will form the substance of what is to follow.

Outros are often used to repeat or emphasise the name and location of the advertiser. They too are frequently announcer-read:

ANNO: So for the best toys at the best prices this Christmas, remember Bloggins; there's a store near you, see the *Yellow Pages* for details.

The same function can be carried out by a character:

MVO 2: I'd better get down to Smith and Jones in the High Street before they sell out.

Remember you are addressing each listener individually, using radio's intimacy to create a bond of friendship with the characters in your script.

Activity

Study the examples of radio commercial scripts. Without copying words or phrases from them, see if they give you some ideas you could use for your client.

– Pulse Productions –

Client: **H. R. Jackson**	*Dur*: 50"
Cart No: 7919	*Writer*: Dan
Title: Amends	*Exec*: Linda
Production Time: 1	*Cost*: £175

Anncr: Remember when you were eleven, and you were playing cricket with a tennis ball and a cardboard tube? You remember – your mum told you not to play. Indoors. In the living room. Near the vase. Near the expensive, fragile vase. You've never been sure if she heard it break, but you've always been pretty certain she smelt the glue. And saw the join. But she never said a word. And you've never quite forgotten. Or forgiven yourself. Have you?

Crystalware, glassware, tableware. Royal Doulton, Royal Albert, Royal Crown Derby. Mother's Day at H. R. Jackson, Darley Street, Bradford. It's time to make amends.

– Pulse Productions –

Client: Calderdale Leisure   *Dur*: 40"
Cart No: 7440   *Writer*: Paul
Title: Video   *Exec*: SS
Production Time: 3   *Cost*: £279

SFX: An aerobics video is playing in the background.
MVO: Well, I've watched this aerobics video twice and
        I've got to say I don't feel any fitter...
FVO: You're not just supposed to watch it – you've got to
        follow what they're doing...
MVO: What?! I'll give meself a Hernia!
FVO: You'll have to do something to get fit.
MVO: Well, I am planning to watch the Olympics.
FVO: Get down the Leisure Centre...
MVO: What can I watch down there?
FVO: Nothing, but there is plenty to do. There's a pool,
        a fully equipped gym...
MVO: I'll just give the video one more try. Where's the
        remote control?
Anncr: At your local Leisure Centre you'll find a pool, a
        gym and all the help you need to lose weight and
        get fit.
        And with Leisure Centres throughout West
        Yorkshire, you won't even have to do much
        exercise to find one.

– Pulse Productions –

Client: Huddersfield Technical College   *Dur*: 50"
Cart No: 4183   *Writer*: Luke
Title: Supermarket   *Exec*: LP
Production Time: 1   *Cost*: to be agreed

SFX: Supermarket musak. Cash tills, etc.

Lily Savage: (Shouts) Till number six – cheesy pancakes!

SFX: Bell rings

                If you do a part-time job people think
                you're either lazy or you're so thick you
                think Saatchi & Saatchi are the twins out of
                'Neighbours'. But who's gonna train a young
                mum with kids so she can get a *proper* job?
                (Shouts) Is someone going to tell me how
                much these faffin' cheesy pancakes cost or
                what?!

SFX: Bell rings

I've had enough! I'm going to get a job I like! I've been on the phone to Joan at Huddersfield Tech. They've got courses in Hairdressing and Beauty Therapy and it doesn't matter if you've got kids because you can learn part-time, night-time, distance learning – they've got a crèche and a nursery. I learn when it's best for me. (Shouts) How much are they? A pound and five p, love – there we go. Have you got the five? No you've given me a *button* there love ... (louder)... Yes it's a button, I can't... have you got any proper money in there! (Fade)
(Intimate, friendly) For a career in Hairdressing or Beauty Therapy, get on the phone to Joan at Huddersfield Tech. Huddersfield 536 521.

You should now take some time by yourself to write down a few ideas, and to develop those which work. Remember the time constraints you are working to; the script must run exactly to time, with a tolerance of less than one second. It will help you to remember that most people speak at around three words to the second – that means a 30-second commercial will be about 90 words long, and a one-minute commercial will be about 180 words long. Don't forget to allow time for music and sound effects if you're using them.

You must remember all the time what your characters are supposed to be doing; they need not stand still or silent whilst someone else is speaking, any more than they would in real-life situations.

Many advertising agencies get their radio copywriters to create a visual storyboard for a radio commercial, as they would for a video production, to keep this sense of reality alive. Remember that dialogue arises from action, and not the other way around. It is essential to provide a description of each character so the voice-over knows what you're trying to achieve.

MVO 1: Smooth middle-aged salesman
FVO 1: Harassed young mother with small child
MVO 2: Elderly, forgetful customer

Assignment: Part 3

You are now ready to begin the process of drafting a script, or several script ideas, for approval by the client. Although you may wish to write out rough ideas in a notebook, the finished script

A man who's supposed to be sawing wood should sound out of breath when he speaks, and his speech will be in rhythm with the sawing sound effect; he may also gasp or grunt whilst someone else is speaking. A customer in a shop may sigh to indicate the difficulty of choosing a style, and this adds to the realism of the situation for the listener.

Keep examples of any ideas which don't work – you should include them with your production brief to show your assessor how you went about selecting a script for your client.

should be typewritten or word processed, according to the following conventions:

- the script must be in double-line spacing, with margins of at least 2 cm at each side.
- The elements of the production (voices, music, sound effects, etc.) are listed in chronological order down the left-hand side of the page.

When you have come up with at least two completed scripts, you should arrange a second meeting with your client to let him/her see the scripts and to make any comments on them. You should make careful notes of what the client has to say, and be ready to modify your ideas accordingly. Be prepared to defend your ideas, but remember that the client has the final say as the person who would be paying for the campaign in the real world.

Once you have agreed which script will be produced, you need to draw up a list of the resources you will require to make it. This will include the number of voices required, and the people you have cast to read those voices; any sound effects you need to obtain, either from pre-recorded sources or by recording them yourself; and any music you require, and how that will be obtained – from pre-recorded tape or CD, or by 'live' recording of musicians or singers in a studio. You are then in a position to specify what technical equipment you will need. You will need to book sufficient time in a studio with an engineer to work the recording desk, and you will need to make sure the studio has all the necessary equipment to play in your tapes and/or CDs as well as the required number of microphones (of the right type).

It will help if you write out a diary or production schedule in which you plan what you will do on each day you have available for the project, and how long each task will take. You can use the schedule to check your progress as you go along.

You will probably find your progress is frustrated by a shortage of equipment or studio time, and that tasks in the studio take longer than you had expected. These problems also exist in the real world of commercial production, and you must plan ahead effectively if you are to overcome the difficulties.

Assignment: Part 4

As the final written element for your assessed radio commercial, you should list the other people who have helped you in the planning and scripting of your audio product, and what their rôle has been (such as 'Jude helped me record the sound effects; Raj went with me to visit the client', etc.)

The radio news feature

You now need to consider the second audio product by which you will be assessed within this unit – a non-fiction programme which we suggest is a radio news feature. This requires a somewhat different approach to the planning process. You will be working in teams, and the finished product will be very much a team effort. It is essential, therefore, that you keep a record of your own individual contribution from the outset.

In writing your commercial you were free to use your imagination to develop ideas and characters. Reporting requires a more disciplined use of the technique as the objective now is to communicate facts. This does not mean that you cannot be creative; but you must not allow your use of the medium to mislead your listeners, who are totally dependent on you as the reporter to be their eyes and ears.

Broadcast regulations

All radio journalists working in the United Kingdom must be aware of the regulatory framework within which broadcasters operate. They must be aware of the laws of **libel** and **contempt of court** (which will be discussed later); they must be familiar with the rules concerning the broadcast of copyright recordings which we discussed earlier in this section – in a news context this also extends to the use of archive material (famous speeches or news events from the past).

These documents are too complex and wide-ranging to discuss in detail here, but in broad terms, they impose an obligation on journalists to be fair and impartial in all their reporting.

But above all they must be aware of the obligations laid out in the Royal Charter which regulates the operation of the BBC, and the Broadcasting Act which regulates all land-based commercial broadcasters (ITV, Channel 4, Independent Radio).

The owner of a newspaper determines the editorial policy of that publication; he/she is in a position to instruct journalists to report controversial issues in a way which is favourable to one political party or another, and on polling day the newspaper will urge readers to vote for the party of the owner's choice. An owner can also seek to influence public opinion by the way in which the publication addresses issues such as abortion, race, crime and the environment. Individual journalists may have greater or lesser degrees of editorial freedom depending on the policy of the publication; but ultimately their employment depends on their willingness to comply with the editorial line set by the owner.

The broadcast journalist on the other hand is free from many of these overt pressures – the station is prohibited from taking an editorial line on any issue of public controversy, and must endeavour to reflect all points of view on the issue. In particular the station may not urge listeners (or viewers) to support a political party, and there are other severe restrictions on comment imposed by the Representation of the People Act, which applies (becomes active) during election campaigns. Among other things, this prevents any discussion of key issues or the publication of opinion polls on or just before polling day; and it obliges broadcasters to balance precisely (in accordance with an agreed formula) the amount of time they allow for politicians of different parties to express their views.

Activity

In a group, discuss the following:

- Do you agree with the principle of the Broadcasting Act and the BBC Charter restricting editorial comment by major broadcasters?
- Why should TV and radio be treated any differently from newspapers and magazines?
- What dangers could there be in publishing an opinion poll of voting intentions on the day of a general election?
- Do you believe that, in everyday situations, broadcasters are really free from political or managerial pressures?

In approaching the topic you are to cover for your radio news feature you must be aware of these rules, and apply them right from the planning stage. You must not allow your own personal feelings to cloud your professional approach to a story.

At a local level, there may be significant opposition to plans for a new road scheme – but if you choose this as your topic you must not fall into the trap of saying in your report that 'everybody is against the road'. That may be the case among your immediate circle of friends and neighbours, but there will be individuals and groups in favour of the scheme; for example, lorry drivers, or motoring organisations such as the AA and RAC. To ignore their views would be to ignore your responsibilities under the Broadcasting Act or BBC Charter.

You may well be opposed to the slaughter of seals for their fur – but as a broadcast journalist you must instinctively seek out the other side of the story, and either let the trappers and dealers have their say within a balanced package, or at least put their point of view to environmental campaigners to draw out a response to the points they make.

Public service broadcasting

For nearly half a century, all legal radio broadcasting in the United Kingdom was controlled by the BBC (the British Broadcasting Corporation, originally founded as the British Broadcasting Company). Its first director general, John (later Lord) Reith, established the principle of public service broadcasting. This means that the broadcaster provides a balance of programmes designed to cater for a wide range of tastes and interests, with the intention that the service should educate and inform as well as entertain its audience.

This public service rôle is underpinned by public funding, as the BBC obtains its income from the TV licence fee. The system requires anyone with a television in his/her home (originally anyone who owned a radio) to buy an annual licence for it, in effect a compulsory subscription for the service whether or not the viewer or listener tunes to BBC programmes. This is in marked contrast to the development of broadcasting in other countries, particularly the United States, where the system ran on commercial lines from the start – stations compete to win the biggest audiences by offering popular programmes which will appeal to a large proportion of the available audience, but which may neglect minority tastes, and may seek only to entertain.

Supporters of the commercial model argue that in time, these minorities will be catered for as new stations enter the market looking for a **niche audience**. Opponents claim that without the secure income provided by public funding, broadcasters are unable to take risks with new programme ideas; and that serious drama and orchestral music, as opposed to soaps and pop, should be made available on the air to everybody as part of the national heritage. Public service broadcasting does exist in the United States, but such channels are normally funded by donations and bequests from supporters, or charity appeals.

Planning

You must now begin the planning process for the second part of your assignment – the radio news feature.

Assignment: Part 5

You are to produce a feature of between two and a half and three minutes' duration based on the subject you decided in Study Unit 2, Section 3, and for which you are (or will be) also producing a radio commercial. You should assume that you are working for a community radio station based at your workplace, which serves the area from which students in your group are drawn. Its target audience is the community living and working within this imaginary transmission area; if it is a large area, you may also wish to subdivide the target audience by age, for example 'young people aged 16–24' or 'older people over 55'.

Work in a group of four, but if this is not possible you may work in a pair. Distribute the following rôles:

- reporter
- producer
- editor
- sound engineer.

If you're working as a pair, the reporter/engineer and producer/editor rôles will be combined. You should alternate the rôles so that each student is the reporter for his/her own assessment piece, whilst taking on the other functions for other group members.

The first stage in the planning process is to hold a production meeting at which you will allocate the key rôles outlined above, and discuss your ideas for the feature. Keep notes of what is suggested at the meeting, the rôles you agree upon, and the various options you discuss before you make your decisions – these notes will form part of your assessment.

Production rôles

The reporter

The reporter must keep notes of all research carried out, including lines of inquiry which lead to nothing, and submit these as part of the course assessment.

The reporter's job is to nominate and research the people to be interviewed. Find out their names, their job titles, where they are based; and (if they are willing to be interviewed) when it would be convenient to see them, or speak to them on the telephone. If someone is too busy to help your assignment, or is on holiday, you must come up with a suitable alternative, or suggest another way of putting over his/her viewpoint. You should also give an indication of what areas your questions to each interviewee will address, but don't write out a long list of exact questions as when you conduct the interview you must listen closely to what the interviewee says, and be ready to vary your questions as you react to the information given in the answers.

The producer

The producer must keep the list of resources identified at the production meeting, together with any later alterations, as part of the assessment.

The producer must identify a list of resources required for the feature. Will it be possible to visit the people you need to interview? If not, do you have the means to record telephone conversations? If so, can the required interviews be carried out on the telephone? Or can the reporter suggest an alternative spokesperson? Is the suggested music available in your own collection, in your workplace library, or can it be borrowed from a library elsewhere? (Many public libraries have large CD collections which are available for loan for a small fee.)

Do you have the necessary music copyright details to include on your music log? Are the suggested sound effects available on tape or CD? If not, is it possible to record them yourself safely and conveniently? Can the feature be made within budget, and within the time allowed?

The editor

The editor should keep notes of the discussions on these topics, and how any conflicts were resolved, as part of the project assessment.

The editor must take on the rôle of professional listener for the project. Given the need for the piece to be balanced, fair and impartial, has the reporter identified all the people who need to be included? Are there any relevant viewpoints which are being ignored? Is the reporter taking sufficient care to address issues of representation, and avoid stereotypes? Is the music (and/or use of sound effects) relevant and appropriate, or is it irrelevant, clichéd and inappropriate? Will the finished audio product be

The engineer must make a list
of the technical requirements
for the project, and submit the
list as part of the assessment.

interesting, stimulating and informative for the audience of your imaginary radio station based in your workplace, or will it be boring and irrelevant to their lives?

The engineer

The engineer's job is to make sure you have all the equipment you need to make the feature; if you will be recording on location, you will require a portable tape recorder with a suitable microphone, enough tape, and freshly charged batteries. If you will be recording in a studio, the engineer is responsible for booking the space, setting up the required number of microphones, operating the mixing desk and checking the finished recording. The engineer must also make sure you have the means to play in all the proposed music and sound effects in the final mix; there's no point getting an effect on DAT tape if you don't have a DAT player to reproduce it from.

The production schedule

Assignment: Part 6

You are now ready to draft a production schedule for your feature.

The schedule should be in the form of a diary, indicating in chronological order what you intend to do on each day (or session) you are devoting to the project. For each day, and in the light of your earlier discussions, you should indicate who you intend to interview, where each interview will take place, and how it will be recorded. Include entries for times when you will visit libraries, or record sound effects on location, and remember to include sufficient time for reviewing your material – listening back to tapes – and editing your recordings before the project deadline. This production schedule must then be agreed with your tutor before you start work.

Once the schedule is approved, you should use it as a guide to refer to as your work progresses. It should be useful both as a checklist, to make sure you haven't forgotten to do anything, and as a time management tool, to ensure you meet the deadlines you have agreed.

Remember, in the real world of newsgathering you can never miss a deadline, as a story which arrives too late for its planned transmission time will often be scrapped, since it is not acceptable in any newsroom to broadcast out-of-date information in a later bulletin.

2 Record audio material for products

You are now ready to move on to the production stage for your audio products. In this section you will take the specifications you drew up in Section 1, and translate your ideas into finished recordings ready for editing. You must maintain a log book throughout this unit in which you record the decisions you make and the reasons why you make them. It is especially important to remember to use your equipment safely at all times, and you must be able to show that you have done so. You will also be faced by a range of ethical and legal issues. Your log must show that you are aware of these issues, and that you have given due consideration to your actions throughout.

Before starting recording, you must first examine the technical options available for you to achieve the effects you require.

Recording medium

Your choice of recording medium may well be dictated by the equipment available to you.

Cassette recorders

Cassette recorders are almost universally available, and are simple to operate. They are seldom used in professional radio stations because the quality of the recording obtained is relatively poor compared to open-reel, DAT tape or data (disk) recorders. This is because in order to create the compact cassette format with conventional (**analogue**) technology, the recording tape has to be made thin, which makes it extremely vulnerable to physical damage. It also moves relatively slowly across the record and playback heads – at $1\frac{7}{8}$ inches (4.75 cm) per second – meaning that a lot of information has to be stored on a small area of the recording medium, and the recording will be severely affected by tiny variations in the speed of the machine's motor. For all but the most dedicated it is impossible to **splice edit** a cassette tape, meaning that all material recorded must first be dubbed on to an open-reel tape (resulting in a **generation** loss of quality) before it can be edited. If electronic editing is used, the material must first be loaded in real time into a computer file before editing can begin. Both these processes involve considerable time delays which can be unacceptable in a busy broadcast environment, such as a newsroom.

Many cassette recorders are designed for domestic use, with automatic recording level controls and built-in microphones, both of which are unsuitable for professional use. Automatic level control can result in sudden drops in recording level if the machine reacts to a sudden sound, such as a book being dropped, which is louder than the speech being recorded; the same intrusion would only cause a momentary overload if the level were controlled manually. Built-in microphones are generally of very poor technical quality, and are prone to pick up a lot of intrusive noise from the sound of the machine's motor going round within the same outer casing. Even if the machine is fitted with a tape counter, it is time consuming and fiddly to **cue** a passage – find the start of a passage – for **dub editing** purposes, and accurate cueing is virtually impossible.

Cassette recorders do however have the advantage of being light and easy to carry around; tapes and accessories are relatively cheap; machines specially designed for professional use, such as the Sony Professional Walkman, do exist, and, when used with an external microphone of broadcast quality, are useful for correspondents working away from a newsroom for long periods in hostile conditions, or where the bulk and weight of open-reel equipment would be inconvenient. Professional use otherwise is generally limited to non-urgent feature production, where the delays caused by the need to dub material are less of a problem.

> When using a cassette recorder it is vital to ensure that the correct tape bias setting is selected for the grade of tape being used; many machines will have the choice of ferric, chrome or metal tapes. If in doubt, refer to the instructions for the particular machine you are using.

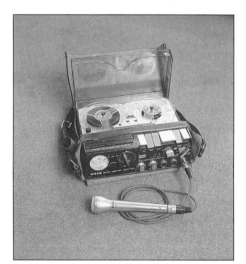

Fig. 4.3
Uher reel-to-reel recorder

Open-reel recorders

Reel-to-reel portable recorders are the mainstay of most professional newsrooms in the UK and continental Europe, although new technology means they are likely to become redundant within the coming decade. They have both advantages and disadvantages; the main advantages being quality and speed. They record at 7½ inches (19 cm) per second which allows for easy splice editing, and the tapes recorded can be lifted off straight on to an editing machine in a newsroom for near-instant use on air. They can be easily cued (with or without **leader tape** on the start – leader tape is coloured plastic tape of the same width and thickness as the recording tape, but you can't record on it) and the tape itself is fairly resilient and can cope with rough handling to a much greater degree than cassettes.

A typical newsroom will be equipped with Uher or Marantz machines, which are designed to be sturdy and hard-wearing. They are however extremely heavy to carry around, are much bulkier than any other recording machine because of the need to accommodate two 5-inch (12 cm) reels, a powerful motor to drive them and a hefty rechargeable battery within the case. They are expensive to buy and maintain, and are less forgiving of student mistakes than other types of recorders available.

DAT tape

DAT tape recorders offer the quality of **digital** recording in a compact tape format which is light and easy to carry around. The main difficulty with DAT is the expense and relative scarcity of the equipment, combined once again with the need to dub on to another medium (although this time without loss of quality) before editing.

Minidisk recorders

As more newsrooms convert to digital editing on personal computers, there is little doubt that some form of minidisk recorder will become the industry norm. At the time of writing, the technology is still new and is susceptible to breakdown; however, once the hardware is fully developed, the minidisk will offer the quality of digital recording combined with the speed of the open-reel systems, as the files created on minidisk can be rapidly transferred to the hard disk of a personal computer (PC) equipped with digital editing software.

Microphones

You can now move on to deciding which microphone (mike) is most appropriate for the recording situation you have decided upon. Microphones come in several types:

- *Omnidirectional* microphones, as the name suggests, pick up sound from all around. They are used most effectively for group recording, when one microphone can be positioned near the centre of the group and sound from all participants will be recorded. Their biggest disadvantage is that they can pick up a lot of extraneous – unwanted – noise from around the room if you are attempting to record just one person.

Fig. 4.4
Omnidirectional
microphone

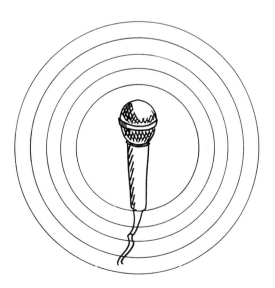

Fig. 4.5
Bi-directional
microphone

Fig. 4.5
Bi-directional
microphone

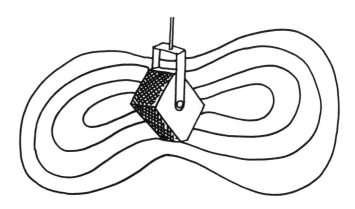

- *Bi-directional microphones* are seldom if ever found outside a radio station. They are designed, as the name suggests once again, to pick up the sound from two directions, and are normally placed between the interviewer and interviewee on or above a table. They usually have two flat faces, or a diamond-shaped body, so it's immediately obvious which sides to speak into.

Fig. 4.6
Cardioid microphone

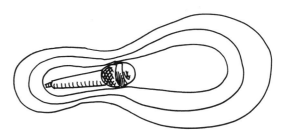

- *Cardioid microphones* are probably the type in most common use today. They are designed to pick up sound in a cone-shape from the front, in an arc extending to about 80 degrees, but they will also pick up some noise from outside this sensitive zone at a lower level.

Fig. 4.7
Rifle microphone

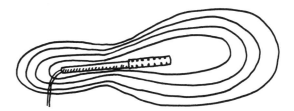

- *Rifle microphones* are extremely directional, picking up sound in a narrow beam from the front of the 'barrel'. They do not pick up sound over long distances, and generally won't pick up a sound you can't hear from where you are standing with the microphone. However, by eliminating

When recording on location away from your normal work environment, you must take every precaution to ensure your own safety; in particular, you must not become so absorbed in the recording process that you fail to look out for everyday hazards.

When choosing a location, you must always assess the potential risks in that location such as those created by machinery or moving vehicles.

As with any electrical equipment, you must be very careful when handling your tape recorder, especially if it is plugged into the mains. *Never* use any tape recorder if the plug or power lead is damaged, or if the lead does not fit properly into the power socket. *Always* switch off your machine and unplug it from the mains when you have finished a recording or editing session. When you're working on location, take care not to get your recorder or microphone wet. *Never* attempt to do repairs yourself if the machine stops working – always consult a qualified technician or engineer.

Remember as well that if you are recording in a public place, you must make sure your equipment does not present a hazard for others; for example, make sure you do not leave microphone cables or power leads trailing across floors or doorways, which could trip people up. If you are recording in the street, you may well attract bystanders who want to watch what you're doing; you must not allow your presence to create a hazard, and remember you must not allow your equipment (or the crowd you attract) to block the road or pavement, or you could be arrested for obstructing the highway.

or minimising other noises in the environment, they can make the sound much clearer and sharper. To use a rifle microphone effectively, you must wear headphones to hear exactly what the mic is picking up; you must also remain still, as a small movement of the barrel can take the desired sound out of range.

You now need to look at some of the practical considerations involved when recording in different situations.

Location recording

When you are to record on location, that is away from your working environment and outside a studio setting, it is important to make sure you take everything you are likely to need with you. To record a simple one-to-one interview you will need a portable tape recorder, a suitable microphone, sufficient tape for the duration of the intended interview and fully charged batteries. Remember you are using delicate technical equipment; you must take good care of it. You must protect your equipment from excessive vibration, and should not leave it to be thrown about unprotected in the back of a van or the boot of a car.

It's always advisable to take a spare set of batteries with you, as battery failure is the most common technical problem experienced away from base. If your tape recorder has a headphone socket, it's also a good idea to use headphones to monitor the recording whilst you are making it. This will help you spot problems such as a faulty connection or excessive **wind noise** whilst you still have a chance to do something about it, rather than afterwards when you review your material.

Always check the complete recording rig before you leave your working base, no matter how many times you have used the machine before, or how experienced you are with recording equipment generally. Plugging everything in and switching on is the only way to be sure that you have all the bits you need, and that all the connections are working properly. Having carried out this test, make sure you turn the power off before you start on your journey to the remote location.

Choosing a location

When deciding on a location for an interview, bear in mind the legal constraints which could affect you. You may not record on private property (such as a bus or train station, or a shopping centre) without the permission of the owner. Getting that permission may often require you to write a letter several days in advance, and even then it may not be granted. Neither can you record in a hospital or a school without permission and, when dealing with schools, remember you may need the permission of each individual parent or guardian before you may speak to children under the age of 16, although some headteachers are willing to take this responsibility themselves.

The choice of location is also determined by both technical and creative considerations.

Technical considerations

The technical points concern the acoustic qualities of the location.

If you are recording indoors, be aware of the echo in the room. If an office is sparsely furnished, with bare walls, lots of hard surfaces (wooden desk tops; metal filing cabinets), no carpets and blinds instead of curtains, there is likely to be a bright (echoey) atmosphere. Our ears are used to filtering out such echoes as we concentrate on what a speaker has to say, but the microphone cannot filter these sounds.

Compare this with a room which is expensively furnished with soft chairs, thick carpet and curtains. If you record in this environment, you are likely to experience very few echoes.

Activity

With your portable recorder, explore different indoor locations within your workplace. Try recording speech in a sparsely furnished room, and in one with lots of soft furnishings. Listen to the differences when recording in a small room, and in a large room like a gymnasium. Try also recording in a noisy environment (like a coffee bar) and in a quiet space (like a library). Keep a log of the differences you notice.

Do not become a victim of 'quiet room syndrome' – many interviewees, perhaps aware of some of the needs of broadcasters, may automatically steer you towards a quiet location well away from any activity in order to offer you what they see as the best possible recording environment. Quiet locations were also important half a century ago, when recording equipment was less sophisticated and any background noise at all could make an interview unusable.

Background noise

Be aware of any other sounds in the recording environment which are likely to affect the recording. If there is a telephone in the room, ask your interviewee if calls can be diverted elsewhere during the interview. Turn off any radios or TV sets, especially if there is music playing.

Listen carefully to the background or **ambient noise** in the room. Everyday sounds such as fans (including the tiny fans within personal computers), water gurgling in pipes, etc. can sound very loud indeed on the finished recording, especially if you are using an omnidirectional microphone or if you are very close to the source of the sound.

You should also beware of the 'silent dangers' which can ruin a recording. The whistle from a TV set with the picture on but no sound or

---

You can test the **brightness** of the atmosphere by making any loud, sharp sound such as clapping your hands – if you are aware of any echo at all, your interview may well sound on playback as if it has been recorded in a bathroom.

You can minimise the effects of a bright atmosphere by using a directional – cardioid – microphone, and by using a closer microphone technique than you would use in normal circumstances, holding the microphone at (say) 10 cm from the speaker's mouth instead of the usual 20 cm. Of course, in some circumstances you may want to use brightness for deliberate effect – if you are in an empty factory, for example, or a supposedly 'haunted' house, in which case you can even exaggerate the echo by moving the microphone further away.

Remember, if there is any recognisable music at all playing in the background, the tape will be impossible to edit as any **cuts** in the speech will also create breaks or gaps in the music – these will be very obvious to the listener.

the hum from a fluorescent light fitting at close range are normally inaudible to the human ear, but can be picked up by the microphone which has a wider **dynamic range**.

Recording outdoors

If you decide to record outdoors, there are other technical considerations you must be aware of. All microphones are prone to pick up wind noise. This is caused by wind blowing into and across the end of the microphone, and sounds as if you were blowing into it on purpose from close range. It is possible to minimise wind noise by using a **wind shield**; this is normally a ball of foam rubber shaped to fit exactly over the end of the microphone.

Intrusive sounds

Background sounds such as ambulance sirens and aircraft can intrude on your recording; like music in the background, they too can make a recording impossible to edit. General traffic noise is less of a problem, as its random nature means that discontinuities are less obvious to the casual (untrained) ear. Some of these problems can be avoided by careful choice of location: don't do a **vox pop** – random street interview – near a hospital or a fire station, for example.

Creative considerations

You can now begin to consider the creative or artistic aspects of your chosen location. You may decide that you can add an extra dimension to the interview by choosing a 'busy' location, where the background sounds will give colour or context to the situation. If you are talking about a busy hospital, for example, it can reinforce the speaker's words if the sounds of a bustling ward can be heard in the background. So long as the ambient noise is not intrusive, it can be a real asset to your feature.

If you have any doubts about the suitability of a location, record in a quiet room and also record some **wildtrack** sound before you leave the location. Wildtrack is a recording of ambient noise without any speech on it; if you record between 30 seconds and 2 minutes of wildtrack, you can then mix the real ambient sound underneath your 'quiet room' interview back at the studio – with the added benefit that you then control absolutely the level of background noise.

If you have no proper wind shield available, it is possible to improvise one using a handkerchief, scarf, or length of cotton wool – any soft, porous material – you can wrap around the end of the microphone to stop the wind blowing directly on to it. Be aware, however, that an improvised wind shield is also likely to muffle your recording.

When recording sound effects on location, make sure there are no background sounds which will interfere with the finished recording. For example, if you are recording the sound of a door opening and closing, make sure you cannot hear conversations or telephones ringing at the same time – unless you want these sounds as part of the effect.

Activity

Bearing in mind the technical and creative considerations which could affect your choice, decide on a good location to do an interview about:

- a new rail service starting in your town
- a new swimming pool opening nearby
- a countryside warden who has reared some baby birds.

Setting up

When you are ready to conduct your location interview, take the time to first set up in a suitable place. If you are recording in an office, you should avoid interviewing your guest across a desk. Not only does the table create a physical obstacle between you, it also creates a psychological barrier. By keeping the reporter at the other side of the desk, the interviewee is less likely to open up or reveal anything about him/herself. The microphone is always in the interviewee's field of vision, and will reinforce the perceived need to be careful (or very formal) about what he/she is saying. It is also uncomfortable for you as the interviewer, as your arm will get tired holding the microphone at full stretch for more than a few moments.

Fig. 4.8
The wrong way to set up a radio interview

Try instead to sit alongside your guest, or at worst, speak to him/her across the corner of a desk. Keep the tape recorder out of the interviewee's line of sight (if you can) but remember you must be able to both reach the controls and watch the meter. It is normally best to try to face your interviewee with the microphone in your right hand, with your body between the guest and the recorder, which is either on the floor (if you are seated) or hanging from a shoulder-strap (if you are standing) at your left side. You can then operate the controls with your left hand out of sight of your interviewee, and you can observe the meter with a swift glance down and to the left.

Fig. 4.9
The right way
to set up a
radio interview

The interview

Putting the interviewee at ease

You must remember that being recorded for broadcast on the radio (or even for a student project) is a stressful experience for many people who are not used to the technology, and who may be self-conscious in front of the microphone and when hearing themselves on tape. The best way to overcome nerves on the part of your guest is to be confident yourself – this means you must be familiar with the controls on your recorder, so that you can switch it on without making a great fuss, and you must know what you are going to ask before you start.

Asking the right questions

Remember Rudyard Kipling's poem:

'I keep six honest serving-men
They taught me all I knew –
Their names are what, and why, and when –
and how, and where, and who.'

You will get a better interview if you ask 'open' rather than 'closed' questions. **Open questions** cannot be answered with a simple yes or no – for example, 'What is your name?' or 'Where do you live?' rather than 'Is your name Sanjiv?' or 'Do you live in London?'. Open questions force the interviewee to say more, and will make editing easier at a later stage.

How much to record

As a rule of thumb, try to record about three times the amount of material you will need for the finished piece, and no more. If you need 20 seconds from an interviewee, record for about a minute. If you need a minute, record three minutes. Never come back from an interview with too little material, and try not to come back with too much.

Think about editing as you record

As you conduct your interviews you should begin to cultivate the ability to decide as you go along how the material will be used; in effect, you can edit in your mind. If you know you are dealing with a nervous or hesitant interviewee, you should decide before you start how long you will require the individual's contribution to be. Ignore any false starts or bad answers the interviewee gives, then begin counting seconds in your head from the point at which the interviewee starts to give you a good, clear and positive answer. Stop counting if the interviewee begins to stumble or dry up and resume counting from the point at which the individual recovers, and continues giving you a good answer. It is better to re-record a question within an interview at the time, rather than attempting to remove imperfections in the edit suite.

You will often feel embarrassed asking an interviewee the same question, or drawing attention to shortcomings in the person's answers; the solution is to paraphrase the question (ask for the same information in a different way), giving the interviewee another chance to get it right.

If on the other hand you have a very fluent interviewee who talks for longer than you will be able to use, be ready to interrupt the answers to steer the interview on to the next point you need to cover – otherwise you will end up with far more material than you will ever be able to use.

Legal and ethical responsibilities

You must remember that your responsibility as a journalist is to be fair and balanced in your questions. You should tell your interviewees what general areas you will be asking about, so that they can prepare their thoughts for giving the answers. However, you should never provide a written list of questions, as 'rehearsed' answers tend to take all the spontaneity out of an interview. You should also avoid making assumptions about your interviewees which tend to reinforce the stereotypes of different groups in society. Older people are not always poor or frail – and people with a physical disability are no more likely than anyone else to have learning difficulties. Approach every interview – and every interviewee – with an open mind.

Accuracy

Your reputation – and the reputation of every journalist and broadcast organisation – depends on the accuracy of the information you put to air.

This means you must take every reasonable care to make sure all the material you include in your programme is factually correct. Remember the journalists' golden rule: 'If in doubt, leave it out.'

Privacy and confidentiality

You must respect everyone's right to privacy, and this includes the right not to be interviewed or to answer questions if they so choose. Other people may give you useful information on the understanding that they will not be named as the source of that material. If you agree to this, you must respect any promise you give.

Exploitation

Be very careful not to use your position as a weapon, perhaps frightening or intimidating people into saying things they really don't mean, but which they feel you are pressuring them to say.

You should beware of exploiting the vulnerable, or exploiting the misfortune of others. Whilst there can be a genuine public interest in reporting issues of homelessness, or reporting tragedy, you must respect the dignity of each individual and not treat people simply as objects to be used for the purpose of your reporting. You are also in a powerful position simply because you are carrying a tape recorder, and the people you speak to know what they say to you will potentially be broadcast to an audience of thousands or millions.

Sensationalism

As a journalist, you are in a very privileged position; you get special access to people and places because you are reporting on behalf of all the listeners, readers or viewers you represent. You must use this privilege responsibly, and not distort the real situation you find in order to produce a more entertaining (or a more heart-rending) story. Ask yourself how you would feel if you, or someone who is close to you, were the subject of an exaggerated or sensationalised story on the radio.

Libel

You must be aware of the laws of libel, which exist to protect the reputation of every citizen. Libel is a very complicated area of the law, which working journalists need to study in depth, but for your purposes on this assignment, just remember that you must be able to prove that all statements made in your programme feature are true. If your guest says 'John Smith is a thief', for example, you must be able to prove that statement. You must know when he was convicted of theft, by reference to documentary evidence (such as a report of the trial). If you can't provide such evidence, you cannot know for certain that John Smith is in fact a criminal; just to claim that 'everyone says he is' does not prove anything.

You must also be careful of attributing blame to someone without evidence. To say 'The car hit the little boy' may seem to be an accurate description of a road accident; but it may later turn out that the child ran into the road, and the driver had no chance of stopping. It is legally safer, therefore, to say 'The car was in collision with the little boy', which avoids any implication that the driver was at fault.

Copyright

As when you made your radio commercial, remember that you must be aware of the source of all material you intend to broadcast, and be aware of copyright considerations. This means, for example, that you will have to pay a **royalty** for most music used in your feature. You may also have to seek permission to use extracts from plays or books, other than very short extracts used for the purpose of reviewing the material.

Activity

Imagine you are a reporter on the scene of an accident where a school bus has crashed, injuring several students. The emergency services are still present, and a number of parents and teachers from the school have arrived to see what's happening, and what they can do to help.

- Who would you try to interview in this situation?
- Who would you avoid interviewing, and why?
- What ethical problems would you face as a journalist trying to get your story?

Someone tells you the crash was the driver's fault because he fell asleep at the wheel. What legal problems does this statement create?

In order to get an authoritative statement of what's happened, a journalist would normally approach the most senior police officer at the scene – unless the officer is very obviously involved in operational matters such as directing ambulance crews, or arranging a traffic diversion, in which case the journalist should wait until a suitable opportunity arises. It would not be appropriate to approach junior officers involved in crowd control activities, as they would not normally have the authority to give any kind of statement to the media. If there has been any sort of rescue operation, the senior fire officer at the scene should also be able to give a statement. You should avoid approaching anyone who is badly injured, or anyone who is clearly distressed unless he/she wants to talk to you. There may be people who although physically unhurt are still traumatised by the crash. There will probably be eyewitnesses who will be only too willing to give their version of events; be wary of their comments, as they may have had only a partial view of what happened and their stories can often be exaggerated. If anyone makes a defamatory statement about anyone involved (for example, suggesting that the driver fell asleep) you must be aware of the dangers of libel – and if a court case is likely to follow the accident, especially if the driver has been arrested, you must beware of saying anything which could influence a future court case or you could be in contempt of court. The public has a right to know what is happening in their community – but you must weigh this responsibility with the need to avoid sensationalism and exploitation, and with individuals' rights to privacy.

Recording material

Monitoring the recording

If your recorder offers the option of **monitoring** 'source' or 'tape', you should switch occasionally to the 'tape' setting for a second or two during a long answer from your interviewee; check the meter, which should be bouncing in time to the peaks in the flow of speech, but just fractionally behind the rhythm of the live sound – this indicates that the recording is registering satisfactorily. If, however, the readings are very low, the meter is pulsing in a pattern unrelated to the flow of speech, or there is no level at all showing, then there is a fault with the recording and you must check your equipment before you continue.

If you have an engineer with you on location, he/she can monitor the whole interview on headphones, and can warn you of any problems such as **handling noise** or failing batteries. If your recorder has the 'monitor tape' option, the engineer should monitor on this setting; but be aware that if you are monitoring yourself you cannot listen on the 'tape' setting, as you will hear your own voice a split-second behind what you're actually saying – this makes it almost impossible to speak, which is why it's probably the worst practical joke that can ever be played on a presenter live on air!

Protecting your recordings

Having made your recordings, it is vital that you protect them against being lost, or recorded over. You should therefore label each tape clearly as soon as you take it out of the machine with the date, the subject (the speaker, or the topic) and if possible a reference number. An interview with a store manager called Vera Jones about shoplifting, which is your third tape for the assignment, could therefore be labelled:

27.4.97 SHOPLIFT/JONES 3

If you are using a cassette recorder it is also possible to protect the material from accidental recording-over by removing the little plastic tabs on the top edge of the cassette; this will stop the record button being pressed on most recorders. To re-use the cassette at a later stage you can cover over the exposed holes with a piece of sticky tape.

Activity

Try recording sound effects at different distances – close up, about a metre away, and several metres away – to obtain the best effect. You may find that the result is less effective if you always record close to the object.

Make sure you allow several seconds of silence (or neutral, non-intrusive background noise) before and after the effect to allow later editing, and to avoid the danger of microphone handling noise or recorder 'clicks' being recorded over the effect, or so close to it that it is not possible to edit easily.

Mono or stereo?

Most external or location recordings will be **monophonic**, using a single hand-held microphone. Mono is perfectly adequate for speech recording, and for most sound effects – although you should consider the value of **stereophonic** (twin-microphone) recording for effects such as a bustling office or a busy train station where there is a lot of movement. However, even a mono location recording can be placed in the stereo picture to creative effect once safely back in the studio.

By using stereo, you can move people and objects around in the theatre of the mind. You can position them within the **sound picture** to create a realistic scene with the listener at the centre of the action. For most stereophonic recordings, you will need the use of a studio.

Stereo picture – the relative positioning of different sound sources within the left- and righthand channels of a stereophonic recording; used to create a realistic sound picture which places the listener at the centre of the action, rather than as a passive observer. The positioning is achieved by panning individual sources to the left or right.

Studio recording

If you decide your commercial will feature two people talking in a pub, think about how you will create the image of the pub in sound. You can position your listener between the two characters at their table. To do this, you **pan** the microphone sources from the two actors, one slightly to the left and the other slightly to the right. Now when they talk you will hear one more loudly from the lefthand loudspeaker, and the other more loudly from the righthand loudspeaker. From a sound effects CD, you can add the sound of pints being pulled at one side or the other, and if you have a second CD player on your mixer, perhaps the sound of a fruit machine or people playing darts to the opposite side. Now, from tape or cassette you can add a general buzz of conversation without panning (so that it comes out with equal volume from both speakers) and when you listen with your eyes shut you will find you have created a realistic pub-type atmosphere.

Remember that you can place characters in the foreground or the background, and move them around, by using the correct microphone, the correct level and the correct microphone position. You can create intimacy by having a character speak softly into a microphone at relatively high **gain** from a close distance – this will sound to the listener like someone speaking close to their ear. By getting a character to speak loudly or shout further away from a microphone with the level turned down, you can create the effect of someone calling in the street, which would be heightened by adding a general outdoor atmosphere. You should experiment with different microphones, different microphone positions and different gain levels until you achieve the effect (or range of effects) you require.

Working with a partner, find a location in or near your school or college where there is some activity going on, such as children playing in a park, or workers repairing the road. Make sure you are sitting or standing in a safe place where you won't get in the way of other people.

One of you should then close your eyes (or wear a blindfold) and listen intently to the stereo sound picture. Working from left to right, describe the sounds you can hear to your partner, who writes them down. Then find another location and swap rôles. Afterwards discuss with other students how you would go about recreating the scene in a studio.

Mixing

To mix the different elements of your commercial together, you will require a mixing desk. This can range from a very simple mono unit with four inputs and a master output, to a much more sophisticated arrangement with eight, 12, 16 or more inputs to two, four or more outputs. In either case the basic principles are the same.

You need to set the **level** of each sound source using the gain control for that input. This determines how loud the voice, sound effect or music will be when the fader for that source is fully open.

Each source must be pre-set at the correct level so that the sound is neither too quiet nor too loud within the overall sound picture. If it is too quiet, it will require the listener to adjust the volume to a higher-than-normal setting; this will amplify background noise and **tape hiss**. If it is too loud, the recording will distort and this problem cannot be corrected at a later stage. Most desks will allow you to check the level of an input on the meter or on your headphones during a live broadcast or a recording by listening to it before you open the fader – this technique is known as **pre-fading**, and the control button will be labelled 'pre-fade', 'PFL' (pre-fade listen) or sometimes 'cue'.

The fader is the slider control which is used to set the level of different inputs against each other in the final mix. As the name suggests, opening or closing a fader slowly will fade the sound in or out. Closing the fader quickly will 'cut' or 'pot' the sound – the term 'pot' comes from the old-style rotary faders used in the early days of sound broadcasting, which were made of ceramic material, or pot.

Fig. 4.10
A simple mixer

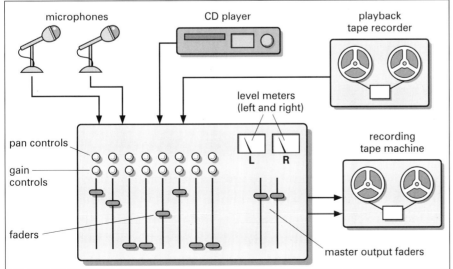

Input level

You should refer to the instructions for the desk you are using in order to understand the input level measurement system it uses. A simple desk may have a line of coloured lights (LEDs) which indicate green, yellow and red; in this case, set the levels so that all the green lights are illuminated most of the time, with the loudest bits (**peak level**) making the yellow lights come on. The red lights should never be illuminated as this indicates **distortion**.

Other desks will have a VU (volume units) meter; in this case the level should be set so that average level causes the needle to bounce up to the zero decibel (0 db) mark, with peaks bouncing slightly above this into the distortion zone. The 0 db position may also be marked as '100%' on the scale. These meters are very difficult to read as the needle usually moves about rapidly during speech and most music, but you must avoid the situation in which the needle is consistently in the distortion zone, or jammed against the end of the scale which indicates significant distortion.

More sophisticated desks will be equipped with a peak programme meter (PPM), which is calibrated from 1 to 7, and gives a much steadier reading. With a PPM, speech should normally be recorded in the range from 4 to 5, with the quietest sections registering no lower than 2, and the loudest peaks no higher than 6.

Special effects

If your desk hasn't got a reverb function, you can still create a simple echo effect using tape echo. To do this, open the fader on the desk slightly for the tape recorder you are recording on to. This will create feedback, normally a fault which will ruin recordings; if, however, you control the level of feedback carefully with the fader it will give you something which will pass as an echo effect.

Your desk may allow you to add special effects to sound sources; You may have 'EQ' controls which allow you to adjust different frequency ranges independently of each other. This will allow you, for example, to minimise an intrusive background hum on a tape by isolating the frequency and reducing it within the overall sound spectrum. You can also make a voice in the studio sound as if it is on the telephone by removing some of the bass (low) frequencies from the spectrum.

Another useful special effect is 'reverb', or **reverberation**. This creates an artificial 'echo' which can give a voice an eerie tone, or create the atmosphere for a cave (or a cathedral).

Assignment

By the time you finish this section you will have recorded all the material you will need to produce two audio products for your assessment – a radio commercial, and a news feature – having used the appropriate equipment throughout.

For your radio commercial you will need to make sure you have recorded all the voices and the sound effects you require. If you are using music, you must have the details of artist, title, composer, publisher and record label you will need for copyright clearance. As it is a relatively short production you should have a

near-finished product to carry forward to the editing stage in Section 3.

For your news feature, you should have all the interview material you require to put together a balanced package on your chosen topic. Make sure you have gathered all the background material you will need to write an informative introduction to the feature, and in particular make sure you have the proper names and titles for everyone you have interviewed – you will always need a first and a second name for everyone, as in most contexts just using a first name will sound over-familiar ('John says the new store will create 50 jobs'), whilst just using a family name will sound too formal ('Mr Iqbal thinks the museum is fantastic').

Make sure your tapes are clearly labelled, especially the master tape, and if possible protect your tapes against accidental erasure (for example, by removing the tabs from a standard audio cassette). Make sure your tapes are stored in a safe place well away from heat and from magnetic interference from TVs, computer monitors or other electrical equipment.

If you have recorded on open-reel tape it is normal practice to store master recordings **tail out**... that is, wound on to the right-hand take up spool so they must be rewound to the beginning before they can be played. This is to prevent the worst effects of print-through which can occur when magnetic tapes are stored for a long time. The magnetic information on each layer of tape can affect the recording on the next layer, thereby creating a phantom recording which will interfere with the signal on playback.

You must also write and maintain a log book in which you record the decisions made at each stage of the process, especially those relating to health and safety, and to the legal and ethical issues which you addressed. This should again be in the form of a diary (as you used for the production schedule in Section 1) noting every day what you did on the project, and what discussions you had before you made your decisions. Entries might look something like this:

'Monday April 29th

9.30

Had a meeting to decide who to interview for the news feature.

We all agreed to speak to John Smith, the store manager, about the new jobs it will create.

Tracey will contact the shopworkers' union to get a comment from them to make sure the feature is balanced with another point of view.

199

Naseem wanted to talk to the headteacher of the school next door to the new store, but we had a vote and decided that could make the piece too long.

Ryan and Gita telephoned John Smith, who said they could go round at 12 o'clock.

They signed out a tape recorder and tested it, checking all the connections.

They told the tutor where they were going, and agreed to stay together whilst they were out of college.'

You must be able to show your assessor that all the relevant health and safety issues have been addressed by your group, and that you are taking care to make sure your piece is fair and balanced, avoiding exploitation, sensationalism, and stereotypes. You must write up your log book neatly to hand in as an important part of your assignment.

3 Edit audio products

It is now time to take the recordings you made in Section 2 and translate them into the finished products for your assessment using a range of selection and editing techniques. Editing is the name given to the process by which the finished audio product is created by selecting and discarding elements of recorded material, and then assembling the selected elements together in the most effective way possible. It is the most creative part of the production process, as it gives you the opportunity to influence the way in which the messages contained within your feature are received by your listeners. As you edit your material you can think of yourself as a surgeon in sound – your skill can remove the imperfections from an individual speaker's words, helping him/her to communicate more effectively.

Editing takes time!

Editing will always take far longer than you anticipate. As a student just beginning to understand the technology you will need at least 30 minutes of editing time for each minute of the finished production.

When you start to edit your material you should ideally wear headphones. If you have to listen through a speaker you must make sure there will be no intrusion from other students trying to listen to their tapes nearby.

Technical considerations

In making your decisions about what material to include and what material to leave out, you are listening for both the content and the technical quality of the recordings. If you have followed the instructions in the last section, most of your material should be of an acceptable technical quality; but you will need to exclude material which shows any signs of:

- distortion – the words are difficult to hear because the recording level was set too high
- **sibilance** – the words are distorted through excessive hissing of 's' sounds in the higher frequency ranges, caused by bad microphone positioning
- tape hiss – the words are difficult to hear over the background hiss of the tape because the recording level was set too low
- noise – you can hear an old recording in the background, or a regular 'whooshing' noise, because the tape you recorded on was not wiped properly before you used it, or your recorder had a faulty erase head

- intrusive background noise – the background noise is too loud relative to the voice on tape, because you chose a noisy location, or the interviewee was too far away from the microphone
- inappropriate background noise – the material can't be used because something happened in the background which would not be appropriate on air; this could be swearing or laughter, or something like an aircraft passing overhead or a police siren passing the window
- **popping** – the interviewee's 'hard' sounds ('p's and 'b's) 'pop' because he/she is too close to the microphone
- handling noise – you can hear the sound of the microphone being moved about
- wind noise – you hear a 'rumble' on tape caused by wind passing the end of the microphone.

Inflection

Inflection is the name given to the rising and falling tones within speech. A speaker who uses little or no inflection will sound very boring as he/she is, quite literally, monotonous; using all one tone.

Rising inflections – the voice going up – usually indicate emphasis, as in 'I *told* you not to do that!' They also indicate, at the end of a phrase or sentence, that the speaker hasn't finished – 'Young people today don't know *how lucky they are*. We never had the chances they've got'. Avoid rising inflections at the end of the passages you cut from an interview wherever possible; most speakers finish their sentences on a falling inflection, which is a culturally understood device to indicate to the other people in the conversation that the speaker has finished saying what he/she wanted to say. Cutting a speaker off on a rising inflection has the same effect, in radio terms, as interrupting a speaker would have in a face-to-face conversation.

Falling inflections within quotes tend to indicate apology, or maybe dejection – 'I'm sorry about *the car*. I didn't know it *wasn't insured for me*. I'll pay you back *one day*.'

Selecting material for editing

In terms of content, you should discard material which you, as a listener, would find boring or difficult to understand. The best material to select is that which provokes a reaction from you when you hear it; if you sit up and take notice, so will your intended listener. Bear in mind the intended duration of the finished product. For your radio commercial, the material is already tightly scripted, and you are probably listening for the best 'take' in terms of the voice-overs (actors) working together well.

Editing conventions

Whatever technical system you use to edit, bear in mind that the objective is to make the editing process inaudible to the audience, who should perceive the finished product as a smooth flow of sound. This means that you should make as few edits as possible, concentrating instead on getting the right material on tape to start off with.

Although it is possible to 'construct' a quote word by word from the material recorded, this is not desirable. From a technical viewpoint, the manufactured quote will often sound jerky and unnatural – the tone of voice may fluctuate, and even if such fluctuations are within the range of normal speech, all meaning or **inflection** will have been removed from the speaker's words. Radio acts as a great amplifier of sincerity; it is also a great amplifier of insincerity. When the listener is deprived of visual clues as to the conviction of the speaker, he/she listens intently (if unconsciously) for the minute variations of tone and stress which can indicate emotion, emphasis or evasion. It can be confusing (or at worst misleading) to create such patterns artificially with a random or distorted selection of words and/or phrases from an interview.

Ethical considerations

Even though it is technically possible, no broadcaster could ever consider removing the word 'not' from the phrase 'I believe the man is not guilty'. To do so would not only misrepresent the speaker, flying in the face of broadcast regulation and opening the possibility of legal action for **defamation**, but it would also seriously damage the credibility of the broadcaster in all future interviews; if such manipulation could happen once, the listener will conclude, it could happen again. When making cuts simply in order to make an interviewee sound more deeply opinionated – by removing qualifying remarks following a strong statement, for example – ask yourself if you are in danger of misrepresenting the interviewee, or exploiting the individual for the purpose of entertaining your audience.

Where to begin

Try to avoid cutting in on passages which start with verbal punctuators – 'Well' or 'Obviously' and 'I think' are some of the most common, adding nothing to the comment and wasting precious airtime. Try instead to cut in on the start of a positive statement. For example, 'This road must be stopped, or children's lives are in danger' has greater impact than 'Well, – er – obviously I believe this road must be stopped or children's lives are in danger'.

When linking phrases together, make sure you leave or insert a natural pause between words – otherwise your edit is glaringly obvious even to the casual listener, as it would be impossible for the speaker to reproduce the vocal pattern you've created in real life without pausing or drawing breath.

If possible, edit on a 'hard' sound – 'p', 'b' or 't' – or on a breath, allowing a natural intake of breath before cutting to the new phrase, but you must be careful to avoid the technical trap of the '**double breath**' caused by leaving a breath on both the end of the first phrase and the beginning of the second. The result of this is a sound as if the interviewee has been startled, which is also near-impossible to reproduce in 'live' speech.

If you have a long-winded interviewee, who never seems to get to the end of his/her comment and repeatedly uses rising inflections, you can sometimes rescue the material by again cutting on a breath – this will sound less like an interruption (see the margin note on inflection). Ensure as far as possible that tone and inflection match in both phrases you are joining together. This is not always possible, especially in a speaker who uses a wide range of vocal tones, but you must avoid a sudden switch from a very high tone to a very low tone which again sounds grossly unnatural and exposes the editing process.

Putting in pauses

If you have to edit in an artificial pause in order to space words out, but there is no breath or natural pause at the end of the first phrase or the beginning of the second, you can still rescue the position by importing a pause from elsewhere in the interview. As a matter of habit you should record several seconds of room atmosphere – or wildtrack – with no speech over it, at either the beginning or the end of your interview – this will appear quite natural to the interviewee, who will assume you are simply thinking of what you are about to say. You can then take a few centimetres of this 'silence' to insert in the point where you need a pause, and on playback it will sound completely seamless. With a little practice you can vary the exact length to match the natural delivery of the speaker, and even tailor it in such a way to add extra emphasis to the phrase which follows by adding a 'dramatic' pause.

Never insert blank tape or leader as a way of creating a pause – the sudden absolute silence, with complete absence of background atmosphere, will be obvious to the listener, and will again expose the fact that the material has been edited.

Activity

In a group, listen to a number of tapes recorded by group members. Discuss which quotes sound the most effective, and decide where it would be best to cut in at the start to give a positive feel to the quote.

Editing techniques

You are now ready to start editing your material. There are three main techniques you can use to do this.

Paper edits

A paper edit involves making the decisions about what to use and what to leave out on paper, without actually cutting or dubbing your material.

A paper edit can speed up the time you spend in the studio actually manipulating your material, and is ideal if there are a lot of students wishing to use the same studio or editing suite. The only equipment you need, apart from pen and paper, is a tape recorder to play back the material you recorded in the last section.

You should **transcribe** – write down what is said on the tapes, remembering that what you write must be accurate if you are to find the material later. If your tape recorder has a counter, set the counter to zero when the tape starts, and log the number showing on the counter alongside the point where important passages start. This will also help you find your material more easily. If there are sections of tape which you know you will be unable to use, don't waste time transcribing these sections; instead just mark down the numbers where they start and finish.

Activity

Listen to about two minutes of one of your interviews, transcribing the words exactly as they are said (including 'ums', 'errs' and repetitions). This will take up about a side and a half of A4 paper. Read back the transcript, and underline or highlight those sections you would want to keep in the finished production. Then put brackets around those sections you would want to cut out. Listen to the tape again, following the highlighted transcript, and check that you will actually be able to make the cuts you want whilst maintaining a natural flow to the interviewee's delivery. There must be no sudden changes of fast to slow speech, and the inflections must be compatible as far as possible.

Dub edits

Dub edits are perhaps the easiest edits to do in a studio; they also avoid the problems which can arise if you make a mistake whilst splice editing, which can destroy your original recordings. However, you must be aware that every time you dub from one tape to another, you lose a 'generation' of quality in the recording. Even with broadcast-standard equipment, the loss of quality is very noticeable by the third or fourth generation, and even a second generation cassette-to-cassette recording can show signs of deterioration.

When dub editing, you must be sure never to **clip** a word at the start or finish of a section you require, as that material cannot be recovered; if in doubt, allow a little too much material to transfer across. Quite often it is possible to tidy up a dub-edited recording by splice editing a junction at a later stage.

The technique of dub editing is quite simple. You will require two tape recorders, linked so that the output socket of the machine you are using for playing back your original tapes feeds into the input socket of the machine on which you are recording your master tape (or you can feed one or more playback machines into a mixer, with the mixer output going to your master tape).

You must first set the output level of your playback machine to avoid distortion, then set the level of your recording machine as described in the last section. Put the recording machine into record mode, but with the pause control engaged. When you get to a section on your playback machine you wish to dub across on to the master tape, make a note of the tape counter reading, or make a note of the words immediately before the section you require. Then rewind your source tape a few seconds, and play it again. As you hear the words just before the section you require, or as you see the counter coming up to the reading, release the pause control on the recording machine. Let both machines run until you reach

Fig. 4.11
Dub edit setup

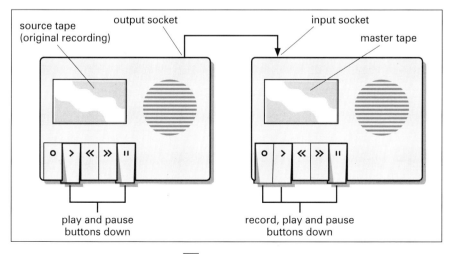

source tape (original recording)   output socket   input socket   master tape

play and pause buttons down

record, play and pause buttons down

the end of the section you require – at which point you should press the pause button on the recording machine again.

With a little practice you will find it is possible to be quite accurate with this technique, although you should bear in mind that it can never be as accurate as the splice method.

Activity

Working with a partner or in a small group, practise doing a few dub edits, using the tapes you transcribed for paper editing in the activity on page 205. This time, try to make the cuts you identified in that activity by using the pause button on your master recorder. You will find it is difficult at first to get the timing right, as you must anticipate when the words you need are coming, rather than waiting until you have heard them (which is too late!).

Splice edits

Splice edits are the norm in all newsrooms and broadcast organisations where speed and quality are more important than the preservation of the original recording, and where quarter-inch tape is the medium commonly used. To carry out splice edits you will require an **editing block**, a **Chinagraph pencil** and a single-edged razor blade or scalpel.

Listen to the playback on headphones if you can; it will help you exclude all other sounds, and concentrate on the job in hand. When you reach the start of the section you require, stop the machine and put it into edit mode. The controls may be labelled 'edit', 'cue' or with a symbol indicating a cut. This causes the tape to be held in contact with the playback head, but without moving either forwards or backwards; the brakes are off, and as you rock the tape slowly backwards and forwards across the heads you will hear the recorded sound at the speed you move the tape – if you move it quickly, you will hear the words too fast, in a sort of 'cartoon voice'; if you move it slowly, the sounds you hear will be very deep, almost unrecognisable as speech. Try to develop the technique of moving the tape at around the speed it would normally play at. This will help you locate the point at which you need to edit more quickly as you will hear the words sounding more or less normal.

When you find the word you wish to start on, stop the tape and wind it back slowly until you hear silence; this will be the start of the word. It's always easier if the word starts on a 'hard' sound like a 'p' or a 'b', as the transition will be very clear; it's more difficult if it starts with an 's' or an 'f' where the sound tends to build more slowly, and it's harder to decide where the gap between words ends. This is also a problem if your interviewee slurs his/her words, or speaks very quickly. Having identified what you believe to be the start of the first word of the passage you require, you should mark the point where the tape rests on the recorder's

Safety

When using a razor blade or scalpel, you must always take extreme care: *never* cut on any surface other than an editing block, and *never* pull the blade towards yourself. Take care with loose blades in your work environment: *never* put blades on a tape spool or the bed of a tape machine – they can fly off at high speed if the machine is started. Make sure there is a policy for disposing of old blades safely (normally in a strong sealed box with a slit in the top just large enough to drop a blade through). Make sure there is a first-aid kit available in case of accidents. Remember as well that when using open-reel machines you should *never* attempt to stop moving spools with your fingers; use the stop control, and wait for them to stop moving before you touch them. This is especially important if you are using metal spools, which can cut your fingers very easily; if possible, always use plastic spools.

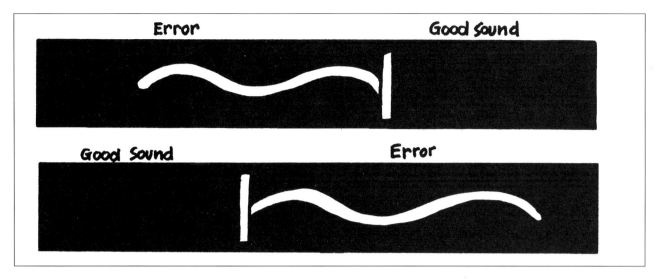

Fig. 4.12
Marking the tape
for a splice edit

Fig. 4.13
Cutting a splice edit

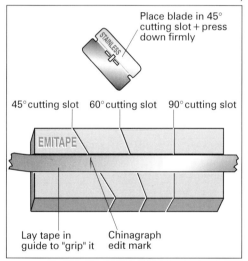

Place blade in 45°
cutting slot + press
down firmly

45°cutting slot   60°cutting slot   90°cutting slot

EMITAPE

Lay tape in   Chinagraph
guide to "grip" it edit mark

playback head with a single vertical line across the tape with your Chinagraph pencil.

Take care not to write on the head itself, and never attempt to mark your tape with anything other than a chinagraph pencil as ball-point pens, HB pencils, etc. will damage the head. Then start the recorder using the play button; if you have found the correct point, the tape will start on the precise word you require. As a double check, rewind the tape a short distance and play it again; watch as your mark passes the playback head. Is it in the right place for the start of the passage you want?

Once you are satisfied your mark is correct, you should lift the tape carefully from the machine, and lay it gently along the edit block with your mark roughly in line with the cutting slot. As you press the tape gently into the horizontal groove, the block will grip the tape allowing you to slide it around until your mark is precisely in line with the cutting slot. Then you should take your razor blade and lay it gently in the slot. The tape should cut cleanly without any need to 'saw' backwards and forwards – if it won't cut easily, you may have a blade which is blunt, or you may not be letting the block do the work for you; you must let the slot guide the blade, and not attempt to slash at the tape yourself.

As this is the start of your chosen extract, you must now fasten a piece of **leader tape** on to it.

Take a length of leader tape (at least a metre) and put one end in the editing block, as you did before. Cut the end using your blade in the editing slot so that it matches the end of your recording. Then slide the two cut edges together, so they are just touching without overlapping. You then need to take a short length of **splicing tape** (about 3 cm), and with your finger and thumb gently lay this along the groove so that half of it lies at each side of the join. This will take a little practice at first, but after a while you will be able to lay the tape neatly in position – the groove will help you ensure it is lying straight. When you are satisfied the splicing

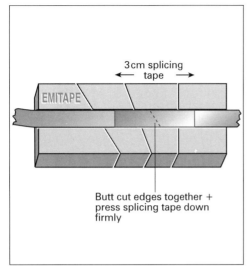

3cm splicing
← tape →

EMITAPE

Butt cut edges together +
press splicing tape down
firmly

Fig. 4.14
A completed splice edit

Full track mono is a mono recording carried on the full width of a ¼ inch audio tape, which will play back through both left and right channels if played on stereo equipment. Half track mono is a mono recording which is carried on only half the width of a ¼ inch audio tape, and will play back through the lefthand channel only when played on stereo equipment. Some portable tape recorders (such as Uher) are designed to record half track to allow the reporter to turn the tape over if it runs out. Be aware that if you do so, playing it back on stereo equipment will result in the second track running backwards on the righthand channel of the stereo – and playing on a full track mono machine will result in the sound being garbled as the 'backwards' track is superimposed on the recording you want. To prevent these problems, make sure that your tapes are erased thoroughly before you start recording on a half track machine.

tape is in the right place, press it down gently. As you apply pressure the splicing tape will stick firmly; but you must make sure you have stuck it down evenly at both sides of the join.

You can then edit further passages to the end of the first passage you have selected, and more leader tape at the end of the selected material.

Activity

If you have access to splice editing equipment, practice a few splice edits using a spool of tape you are not going to use for your assignment – maybe an interview you have discarded, or an old interview someone else has done. Take great care with handling the blades, and read the safety note before you start. You should also wash and dry your hands before you start, to reduce the chance of putting grease or moisture on to the tape. Make sure you place the splicing tape neatly over the edit, so as not to leave any sticky surface exposed – and use at least 3 cm of tape for each edit, so there is less risk of the edit pulling apart by the force of the spools going around.

Which leader tape should I use?

The following will help you select the most appropriate leader tape to use.

White:	Start of mono *full track* tape
Green:	Start of mono *half track* tape (Uher tape)
Red and white striped '*tiger tape*':	Start of stereo tape
Yellow:	Interbanding (gaps between bands)
Red:	End of tape (all formats)

In practice, colour coding conventions vary between broadcast organisations.

The one important rule is never to use red leader other than at the end of a tape, as to use it at the start could cause the tape to be played out back-to-front if an engineer assumes he/she has been given the tape 'tail out'.

Electronic editing

With the widespread adoption of personal computers in news organisations, a number of software packages are now available for digital editing of recordings. The material is first loaded into the computer as a sound file, either in real time from an analogue tape (such as a cassette

Fig. 4.15
Electronic editing

recorder) or in data form from a floppy disk. The file can then be played back and manipulated in many ways by using a cursor on the PC screen. This new technology combines the best qualities of splice editing (precision, no loss of quality) with the benefits of dub editing (if you make a mistake, your original material can be recovered). There is no doubt that digital sound editing will be the norm in broadcast organisations within a very few years; however, at the moment no one software system has emerged as the clear standard for the industry.

Editing your own work for assessment

The radio commercial

Remember that your edited commercial must be exactly the right length, as you agreed when you negotiated the brief with your client. As it is a relatively short product, with the opportunity to re-record it if anything goes wrong, your assessor will be looking for a high standard of technical quality. Make sure the finished commercial starts and finishes cleanly, with leader tape of the correct colour if you have done it on reel-to-reel tape. You should label it with the name of the client, the title of the script, your name, the tape speed and format (if a reel-to-reel recording) and the duration. For example:

ACME TOYSHOP, 'ELVES'. JO SMITH 7 1/2 ips Stereo Dur 30".

The news feature

Editing the news feature is likely to be a much more time-consuming process, because unlike your commercial the feature will not have been scripted in advance. You must construct the feature from the interviews you have carried out. The simplest form of feature would consist of a single interview, edited to the required duration. Aim for a good, strong beginning to such a piece, which is going to grab the attention of the audience. A long interview of this sort will have a logical flow to it, and will have a beginning, a middle and an end. Such a flow is likely to be chronological, explaining what has happened in the past, what is happening now, and what could happen in the future. If you edit your material in this form, you will have to write a brief cue – introduction – which a presenter could read out on the air before playing the tape.

Look at the example of a cue below.

---

(1) PETITION   **(2)** RH for **(3)** 27 April

(4)
Protesters from Happy Valley in Harrogate are to present a 500-name petition to the district council next week... demanding a start on the estate's long-awaited by-pass.

(5)
They say politicians of all parties have failed to back promises with action...

Ann Angry, who chairs the residents' action group, says they now fear for the safety of youngsters who live near Valley Drive...

(6)
PETITION

dur: 2' 31"   **(7)**

o/c we wait?   **(8)**

---

(1) TITLE for the story
(2) YOUR NAME or INITIALS – who wrote the story that went to air?
(3) DATE story is to be USED
(4) MAIN TEXT, separate from heading, double spaced with at least 2 cm margins to allow for any late corrections and additions by hand
(5) NEW SENTENCE = NEW LINE helps the presenter to cut the story short if time is a problem by creating 'natural breaks' in the text. Always put the in-line – the line which introduces the audio – on a new line.
(6) LEAVE SPACE before tape details – note repeat of title (1)
(7) DURATION of the feature in minutes and seconds
(8) **OUT CUE** (O/C), the last words the newsreader will hear before he/she is to begin speaking again.

If you have done two or more interviews for your feature, you will need to wrap them together by writing and recording linking scripts. You will still need to write a cue, as above, but your **in-line** – the line which introduces the feature – will introduce your report.

PETITION   RH for 27 April

Protesters from Happy Valley in Harrogate are to present a 500-name petition to the district council next week... demanding a start on the estate's long-awaited by-pass.

They say politicians of all parties have failed to back promises with action...

Jo Smith reports...

PETITION

dur: 2' 31"

o/c next week

Your reporter – Jo Smith – will then write and record on to tape a brief introduction to the piece, along the lines of:

> 'It's been three years since Harrogate Council promised a by-pass for the Happy Valley estate – and protesters, like Ann Angry, a mother with three small children, says she fears for the safety of all youngsters in the area...'

You then edit the introduction on to the start of the interview with Ann Angry. At the end of the first interview, you then record another **link**, which introduces the second interviewee and explains his/her part in the story:

> 'But the Chair of Harrogate Highways Committee, Councillor Bill Bloggs, says the money just isn't available to start work on the by-pass immediately... although they still consider it a priority...'

You then edit this link on to the start of the second interview, and so on until you have included all the speakers you are going to use. In a short news feature you are unlikely to use more than two, or at the most three, interviews. At the end of the last interview your reporter must record a few words which sum up the story.

> 'So whilst the mothers of Happy Valley are unhappy with the situation, councillors claim everything possible is being done to make the roads in the area safe for young families. This is Jo Smith reporting from Harrogate.'

Assignment

You must now prepare your two final tapes for assessment – edited, labelled and cued. You will also need to provide your assessor with a copy of the script, notes of what editing was required and what techniques were used to carry it out, and log sheets with notes on the technical recording quality.

Check that your feature is:

- well balanced
- edited in a smooth and logical way
- easy on the ear
- informative
- of interest to the target audience.

Review and evaluate audio products

Having completed production of the two audio products required for your assessment, you must now evaluate the effectiveness of the audio products in serving their purpose. For this you will need to arrange a playback session involving students, tutors and a representative group of outsiders who have not been involved in the production process. You should give each participant an evaluation sheet – see below.

Ideally, you should invite your clients to attend the playback session. It may be difficult for all clients to attend, but even a few would add greatly to the reality of the assessment. You could also invite one or more professionals – a journalist or commercial producer from your local radio station, or someone with experience of running a student or hospital broadcasting service.

The audience will need to hear the tapes played back through good quality speakers in order to evaluate technical quality; ideally, they should be in a room with few visual distractions so as to concentrate their attention on the audio messages.

As an alternative, if it is not possible to gather people together for review purposes, you could consider duplicating copies of your material and distributing it to them for review, together with an evaluation sheet.

The evaluation sheet

The evaluation sheet could, for example, ask your audience to give marks out of ten in the following categories.

For the news feature

Recording quality (1 = poor quality, 10 = broadcast quality)
Quality of editing (1 = poor quality, 10 = broadcast quality)
Quality of mixing (1 = poor quality, 10 = broadcast quality)
Interest to the assessor as an individual (1 = boring, 10 = very interesting)
Relevance to the general community served (1 = irrelevant, 10 = very
    relevant)

Relevance of interviewees (1 = wrong people interviewed, 10 = all the right people interviewed)

Journalistic balance (1 = highly unbalanced, 10 = fair and impartial)

Appropriate use of language in the script (1 = wrong language used, 10 = right language used)

Appropriate use of music and sound effects (1 = inappropriate use, 10 = appropriate use)

Originality of subject and/or treatment (1 = clichéd, 10 = original and unusual)

Giving a total mark out of 100.

For the radio commercial

Recording quality (1 = poor quality, 10 = broadcast quality)

Quality of editing (1 = poor quality, 10 = broadcast quality)

Quality of mixing (1 = poor quality, 10 = broadcast quality)

Appropriate use of language in the script (1 = sounds like reading aloud, 10 = sounds natural)

Casting of voices (1 = wrong voices used, 10 = right voices used)

Use of theatre of the mind (1 = little use of images, 10 = good use of images)

Relevance to the assessor as an individual (1 = boring, 10 = very interesting)

Relevance to target audience (1 = irrelevant, 10 = very relevant)

Originality of subject and/or treatment (1 = clichéd, 10 = original and unusual)

Would this ad make me more likely to try the product? (1 = very unlikely, 10 = highly likely)

Giving a total mark out of 100.

Assignment

1 **Members of the audience, or your review panel, should be invited to make brief comments – written or verbal – about the audio products after they are played, and these comments should be noted down and submitted, together with the evaluation sheets, as part of your assessment. Clients, in particular, should be invited to indicate how closely they believe the product you have created matches up to the original production brief, and to their own 'self-image' of their organisation.**

You should also make separate notes about the audience reaction as your piece is being played. Where do the audience laugh? Where do they give their full attention to the piece, and where do they yawn or fidget?

This observed reaction can be as important as the comments and marks you receive on your evaluation sheets, and your notes on it should be included with your work for assessment.

2 Now try to compare your audio products with real broadcast products. In what areas are your efforts as good as those you hear on the radio, and in what areas are they not as good? Write a brief self-assessment of your audio products (about 300 words) in which you are as honest as you can be about your own faults. How far can these be explained by using inferior equipment, or by lack of experience? What would you do differently next time?

3 Finally, you should write another self-assessment (again of around 300 words) in which you state what you've learnt about your own abilities whilst you've been doing this unit. What aspects of the audio production process do you enjoy the most? What do you enjoy the least? Where do you feel you were able to contribute the most to group efforts? Where will you have to concentrate your efforts in future? It may help if you discuss these questions privately with other group members, and share your feelings, before you write your self-assessments.

Having completed your audio products for assessment, you may wish to consider taking the material to a wider audience. One way of doing this would be to approach a local community broadcaster in your area. Although the 'established' BBC and Independent Radio stations are unlikely to be interested in broadcasting a student-produced tape (for a number of good reasons, including issues of editorial control and copyright as well as considerations of technical and journalistic quality) you may find a student or hospital station, or a **Restricted Service Licence (RSL)** community broadcaster which would be happy to use the material. But before you pass any tape you have recorded to any broadcast organisation, you must make sure that everyone who appears on the tape is willing for you to do so; some organisations have strict rules about who may speak to the media, and whilst local representatives may be willing to speak to you on tape to help a student project, they may not give their consent to a 'real' broadcast.

You must also have (and pass on to the broadcaster) full **Performing Rights Society (PRS)** details for any pre-recorded music which you use in your feature, and written permission to broadcast any original music (such as a musical written and performed by schoolchildren) you include.

If you pass on your radio commercial to a broadcaster, again be aware of the copyright issues, especially those relating to commercially recorded music (for which the penalties for unauthorised commercial use can be severe) but also watch out for problems which could arise if your commercial is very similar to one already in use by an established broadcaster; you could be accused of infringing copyright on the idea.

Summary

In this unit you have examined the processes that go into the making of audio products which are received by mass audiences across an ever-increasing range of outlets; not only on broadcast radio stations, but in other situations such as public address systems in stores and shopping centres, pre-recorded audio magazines for specific audiences or consumer groups and talking guides for tourists. You should now appreciate the planning which goes into the production of such materials, both in the choice of appropriate styles for putting specific messages across, and the selection of suitable interviewees.

Glossary

ambient noise the pre-existing background noise in a location

analogue recording or transmission in which sound is represented by means of variations in voltage or wave-form

brightness an expression of the degree of echo present in a location – very bright = lots of echo

Chinagraph pencil soft, waxy pencil used to mark the position of edits on audio tape. It will not harm the playback head on the tape recorder

clip, clipped a mistake in editing which causes part of a word to be lost

commercial producer (comprod) a producer engaged in the making of radio commercials, as opposed to the making of programmes

contempt of court actions which interfere with the legal process and/or the authority of a court of law

cue either a script which is read by a presenter or newsreader before an interview or package is played or the action of locating the exact point at which a piece of audio begins, and/or preparing the piece to be played when instructed

cuts material which is removed during editing

defamation injury to a person's reputation by means of libel or slander

digital recording or transmission in which sound is represented in numeric data, as in a computer file

distortion a fault in recording or transmission in which sound quality is lost because the level is too high

double breath a fault in editing in which an interviewee's breath at the end of one statement is edited onto a breath at the start of a second statement – giving the impression of two intakes of breath

dub editing the process of editing by recording selected passages from one tape to another

dynamic range the range of sound frequencies which can be detected or handled by a piece of equipment

editing block a device to hold audio tape firmly whilst it is cut, which also has grooves to guide the editor's blade so as to ensure a consistent angle of cut

fader a control which allows the level of different sound sources to be manipulated on a mixing desk; thereby allowing individual sound sources to be introduced or removed from the overall sound picture

feedback the noise created when the output of a sound recorder is fed straight back into the input channel of that recorder, thereby creating a sound loop (or screech)

gain the degree of amplification applied to a sound source during recording or mixing

generation the number of times an original recording has been copied, usually during mixing or dub editing

handling noise noise on a recording caused by handling the microphone, microphone stand or cables

in-line the words in a cue which come immediately before an interview or package is to be played

inflection the tone of voice of an interviewee which can determine the meaning of the words used

leader tape coloured non-magnetic tape of the same width and thickness as magnetic recording tape used to indicate the beginning and end of a recording on open reel tape

level the measured loudness of a sound recording

libel an untrue statement which injures a person's reputation in published (written or broadcast) form

link a scripted passage which links together two pieces of audio; the bridge between two elements of a package or wrap

location a place chosen for conducting a recording other than a recording studio, either indoors or outdoors

monitoring listening to a recording in progress so as to check that the sound is being recorded properly

monophonic a recording designed to be heard on a single loudspeaker, or where there is no variation of sound between multiple speakers

niche audience a specialised, usually small audience sharing strong common tastes or interests

omnidirectional a microphone which picks up sound evenly from all directions

open questions questions which cannot be answered yes or no – normally those beginning Who, What, Where, Why, When or How

out cue the last words or sounds heard on a recording before it finishes

pan moving a sound around within a stereophonic audio picture so as to give in a specific location to the left or right; can be used to indicate movement

peak level the highest audio level of a recording or sound source

popping a fault in recording in which the interviewee's plosive sounds ('p's and 'b's) distort; usually caused by having the microphone too close to the interviewee's mouth

pre-fading checking a sound source on a mixing desk separately (on headphones, meter or loudspeaker) before introducing it to the audio picture being recorded or transmitted; usually done to ensure that the correct sound source is present, and at the correct level

PRS Performing Rights Society; PRS details = the information required from users by the Performing Rights Society

RSL Restricted Service Licence: a licence granted by the Radio Authority for a specific short-term broadcast or series of broadcasts, usually of 28 days

reverberation an audio effect in which an 'echo' is electronically applied to a sound source during the mixing stage; used to create atmosphere, or to add extra power to a singing voice

royalty payment due to an artist, musician or writer for use of his/her copyright material

sibilance a fault in recording which emphasises the interviewee's 's' sounds; often caused by bad microphone position

sound picture the image created in the mind of a listener by a sound or combination of sounds

splice edit an edit in which recording tape is physically cut with a blade and reassembled using sticky tape

splicing tape special sticky tape used for splice editing. It has the correct width to match the audio tape, and peels off easily until it is pressed down firmly, after which it is very difficult to remove

stereophonic a recording made using two or more microphones which is designed to be heard on a pair of loudspeakers, or headphones in which a different signal is sent to left and right ears. Used to create a realistic audio picture in which the listener has the illusion of being present at the scene of the recording.

tail out an open-reel tape which is stored with the end of the recording, or tail, on the outside of the spool so it must be rewound before being played

tape hiss a fault in recording in which the normally inaudible background noise of the recording tape is amplified to a high level, caused by the recording level being too low

transcribe to write out the words spoken on a recording

vari-speed to alter the playback speed of a recording, either to compensate for an error in the recording speed so as to make the speech sound normal, or to modify the speech for creative effect

voice-over an actor in a radio commercial

vox pop interviews in which members of the public are asked to comment on a subject for inclusion within a feature; normally edited so as to reflect varying points of view. From the Latin 'vox populi' = 'voice of the people'

wildtrack recording of background noise from a specific location, usually without recognisable speech; used as a background to an interview or series of interviews recorded elsewhere when mixed at a later stage

wind noise fault on a recording caused by wind blowing onto or across the end of a microphone; creates a 'booming' or 'crackling' sound

wind shield device used to prevent wind noise by protecting the end of a microphone from exposure to wind currents, without muffling other sounds; usually a shaped ball of foam rubber

Producing moving image products

Contents

LONGMAN

Introduction

In the first section of this study unit you will be looking at how you plan a moving image product. You will be able to use some of your ideas and plans produced in Study Unit 2. You will be able to demonstrate that you understand basic research and planning and that you can write down evidence of your own work and your team's work.

You will find that in every visual production process there are preparatory tasks which involve both writing and recording using different media. You will investigate these processes by undertaking activities and assignments that will give you the chance to produce real media products. You will learn why it is important to keep detailed written records of planning, progress and production.

In Section 2 you will learn how to record using video equipment and professional techniques. The same techniques can be translated to the making of a film or animation programme. You will be able to make decisions about the suitability of material that you record, rectify any production problems that you identify in the recording process and keep records of health and safety issues.

In Section 3 you will learn about the editing processes which are vital to the production process. You will be able to make decisions about your recorded material, identify issues relating to the recorded material and add special effects to your work. You will deal with any issues that were discussed earlier and develop new skills both as an individual and as a team member. By the end of this section you will have produced two moving image products.

At the end of this unit (in Section 4) you will develop skills in reviewing and evaluating your work. This is vital for all media professionals who rely on the feedback from an audience. You cannot be sure of the quality of your product without your audience's evaluation. How to go about getting their views is discussed, and you will be given guidance on how to react to their criticism.

1 Pre-production: Planning the production process

Every one of the programmes you watch on television tonight, or every newspaper article you read today, has been through a process of research, planning and recording with an audience in mind. For example, a programme detailing the development of the motor car may not appeal to small children, whereas a comic strip cartoon may not appeal to a teenager thinking about purchasing his/her first car. The target audience for visual products will have been carefully researched before any scripts have been written, photographs shot or sound recorded. In broadcast television the competition between the BBC and Independent Television companies can dictate the station's output. Every Christmas there is a battle between the two to see who can win the bigger audience with their programming. Why do you think that the ITV companies want their viewing figures to be high? They are reliant on their income from advertisers and if viewers do not watch their programmes then they do not see their advertisements. In the USA the audience reaction to programmes is very carefully monitored and if the viewing figures of a programme drop then that programme is taken off the air. Matching the audience to the product is very important.

The target audience

Activity

Choose a television programme that has been broadcast (via terrestrial TV, cable or satellite). The programme should be from a particular genre (type) of programme. For the purpose of this activity choose something that is quite short. Watch the programme and then answer the following questions:

1 **At what time was the programme broadcast?**

2 **What channel was it broadcast on?**

3 **Who do you think the target audience was?**

4 **Why was it shown at this time?**

Were you able to decide the target audience and did the time of broadcast influence your decision? There are restrictions about when certain things can be broadcast on television and what can be shown in a film. Later in this section we will be looking at this in greater detail. Obviously the audience for different programmes may be determined by the nature of its contents. Some television channels show minority types of programmes, subjects that do not appeal to mass audiences. Sometimes channels deliberately place one programme in direct opposition to programmes on other channels.

Activity

1 Using a national newspaper and a local newspaper, carefully examine the news coverage of both of them. Make a note of the kind of news stories that each one covers. Note down the geographical area that these stories relate to and if possible the name and title of the reporter. What indications are there to the nature of local and national newspaper reporting?

2 Do the same exercise for a local and national news programme on television.

A local newspaper will present issues that are important to its local readership whereas a national newspaper will be giving a much wider scope to its readers. This will also be reflected in its advertising. There is no point in advertising a local service in a national newspaper. Advertisers carefully plan their campaigns to target an appropriate audience. This applies to commercial television stations that need to attract viewers. One of the most expensive slots for advertisers is the break in *News at Ten*. In the past companies have tried to outbid each other for this prime slot. An average cost for a 15 second advertisment in this slot can be as much as £25,000.

Activity

Why is the *News at Ten* slot so popular with advertisers? Write down your thoughts and discuss them with your group.

Is it because the programme has credibility and this reflects on the product? Is it that the programme is watched by millions of viewers and the advertiser can reach more people? An average audience for *News at Ten* is 8.5 million compared to the BBC equivalent news broadcast at nine o'clock which does not even appear in the ***Broadcast/BARB*** top 70.

By now you should understand that the audience for a moving image product will impact upon the planning and production of the product. If you have a school or college prospectus read it carefully and then think about its target audience. Does the prospectus have photographs and if it does what do the photographs show? Are there images of people being unhappy? Is your school or college shown as being dirty and inhospitable? The answer to these last two questions is no, of course: the audience for these publications is prospective clients. A great deal of planning has gone into these publications. See if you can find out who did the research and planning and ask him/her about why this material in particular was used.

If your school or college has a video programme or tape/slide presentation that is shown to prospective students, do the same criteria apply? What other aspects could be shown in a video or tape/slide presentation that are missing in a paper prospectus?

Production rôles

When you begin to look into the research and planning of moving image products you will see that an individual working alone would find it very difficult to produce a quality product. In a typical video production there will be a considerable number of people involved in the production process. The following are just some of the people involved in *Road Safety for Primary Schools*, a programme that you will be following later in this section.

- *The director* is responsible for turning the script into the visual medium of television or film.
- *A camera operator* works with the camera getting the best possible camera shots under the guidance of the director.
- *A sound recordist* is primarily concerned with recording the best possible sound and working as a team with the camera operator.
- *An editor* works with the **camera original** material and links together the shots required for the finished film or video programme, working closely with the director in the editing suite.
- *A vision mixer* operates the equipment that mixes and **wipes** the television signal that comes from each camera. He/she would normally work in a television studio but is equally at home in a location outside broadcast vehicle.
- *A production assistant* is the vital link between the director and the crew, keeping notes of the requirements of the production and ensuring that everything runs smoothly.
- *The lighting director* is responsible for the design and control of the lights being used in a production. He/she will work closely with the director to create the right effect for each scene.
- *The floor manager* has control over the studio floor and acts as the director's eyes and ears with the responsibility of making sure that actors and crew are at the right place and on time.
- *The presenter* fronts a programme, making links between sections and introducing acts.
- *The interviewer* prepares and asks questions in a studio or location setting.

All these people have their own jobs to do to the best of their ability. Some people are good at research and some are good at planning. Other people have the ability to produce excellent camera shots and others can record good quality sound tracks. Bringing all of these people together to form a team should lead to the making of a quality product.

Remember that if you work as a team member you should keep your own records of the work that you do. Later you will look at evaluating your work and the work of your team. It is a good idea to keep a diary of all the skills that you learn and all the work that you undertake.

223

Activity

Working on your own, produce a list of the production rôles for the following:

- a television production, for example a drama
- a feature film.

To help you make a list of rôles watch a television programme and a film, then note down all of the jobs listed. It may be easier to list all of the jobs if you watch a video copy, play through the credits at the end, stopping and starting the tape as necessary. Once you have listed them do some initial research into each job and give a brief description of what it involves. To do this, use the resources of your library to help you find out the names and addresses of organisations that work in the media, for example the Independent Television Commission or broadcast trade union (BECTU).

You have begun to carry out your own research into a job rôle that you might want to develop later.

Teamwork

It is essential that you develop skills in working as a team member. Media teams rely on all the members working together in a professional manner. Imagine the scenario of arriving to film the local Member of Parliament in your studio. You will need a crew to operate the cameras, sound and lights. What would happen if your crew members were not able to work together or were constantly doing each other's jobs? What type of product would result? What impression would this give to the client?

What do you think are the benefits or drawbacks of working in a team? Will you be able to share out the rôles within your own moving image products?

You will have to take part in meetings to plan your products or to allocate production rôles. The following outline may help you to arrange effective meetings.

- Arrange a time and suitable room for the meeting.
- Decide who will be in the chair and, if necessary, hold a ballot for this job.
- Arrange for someone to take over in the absence of the chairperson.
- Decide who will take notes and distribute them to the team members.
- Allocate rôles according to individual skills or preferences (these rôles can be changed for later projects).
- Plan a date for the next meeting when an initial project can be discussed.

The following example is taken from the minutes of a production meeting held to discuss the initial stages of *Road Safety for Primary Schools*. You will be following the development of this programme as you work through this chapter. These minutes give you an idea of the format to use and the information that you need to record.

Fig. 5.1
Minutes of production planning meeting

Minutes of meeting held on Friday 4th July 1994 in Room 44, Main Studios, High Street, Birmingham

Present John Smith (Director), Bill Jones (Producer), Ann Robinson (Cameraperson), Don Chow (Sound), Yasmin Hassan (Lighting), Mary Boulton (Production Assistant)

Apologies Mary Jones (Publicity)

1 J. S. requested that all crew members be made aware of the nature of the next production, namely a documentary on road safety, currently undergoing a final script edit.

2 A. R. stated that the new camera equipment would be available for the shoot and that all resources had been booked.

3 B. J. reported that all actors had confirmed their availability.

4 Y. H. had inspected the locations with B. J. and could confirm that all necessary Health and Safety issues identified at the last meeting had been recorded and resolved.

5 Next meeting to be held at 11.00 am on Monday 3rd August at Main Studios.

The product

In order to satisfy the evidence indicators for this part of the unit you must produce two production/shooting scripts that are supported by an agreed programme brief, lists of resources and technical requirements, reconnaissance notes and a production schedule. You will have undertaken preliminary planning and research in Study Unit 2 and these ideas could now be developed as part of this section.

Before you can start the planning process you need to be clear about the nature of the products you can produce. Although the emphasis in the following pages is on video production you will still be able to work in film in order to satisfy the following criteria:

- *Video* This may be in any video format that you have available. You may be able to use a video camcorder to record your material. You may have a more professional camera and recorder using **Low** or **High band UMatic formats**. It does not really matter which format you use.

225

Emphasis will be on developing production techniques that allow you to make two or more programmes.

- *Film* Film formats could be 8 mm film or even 16 mm if you have the resources available. The production processes for film and video are similar and you may be able to make one film and one video programme.

Agreeing the brief

The work undertaken in Study Unit 2 will have produced some ideas which could now be developed into production scripts to enable you to move the script on to the screen. They should be discussed with your team and with your teacher. Your teacher could undertake the rôle of a client, or it may be possible to find a client who really does want a video or film programme. Does your school or college have a promotional programme to show to prospective new students? If not, why not make one? Is there a local group of people desperate for someone to make a short film for them?

To satisfy the requirements of this unit you should undertake the production of:

- one non-fiction product – this could be a documentary, and
- one fiction product – this could be a play.

At the end of this section there is an assignment that will help you to provide evidence for your assessment.

Audience

You should always bear in mind the intended audience for your products. Advertisers quantify the quality of a programme by the number of potential viewers. There is no point in trying to show material that is not relevant to a particular audience in an inappropriate **time-slot**. You will be looking at this issue later in this unit.

Resources

A major constraint for your team will be the availability of physical resources and the time that you have available during your course. In order for you to begin to analyse these constraints you should undertake a resources survey.

Activity

Organise a team meeting and at this meeting allocate rôles to each team member. These rôles could be to find out:

- what video camera resources are available and when they can be used
- what sound equipment is available and when it can be used
- the time available for resource use, both on and off the timetable.

Compile the information into a form that allows the team members to see what is available and when. You may be able to make a chart using appropriate computer software.

These are only three examples of tasks. You may have to undertake more than one task if your team is small. All of the team's members should have a task that they can record and bring back to a meeting. The results of the survey should allow you to plan effective productions. Later in this section you will see how to plan a production schedule and the results of your survey will be very helpful.

You now know what resources you have and the time available. Next you need to consider the production process that you go through to make a complete moving image product. Whatever moving image product you select there is a similar production process to be followed.

The following chart shows a production planning cycle which illustrates the process a production company would undertake. You may find it helpful to view the whole process when you plan your programmes.

Fig. 5.2
Production planning chart

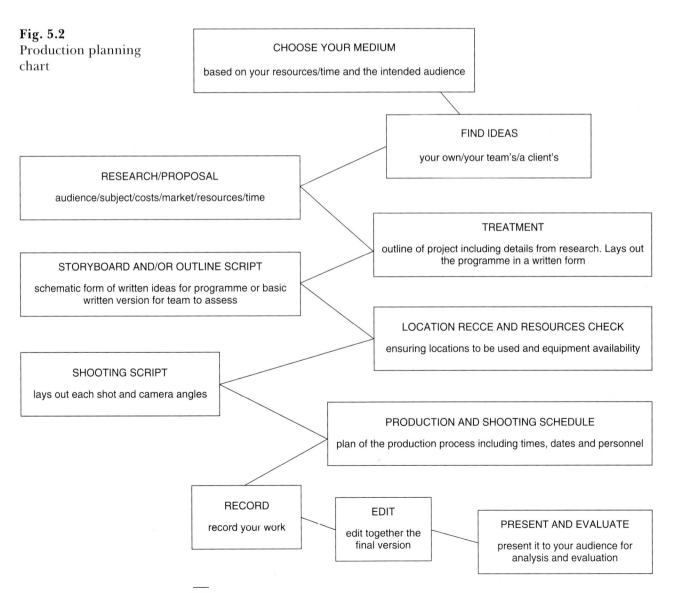

CHOOSE YOUR MEDIUM

based on your resources/time and the intended audience

FIND IDEAS

your own/your team's/a client's

RESEARCH/PROPOSAL

audience/subject/costs/market/resources/time

TREATMENT

outline of project including details from research. Lays out the programme in a written form

STORYBOARD AND/OR OUTLINE SCRIPT

schematic form of written ideas for programme or basic written version for team to assess

LOCATION RECCE AND RESOURCES CHECK

ensuring locations to be used and equipment availability

SHOOTING SCRIPT

lays out each shot and camera angles

PRODUCTION AND SHOOTING SCHEDULE

plan of the production process including times, dates and personnel

RECORD

record your work

EDIT

edit together the final version

PRESENT AND EVALUATE

present it to your audience for analysis and evaluation

Terms to learn

- **The proposal** is your initial idea set down on paper. You should include in the proposal enough information for the reader to understand what you intend to do. The proposal has been described as a 'sales tool' – in other words, it is used to whet the appetite of a potential client. You will have looked at proposal writing in some detail in Study Unit 2. An example of a proposal is given below to enable you to follow through the production process for *Road Safety for Primary Schools* from beginning to end.

Fig. 5.3
Programme proposal

PROPOSAL

Programme title: *Road Safety for Primary Schools*

Client: Derbyshire Constabulary

Writer: Ian Smith

Date: 01/08/95

- -

Media Productions will produce a ten-minute video programme on the theme of road safety aimed at an audience of young people aged between 8 and 11 years.

The programme will be shot entirely on location using broadcast standard recording medium. The programme will be edited by Media Productions at its Birmingham facility.

The programme will be based on a drama scenario involving a young boy, approximate age 10 years. This boy enjoys sport and outdoor activities and is looking forward to moving to a new secondary school. A momentary lapse in concentration when crossing the road to see his friends results in an accident involving a car. The boy is seen in a wheelchair unable to participate in sport and wishing that he had used the Green Cross Code.

The programme budget will be approximately £10,000.

- **The treatment** is a written description of the programme idea, including the title of the project, the proposed length of the programme, the format of the programme – for example, a video, tape/slide presentation or multimedia programme. You should identify the intended audience and try to give an idea of estimated costs. It should be written in a way that allows the reader to visualise the content of the programme and to make an evaluation of the programme's worth. The treatment should provide enough information to enable the client to commission further development work.

The treatment below has been taken from a real programme. The original idea came from a client who had a very old-fashioned programme that he was showing to school groups. Most of the message was lost as the audience spent time trying to guess the programme's date. The client wants to make an up-to-date programme on road safety.

Fig. 5.4
Programme treatment

TREATMENT

Programme title: *Road Safety for Primary Schools*

Client: Derbyshire Constabulary

Writer: Ian Smith

Date: 02/08/95

The programme will open with shots of John Smith enjoying himself playing football at lunchtime on the school playing fields. He is later seen working hard in the classroom and in the school library where he helps to keep the books in order.

Later on the same day we see John walking in the High Street where he goes into a McDonald's restaurant and emerges with a Big Mac and a drink. His friends see him on the other side of the road and call to him as they are going to play football at a local park. John forgets about checking the road for traffic and is knocked down by a car.

The scene changes to the local hospital where John is in bed attached to monitors and drips. Doctors are discussing his condition and they are heard saying he may not walk again. The final scenes show John trying to adapt to his life in a wheelchair and wishing he had used the Green Cross Code.

The action will be enhanced by appropriate use of visual and sound effects.

The programme will be shot on broadcast video format and will cost approximately £10,000.

- **The outline script** is sometimes called a scene script and it gives an outline of each scene without going into detail about each shot. It can indicate whether daytime or night, the characters used and dialogue or narration.

On the next page is part of an outline script, taken from *Road Safety for Primary Schools*.

Fig. 5.5
Outline script sheet

OUTLINE SCRIPT

Programme title: *Road Safety for Primary Schools*

Client: Derbyshire Constabulary

Writer: Ian Smith

Date: 01/09/95

----

7 Exterior of Bath Street: Daytime

John walks down the street and looks into McDonald's. He sees two friends sitting at a table. He enters the restaurant through the front doors.

8 Interior of McDonald's restaurant: Daytime

John greets his friends and walks to the counter to order his meal. He chats to the waitress as he waits for the food to arrive. He is obviously in a good mood. He moves away from the counter with his meal and joins his friends. They discuss the football match that John will be playing in next day.

9 Interior of McDonald's restaurant: Daytime

John finishes his meal and leaves the table with his friends. He exits through the front door carrying the milkshake that he did not finish.

10 Exterior Bath Street: Daytime

John leaves the restaurant and walks up Bath Street where he sees his friends across the road. He calls to them and they shout back that they have some important news.

11 Exterior Bath Street: Daytime

John runs across the road without using the Green Cross Code.

- **The storyboard** is a paper visualisation of the production. It helps to form ideas about the way that the visual and sound elements work together. Many feature films will make a complete storyboard of the film before shooting starts.

Activity

Using the material in the outline script complete five frames of a storyboard. You do not have to be the best artist in the world to make a storyboard. You should, however, make the pictures clearly identify what is going on.

Once you have made the storyboard you should then present this to your client, who may be your teacher, another student or an outside body. Using the storyboard, the client should be able to visualise just what the programme will look like. The client may make suggestions of changes to be made. Remember to record all of the changes that you agree to make. This may be in the form of minutes of a meeting, written evidence from a meeting with the client or a letter confirming acceptance of the storyboard.

Once the storyboard has been approved then the shooting script can be drawn up.

- **The production shooting script** is a detailed version of the outline script. It shows each shot sequentially numbered and in order. The framing of each shot, i.e. whether close-up or medium, etc. is indicated but there is room for the director to make changes.

Although the examples used so far relate to a video programme the same procedures are applicable to film production. The client can still see the way that the story is developing whether it is a film or video product.

The following example of a shooting script is taken from the *Road Safety for Primary Schools* video. You can see the development of this script from the outline script.

Fig. 5.6
Shooting script sheet

SHOOTING SCRIPT

Programme title: *Road Safety for Primary Schools*

Client: Derbyshire Constabulary

Writer: Ian Smith

Date: 09/09/95

Shot	Camera position	Scene/Action/Sound
	Scene 8. Interior McDonald's: Daytime	
15	Near counter (*follows John from door to counter*)	(*John enters and walks to counter*) Buzz track interior
16	Near counter (*John addresses waitress on 2 shot*)	(*John orders meal*) *John*: Can I have a Big Mac please?
17	Near counter (*Waitress replies in close up*)	*Waitress*: Do you want fries?
18	From doorway (*wide shot as John waits for his meal*)	(*John by counter, friends wave to him. He waves back and then walks to table*)
19	By table (*mid shot of John and friends*)	*John*: Hi, what are you doing here?

You should be recording all of your decisions to be used as evidence which should show how you have arrived at decisions in the team and how these decisions are affecting the programme you are making.

It should be possible for the shooting script to be given to a director to interpret the action into real images.

Earlier you looked at available resources in terms of equipment, time and personnel. The next step is to produce a production schedule that allows you to plan effectively. There is no point in planning to make a product if you do not have the resources or if the resources you do have are not available at the right time. If you are using actors you must plan a timetable that gives them an indication of when they are required.

Imagine this scenario. You are asked by your local community centre to record the opening of their new premises, with the local MP performing the ceremony. The day of the opening is approaching fast and you must be sure you have a camera and all of the necessary equipment and a crew.

- How do you ensure that all of the equipment is available?
- How does your crew know where to be and at what time?
- Where will you put the camera when you get there?
- What type of lighting is there and is there any mains power supply?

Location reconnaissance

This is the first step towards planning the production. It is where you can visit the location and check the lighting and power supply. You may be able to find a contact person to let you in early to set up your equipment. You will be able to see if there are any health and safety hazards to overcome. All this information should be recorded in a location visit sheet (see page 233).

Safe working practices

Throughout this unit you will encounter topics on safe working practices. The production of moving image products involves you in working with equipment, working with other people and working with an audience. No-one wants to work in a dangerous situation if this can be avoided. The location recce (reconnaissance) can identify potential hazards so that you can begin to compile a risk assessment document vital to the completion of evidence for this unit. The same can be applied to studio shoots although you may want to adapt the following location visit sheet for this situation. It will help you to write down the details that you need to remember from a location visit. Once again the source of this material is the *Road Safety for Primary Schools* video.

When you have established the location then you can make precise plans for the shoot. The producer's or production manager's job will be to organise the crew, actors and resources to be at the right place at the right time.

Fig. 5.7
Location visit sheet

LOCATION VISIT SHEET

Programme title: *Road Safety for Primary Schools*

Client: Derbyshire Constabulary

Location visit undertaken by: Isabelle Zahar, Production Manager

Date: 01/08/95

Location 1: Interior of McDonald's restaurant
Rough sketch of location (include windows, doors and furniture layout)

Electricity points located at: regular intervals on side walls/double 13 amp sockets

Access gained by: front entrance on Bath Street

Telephone number of contact: 01559 745342

Health and safety issues to note:

1 customers will be in the store during shooting

2 trailing electrical cables on floor

3 lighting stands will need one person by each stand

4 hot drinks/food will be used in the shoot to add realism

The production schedule

This should include details of when the production started and when various activities have taken place. This information, although not necessarily industry standard, is vital for your records. It will be useful when you come to evaluate your work later in this unit. Below is an example of a very detailed production schedule and is from the *Road Safety for Primary Schools* video.

Fig. 5.8
Production schedule

PRODUCTION SCHEDULE

Programme title: *Road Safety for Primary Schools*

Director: John Norris   Producer: Sue Ullstein

Date production started: 25/11/94
Treatment started: 01/08/95   completed: 03/08/95
                                           sent to client: 04/08/95

Storyboard started: 15/08/95   completed: 20/08/95
Shooting started: 20/10/95   completed: on-going
Post-production started: to be arranged   completed:
Rough cut submitted: agreed with client:
Final show tape completed:

Location equipment required
Sony camera / tripod / batteries x 2
Microphones: 1 rifle and 1 radio
Lighting kit: 3 x lights (2 800 & 1 2000)
Tapes x 5

Transport requirements
1 x minibus for cast – days 1, 2 and 3
1 x crew car – days 1, 2 and 3

Crewing requirements
Cameraperson: Terry Smith
Sound: Vanda Zebrak
Lighting: Mazin Aldevsy
Production assistant: John Wright
Technician x 2: Linda Moore and Barry Betts

Actors
John Smith – Brian Wilson
Friends – Brian Smith / Graham Woodhead / Tom Sharpe / Ayesha Sheik
Policeman – Fred Harris
Doctor – Paula Dennis
Nurse – Joan Fullerton

Props
Football kit – day 1 / Library books – day 1
Supply of Big Macs and drinks – day 2
(note continuity of clothes from day 1 to days 2 and 3)
Costumes list from: Mary Smith
Other props on set as per daily schedule

Post-production requirements (state format, effects needed, etc.)
All shooting on **BVU High Band SP**

The production schedule can be complemented by a daily schedule that shows the resources required for just one day. This is known as a call sheet and gives details of where to be and at what time. It details arrangements about transport and lists times and places to meet. The following two call sheets are taken from the *Road Safety for Primary Schools* video. Look at the detail on the sheets and note the way that meeting places and times are carefully recorded.

When you do your planning remember to keep everyone informed about the schedule. If someone does not attend when expected there is no excuse if he/she had been given a call sheet.

Fig. 5.9
Crew call sheet

CREW CALL SHEET

Programme title: *Road Safety for Primary Schools*

Programme number: 0014

Director: John Norris   Producer: Sue Ullstein

Crew

Camera: Terry Smith

Sound: Vanda Zebrak

Lights: Mazin Aldevsy

Production assistant: John Wright

Technicians: Linda Moore and Barry Betts

Venue: McDonald's restaurant

Meeting place: Production HQ – foyer Market Hotel, Bath Street

----

Call date: Tuesday 23rd October

Call time: 08.00 expected finish 16.30

Transport: Crew car

Other instructions: Warm clothes / packed lunch

Fig. 5.10
Actors' call sheet

ACTORS' CALL SHEET

Programme title: *Road Safety for Primary Schools*

Programme number: 0014

Director: John Norris   Producer: Sue Ullstein

Actor	Character
Brian Wilson	John Smith
Brian Smith	Friend
Graham Woodhead	Friend
Tom Sharpe	Friend
Ayesha Sheik	Friend

Venue: McDonald's restaurant

Meeting place: Production HQ – foyer Market Hotel, Bath Street

----

Call date: Tuesday 23rd October

Call time: 08.30 for make up and wardrobe

Transport: Minibus provided from hotel pick up at 08.00

Other instructions: meals provided (Big Macs!)

The budget

So far you have not taken into consideration the cost of producing your moving image products. There is no average cost for producing television programmes – some can cost very little to produce and some, particularly costume drama, can be very expensive.

The *Road Safety for Primary Schools* video that we have been following in this section was made on a low budget. It was not intended for broadcasting so it could be made on non-broadcast format video. The programme budget was finalised *after* agreement had been reached with the client on the content of the programme.

- *A budget proposal* specifies all costs to be incurred in the making of the product, giving a total cost at the bottom.

You should produce budget proposals for your programmes that are realistic. In order to do this you will have to find out how much it costs to hire equipment. You may already have equipment in your school or college but it might not be hired out for a fee.

Activity

Produce a rate card that identifies each piece of equipment that your school or college has for programme making. For each piece of equipment find some way of identifying what it would cost to hire it. Produce your rate card in a way that would be easy to understand.

You could start by contacting your local equipment rental shop. If it does not specialise in video or film equipment then ask for the address of the nearest supplier. You will find that there are a number of companies that hire film and video equipment on a daily or weekly basis.

When you have completed your rate card you can begin to prepare a budget for your programme. Below is the budget sheet for the *Road Safety for Primary Schools* video.

Fig. 5.11
Budget sheet

BUDGET SHEET			
Programme title: *Road Safety for Primary Schools*			
Producer: Sue Ullstein			
Date:			
Writing a treatment	1 day	£40 per day	£40
Writing a script	3 days	£40 per day	£120
Writing a production schedule	1 day	£40 per day	£40
Director's fee			£750
Producer's fee			£750
Actors' fees			£900
Camera hire	3 days	£75 per day	£225
Video recorder hire	3 days	£50 per day	£150
Microphone hire	3 days	£20 per day	£60
Video tapes 10		@ £5 each	£50
Special effects	1 day	£30 per day	£30
Using an edit suite	3 days	£75 per day	£225
Producing graphics	1 day	£100 per day	£100
Providing music		£50	£50
Voice-over		£40	£40
Total cost			**£3,530**

It probably seems that there is a lot of paperwork to do before you can handle a camera. If you delegate some of it to your team then it can be carried out quickly.

Use the following activity as a starting point for a non-fiction product which could be used as one of the two production scripts needed to complete the evidence indicators for this unit.

Activity

Work in a group. You have been asked to produce a short video programme that records the environment of your classroom or studio. Call a team meeting to discuss this commission and produce a proposal for a client. The proposal can be produced by the team but you should also try to produce a proposal on your own. Each of the team members should choose a production rôle.

When you come together to discuss this programme you should write down all of the ideas on a large piece of paper. Some of the ideas may seem silly or outlandish but give them all your full consideration. When you have discussed all of the ideas, go back over each one and consider its possibilities. Cross out ideas that will not work, maybe because you have used your resources survey, and you will be left with some feasible ideas. This system is known as brainstorming.

When you have compiled your ideas and written a proposal ask someone to take the rôle of a client and see if the proposal makes sense. Do not worry about which equipment you plan to use – you will decide on this later.

Activity

Using the proposal that you developed earlier, write a treatment for a client detailing the way that you intend to make the environment programme about your classroom or studio.

In the treatment you should show clearly the method by which the programme will be recorded. The treatment should indicate the shape that the programme will take, including an estimate of cost. Look at the example of the *Road Safety for Primary Schools* video and prepare a budget.

You now have a proposal and treatment for the environment programme. You should have agreement from your team and the client about the content of the programme. Now take this a stage further.

Activity

Using the proposal and treatment from the previous activities plan out the production process with your team. Now try writing a simple outline script.

So far you have looked at ways of planning your moving image ideas. You have identified the planning process and the way that you should write down your ideas. Now you should identify the equipment that you are going to use. You need to identify how you will proceed, given your resources and timetable. Before you do this you should understand some of the constraints that there are on the process of producing your product. In Study Unit 2 you looked at codes, conventions and issues relating to ethics. You will now consider basic visual codes that you will be using throughout the production process.

Basic visual codes

There is a range of visual codes that you need to learn before you undertake the planning and production of your visual product. These codes are relevant to all of the visual media that you have looked at.

Camera angle

The position of the camera is very important to the viewer. If it is positioned at a low angle then the subject appears to dominate the scene. If however the camera is positioned at a high angle then the subject appears to be weaker or smaller.

Camera movement

When the camera moves with the subject, known as doing a tracking shot, an intimate feel is created, almost as though the viewer is part of the action. Moving from a wide-angle shot to a close-up directs the viewer's attention to a particular point. Generally camera movements are made slowly to avoid disrupting the viewer. There are several types of movements:

- the camera **pans** left and right
- the camera focus in on the subject, with the camera moving
- the camera **tracks** the action
- the camera tilts up or down from a fixed position
- the camera is raised above the subject on a support for an overhead view
- the camera operator holds the camera.

It is usual in film and television production to move the camera rather than alter the **zoom**. If you use a camera on full zoom then every shake or wobble is exaggerated. If you use an ordinary lens setting and move the camera in you can avoid the shakes and also retain a good **depth of field**.

Depth of field

This refers to subjects in the picture that are in focus. Using a **wide-angle lens** you can normally achieve a good depth of field and all of the subjects both in the foreground and background are in focus. A **telephoto lens** will bring the image magnified into the frame but this is sacrificed by a poor depth of field. The image in the foreground may be sharp but the detail in

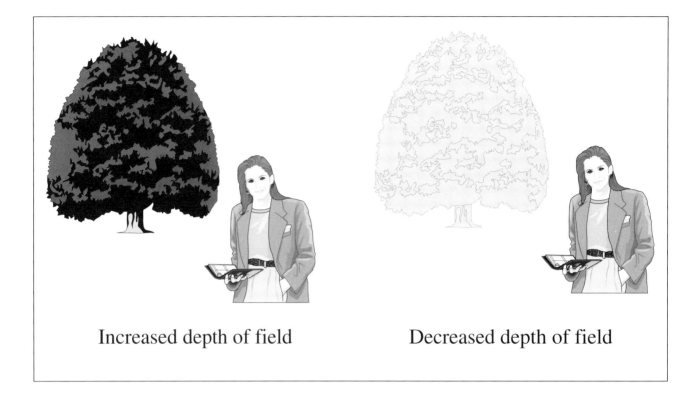

Increased depth of field   Decreased depth of field

Fig. 5.12
Depth of field diagram

the background will be fuzzy. This can be used to good effect when you want the subject in the foreground to be emphasised. Depth of field is important in both film/video and still photography and the same principles apply to all camera lenses.

Framing

The image in the frame is important to the viewer whether it is a still image or a moving image. The position of the subject within the frame can make the scene look interesting or boring. There is a simple technique called the 'rule of thirds' that breaks up the frame into three equal horizontal and vertical bands. You compose the shot so that the main subjects sit on these lines or where they cross. This rule can be broken intentionally or by necessity, but if you try this technique, eventually you will begin to use it naturally when you compose your shots.

Types of camera shots

The abbreviated names of these shots can be used in your scripts.

There are a variety of camera shots that are used in both film and video:

– close-up: for example, a person's face where you can clearly see emotion
– medium shot: the most common camera shot with two or more people seen from the waist up
– long shot: the shot that could establish the scene, possibly containing groups of people in full figure
– high-angle: looking down on the action from the top of a ladder; subject seems dominated by the camera

- low-angle: taken as though you are looking up at the action; subject seems to dominate the action
- wide-angle: a wide view showing where the action is taking place and what action is taking place around the actors; not good for involving the actors as they appear too small in the scene
- top shot: where the subject is seen from directly overhead as though the camera was in a balloon.

Activity

Take a piece of black cardboard and cut an aperture in it to the proportion 5:4 (5 units long by 4 units high). Make sure that you have enough room left around the aperture to block out any extraneous light. Use this card to view the room you are working in. What does the limitation of the aperture show you about framing for a television screen?

What will you have to be aware of when you record through the camera? Move close into a subject and then move out for a wide-angle shot.

The frame you used gives a good idea of what will be included in the frame of a television or cinema screen. Directors use a similar technique to judge what they want to appear on the screen. You will probably have seen microphones appearing in shots when they should not be there. It is normally good practice to stop filming when the camera operator sees the microphone in the viewfinder. Of course it is not always practical to stop filming in a live situation.

Lighting

The lighting of a scene, whether natural or artificial, can add or detract from a subject. Dramatic lighting can give real depth to a subject and soft lighting can give a sympathetic feeling. Look at films featuring 'fading' stars and see how the lighting director has used soft lighting to dissolve away the years of wrinkles. Dramatic lighting can be used to good effect in action or horror movies, for example, the scene in *Close Encounters of the Third Kind* (Steven Spielberg, 1985) when the young boy, after finding his toys coming to life, is surrounded by shafts of bright light from a spaceship and vanishes.

There is a whole range of lighting gels available to transform white light into all colours of the spectrum. You could ask for a sample card of gels from a stage lighting company or from your local theatre.

Activity

Find as many colour filters as you can. These may be simple filters, for example, transparent sweet wrappers, or you could use lighting gels. Look at the world through these filters. Describe the atmosphere produced. Does red give a warm world? Does a blue filter give a cold world?

Studio lights tend to be secured to a **lighting rig** attached to the ceiling. Most studios will use either broad lights, spots or redhead.

- *broad*: a light that gives a very wide light dispersal that is useful for lighting the background
- *spots*: a light that gives an intense pool of light that can be varied in size
- *redhead*: a multipurpose light that can be used as a wide beam but can also be set up as a spot light. A larger version (more powerful) is the blonde. These last two lights are used extensively on location shoots.

There are many lighting set-ups for a variety of recording techniques. One set-up used extensively in the studio is three-point lighting. The main or key light is positioned slightly above and to one side of the camera. This is normally a spotlight to give a hard light. A broad or fill light is positioned on the opposite side of the camera to light the shadow areas. A back light placed behind the subject and angled down brings the subject forward from the background. Extra broad lights should be used to light the background area.

Fig. 5.13
Three-point lighting
set-up

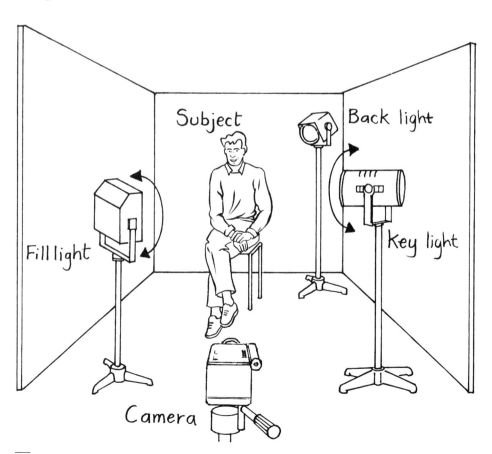

242

Activity

Try to light a subject using the three-point lighting system described above. What happens to the subject as you turn off each light, one at a time? Try using only two lights to light the subject. What happens to the subject and what happens to the background?

Try lighting with this system but add coloured gels to the lamps. What kind of atmosphere can you generate with coloured light?

When lighting is too harsh a diffuser can be used to tone down its intensity. This diffuser might be a metal screen that fits over the front of the lamp or it could be heatproof **scrim** that is fixed over the light. Some studios will have variable lighting controls that regulate the amount of power going to each light. If the power is reduced the colour temperature of the light will change as the power decreases.

Many of the lights used in the studio can also be used on location, in particular the redhead (1 Kw) and the blonde (2 Kw). These lights are placed on stands or attached to the walls or supports by a **gaffer grip**.

Location lighting is more difficult to control than studio lighting since daylight is so variable. For example, light coming in from a window has a daylight (bluish) tint but lamps produce an orange tint. The camera does not know which one to prioritise. In this instance the lamps would have a blue filter gel attached to them to match the light from the window.

Safe working practices

One of the biggest hazards in film and video production is in the handling of lights. Not only can they get hot but they have trailing cables that people can trip over. Lights on stands can be knocked over and the resulting broken bulb could cause a fire or severely injure someone. It is essential to use the following rules.

- Always ensure that any trailing cables are firmly attached to the floor with **hazard tape**.
- Make sure that someone is positioned beside each light on a stand so that no-one can walk into it.
- Wait for five minutes after you have turned the lights off before you touch them.
- If you are working with studio or location lights always isolate them from the mains supply before attempting to change bulbs or move lights.
- If you are working on studio lights on a lighting rig always have someone holding the ladders.

Graphics

Title sequences in programmes can help you to understand the questions of where, who and what. The nature of the lettering at the start of a programme can identify in your mind the genre of programme you are watching, for example, a comedy where the use of quirky lettering indicates that this is not a serious film.

Activity

Design a title graphic for the following programmes:

- a children's programme aimed at the under-six audience
- a horror programme aimed at teenagers
- a comedy about life in the countryside
- a programme about journeys into space.

Titles and end credits can be easily created for your programmes by drawing them with white or coloured chalk on a chalkboard. This could then be filmed and edited into your programme. Other ideas include using Letraset (using transfers) or stencils on white or coloured card. For a really sophisticated result, computer software packages are widely available for titling – your work could be printed out and filmed or downloaded straight on to video tape.

Activity

1 Design a title package for the environment programme. Use a variety of different techniques and then choose which one you think looks suitable for the programme.

2 Do the same for the end credits, putting the names of all your team members and the job that they decided to undertake.

Keep records of your designs in your **log**. Remember to have your own design ideas as well as the team's designs. If you have produced them on tape keep it safe for later assessment.

Editing

Almost all visual material is edited at some stage. Your film or video images will probably have to be shortened to fit into a programme. Being able to edit film and video means there is much greater flexibility when shooting the programme. It would be very hard to arrange for all of the shots in a film to be filmed in sequence. For example, if there is a shot outside followed by a shot inside then followed by another shot outside, you would have to bring the camera inside then take it out again, thus wasting time. Before editing, the outside shots can be done first and then all of the inside or vice versa if the weather is not so good. When you use the medium of film you literally cut the film up and then join the scenes together. In video you have to transfer the material electronically between tapes.

There are various editing codes that you need to know when you start to shoot your material:

- *cuts*: shots are joined together to give an impression of continuity
- *fades*: give the indication of time passing
- *dissolves*: a subtle fade
- *wipes*: where the image is literally wiped off the screen by a new shot
- *camera effects*: produced in the camera, for example, zooming into a scene and defocusing to a blur. The next shot refocuses into a clear shot in a new location.

Within the editing codes there are rules that govern good technique:

- Do not cut between similar shots – for example, from one long shot landscape to another long shot landscape.
- Do not cut whilst zooming in or out.
- Avoid cutting into a black screen – try a fade instead.

Of course you will want to experiment with these techniques and you will soon see what works and what does not. Later in this unit you will look more closely at editing techniques.

Sound

No film, video or audio visual programme would be complete without a **sound track** (unless you are making a silent movie). Sound can enhance a production or it can detract if the sound recording is particularly poor. The marriage between sound and vision should be so subtle that no one element should overtake the other. There are three basic sound codes.

Music

Music has been very important from the early days of cinema. You may have seen silent movies which are accompanied by a pianist or orchestra. Music can add an extra dimension to a programme by its intensity, its mood or its vitality. Horror films are an example of where music can enhance the horror by its ferocity or sense of impending doom.

Activity

Record three different programmes on video tape, for example, a comedy, a thriller and a science fiction programme. These programmes should contain various kinds of music. Play parts of the sound tracks to a small group of people without showing them the screen. See if they can identify the programmes' themes.

How did the group do? It is relatively easy to judge moods by the nature of the music being played. They will be accustomed to hearing danger music when the mood is threatening. Music greatly enhances the visual element of your programme.

When you plan to use music in your programme you should be aware that all recorded music will be subject to some form of copyright control. The writers of the music will expect payment for the use of their music. The performers will also expect payment and the publisher will want the appropriate cut.

There are several organisations that will help with music copyright. The Mechanical Copyright Protection Society (MCPS) acts on behalf of publishers and writers to collect licence fees. Their library music is published on tape or CD and is normally distributed free. However you do have to pay a licence fee to use it in a programme. It is possible to buy a special licence for use in schools and colleges and you should check with MCPS about current costs. Phonographic Performance (PP) act to collect licence fees for the use of music from records, CDs and tapes when they are used in the broadcast industry.

Activity

Find several examples of records, CDs or tapes. Note down from the label the name of the writers, the name of the publishing company and the names of the performers. How would you find out how much these people want for using their music?

The music track for the *Road Safety for Primary Schools* video was cleared for copyright through the MCPS. The client wanted to use the music from the 'Birdy Song' over the end credits. The MCPS contacted the publisher and writers and arranged for the use of this music for £100. Music licences can be very expensive.

Of course you could write your own music track for your video and then you would own the copyright and there would be no fee to pay.

Activity

What kind of music would be suitable for your environment project? With your group find some appropriate music, or commission someone to write a piece for you. Record details of the composer, publisher and date, and ascertain how much it would cost to use this music or agree a cost for your commissioned piece.

Sound effects

These are sounds not recorded normally as part of the programme. They can be added later to enhance the viewer's or listener's perception of what is happening on screen or through the radio. Sometimes the effects are recorded on location as 'wildtrack' but not in **sync** (synchronisation) with the action, for example, the interiors of buildings with lots of noise or traffic noise. These ambient sound tracks or buzz tracks are useful when you are editing together your programme and you want to create an atmosphere.

Many sound effects can be purchased on tape or CD but it is more fun to record your own wherever possible. It is also necessary to clear copyright of the spoken word with an appropriate agency before use.

Activity

It is interesting to close your eyes and listen to the sounds around you. You could do this in the classroom, studio or outside in the street. Take a notepad and note down some of the sounds that you hear. Listen carefully for the background sounds that are not always obvious to the human ear but would be picked up by a sensitive microphone.

Activity

For each of the following programmes try to think of appropriate sound effects:

- a play set on a summer's day
- a drama set near a seaside resort
- an interview taking place near Westminster, London
- a comedy programme set in a nightclub.

What kinds of sound effects would you use for your project in the classroom or studio?

Dialogue

Dialogue can be delivered by a person on the screen, an actor saying lines or a voice-over. In the early days of film there was no dialogue because there was not the technology to record the sound and play it back in sync. Captions were used between the scenes to explain the action that was taking place.

When you record on video the sound is laid down on the tape at the same time as the picture and this means that the two should never be out of sync.

Most film formats rely on recording the sound on a separate sound tape. This can lead to problems with the synchronisation of sound and vision. This is achieved by using a clapperboard device at the start and sometimes the end of every scene. The clapperboard, with the details of the production and the scene and take number written on it, is placed in front of the camera before the scene starts. The following sequence of events then happens:

- The director asks the camera operator to 'turn over' or 'run camera'. This means start filming.

Fig. 5.14
A clapperboard

SCENE   TAKE

ROAD SAFETY

CAM   DIR

247

- At the same time the sound operator turns on the sound recorder. When the recorder is running at the correct speed the sound operator says 'sound running'.
- The camera operator, when all the equipment is running smoothly, says 'mark it'. This is the cue for the person holding the clapperboard to call out the scene/take number and then to bring the two parts of the clapperboard together.
- When the director is sure that everything is running he/she will then ask for the action to start by shouting 'action'. Their words can be removed at the editing stage.

The action of bringing the clapperboard arms together is now recorded on vision and sound. When the editing takes place the visual point where the arms meet can be synchronised to the noise of the arms meeting on the sound track. Even though the sound synchronisation on video may not require a clapperboard it is still advisable to use one. It gives you information about the programme and can help you to edit by allowing you to identify scenes and takes of scenes. *Road Safety for Primary Schools* had 45 scenes and in some instances these had up to five takes. By using a clapperboard the scenes could be found easily.

The same sequence of events used in film is equally applicable to video production with the only difference being that the sound recorder is replaced by the video recorder.

Your project on the classroom or studio environment may require someone to front the programme. You may decide to use a voice-over. What type of person and voice do you need?

You now have an understanding of basic moving image language. This will help you to plan an effective moving image product. You should now consider some of the basic elements to make a successful recording.

Video tape recording

Using a video camera you could plan and record your material in two ways:

- recording all of the sequences in order, making a complete programme. This is called 'in camera' editing.
- recording all of the sequences but not in the order that they will finally finish in. The material is edited later.

Film

- Recording on film will almost certainly require shooting out of sequence.

To record the sequences or scenes in order your script must be very carefully worked out. This is not always possible on long programmes but with a short programme you may be able to complete all of the filming very quickly. As you have seen, most commercial video productions are made by recording the scenes out of order. How do you plan to make everything run smoothly? One simple way is to construct a chart like the one below which lays out each day with columns for actors, resources and locations.

Fig. 5.15
Location planning chart

	LOCATION	ACTORS	CREW	PROPS
DAY 1				
DAY 2				
DAY 3				

Activity

Use the chart above and plan a filming schedule for three days. Look at the production schedule on page 234 and place the actors and locations with crew and props on the appropriate days.

Actors available:	**Brian Wilson – days 1, 2 & 3**
	Fred Harris – days 1 & 2
	Paula Dennis – days 2 & 3
	Joan Fullerton – day 2
	Brian Smith – days 1 & 3
	Graham Woodhead – days 2 & 3
	Tom Sharpe – days 1 & 3
	Ayesha Sheik – days 2 & 3
Camera kit available:	**days 1, 2 & 3**
Locations available:	**McDonald's days 1 & 3**
	Bath Street – day 1
	Hospital – day 2
Crew available:	**days 1, 2 & 3**

From these details plan who, what and where to shoot.

You can see that sometimes you have to shoot some sequences out of order. It can be very difficult for production staff and actors to remember just what part of the production they are working on. What problems do you think might occur when you shoot different scenes on different days?

You have probably seen examples on television or at the cinema where there are **continuity** errors. This happens when someone changes clothes halfway through a scene or a prop appears and disappears. The production assistant would normally keep a note of continuity in order to make sure that this does not happen. It does happen to the most professional of directors. Whether you work in film or video the same rules apply.

Studio shooting

You would undertake a similar activity as before when planning a studio shoot. Your actors and studio crew may only be available at certain times. What happens if you have to miss a day's shoot because one of the actors is not available? The studio may be required for other work and you cannot afford to pay for the studio to stay unused. How do you remember what went where and which camera was in which position? The answer is to make your own studio **floor plan** which records where everything is in the studio, including each camera position, the position of props and scenery.

A **lighting plan** can also be included on this and it will help you to remember where all the lights went and what kinds of lights were used. Of course, the type of plan you use will depend upon the studio area you have available and the lighting rig you are using. It may be useful to make a floor plan for all of your location work as well.

In this section you have looked at the planning and preparation required before starting to produce your moving image product. It probably seems like a lot of paperwork but it is important to have all the information you need, resources identified and booked, before you undertake the next step.

The following assignment will help you to develop appropriate evidence for assessment.

Assignment

You have been contacted by a local cable television station who have heard that you have a television studio, location recording equipment and post-production facility. They would like you to produce television programmes for them. These programmes will be for two purposes. One will be for local community groups to put forward their views about local issues. The second will be a children's drama series about life in your town.

Before they can give the go-ahead for you to make the programmes they would like to see examples of your work. You suggest making two pilot programmes for them, one for each type of programme. Your teacher has agreed to act as the client liaison and has been given the power by the cable station to make decisions on their behalf.

Remember that evidence of planning should be included in your portfolio. Keep your work in a filing system that allows you easy access to the information, for example, a ring binder with dividers between each section. It is also important to keep your own notes as well as any team meeting minutes. You may well be able to share copies of scripts and planning notes but you should always include some of your own material. This could be in the form of a diary that lists all the activities you have undertaken. You could keep notes of any new skills that you have learned.

The client suggests that the pilot programmes should be no more than five minutes long and should contain both studio and location material.

- Working in a group think of an idea for each pilot programme and develop this into proposals and subsequent treatments.
- Present these to the client and amend as necessary.
- Develop team rôles, and undertake resource and technical research. List the resources and technical requirements you will need for production.
- Develop production scripts and production schedules.
- Write notes on what your contribution was to the team's development of the proposal.

2 Production: Recording moving images

In this section you will look at the techniques and practices of recording moving images. You will have planned the production process earlier in this unit and will have developed firm programme ideas. The next step is to turn these ideas into a reality.

Selecting appropriate equipment

Before recording can commence you must be sure that you have the right equipment for the job. Choosing equipment for recording depends upon the way in which the recording will take place.

In the studio

Studio-based programmes may be able to use more than one camera for the recording. A **vision mixer** enables you to cut or mix between the cameras as you are recording. Cameras can be mounted on a tripod or **pedestal** on a dolly (wheels) that can be moved easily around the studio. Lighting in the studio can be controlled to good effect. Studio recording also helps to obtain a good sound recording. There will be no unwanted noise if the studio is soundproof.

On location

Normally, location work involves only one camera which may be hand-held or mounted on a tripod. Recording using more than one camera on location would involve using portable vision mixers and monitors. It is simpler to use only one camera with techniques that suggest to the viewer that you are using more than one camera.

Activity

Watch a news item that is recorded on location where an interview is taking place. Does it look as if there are two cameras being used, one for the interviewer and one for the interviewee?

It is almost certain that in this situation there is only one camera being used. In this technique, the camera focuses on the interviewee and the reporter stands by the side of the camera asking the question. The answers are recorded on vision and sound. The camera is then moved to the point where the interviewee stood and the interviewer asks the questions again. This is recorded on vision and sound. Later, the two parts are put together in the editing suite.

Activity

What are the implications of recording an interview in this way? What could happen to the content of the questions and answers?

In a technical sense you have to be careful that you do not 'cross the line', i.e. having the reporter looking in the wrong direction when asking the questions. Since the interviewee has probably gone away, the camera operator has to be very sure to get it right.

Ethical problems may arise where the context of the interview is affected by changing the nature of the questions after they have been answered. The way that the interview is edited may also alter the reality.

Video cameras

There are a number of cameras available today. The one that you will probably find in your school or college is the camcorder. This is an integrated unit that has a camera head and video recorder built in. They are normally lightweight and ideal for location recording. Some cameras are literally a camera head that is linked to a separate recorder. These systems are not so easy to use and require two people to operate them, one to operate the camera and one to operate the recorder.

Film cameras

The most commonly used cameras are in the 8 mm and 16 mm format. These cameras are either battery or clockwork powered. The 8 mm camera may have a sound recording facility but the 16 mm camera will almost certainly need a separate sound recorder.

Tripods

At some time you will need to use a tripod to support your camera. Lightweight cameras are easy to hand-hold but when you zoom in to a close-up then every movement you make is magnified. This results in camera shake (the shots will wobble as you wave the camera). The tripod will hold the camera steady and will allow you to do slow panning and tilts.

If you do not have a tripod you should find a solid structure to lean against. This will help you to steady the camera.

Batteries

Much of the equipment you will be using will be battery powered. Cameras and video recorders have a compartment for batteries. Many of the microphones will be battery powered either from an external source or through a small integral battery.

Rechargeable batteries are essential if you are using your equipment on a regular basis. Always ensure that your batteries are fully charged before you try to use them on location or in the studio. It is a good idea to carry at least one spare battery with you at all times.

Microphones

See Study Unit 4 for more details on different types of microphone.

There are two main types of microphone used in video and film recording. These are omnidirectional (picking up sounds from a wide area) and unidirectional (picking up sounds from a very narrow area).

Omnidirectional microphones are normally used on video camcorders as they will pick up all the sounds around. They work well when you want a general sound such as a group of people talking. Hand-held microphones can be omnidirectional and these need to held quite close to the subject to get a really good sound recording. Hand-held microphones can produce handling noise (scraping, thumping) as the mike is moved around. They can also look unsightly.

Unidirectional microphones pick up sound from a narrow angle and therefore can differentiate between individual voices in a crowd. As you move it around you can pick up different sounds and different voices. There are two types of unidirectional microphones commonly used in video production:

- *The rifle mike* is used for long-distance sound pick-up from a subject in the picture. It can be attached to a 'fishpole' or long pole that can be placed overhead near the subject but out of camera shot. This can be moved from subject to subject as they talk and is used in both studio and location work.
- *The personal mike* is attached to the clothing of the subject and gives a very clear pick-up. It can also be used in both studio and on location. In the studio it may be attached to the recorder by a long lead. It may also be a wireless type where the signal from the microphone is relayed to a receiver. For this the subject has to carry a transmitter rather than use a long trailing wire.

Activity

In what circumstances would you use:

a   an omnidirectional microphone

b   a unidirectional microphone?

Write down a list of the uses of both types.

Obviously there are many uses of each microphone type. Each one has its good and bad points. Hand-held microphones can produce handling noise but they are good for close interviews. Rifle microphones are good for recording individual sounds but record very little **ambient** sound. Personal microphones can produce rustling noises as they brush against clothing. It would be good to experiment with different microphones before deciding which one to use for a particular programme.

Lighting

For a description of lighting effects and equipment see pages 241–243.

Getting the recording right

You have identified appropriate equipment to use and have arrived at a location to record your programme. What must you do to ensure that you can record the material accurately and with a quality image and sound track? There are technical details that you need to take into account to ensure that you can produce a quality recording.

Camera

All cameras need to be able to reference a white signal or **white balance**. If the camera knows what white looks like it can then differentiate between all other colours. Most simple camcorders have an automatic white balance setting. The camera takes in the signal and corrects the colours according to a pre-set programme in its memory. Professional cameras have to be set up by pointing the camera at a white subject and pressing a button that tells the camera to balance to this white subject. If the camera is moved from inside to outside or vice versa then the colour balance will have to be reset.

Because the brain compensates we tend to assume that most everyday light sources such as sunlight, fluorescent tubes, tungsten light and candlelight are all producing white light. In reality they are very different. The camera will see them as bluish or orange light according to the source and intensity of the light. White balancing the camera ensures that it will compensate for the prevailing lighting conditions.

Focus

Some camcorders have automatic focus. This system adjusts the lens focus for maximum sharpness on a preselected area. Sometimes the subject you want in focus is not the one the camera chooses. Whilst autofocus allows you to concentrate on other camera functions it is advisable to use manual focus for the majority of the time. The focus can be found at the end of the lens housing and the image in the viewfinder will allow you to see whether or not the image is sharp.

255

The recorder

Whether you use a camcorder or separate video recorder you must remember that video tape needs time to reach maximum operating speed. Modern camcorders have a facility in the pause mode to backspace the recording to allow time for the next shot to come in while the video tape comes up to speed. This means that you should remember to allow a little extra time at the end of every shot to allow the camera to backspace. Professional recorders do not have this facility and therefore you should allow approximately ten seconds from going into record mode before you start the action.

Sound

For a detailed discussion of sound and the types of microphones see page 254. During the recording it is vital that someone monitors the sound levels from the microphone. It is all too easy to forget the sound when you are concentrating on the visuals. Camcorders have a socket into which you can plug a set of headphones. This will allow you to check whether sound is being recorded. Professional recorders will have similar sockets and they should also have a visual display that is a meter of some description. This shows the level at which the sound is being recorded so you can alter the level if necessary.

Keeping a record

Once you start to record it is useful to keep a careful record of the shoot as it progresses. This is normally undertaken by the production assistant who records each scene as it is shot, with a brief description of the action and the time that each shot lasted. The record will also indicate whether there was more than one take of each shot and if so which one will be used in the final programme. A chart similar to the one below could be used.

Fig. 5.16
Field footage log

FIELD FOOTAGE LOG

Programme: *Road Safety for Primary Schools*

Producer: Sue Ullstein

Scene no.	Take no.	Good/N Good	Description
10	1	N/Good	John enters through door
10	2	Good	"
11	1	Good	John on long shot
12	1	N/Good	John talks to Brian (noisy)
12	2	Good	"

Throughout the production process the recording of information in the form of a log is essential for your evidence.

The **field footage log** enables an accurate record to be made. This information can then be stored with each tape or film to enable the editor to identify each scene particularly when undertaking a paper edit. The editing process is explained in detail in Section 3.

Content considerations

In Study Unit 2 you looked at factors that might influence the material that you record. Sometimes these factors are not evident until you actually arrive at your location or start to prepare your studio shoot. Imagine a situation where you and your camera crew arrive at your location, having done careful reconnaissance, to find that the owner of the land on which you have planned to film no longer wants you to film there. Do you continue to film and ignore the owner's wishes? Do you attempt to negotiate even though a huge sum of money is demanded?

Filming in the street can provide many problems for directors and camera crews. Most broadcasters insist that everyone who appears on the screen has given permission for you to use them. **Release forms** need to be signed and fees paid. What about the busker playing in the background? Should you pay a fee for the performance and what about the copyright of the song being played?

Anyone can withdraw filming permission at any time and there is little you can do about it. It is always advisable to have a fallback position just in case you cannot film in your chosen location.

Activity

Using the material you developed for the environment of your classroom or studio assignment, record sufficient footage to make a three-minute programme. Consider all of the issues raised in the planning stages and use the resources that you identified earlier in this unit. Keep all of the material that you shoot for an activity later. Before you begin this activity read the following information about safe working practices and adhere to good practice at all times.

Health and safety

You have looked already at working safely with equipment and people. In all aspects of the planning and recording process in both video and film it is vital to take account of health and safety issues. When you plan your productions you will have to be aware of health and safety issues that will mean you can or cannot record your work in some conditions. It may be as

257

simple as having sufficient electrical cable to run your machinery without trailing wires for people to trip over. The following are examples of some of the things you need to be aware of:

- handling recording and editing equipment safely
- using lighting equipment safely
- recognising the dangers of prolonged use of VDU screens
- working in a sensible way and responding to directions.

Activity

A record of all health and safety issues that you encounter during the planning, recording and editing processes must be kept. You will be able to do this through the minutes of your meetings.

Find out about health and safety procedures by contacting as many agencies as you can. Your research should be collated into sections that correspond to safety of equipment, safety of team members and the safety of the public. When you have obtained as much information as possible use this as reference material for the productions you will undertake.

In this section you have looked at the technical aspects of producing a recording. By now you should be able to make decisions on appropriate equipment and formats. You should be able to handle equipment safely and make accurate **logs** of material produced. Finally, you should have practised recording material. The next stage, post-production, involves using your recorded material from the classroom or studio environment activity.

Assignment

You should have completed the planning and preparation for the cable channel pilot programmes. You will have identified and secured resources. You should now be at the stage of recording the programmes.

1 **Record the programmes in accordance with the agreed script and production schedule.**

2 **Demonstrate your ability to record using appropriate equipment and techniques.**

3 **Make detailed notes on any health and safety issues raised and resolved.**

4 **Keep a log of any content considerations identified and resolved in the recording process.**

3

Post-production: Editing moving image products

In this section you will consider the post-production process involving the various editing techniques associated with moving images. As you have already learned in Section 2, almost all visual material is edited at some stage. Generally, editing in film and video is used to provide greater flexibility when shooting. It also provides you with ways of correcting and improving your finished product. You can:

- correct errors in the recording by omitting them from the finished programme
- use retakes of a scene that did not go right first time
- shorten sequences that are uninteresting or repetitive
- control the overall length of your programme by shortening or lengthening individual scenes
- introduce special effects in vision and sound effects.

Logging the scenes

Before video editing can start you will need to log all of the camera original tapes that you have shot when you recorded your programme. It is essential to know what you have on each tape. Imagine having 20 camera original tapes each with 30 scenes. You must keep a written record so that you know what is on each tape. You can review your camera material by watching the tapes and at the same time logging all the scenes (or **rushes**) with some notes about the quality of the work.

A typical tape log, as shown in the example below, would include the scene number, a brief description of the scene and comments on the visual image and the sound. Each tape log sheet, one for each camera original tape, should be kept with the tape or carefully labelled and stored ready for editing.

Fig. 5.17
Tape log sheet

TAPE LOG SHEET no.			
Scene no.	**Take no.**	**Description**	**Comments**

You will now be able to use the material on the environment of your classroom or studio that you recorded in Section 2 of this unit. All of the material you recorded should now be logged on paper. Go through all of the footage you shot and complete the details as discussed in the last paragraph.

It is interesting to go back and look at old footage. You may have shot it only hours or days before but it is amazing what different things you see in it when you look again.

The editing process

The editing process in video consists of electronically transferring a video signal from one recorder to another. Sound and vision can be transferred together or separately. Visual effects can be added to make the transition between shots smooth.

In film editing the film is literally cut up into individual scenes and then the scenes are glued together in the right order. Sound is normally recorded on a separate recorder and transferred to match the picture at the end of the process.

Many feature films are now edited on video although they are shot on film. The film is transferred to video and an 'off line' edit is produced that allows the director to see the initial edit before the costly process of film editing commences.

Systems of editing

Two-machine editing

In this system the camera original tape is put into a player and the video and sound signal is transferred electronically to another tape, the **edit master**. If you are using film then you have to physically cut it and join the

Fig. 5.18
Two-machine editing

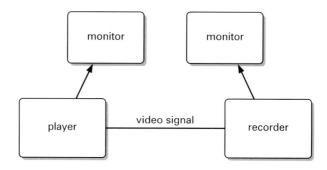

two sections together. Video tape cannot be cut and joined in this way. If you were to run a joined tape through the machine it would cause irreparable damage to the **video heads**.

The video and sound signal is transferred from the player to the recorder directly. This system is sometimes called **crash editing** and gives very little accuracy as to where the edited sections start and finish. A more precise system uses an **edit controller** linked to the player and recorder to enable accurate edits to be achieved.

Fig. 5.19
Editing using an edit controller

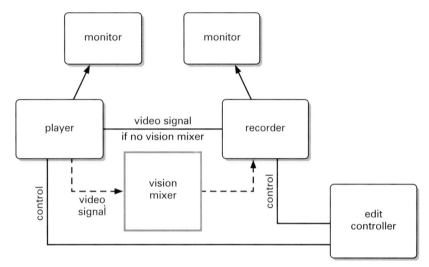

A vision mixer could be incorporated into the system to enable **electronic effects** to be added to the edit. The vision mixer takes the video and sound signal from the player to the recorder and on its journey adds electronic effects. These effects could be:

- *freeze frame*. The image from the player is stored electronically and shown as a single frame.
- *strobe*. The image from the player is stored for an instant then replayed giving the appearance of jerky images much like early film movements.
- *colour correction*. The image from the player can be changed from the original colour and even made black and white. This is a useful effect if you have problems with the colour balance in the camera.
- *mosaic*. The image from the player is seen as a pattern of small squares. This is often used to obscure certain parts of a scene or to give a creative effect.
- *sound level*. Some vision mixers allow the sound from the player and other sources (for example a record or cassette) to be mixed together.

These visual effects should be used sparingly. It is exciting to add effects to make your programme look different but adding too many will confuse the audience and detract from the original theme.

Three-machine editing

It is sometimes desirable to mix between scenes. To achieve this a three-machine edit suite is used, with two players and a recorder. The edit controller informs the players and recorder when to start and finish each

Fig. 5.20
Three-machine editing

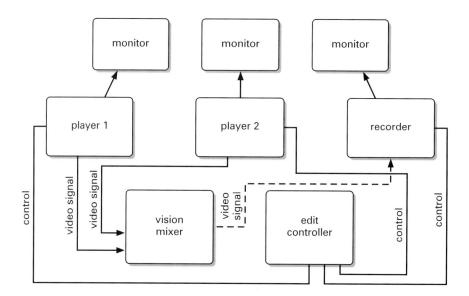

edit. The material from the two players can be mixed together as they are recorded. This allows a **transition** from scene to scene to be smooth rather than a direct cut.

These configurations you have seen allow the linear editing of video and sound. This means that you have to edit the programme scene by scene, making scene 1 follow scene 2 and so on. If you find later that you have edited the wrong scene or you need to replace some material it can be very difficult. Sometimes you have to start the editing process all over again.

Non-linear editing

The editing of video material has entered a new phase with the introduction of new technology. Computer technology allows video and sound signals to be digitised from video tape into language that the computer understands. This information can be stored on hard disk and manipulated through the computer controls. It can be changed easily and the order of editing can be re-arranged. The material is transferred to tape only at the end of the editing process. This system is called **non-linear editing**. This can produce many effects that would normally be provided by a vision mixer. The drawback of this system is the high volume of hard disk space required to store video and sound material. A typical system would require seven to nine gigabytes of hard disk space for a 30-minute programme of broadcast quality.

Fig. 5.21
Non-linear editing

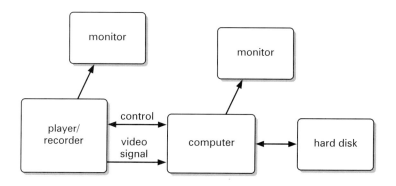

Editing techniques

There are two distinct types of editing techniques that are present in all systems of editing video.

Assemble editing

In assemble editing, video, audio and control track material is laid down on the recorder. The control track is the electronic pulse that synchronises the video heads for playback. The video signal and sound are recorded simultaneously. This system is good for recording large pieces of material.

Insert editing

In insert editing, video and audio material can be added to a tape that has previously recorded material on it by overlaying new pictures or sound to replace existing material. This can be very useful if you have to change any details in your programme. Remember that the material you are replacing must be the same length as the material you are inserting.

Types of editing

Off-line editing

This process, also known as the 'rough cut', is the initial version of the programme made on the lowest quality system. The off-line version can be shown to a client to identify any potential problems.

On-line editing

This is the most expensive editing process. It involves adding all of the effects and mixed down sound tracks prior to release. By this stage the final specifications of the programme will have been agreed and no changes will be made.

Paper edit

This is the process where you write down all of the shots you want in the programme and visualise them cut together. It is also known as an edit decision list. The paper edit should record the first editing decisions that you take. You should watch your camera original footage and make notes on which scenes should go where and how long these scenes may be. You should be able to use the numbering from your video recorder to give approximate in and out points. The details in the sample paper edit overleaf are taken once again from *Road Safety for Primary Schools*.

Fig. 5.22
Paper edit sheet

PAPER EDIT SHEET

Production title: *Road Safety for Primary Schools*

Director: John Norris

Editor: Pip Smith

Date: 1/11/95

- -

Scene	Tape in	Tape out
15 Near counter (*follow John*)	0047	0089
22 Cut away from other camera angle (*John walking to counter*)	0187	0198
16 Near counter (*John addresses waitress*)	0090	0115

This form of editing allows you to make decisions before you need to use an editing suite and this could save you money.

Activity

Using the material recorded for the assignment on your classroom or studio environment, make a paper edit of your programme. Use the suggested layout or make your own paper edit form.

How easy was it to make decisions about the editing process? Editing can be a long process but the paper edit helps you to make decisions.

Additional material

You may find, having done the paper edit, that you need more material for your programme. It is not always possible to revisit a location or book a studio. One answer would be to use still photographs or library material. Still photographs can be added to the programme by filming them on a rostrum camera. This means placing your photographs on a flat surface and pointing the camera at them. You should ensure that the camera is pointing straight at the photograph. One method is to use a suitable tripod and place the photographs on the floor. Ensure that the lighting allows for each area of the photograph to be evenly illuminated.

A number of companies keep **footage** in their libraries but using it can be very expensive. For example, if you are looking for archive footage of your town then the Pathe Library would probably have some early film and they would transfer this to video tape if needed. Unfortunately just a few seconds of film can cost in excess of £100.

Sound editing

Like visual editing, sound editing is an important part in the post-production process. You may have seen films or programmes where the sound quality was poor or the sounds did not match the action. In video recording there is little need for recording sound separately. The video tape will have recorded synchronous sound on to a separate sound track. Sometimes there are drawbacks in having the sound on the same tape. The editing out of sections of sound can be difficult. In broadcast television it is normal to copy the sound track from the video tape, work on the sound and then return it to the finished master edit. You may not have the equipment to do this and therefore you will have to work on the sound track as you edit the picture.

As mentioned earlier, the insert edit mode allows you to put a new sound track on previously recorded video tape. This is useful when you want to add a voice-over or music to an existing programme. A useful addition to the editing suite is a simple sound mixer that allows you to input two or more sound sources. This gives you the opportunity to mix voice, music and the original track with some control over the volume level. Non-linear editing systems give you a good level of control over sound editing. Some systems have six to eight sound tracks allowing you to put down different sound on each track. These can then be mixed down on the final version of the programme.

Having completed a paper edit you will know the order of shots. You will know approximately where each shot is located on your camera original tape. You will now have to transfer the camera original material electronically on to the master edit tape.

Cutting points

Your master edit tape should begin with a black section before the programme starts. The viewer does not want to look at a screen full of 'noise' (the inherent video signal on blank tape). The black screen should signify that something is about to happen. The first thing that you put down may well be the title of the programme. The sequence for editing this should be:

1 Find the start of the title section you want from your camera original tape and mark this on your edit controller.

2 Find the place on your edit master where you want the title sequence to start and mark this on your edit controller.

3 Look at the sequence using the preview facility on the edit controller.

4 If the sequence looks satisfactory then complete the edit using the edit function on the edit controller.

This should now be the first edited sequence. You should now proceed with editing scene after scene. It is important to remember that when you edit scenes together you should be aware of continuity. If a woman in scene 1 walks away from the camera holding a stick, she must have the same prop in scene 2. Similarly if she is holding a door handle in scene 12 and you cut to scene 13 and show her walking through the doorway, she should still be holding the door handle. The viewer will notice any discrepancies in continuity.

There are occasions when you can save time by taking out the irrelevant parts of the action to avoid the audience becoming bored with the story. For example, in *Road Safety for Primary Schools* the shot of the main character walking across the restaurant to the counter could take several seconds. The audience knows that he is walking across the restaurant and therefore it is not essential to show the whole of his journey. As long as the audience is not confused by the messages that you give them it is safe to save time in this way. Similarly you can extend time to create impact. John is seen on the side of the road after leaving the restaurant. In just ten seconds he has walked into the road and been hit by a bus. This is a dramatic scene that can be enhanced by cutting from John on the road side to a shot of his friends calling. Cutting to the bus approaching, John starts to run, the friends sense that something is wrong. John is now leaving the pavement and the shot cuts to the bus looming large... and so on. The scene is extended and the drama increased by this use of 'extended time'.

Activity

Now assemble edit the first ten scenes of your programme. This may include the title sequence that you prepared earlier. Once you have made your assemble edit try to replace a scene using the insert edit facility.

Sound dubbing

You will have recorded direct sound from the microphone on your camera during your shoot. This may be speech or background noise. It is not always desirable to have this sound track in the finished programme. You may want to add a new sound track that removes the background noise and puts in a new sound. Most editing suites will have a facility for removing a sound track and laying down a new one. Problems will occur if you want to insert a new sound track with someone speaking who is in vision. To enable you to '**lip sync**' the person in vision exactly to the new sound track would require a high level of sophisticated sound equipment.

The simplest form of sound dubbing is when you insert a new sound track of a voice-over or music track over existing visual material. In *Road Safety for Primary Schools* a new sound track was added over the scene outside the restaurant. The noise from the traffic was so bad that it detracted from the visual impact of the scene. Sound effects of traffic were added later and a voice-over calling John from the other side of the road was re-recorded and mixed on to the master edit.

Activity

Using the footage you have just edited of the classroom or studio environment assignment use the sound dubbing facility to record:

- music over the title sequence or first few scenes
- a voice-over explaining what the video is about over the remaining scenes.

Activity

Having produced the first few scenes and tried sound dubbing now go on and edit together the whole programme. It may take some time to make the whole programme but keep trying your new skills in this exercise.

Editing video tape electronically has the disadvantage of **generation loss** every time you copy the signal. You must have seen a VHS video tape that has been copied once or twice. The picture quality deteriorates rapidly every time you copy the copy. Sound recording does not suffer quite so much as the picture grain and colour bleed. The higher the quality system that you use for the editing process the less there is grain increase and colour bleed. Recent advances in editing equipment and materials have seen the introduction of **digital recording**. This system relies on the recording of data signals and less on the quality of the tape and recording process used. A recent experiment by a leading video equipment manufacturer showed that a digitally recorded tape could be copied and copies made from the copies 120 times with no loss of quality. Digital recording equipment will be the recording medium of the future. Already news crews are using cameras fitted with hard disk drives that download their footage straight to a computer for non-linear editing.

The master edit tape

The only record of your finished edit is the master edit tape. This tape should be clearly labelled and stored safely. Any record disabling device on the cassette should be used to ensure that no-one records over your material. As discussed earlier the programme should start with a black screen, or if you have the technology, you could use a video clock that counts down to the start of the programme. Many video graphics computer programmes have this clock in their memory. Whether you use a clock or black space you should note down how much time you have before the programme starts.

It is advisable to make a copy of your master edit tape after completing the edit. Running a tape through a video playback machine can result in damage to the tape. Damage from worn video heads and mechanical parts can ruin a tape. Always use the copy for playing back material and only use the master edit sparingly.

Tape cueing

In the next section you will be looking at ways of showing your work to a client and an audience. When you come to show your programme it is preferable to have the tape in the right place to start the show, or 'cued up'.

Remember to remove the safety recording tabs from your tapes before you put them into your playback machine. By doing this you will ensure that you do not record over your material by mistake.

In this section you have looked at the editing process from paper edits to new technology in computer-based editing. You will have experienced manipulating material and changing the order of both sound and visual material. For some people this part of the production process is the most exciting and for others it is very tedious. One thing is certain, every moving image programme will need editing at some stage. Remember to keep records of all the skills you have developed in this section. Keep examples of all the material you have produced on paper and on tape or film.

Assignment

Your on-going pilot programmes for the cable channel can now be edited and two master edit tapes prepared. Produce:

- two edit master programmes together with notes on the editing process used
- a copy of your edit decision list
- a log of all recorded rushes that indicates their relevance to the script and their technical quality
- a record of any additional material that you used.

Review and evaluate moving image products

In this unit you have considered the process of planning, recording and editing a moving image product. In Study Unit 2 when you undertook research for your moving image products you looked at audiences. You will remember that the audience for your product is important. From the very earliest stage you should have taken into account the type of audience you are aiming at. Now that your product is complete you should address the issue of audience again.

The product you have made has been produced for an identified target audience. It is important that you address this group to find out their views on the completed product. If it is possible to arrange a viewing of your product you could invite a suitable cross-section of the target audience to see your work and ask them to comment on it. If it is not possible to arrange a viewing then you will have to find alternative ways of showing it to the audience.

Presenting your work

Activity

Bearing in mind the possible target audience for *Road Safety for Primary Schools*, how would you find out the views of the audience? Produce a list of possible ways of finding out people's views.

It may be possible to get a number of people to see the programme and then to comment. In this case the audience would have been schools across a wide area. To gather their views a number of pre-release copies of the video were sent by post to a cross-section of schools. The cassette was accompanied by a questionnaire that asked the viewer very specific questions about the content of the programme. It would be unreasonable to ask questions on technical matters to people who may not have any technical expertise. The questionnaire was accompanied by a stamped addressed envelope and a short thank-you letter.

On the next page is a sample of part of the questionnaire about the viewer's perception of the programme used:

Fig. 5.23
Audience questionnaire

ROAD SAFETY FOR PRIMARY SCHOOLS

QUESTIONNAIRE

Having seen *Road Safety for Primary Schools*, could you now answer the following questions. Please indicate your answer by ticking the appropriate response.

What age groups viewed the programme?

| under 16 | 16 to 19 | over 19 |

Do you think that the programme was suitable for this audience?

| Yes | No | Maybe |

Did the programme spell out the dangers of crossing the road safely?

| Yes | No |

Was the programme length:

| too long? | too short? | about right? |

You may wish to devise questions about the entertainment value of the programme. If your programme, or part of it, has been made as a drama, you need to find out whether or not people have enjoyed it. Does the programme come over as up-to-date? Is it relevant to the audience that you are showing it to?

Activity

Devise a suitable questionnaire for the programme that you produced on the environment of your classroom or studio. Use techniques that make answering the questionnaire as straightforward as possible, such as tick boxes or ringed answers.

People sometimes find it difficult to complete questionnaires, particularly if they have to write their views in long sentences. It is much easier for them to tick a box or ring an answer. If you are asking for a more detailed answer then you may have to suggest the viewer writes a short sentence. It may be better to have some tick boxes and some written answers in the same questionnaire.

The questionnaires sent out with *Road Safety for Primary Schools* only began to arrive back after two weeks. Only 50 per cent of the questionnaires were returned, with the final one arriving two months after it was sent out. So this method achieves results but at a cost of time and limited response. The most successful method of gauging an audience's reaction must be a viewing of the programme with an invited audience.

Do not be disheartened by people's negative views of your work. See them as a pointer to doing better next time. You could always use their comments to re-edit the programme or even re-shoot some of the material. Sometimes it is better to sit down with the audience after a viewing and ask for their immediate response. Their views could be recorded on a tape cassette for later transcription. Some people will be more lucid in a face-to-face situation than in a written questionnaire.

Activity

1 How would you arrange a viewing of your programme to an invited audience? Make a list of all the preparations you would have to make.

2 How would you ensure that a suitable number of people attended the viewing? How would you ensure that all of the audience completed a questionnaire after the viewing? What would you have to do to ensure that the audience was in the right frame of mind for viewing the programme?

In the case of *Road Safety for Primary Schools* it was decided to hold a viewing of the programme for local school teachers, road safety experts and young people from two age groups , 11–13 and 15–17. All of the intended audience were sent personal invitations asking them to attend and giving sufficient directions.

The room to be used was laid out in a manner that meant that all the audience could see the screen and the sound levels were suitable for a room full of people. The room was clean and business-like with comfortable seating, warm enough for comfort but not too hot or cold to distract the viewer.

Before the programme started the guests were given refreshments in a separate room and they were given an opportunity to meet the cast and crew. A short address was given before the programme started and the tape was aligned to start exactly on cue.

The audience were notified, before the programme started, that they would be asked to complete a questionnaire. The audience was issued with pens, questionnaires and clipboards to lean on after the programme had finished. The level of feedback from this session was excellent, with 95 per cent of the audience completing a questionnaire.

This session only provided information about the content. You need to obtain feedback on the technical quality of the programme as well.

Activity

Try to think of ways of obtaining feedback about the technical quality of your programme. Who could you approach to give you an objective view of your work?

One way to do this is to invite someone from a local video production company to view your work. He/she would be able to comment on the technical quality of the programme and possibly suggest strategies for improving your work.

Activity

Compile a questionnaire about the technical quality of your programme. When you have designed the questionnaire try it out with your teacher. Ask your teacher to watch the programme and answer the questions.

A questionnaire about technical quality might include questions on:
- camera work
- composition
- sound levels
- editing techniques
- graphics.

Analysing audience feedback

Once you have obtained as much information as you can from the audience, what then? The information on the questionnaires needs to be analysed and recorded in a way that will show just what people think about the programme. For example, it was found that 75 per cent of the audience thought that *Road Safety for Primary Schools* was just about the right length. 15 per cent thought that it was too short and 10 per cent thought that it was too long. From these figures you could assume that you have got the programme length about right.

It is interesting to note that in feature film making the producers invariably go to audience research for information before their film hits the cinema. A classic example is the movie *Star Trek: Generations*. In the film Captain Kirk, the previous captain of the Enterprise, returns to fight alongside the new captain, Jon Luc Picard. In the original cut of the film Captain Kirk is seen going alone to an area of the ship that is then destroyed and he is blown into space. After an audience viewing, the whole scene was filmed again. The audience decided that this scene was inappropriate and that a more tasteful death scene was required. This would have cost the production company many thousands of pounds. Why

You may have heard of a version of a film being 'the director's cut': this is a new version of the original film where the director has added as yet unseen film footage or new material.

would they go to all this trouble and expense if it was not essential to satisfy the audience?

When you begin to evaluate your programme using the feedback from an audience you must accept both positive and negative views. It is always good to have positive feedback and it can be equally good to use the negative feedback to form an action plan for further work. You could use the feedback to analyse the way that you have represented groups or individuals in your programme. You will remember the work that you undertook in Study Unit 2 on representation. This will be an opportunity to find out whether or not you have been successful in putting this into practice.

Evaluating your work

At the beginning of this unit there was a suggestion that you should keep some type of record of all the work you undertake. Whatever system you are using you should have a complete record of all the activities you worked on. You should have a record of the job rôles you undertook and a list of the skills you have learned. If you have not already undertaken a review of your work then the following questions may help you to assess what you have done and the skill level you have achieved.

- What did I do?
- What skills did I learn?
- What went wrong?
- What went right?
- What would I do if I could start again?

At all times remember to 'sell yourself'. If you have done some good work then write it down. If you have had problems then identify these.

If you have any problems with writing them down why not record your thoughts on tape, either video or sound? It may be possible to have this transcribed later or this taped evidence could be used in your assessment.

What about the team's rôle?

The rôle of your team members should also be identified. At the start of this unit it was suggested that all team meetings should be recorded in the form of minutes. These minutes will contain evidence of who said what and who will undertake which rôles. It is important that these minutes are accurate and kept up to date. These minutes will form a valuable part of your assessment not only in this unit but also towards your core skills.

Debriefing sessions are an important part of any media team event. It is common practice in the television or video industry to have a debriefing after a programme has been completed. This session must be attended by all of the team. It allows everyone's view of the programme-making activity to be heard and gives everyone an opportunity to ask questions. One of the hardest parts of being a team member comes when something goes

273

wrong. Imagine having to have your programme on air at 9 pm and one of your team members does not arrive. Obviously you do your best to fill in for the missing team member but the quality of the programme may suffer. You need a forum to discuss this and if necessary to apportion blame. In the world of live television there is no room for team members who let you down. The harsh reality is that if you are unreliable you may not get any work. There is always someone waiting to take your place.

Assignment

You have completed all the planning, production and post-production work on your two pilot programmes for the cable channel. It is now time to evaluate these programmes with the client and an audience.

- You should undertake research into audience reaction and the views of your client. You should present the findings of your research in the form of a presentation to an invited audience.
- Organise a debriefing session and at this provide an evaluation of the pilot programmes that looks at technical quality and content. The evaluation should include an appraisal of the finished products compared to a broadcast or independent film or video production.
- Produce an evaluation of your individual rôle in the planning and production process. Detail your production rôle(s) and the contribution of the team to the production process.
- All of this work should be supported by minutes of production meetings, detailed notes where applicable and a personal record of skills development.

Summary

In this final section you have been able to show your work to the client and to an audience. You have developed questionnaires and analysed the results. You will have analysed your own rôle in the production and also the rôle of the team members.

Remember to keep all of the material that you generated through this section for assessment. This may be cassette tapes of interviews, completed questionnaires, analysis of results and your own actions plans for changes.

It is always great to show your work to an audience. There is a real buzz about having people watch something that you have created. Listen out for the appreciative whispers as the programme goes on. Watch out for the shuffling of feet or bottoms if they are getting bored.

Throughout this unit you have been able to plan, prepare, record, edit and evaluate two moving image products. Much of the work you have undertaken has been practical in nature and some of the work has involved written skills. Media professionals have to have practical skills as well as the ability to communicate effectively orally and in writing.

You will have developed many new skills in programme making and you have experienced making real media products. You have undertaken professional practice in this unit and you should be proud of the finished products.

Glossary

ambient refers to background noise picked up unintentionally during recording

Broadcast/BARB a chart of the top television shows which is compiled by *Broadcast* magazine and a research organisation that represents advertisers

buzz tracks the ambient 'noise' that occurs wherever you record which can be used in a section of a programme that has no voice or music

BVU High Band SP a video recording system developed from the **High Band** system. SP stands for superior performance

camera original material that has been recorded by the camera onto film or video tape. It is the only record of the shoot. It should be given a sequential number for reference and stored carefully

commission a generally accepted term in the media industry meaning that you have been given a brief for which you understand you will be paid

continuity ensuring all necessary details such as props and costumes stay the same from scene to scene

crash editing this is a system of editing together video footage with only two video machines and no edit controller

debrief when the team gets together to discuss any problems that have occurred during the recording session

depth of field the range of distances from the camera within which subjects remain in acceptable focus

digital recording a binary based system that records a series of electronic pulses which are stored and then re-digitised on playback

edit controller this device takes over the mechanical operation of the player and recorder, telling each machine where the edit point is to be and running each machine back just the right amount to make a clean edit point

edit master the tape that you have made by editing your camera original footage

electronic effects these effects are produced in a vision mixer or computer and include simple effects like freeze frame (still image) or mosaic where the image is split up into tiny squares, and more complicated effects such as page turns

field footage log a production assistant or assistant director keeps a log, noting details of all the footage that is shot whilst on location or in the studio, including the scene number and take with an outline of the scene and the time that the scene runs, and an indication of whether this scene/take will be useful in the final edit. In film production the log may include details of lighting conditions to enable the laboratory to correctly balance colours in the rush print

floor plan a schematic diagram of the studio floor that shows the location of the scenery, props, microphones and cameras

footage a length of filmed material, possibly a scene, that is waiting to be spliced together with the following scene. Used for any medium

gaffer grip a device that can be attached to walls or scenery allowing a lamp to be positioned in awkward situations

generation loss the reduction in quality every time a tape is copied

High Band Umatic format a high quality video recording system introduced after Low Band Umatic. It has greater picture quality and definition. It has been superceded by Betacam and Digital Betacam both broadcast standard for picture and sound

hazard tape used to secure trailing cables to the floor or as a warning around a secure area. Brightly coloured

lighting gels pieces of plastic or cellulose that have been dyed to very accurate colour, used to change the colour of the light coming from lamps

lighting plan a schematic diagram of the television studio that shows clearly where lamps have been placed and which lamps have been used

lighting rig the support system in the ceiling of the television studio which allows lamps to be positioned above and around the set at a safe distance from the crew and actors

lip sync the link between the subject and the sounds he/she makes which should always be in synchronisation

logged a written record of visual or sound recording activity

Low Band Umatic format the industry standard video recording format using $^3/_4$" video tape. The first high quality system to be introduced, and still in use today

non-linear editing a system where the camera original material is transferred from tape on to a computer hard disk drive, enabling it to be accessed and scenes located and moved around very quickly

pan camera movement from left to right or right to left, used for following a moving object

pedestal a hydraulic or counterbalanced studio camera mount which allows smooth movement across the studio floor and camera movement directly up and down with little effort

rate card companies that hire out equipment or editing suites will produce this list of their charges, normally based on one day's hire with a discount for more than one day

release form everyone appearing on screen gives the broadcaster their permission to be filmed by signing a form, sometimes also agreeing a fee

rushes all film footage shot each day is processed overnight and 'rushed' to be viewed before the next day's shooting. In video terms, a review of footage to ensure that everything is going smoothly

scrim a translucent, heat resistant material placed over a lamp to restrict the flow of light to produce a soft lighting effect

sound track the part of the programme that provides sound, whether music, voice or sound effects

sync (synchronisation) the link between the picture and the sound. When picture and sound are recorded together they are 'in sync'. With video the two are recorded at the same time but in film the sound is recorded on a separate tape and synchronised with the picture later

telephoto lens also called a narrow angle or long focus lens, this gives a telescopic view of a subject with a very narrow field of view, making the subject look flat or foreshortened

time-slot a particular point in the running order of a broadcast company's programming

track a technique whereby a camera runs on something approaching railway tracks, allowing it to follow the action whilst remaining steady

transition the movement between one scene and the next

video heads a video recorder or camcorder records the video signal on to a tape by placing an electronic signal on the tape via small, sensitive heads mounted on a drum mechanism

vision mixer this device allows two or more channels of video picture to be mixed together to one output. It will also allow effects to be added to the picture and some can incorporate sound mixers of two or more sound inputs that can be linked to vision for fades in and out

white balance an electronic system that matches the colour temperature of the light source to the cameras circuits

wide-angle lens a lens which shows a greater area of the scene, giving a feeling of distance and, in an extremely wide angle, a distorted view

wipes the ways in which one picture on a T.V. screen can change into another. The first image is moved or wiped across the screen to be replaced by another

zoom movement of a camera lens into a close up of a subject

Audience research

G
N
V
Q

Contents

Introduction

In Study Unit 2 you focused on the way in which research is used in the media industries to establish content and to investigate practical production requirements. In this unit you will see how the same research principles and procedures are extended to obtain information about audiences.

Audience research is used for a wide variety of commercial, social and academic purposes. Reliably conducted, it can provide essential data, not only about the size and nature of the audience for a particular media product, but also about the response of the audience to that product.

You will explore a number of theories about the relationship between media and audiences and the ways in which research is planned, conducted and evaluated. You will also have the opportunity to carry out your own audience research.

In Section 1, you will investigate the range of uses of audience research in the media, identifying the principal methods of research and assessing their strengths and weaknesses. You will also find out about the work of official research bodies and independent research agencies.

In Section 2, you will compare models which view audiences as passive receivers and as active users of media texts. You will gain a basic understanding of the theoretical positions underlying these models and conduct a small-scale research task to explore their validity.

In Section 3, you will focus on the analysis of published data to identify trends and changes in media consumption. Finally, in Section 4, you will apply what you have learned about research methodology to two pieces of audience research, one relating to an existing commercial product and the other to one of your own products.

1 Uses and methods of audience research

Uses of audience research

> 'Market research tells us that the average classical music CD buyer purchases as many as 100 CDs a year, this can add up to well over £1000. Some buyers have been known to purchase up to 10 CDs per week, that is over £5000 a year!'
>
> Advertisement for Thru the Looking Glass music club in *BBC Music Magazine*, February 1996

> 'We've done extensive research... There's a growing young, highly intelligent, very demanding and highly sought-after **demographic** group appearing in our figures.'
>
> Jerry Johns, spokesman for BBC Television's *Pebble Mill* daytime programme, quoted in the *Independent*, February 1996

> 'In many market places, consumer dissatisfaction presents a very important opportunity for a new product... The research showed that listeners were very dissatisfied with current radio stations ... and showed considerable demand for a talk-based radio station.'
>
> QuestionAir for Talk Radio

Fig. 6.1
Selection of newspapers

'Research shows that there is widespread public support for the continued existence of advertising-free services. That support is particularly for those services which appeal to young people and children, in contrast to the large and increasing number of advertising-led commercial services that are strongly targeted at those groups.'

Extending Choice – The BBC's Rôle in the New Broadcasting Age,
BBC, 1992

'... A recent study shows how traditional print publishers are not the only people producing well-respected on-line news services. Only five of the web news sites in the 1995 top 10 are from newspaper publishers – others come from dedicated on-line providers and broadcasters.'

Simon Waldman in the *Guardian*, 8 January 1996

'Most people (75 per cent) think that there is more violence now than there was about ten years ago. However, most people are mistaken. Violence and concerns about violence have clearly increased in society in the last decade, but this has not been reflected by a proportional increase on television.'

G. Cumberbatch, *The Portrayal of Violence on British Television,*
BBC, 1987

Activity

Each of the above quotations illustrates one use of audience research. Discuss the quotations, bearing in mind the following questions:

- What product has been researched?
- Who do you think commissioned the research?
- Why do you think the research was commissioned?
- What use was being made/could be made of the research?

You may find it helpful in considering the last question to divide the uses into commercial and social.

In your discussion you probably decided that research is commissioned by a wide spectrum of the media industry: media commentators, advertisers, and the companies themselves. The commercial uses you may have considered include information for **product launches**, for product development and in assessing existing products, for marketing promotion and to inform advertisers. You may have discussed how the social uses of audience research include the provision of data to inform the public on issues relating to the effects of the media, for example, violence in the media and how people use or are used by the media. Social research may also be used to inform the government and the public about media industries and their relationship with their audiences.

Most money on audience research is spent for and by potential advertisers. Buying media space today is a very precise business. Before media buyers book any advertising space/time, they will need the figures to show that they are using their companies' money wisely. The research data they consult will enable them to decide which medium or combination of media to use, which individual product(s) within those media to choose (i.e. the one that is most effective in reaching their target markets), how they should address those markets and when, where, how and how often they should place their advertising for maximum benefit. Most advertising packs from media companies will provide not only the numbers of their viewers/listeners/readers/consumers, but also detailed information about their buying habits and **lifestyle profile**, so that the media buyers can make an informed choice. They will also study **ratings** each week, such as the *Broadcast*/BARB Top 70.

Ratings are the 'currency' used to negotiate advertising space and time.

Fig. 6.2
Broadcast/Top 20 from the BARB top 70 ratings

Title	Day	Time	Viewers (millions)	% Change (week)	Broadcaster/ producer	Last year
1 Coronation Street	Wed	1930	13.71	-0.7	Granada	2
2 Coronation Street	Mon	1930	13.44	-10.0	Granada	1
3 EastEnders	Tue	1930	13.32	4.0	BBC 1	4
4 Euro 96: England v Scotland	Sat	1500	11.68	●	BBC 1	–
5 Emmerdale	Tue	1900	10.92	0.7	Yorkshire	9
6 EastEnders	Mon	1845	10.57	-25.2	BBC 1	6
7 Summer Holiday	Tue	2000	10.44	■	BBC 1	–
8 Euro 96: post-game	Sat	1645	10.03	●	BBC 1	–
9 Coronation Street	Fri	1845	9.99	-27.5	Granada	5
10 National Lottery Live	Sat	1950	9.77	-2.3	BBC 1	7
11 The Bill	Tue	2130	9.33	1.0	ITV (Thames)	14
12 World in Action	Mon	2000	9.24	40.2	Granada	–
13 The Knock	Sun	2105	9.11	-7.3	LWT (Bronson Knight)	–
14 Touch of Frost	Wed	2000	8.93	12.6	Yorkshire	15
15 Emmerdale	Thu	1900	8.46	-16.9	Yorkshire	26
15 News, Sport & Weather	Sat	2055	8.46	33.9	BBC 1	21
17 Wycliffe	Sun	2000	8.28	-19.3	HTV	16
18 Take Your Pick	Mon	2030	8.11	-7.2	ITV (Thames)	–
19 Euro 96: Holl v Scotland	Mon	1630	7.97	●	ITV Sport (Cen/API/ISN)	–
20 Casualty	Sat	2005	7.76	●	BBC 1	–

Assignment: Part 1

This is the first part of an assignment which will enable you to provide evidence for your portfolio (parts 2–4 appear later in this section). You will build up a portfolio which will include all your investigations into audience research in the print and audio-visual media industries.

- Make notes on the uses of research covered in the text above and in your discussions so far.
- Using this information, choose two examples of the uses of research – one print and one audio-visual – and analyse them in terms of who has commissioned the research and for what purpose it is used or will be used.
- You will find it helpful to use tables and/or diagrams to illustrate the data you describe in your case studies.
- Keep your notes in your portfolio.

You may wish to use articles in recent newspapers and trade magazines to find examples of media research or you may wish to begin with a table of data and investigate who commissioned it and for what.

Methods of audience research

The two major approaches to audience research are *quantitative*, which only produces numerical data, and *qualitative*, which obtains more subjective data about audience response to media products. Quantitative measurement will be limited in the type of information it provides. Advertisers and other commercial organisations require much more information about the nature of their audiences.

The methodologies used to interpret the relationships between the media and their audiences are discussed fully in the next section.

Research guidelines

Trade magazines publish weekly or monthly results of research, including the names of the relevant research bodies and organisations which are responsible for providing the data. The organisations themselves can be approached for information, but it is important to be aware that some of them consider such information to be confidential and will not release it.

There are some forms of media, such as advertising poster sites, which cannot be monitored by traditional methods. To overcome this problem, the Outdoor Advertising Association (OAA), which includes all the main contracting companies who own the sites, made an agreement with the Joint Industry Committee for Poster Audience Research (JICPAR). Together they set up a system known as OSCAR – Outdoor Site Classification and Audience Research. Launched in 1985, OSCAR sets out a standard means of measuring poster sites according to a number of criteria – see margin. These include a location code, which defines areas as principal shopping, minor shopping, residential, commercial, etc.; junction type, which includes any pedestrian crossings; and special features, which includes nearby pubs, offices, schools, railway stations and sports grounds. There is also an estimate of traffic during a two-minute count. In addition to this survey, OSCAR also judges sites according to their visibility.

Refer back to the work you did on audience research and audience types in Section 1 of Study Unit 2. This will form part of your evidence indicators for this section.

Many media studies books cover research methods, while detailed information on how media research is carried out can be found in Raymond Kent, *Measuring Media Audiences* (Routledge, 1994). Other sources for research can be found in Section 3.

Key site characteristics for OSCAR models

Vehicular audiences
- Town type
- Distance to next larger town
- Distance to town centre
- Location code
- Special features
- Junction type
- Road classification
- Number of traffic lanes
- Bus routes
- Traffic lights
- Estimate of vehicular traffic

Pedestrian audiences
- Population
- Town type
- Distance to next larger town
- Shops nearby
- Location code
- Special features
- Number of pedestrian entry points
- Estimate of pedestrian traffic

Fig. 6.3
Poster site

Select a site as a potential poster site. Take photographs or make a rough sketch of the site and indicate its key features. (You may wish to video the site and add a voice-over indicating key features.) Present your site to the class, demonstrating how it would fulfil the OSCAR requirements and why it would be an effective poster site.

Strengths and weaknesses in audience research methods

Today there is a growing demand for more detailed research into the media, which is producing more data than ever before. There are a number of reasons for this increased demand. These include:

- changing technology – the growth of new media such as CD-ROM and the Internet
- the surge of new media products, for example, the huge growth in specialist magazines
- increased viewing and listening opportunities through the growth of cable and satellite television and commercial radio stations
- **audience fragmentation** through the development of local and minority channels
- the need for media to respond to any new government legislation
- the need for more precise targeting of a reduced amount of advertising money as a result of economic recession
- the development of media studies.

This demand has led to a better understanding of what methodology is required to provide reliable data. The guidelines for research have been tightened up and are overseen by a number of industry research bodies. The need for accurate research has never been greater. It is, however, an imperfect science.

Every method of research has its own inherent weaknesses. Entire projects can be devised in such a way as to provide misleading information through targeting too small a group of people or by not covering a wide enough demographic. Equally, a **random survey** by a news programme on the topic of violence in children's comics may provide the 'evidence' for a studio debate and be given the same status as more rigorous academic research on the same subject, which has canvassed a wide spectrum of the public, in depth and over a period of time, and which has come to an opposite conclusion.

However, whenever there is any event which sets off a **moral panic**, tabloid newspapers and politicians alike use this questionable data to justify calls for media censorship.

'Research is often used to avoid making a decision for which one can be blamed. This would not be a problem if a great many research findings were not either flawed or plain wrong... I have never found anybody who admits to liking, let alone reading *Reader's Digest* mailings – [yet these] mailings... propelled the *Digest* into the pre-eminent position among the world's magazines...'

Advertising executive Drayton Bird commenting in *Marketing*, 15 February 1996

One example of unreliable research is the Parliamentary Group Video Enquiry, which suggested that large numbers of very young children were at risk as a result of watching 'video nasties'. Academics and media analysts subsequently revealed that both the methods used by the Group and the data obtained were unreliable. They had relied on self-completed questionnaires, which had allowed children to claim that they had watched non-existent videos and much of their work was based on problem families listed by the NSPCC.

Activity

Using the above information, together with what you have learned about different research methods, make notes of examples of occasions when research data might be unreliable. Make suggestions on what a researcher might do to counter these problems.

You might have made the point that research which arrives at conclusions from information provided by the public has to allow for the fact that people are often unreliable sources of information. They forget, they exaggerate, they may even lie. Diaries, in particular, can be unreliable for these reasons.

To counter such problems, you may have noted that researchers need to involve a sufficiently large **sample** size to make allowances for such factors. You may also have noted that questionnaires often attempt to obtain information through indirect questions. Members of the public are not asked whether they are part of a particular social group, but the information is generated by asking them what kind of products they buy, what kind of car they drive, where and how often they take holidays, etc. You may also have come to the conclusion that a combination of different forms of research is the best way to ensure that the research provides a balanced view. Thus, for example, the results from **audience panels** can be checked against quantitative methods, such as those using electronic data.

Activity

Read the two research projects described below and discuss the reasons why one was successful while the other was unsuccessful. What can you learn from this about the strengths and weaknesses of research methodology?

Research project A: cinema audience survey

A small regional cinema decided to find out more about its audience to enable it to target potential cinema-goers more accurately. It produced a lengthy questionnaire about audience attendance: How often did respondents come to the cinema? What kind of films did they enjoy? It also included questions about how respondents found information about the cinema, and about their occupations and their other leisure pursuits. The questionnaires were left on seats and a box was provided at the back of the auditorium for completed forms. Few people filled in the questionnaire and the cinema decided that it had not been very helpful.

Research project B: 'Video in View'

This research project was carried out by Media Monitors Market Research Consultancy for the British Board of Film Classification (BBFC). Its aim was to find out how people use video and how they react to the potentially controversial or offensive elements videos may contain, and also to gain insights into how the public uses the BBFC's classification decisions. The methodology of the research project involved two stages:

'1 An initial, in-depth qualitative stage that allowed video viewers to freely discuss their attitudes and opinions towards film classification, as well as allowing those who are involved with the classification of videos to actually meet and talk to the video film viewers;

2 A second, larger scale quantitative stage, that set out to validate these opinions amongst a nationwide sample of VCR owners and video film renters.

... As much as was possible within budgetary constraints, in the overall sample of 6 **focus groups**, we also attempted to match the age, social class and demographic profile of video renters. In addition, amongst our respondents we included a reasonably representative sample of racial minorities and those who were regular attendees at religious services.'

Having ascertained a range of attitudes and opinions from this qualitative research, the project then undertook quantitative research 'to provide an indication of the extent that these attitudes and opinions towards video film classification [were] held by a larger body of individuals (video renters)'. The sample was designed in accordance with British Video Association (BVA) data, to reflect the UK population of video renters and in order to ensure the statistical validity of the results, a sample size of 1,000 respondents (998 valid responses) was chosen. The results were analysed and the findings published by the BBFC project. The director of the BBFC commented that the publication was an important step in the Board's attempt to keep in touch with the views of the public and that the research offered 'valuable insights into how viewers actually use the system and what they think about it'.

In discussing Research project A, you may have decided that the cinema began the research without adequately assessing its objectives. The questionnaire included too many different kinds of questions. However, the main problems were simply practical ones: few of the audience had pens with them and in any case, it was not possible to fill in the questionnaire in the dark. Investing in freepost envelopes, with a prize draw for all those who responded, would have elicited a much greater response. If that was beyond the resources of the cinema, volunteers stopping one in ten members of the audience over a period of a week and asking them the questions in person would have also been effective. Also the cinema did not allow in its calculations for the time required to assess the information once it had been calculated.

Research project B was successful because it was well planned. It had clear objectives and adequate resources to carry out the research and analyse the results. Within a limited budget it balanced both quantitative and qualitative research and could be considered to be a model piece of audience research.

In discussing strengths and weaknesses in general, you may have also decided that research which uses a wide variety of methods from a large sample of the population is ideal. However, this is the most expensive way to carry out research and is not within the resources of every project.

Assignment: Part 2

Using your notes from the above activities and from your discussions, write a short report assessing the strengths and weaknesses of audience research. Find and analyse two examples of research, one into a print product and the other into an audio-visual product. Keep the report in your portfolio.

Industry research bodies

If in your research you have been using books published more than five years ago, you may have come across a number of other organisations which no longer exist.

As you have carried out your investigations for this section, the names of several research bodies will have emerged. For example, in studying the placing of posters, you have come across JICPAR. Similarly in studying the methods of research, you may have encountered the Audit Bureau of Circulations (ABC), BARB, CAA, JICREG, National Readership Surveys and RAJAR.

The joint industry bodies were set up to share the costs of market research and at the time of writing they are as follows:

- *Television* is monitored by the Broadcasters Audience Research Board (BARB), which replaced the Joint Industry Committee for Television Research (JICTAR), and is jointly run by the BBC and the Independent Television Commission (ITC). In addition to measuring television audiences, BARB also runs the Audience Reaction Service (ARS), which uses panels to evaluate all terrestrial television programmes and ASTRA to monitor satellite television. BARB has also recently taken over the measurement of cable television audiences which had previously been carried out by the Joint Industry Committee for Cable Audience Research (JICCAR).

- *Radio* audiences are measured by Radio Joint Audience Research (RAJAR), which replaced the Joint Industry Committee for Radio Audience Research (JICRAR).

- *Print media – newspapers and magazines* use National Readership Surveys, which replaced the Joint Industry Committee for National Readership

Fig. 6.4
Advertisement for
Audit Bureau of
Circulations

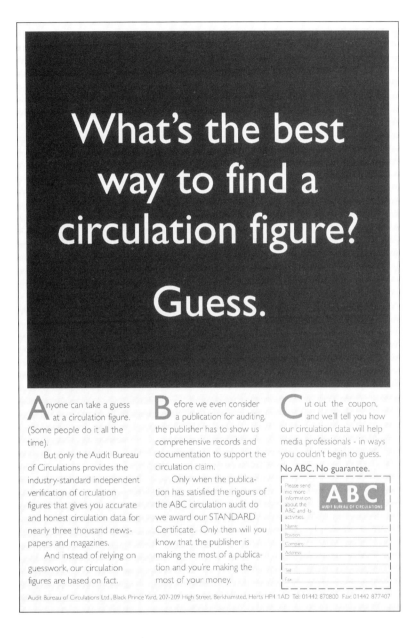

Surveys (JICNARS), and the Joint Industry Committee for Regional
Press Research (JICREG), which is administered by The Newspaper
Society. However, circulations alone are also monitored by the
publishing regulatory body, the Audit Bureau of Circulations.

- *The poster industry* is monitored by the Joint Industry Committee for
  Poster Audience Research (JICPAR).
- Cinema attendances are estimated each week by the Cinema Advertising
  Association (CAA), from figures supplied by the major circuits. These do
  not include figures for the **independent cinemas** (around 20 per cent of
  the total) nor for screens which do not accept advertising. In addition,
  cinema audiences are measured according to the CAVIAR survey.
  CAVIAR (Cinema and Video Industry Audience Research) has been
  running for over ten years and includes a range of qualitative research
  on cinema attendees and the purchase and rental of videos.

Assignment: Part 3

As a class you are going to produce a report on industry research bodies. Working in small groups, divide the industry research bodies into categories according to the media researched. Each group should then research and write brief explanations of the rôle and practices of the bodies for each of the different media industries, using the following guidelines:

- Who commissioned the research – the industry, advertisers or both?
- How independent are the research bodies from the industries?
- What methods are principally used by these bodies to measure audiences?
- What additional methods are used by these bodies to carry out qualitative research?

You may wish to contact the bodies directly or to use published material for your research. Each group should present its report to the class for evaluation to see whether there are any gaps, whether some groups have presented more information than others, what needs to be added, etc. Groups should allocate new research tasks if necessary to ensure that the report covers each body and that the rôle and practice of each is covered.

Independent research agencies

Activity

Make a list of who else – in addition to the joint research bodies you have investigated – would need to commission media research. What purposes would they have for the research? Remember the uses of research that you studied at the beginning of this section.

There are a great many bodies which might commission or undertake research. Your list might include: advertising agencies, the media companies themselves, university research departments, media and communications studies classes and campaigning and **lobbying organisations**. You may also have added a few others such as political groups, media bodies wanting external evaluation, etc. However, the majority of research not carried out by the official research bodies can be considered collectively under three general headings:

- commercial research agencies working on behalf of clients such as advertising agencies and media companies
- university research departments
- campaigning organisations.

Fig. 6.5

Readership of national daily newspapers by sex, social class and age 1993

(Percentage of adults)

| | Total | Sex | | Social grade | | |
		Men	Women	ABC1	C2DE	16–44
Daily newspapers						
The Sun	21.2	24.4	18.2	12.8	28.2	24.3
Daily Mirror	17	19.2	14.9	10.6	22.3	16.5
Daily Record	4.3	4.6	4	2.9	5.4	4.8
Daily Mail	10.5	10.7	10.2	14	7.6	9.2
Daily Express	8.5	9.2	7.9	10.8	6.6	7.2
Daily Telegraph	6	6.9	5.1	11	1.8	4.3
Daily Star	5.4	7.2	3.7	2.7	7.7	7
Today	4.1	5.4	2.9	3.7	4.4	4.7
The Guardian	3.2	3.5	2.8	5.5	1.2	3.8
The Independent	2.6	3.1	2.1	4.6	0.9	3.3
The Times	2.7	3.2	2.3	5.2	0.7	3
Financial Times	1.8	2.5	1.1	3.4	0.5	2
Any daily newspaper	**61.5**	**65.8**	**57.4**	**61.1**	**61.7**	**59**

Source: NRS Jan–June 1993

Assignment: Part 4

The final part of the assignment is both a class and individual project.

Working in groups, write a report on independent research agencies, making sure that examples of all three categories on the previous page are covered. Each group should research and write brief explanations of the rôle and practices of each organisation, using the following guidelines:

- Who commissioned the research – the university, an external industry body, a commercial company, the media body itself?
- How independent are the research agencies? (Bear in mind who is financing the research.)
- Is their research quantitative and if so, what methods are principally used by these agencies to measure audiences?
- Is their research qualitative and if so, what methodologies are being used by these agencies to elicit audience responses?

You may wish to contact some agencies directly or to use published material for your research. Each group should present its report to the class for evaluation to see whether there are any gaps, whether some groups have presented more information than others, what needs to be added, etc. Allocate new research tasks if necessary to ensure that the report covers each category and that the rôle and practice of each is covered.

Finally, make a copy of all the work that you undertook yourself and put it into the central class file, together with any notes that you made while you were researching this work. This may include notes on who you contacted, copies of letters to research bodies and notes on their replies or any absence of replies. Put all this evidence into your personal portfolio.

2 Media and their audiences

Ever since the beginning of the twentieth century the 'effects' of the media on audiences have been debated. All forms of media have been included in this controversy. In the 1920s, Hollywood gangster films were accused of corrupting the young; pop music and 'horror comics' were attacked in the 1950s and 1960s; horror movies in the 1970s and 'video nasties' in the 1980s. The 1990s saw new media such as the Internet joining the ranks of the accused. In this section you will study the evidence that is often obscured by moral panics. You will also study the nature of audiences themselves and their relationship with the media and observe the relationship of an audience to a media product.

To study audience behaviour you first need to think about the concept of what makes up an audience. In Study Unit 2 and in Section 1 you studied the various ways in which audiences can be measured and researched. Now you will explore the audience itself.

Activity

Make a list of all the possible ways in which you could be categorised as an audience. Use all the various ways in which audiences are measured.

You will almost certainly have included basic categories such as gender, age and your occupation as a student. You will have decided that there are a number of different ways in which you can be categorised, for example, in terms of lifestyle (using the Acorn and TGI models which you studied in Study Unit 2).

Activity

You have thought about *who* you are as a media audience. Now think about *how* you consume media. Monitor your family's media consumption over a 24-hour period. Keep a diary and note when the television is switched on and what those in the television room are doing at the same time. Note, too, what your family do while the radio is on and while they play music and how they read books, newspapers and magazines.

291

In your family media survey, you may have noted that although the television is often on for long periods of time, people do not watch it consistently. They do other things at the same time and wander in and out of the room. They may cook, clean or do homework while the radio is on or while music is played. They may read newspapers during television programmes, picking them up and putting them down as items of interest appear on the screen. They do not consume media products in the home with the same concentration that they watch a film in a cinema. They also talk while they are watching.

Jeremy Tunstall, *The Media in Britain*, Constable, 1983

These different modes of media consumption have been described by the sociologist Jeremy Tunstall as primary, secondary and tertiary.

- *Primary* involvement is when the media product is the sole focus of activity – for example when you are totally involved in the book you are reading or the video you are watching.
- *Secondary* consumption is when you are doing other things – for example listening to the radio or music while doing the ironing.
- *Tertiary* consumption is when the radio or television is on, but you are taking very little notice of it.

Models of audience behaviour

The concept of the 'mass' audience which could be influenced by 'mass' media belongs to this century, although many of the concerns regarding mass media are very much older.

Vance Packard, *The Hidden Persuaders*, Penguin, 1956

In the 1950s writers such as Vance Packard claimed that audiences were being unconsciously manipulated by advertising to buy products. Television, in particular, has been singled out for reducing its audience to the level of zombies or '**couch potatoes**'. Those who assert these theories hold that audiences absorb messages from the media in a passive form which is then reproduced a short time later. There are others who believe that the media offer audiences a wide range of more active responses.

Fig. 6.6
Cartoon by Steve Bell

'We must get away from the habit of thinking in terms of what the media do to people and substitute for it the idea of what people do with the media.'

James Halloran cited in T. O'Sullivan, B. Dutton and P. Rayner, *Studying the Media*, Edward Arnold, 1994

Activity

In class make a list of a dozen characters from popular serials such as *Brookside*, *EastEnders*, *Grange Hill*, etc. Create a questionnaire to obtain opinions on the characters and to find out how these opinions have been formed. These might include:

- by myself from watching the programme
- from talking with my family
- in discussions at school
- reading about them in the press.

Use the questionnaires to interview fellow students, family and friends. Collate all the answers and use pie charts to present the results as percentages.

As you discovered in studying the weaknesses of research (Section 1), all research into audience behaviour is to some extent subjective. In addition, audiences faced with a variety of media experiences can behave very differently. Researchers themselves have a variety of points of view which can influence how they look at the media and the results they produce – see this feature from the *Radio Times*, for example.

Who is television's biggest love rat?

**DES BARNES (Phillip Middlemiss),
CORONATION STREET**

Early signs Newlywed Des moves into the street with wife Steph. She has an affair and leaves him. Des retaliates by burning his boat. He has a lot to learn. **Rat rating: 0/10**

Unfaithful urges Cheats on *Street* favourite Raquel with scheming Tanya. **Rating: 8/10**

Malicious meddling Steals Terry Duckworth's estranged wife Lisa while hubby's in jail. Raquel calls off her wedding to Curly after Des declares his love – at their engagement party! Tries to woo married Liz MacDonald, who has "been there" with his brother Colin. **Rating: 10/10**

Relative ructions Terry hires some boys to see to him. He also comes to blows with Curly and brawls with Alex Christie, Tanya's other lover. **Rating: 9/10**

What the tabloids say 'Phil Middlemiss – an ace bird puller on and off the box – doesn't see himself as one of Britain's luckiest men. He reckons he is missing out on ... true love.' **Rating: 6/10**

RAT TOTAL: 33/50

**DAVID WICKS (Michael French)
EASTENDERS**

Early signs Schoolboy affair with Carol Jackson produces daughter. David leaves. Later marriage produces two more children. David leaves.
Rat rating: 10/10

Unfaithful urges Affair with Cindy Beale, behind husband Ian's back. Cindy has dubious distinction of cheating on Ian with both Wicks brothers, David and Simon.
Rating: 5/10

Malicious meddling He asks Cindy to leave Ian. She offers to bring the children.
Rating: 1/10

Relative ructions Fights with Mitchell boys over his "seeing" their sister Sam in Spain. Holds a torch for Bianca, before he knows she's his daughter.
Rating: 7/10

What the tabloids say 'His piercing eyes and disarming smile have ... charmed the pants off half the [women] in Albert Square.'
Rating: 7/10

RAT TOTAL: 30/50

Radio Times, 10 February 1996

Passive models of audience behaviour

Hypodermic needle theory

'[Children] watch the screen and passively soak in images, words and sounds hour after hour, as if in a dream.'
Marie Winn, *The Plug-in Drug*, Penguin, 1977

The 'hypodermic needle' view of audiences is that the material from the television set goes directly into the veins of the audience, who absorb it and then immediately reproduce it. This is the fear of the media as dangerous propaganda, and the effectiveness of television advertising is often cited as an example of this effect.

For supporters of this theory television has been the principal culprit – children are passive viewers – there is no interaction with the material watched. However, television is not the only medium to face this criticism. In recent years, video and computer games have been attacked for 'hypnotising' audiences.

Activity

Discuss the hypodermic needle theory, using your own experience as members of media audiences. Bear in mind the following questions:

- What groups might prefer to believe this theory and why?
- Does your family's viewing behaviour bear out this theory?
- Is the information you have learned about how people watch soaps consistent with this theory?

In your discussion you probably noted that it tends to be politicians and the tabloid press who use this theory when they want to attack the media. From your own family's viewing behaviour and from your discussion about soaps with family and friends, you may also have commented that this theory is not reliable. Audiences are not the 'sponges' that the theory suggests and they do not 'simply watch' television.

Subject position theory

Activity

Read the advertisements on pages 295-6 and discuss what possible responses the advertising copy invites. Include in your discussion a profile of the personae addressed in these advertisements and how advertising researchers might have categorised them.

You may have decided that while the advertisements themselves would not necessarily make you purchase the product, the way in which the copy was written could only generate one response. The rhetorical questions that introduce the Ford Fiesta advertisement and the assertion of individuality in the Lux advertisement do not allow for other readings. The Health and Safety Executive (page 296) presumes that the readers of its advertisement would prefer not to die suddenly in their sleep.

Fig. 6.7
Ford Fiesta
advertisement

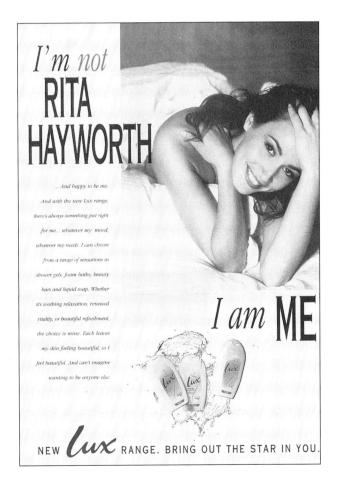

Fig. 6.8
Lux advertisement

Fig. 6.9
Highland Spring
mineral water
advertisement

Fig. 6.10
Health and Safety
Executive
advertisement

These forms of media text create their subject and then address that subject. They are the result of marketing research and they have a fixed objective – to sell a product. The theory of subject position holds that all media texts do this. It maintains that people's need to belong – to find a niche where they feel at home and comfortable – is satisfied by the mass media. The media offer an imaginary image of ourselves with which we can identify. When we are addressed as being that image, we can have only a limited set of responses.

It is easy to see how the audience is created and addressed by some advertisements, but in terms of other media, the manner of address is altogether subtler. Watch television or listen to the radio closely and you will be able to identify a variety of modes of address. These include:

- *Teacher/pupil* – giving the audience information.
- *Parent/child* – giving the impression that the media represent an authority which knows best. This follows the Reithian principle – laid down by Lord Reith who founded the BBC – that radio existed 'to Educate, Entertain and Inform'. Such an attitude is implied in the nickname of the BBC as 'Auntie'.
- *Peer* – the concept that you are one of us, for example, sports commentary, *Top of the Pops*, etc. On regional radio the concept of being part of the same audience is also emphasised by the use of 'we' to include the listeners.
- *Fluctuating* – offering the audience changing allegiances, for example, in a game show when the audience is invited to switch between identifying with the contestants, the studio audience or the quiz compere.

Activity

Find examples of different modes of address from television, radio or the press and identify them according to the terms above or by adding some modes of address of your own. Keep your notes in your portfolio.

In your examples you may have found that there is a wide range of modes of address. You may have noted that broadcasters and writers often make assumptions about who their audiences are, which might not be accurate. You may also have observed how the use of local as opposed to national modes is emphasised by the use of regional accents and shared local knowledge. You may also have been surprised by the number of times the viewer is addressed directly as 'you'. You may have decided that this form of direct 'hailing' sometimes limits the number of audience responses, but not in every case.

Stimulus-response theory

Many theories which allege a passive response to the media come from the background of behaviourist psychology. They allege that audiences can be conditioned to respond to any form of stimulus.

The theory of subject position was promoted by the French intellectual Louis Althusser. In his influential essay, 'Ideology and ideological state apparatuses' Althusser maintains that 'ideology represents the imaginary relationship of individuals to their real conditions of existence'. He argues that this ideology transforms individuals into subjects by 'hailing' them: '...along the lines of the most commonplace everyday police (or other) hailing "Hey, you there!"... Assuming that the theoretical scene I have imagined takes place in the street, the hailed individual will turn round. By this mere one-hundred-and-eighty degree physical conversion, he becomes a *subject*. Why? Because he had recognised that the hail was *really* addressed to him, and that it was *really him* who was hailed (and not someone else).'
From Louis Althusser *Lenin and Philosophy and Other Essays*, New Left Books, 1971

'In making a media artefact ... the producers are not neutrally or innocently concerned with simply assembling these elements ... but are involved in the process of inscribing into the texts a limited number of possible positions which the reader/viewer can adopt.'
M. Alvarado, R. Gutch and T. Wollen, *Learning the Media*, Macmillan, 1987

An example of a paternalistic, nannying style is the reassurance at the close of *Crimewatch UK* that violent crime is actually quite rare, ending with 'Please, don't have nightmares'.

When the character 'Gill' in the soap EastEnders died of AIDS, many viewers responded to the actress as if she was the character and not an actress. The identification was so strong that she felt that she herself had to respond to it. 'I got amazing abuse, I got slapped in the face, I got spat at ... the reaction was enormous. It became very clear to me from the numbers of letters I got from people asking questions that there was a need for me to make a video about HIV awareness' (comment made during a debate on soaps on *Esther*, BBC2, March 1996).

An example often cited in support of such theories is the audience reaction to Orson Welles' radio production of H G Wells' *War of the Worlds* in 1938. The American radio audience believed that they were being invaded by Martians and thousands of people panicked and tried to leave New York.

Media propaganda draws on the stimulus-response theory. Propaganda is as old as the media themselves: the leap from eighteenth-century cartoons and political pamphlets to the **knocking copy** in American television commercials for political parties is one of technology not of content.

Activity

Discuss the stimulus-response theory, bearing in mind its essential assumption that if the stimulus is strong enough, audiences will respond as directed: for example, audience reaction to shopping channels on cable television. Suggest your own examples to illustrate the theory. Make notes from your discussion.

You may have decided that there are some occasions when some people will respond to direct stimuli, but that it should not be seen as an exclusive theory – many people will not respond. You may also have considered the importance of the context and that this itself can sometimes exert just as much influence as the text itself. Another point you may have mentioned is that audiences are made up of a number of different groups and should not be considered simply as one mass entity. Your examples may have included advertisements, party political broadcasts, telethons and motoring organisation weather warnings.

' ... audiences work upon texts in complex and different ways, just as much as texts work upon audiences.'

Len Masterman, *Teaching the Media*, Routledge, 1985

Active models: what people do with media

The quotation from James Halloran referred to on page 293 is at the heart of all the active models of audience behaviour. There is a great deal of confusion about active and passive responses in media studies, but you will be able to cut through the muddle if you refer back to Halloran. Thus if an article tells you that your health will suffer if you do not take some exercise and gives you the phone number of a gym which you immediately ring up, this is a passive reaction (stimulus-response), however active you may subsequently become. But if you read the same article and then discuss it with friends and think about it before deciding whether or not to take up some exercise, it is an active response. In this case you have not shown a knee-jerk reaction, but have assimilated the information into an ongoing personal debate. The media have made a contribution to what you think.

'It certainly seems that, over the last few years, things have changed in the world of media studies. As we all know, in the bad old days television audiences were considered as passive consumers, to whom things happened as television's miraculous powers affected them. According to choice, these (always other) people were turned into zombies, transfixed by bourgeois ideology or filled with consumerist desires.'

David Morley, *Television, Audiences, and Cultural Studies*, Routledge, 1992

However, as David Morley has pointed out, the current trend in media studies is to say: passive models – out, active models – in. As you study active models, you should remember that audiences do not all behave in the same way and that different theories offer different readings of similar behaviour.

Uses and gratifications theory

This theory maintains that instead of passively absorbing the media, consumers actively use media texts to gratify a variety of personal needs. This reflects Lord Reith's desire to educate, entertain and inform, but it goes further. It incorporates the lives and personalities of the audience themselves. Thus there may be some people who become devoted followers of soap operas to fill gaps in their own lives. Similarly there are people who buy and read newspapers, magazines, books and more recently CD-ROMs to obtain information they do not already possess.

J. Blumler and E. Katz, *The Uses of Mass Communications*, Sage, 1974

Blumler and Katz developed a theory which was quickly taken up by a number of media studies writers and is still used to assess the needs of television audiences. This theory proposes that audiences' gratifications can be categorised in the following manner:

'1 *Diversion* – a form of escape or emotional release from everyday pressures.
2 *Personal relationships* – companionship via television personalities and characters, and sociability through discussion about television with other people.
3 *Personal identity* – the ability to compare one's life with the characters and situations within programmes, and hence explore personal problems and perspectives.
4 *Surveillance* – a supply of information about "what's going on in the world".'

Summarised in T. O'Sullivan, B. Dutton and P. Rayner, *Studying the Media*, Edward Arnold, 1994

Activity

The following remarks were made during a debate on soaps on the BBC2 talk show *Esther* in March 1996. Compare them with the data you obtained from your own soap survey. Then analyse them using Blumler and Katz's four headings.

'I think *Neighbours* educates children while watching it. Bullying came up and at the moment there's bulimia – and that's educating parents.'

A teenage viewer

Esther Rantzen to member of *Emmerdale Farm* fan club: 'How much does *Emmerdale Farm* occupy your life?' Fan: 'All of it. I've got an *Emmerdale* cabin in the garden which is full of *Emmerdale* photos... I've got *Emmerdale* curtains in the kitchen... made from *Emmerdale* tea-towels. Everything is *Emmerdale*. We spend all our holidays on location with the film crew and just everything is geared around *Emmerdale*. We never miss it. Not ever... I think it's basically we're fond of the actors as well as the characters... we'd follow them anywhere.'

> 'I think the interesting thing is that different people watch different soaps and they find something to fill their lives which might be empty. Some people will love one soap and some people will love another soap and it gives them something to talk about and it gives them something to look forward to. There are a lot of lonely people in the world... and [soaps give them] a feeling of identity.'
>
> Julia Smith, BBC producer, *EastEnders*

> 'I think it's harmless fun after a day at work, like dipping into a favourite novel.'
>
> A viewer

> '*EastEnders* has never once said "This is right, this is wrong". What it has always done is to present different people in the programme saying "Well, I think she should have an abortion", then someone else says she shouldn't. They all give their points of view, which opens out conversations in the home and in schools.'
>
> Julia Smith

Reflecting on soaps in relation to the uses and gratifications model, you probably decided that while it works well for some programmes, it has serious limitations as a model which covers all forms of audience behaviour. It does not take into account the various ways in which audiences take in the media, such as listening to music while doing another activity. It assumes that audiences have a number of innate needs which media products fulfil – a belief which is held by many who work in the media.

Positional models

In opposition to this theory are a number of models that argue it is the media texts themselves which create the audience – who then react to these texts in a number of different ways. You have already seen how this theory has been taken up by film studies and it is now the basis of most media studies models. The theorists who use these models tend to have political and sociological backgrounds. The question these theorists ask to analyse these models is 'How are we positioned by this text?' You might therefore find it helpful to call them **positional theories**.

Dominant, negotiated and oppositional theory

The sociologist Stuart Hall used the concept of hegemony, arguing that media products – television programmes, newspapers, etc. – contained the basic assumptions held by their producers – invariably white, middle-class males. These produced dominant meanings which limited the scope for audience reaction. Hall set up a model which offers three ways in which

Underlying most positional theories is the concept of **hegemony**. Graeme Burton explains this concept as 'the social and cultural power which the elite and privileged members of society have over the rest. Hegemony naturalizes this power to the extent that it becomes invisible. No one stops to question notions of high art or of good taste, as taught in schools and colleges ... Similarly, the class structure of the social system tends to be taken for granted. Ultimately the concept of hegemony underpins Parliament itself, creating an assumption that what it does must be right and good for society as a whole'.

(*More Than Meets the Eye*, Edward Arnold, 1990).

audiences can react to media. These are:

- the *dominant* – sometimes called preferred – hegemonic position, where the audience agrees with the viewpoint projected by the media
- the *negotiated* position – sometimes called alternative – where the audience argues with the position and reaches a compromise with the hegemonic position, partly agreeing, partly disagreeing
- the *oppositional* position, where the audience disagrees completely.

Activity

Discuss the theory of dominant, negotiated and oppositional positions, bearing in mind:

- its use for a variety of media texts, such as television news, current affairs programmes, advertisements
- the question of whether the theory offers enough scope for all kinds of audience behaviour
- other factors which affect audience behaviour and are not accounted for by this theory.

Make notes from your discussion and put them in your portfolio.

In your discussion you will have concluded that while some media texts fit the theory very easily – for example, BBC Radio News having a dominant hegemonic position – a great many texts can be read in different ways, depending upon the audience. You may have felt that the theory was over-simplistic and that the negotiated position was rather vague and could include a variety of different views. There is also the possibility of members of the audience completely misreading a text and coming to a viewpoint of their own that neither agrees nor disagrees, but simply misses the point.

Other factors not accounted for in this theory include the information that the audience have from other sources and from their own experience. This is the key argument in the *two-step flow theory*, which describes how information reaches its audience in two stages: through the media but also from opinion-makers and peers. This theory, however, does not include personal experience which many field researchers have noted should not be ignored.

There are readings of media texts, of course, that set out deliberately to subvert the original text, for example, the graffito on the Uniroyal advertisement on the next page. Other texts, especially those using humour and irony, deliberately turn expected readings on their head.

One area that is worth further research is the positioning of minority groups by media texts. You might wish to consider this in respect of women and ethnic groups and in terms of how opinions are often perceived to be centralised in London and ignore local variations.

'It would be wrong to see people as being totally dependent [on the media]... as if they are simply empty vessels which are being filled up by *News at Ten*. To accept and believe what is seen on television is as much a cultural act as the rejection of it. Both acceptance and rejection are conditioned by our beliefs, history and experience.'
Greg Philo/Glasgow University Media Group, *Getting the Message*, Routledge, 1993

'Our lives as women and men continue to be culturally defined in markedly different ways, and both what we read and how it is presented to us reflects, and is part of that difference.'
Janice Winship, *Inside Women's Magazines*, Pandora, 1987

Fig. 6.11
Graffito on a billboard

Assignment: Part 1

This is the first part of an assignment which will enable you to provide evidence for your portfolio. Parts 2 and 3 appear later in this section.

Using any of the models you have studied in this section, choose two examples of published evidence on models of audience behaviour and analyse them. Use the following questions as guidelines to help you:

- Why was this subject chosen by the writer/s for investigation? Is it a typical media text or is it a unique example?
- What methodology is being used? Do you know the background of the writer/s, for example, sociological, psychological, political?
- How accurate do you think their data are? Do they provide any hard evidence to help you evaluate the research?
- Do you think that their conclusions are valid?

Activity

Read the newspaper article from the *Guardian* (opposite) and discuss it in terms of the different points of view which it portrays. Say whether or not you feel the arguments stem from actual research – and if so, what kind of research.

In your discussion you may have commented on the fact that the article highlights the existing debate on the influence of the media. You may have noted how the opinions of pressure groups such as the National Viewers' and Listeners' Association are presented as facts, although no actual data is given. You may also have recalled (from Section 1) that unreliable

Winship's study of women's magazines offers a clear portrayal of how the 'woman's world' is presented in magazines. Other books that you may find useful include: Christine Geraghty, *Women and Soap Opera* (Polity Press, 1991); David Morley, *Television, Audiences and Cultural Studies* (Routledge, 1992) and P. Schlesinger et al., *Women Viewing Violence* (BFI, 1992). A clear review of the debate can be found in O'Sullivan et al., *Studying the Media* (Edward Arnold, 1994).

Film company delays video release of Natural Born Killers

Campaigners reignite debate about impact of TV violence

WARNER Brothers yesterday deferred the video release of Oliver Stone's controversial film Natural Born Killers, in which a couple go on a two-week random killing spree.

The killings yesterday at Dunblane have rekindled the debate about the impact of violence seen on television and at the cinema and are certain to unleash a torrent of self-searching about moral and social breakdown.

The decision to hold back the film by Warner Brothers Videos, conveyed yesterday to David Alton, the Liberal Democrat MP who has led the campaign to prevent its release, will strengthen the hand of campaigners over violent videos.

Michael Heap, managing director of Warner Brothers, told Mr Alton by phone from California that it would not be appropriate to release the film at this stage in the light of the Dunblane massacre.

More than 80 MPs, including former ministers, had planned to table an Early Day Motion condemning the video release – due on March 22 – after it was given a certificate by the British Board of Film Classification.

A furious Mr Alton said: 'If this film is not appropriate to be released as a video because of this horrific incident, it is not appropriate to be shown at any time. All the evidence shows that these videos lead to a culture of violence and we need to stop it.'

Mary Whitehouse, former chairwoman of the National Viewers' and Listeners' Association, said yesterday that the use of violence as entertainment desensitised people. 'There have always been lonely, bitter individuals. The difference now is that they are particularly vulnerable to the images of violence as entertainment which is an approved and accepted part of our society.'

But David Selbourne, a writer on civil ethics, argued that the killings were a ghastly illustration of social breakdown in which individuals could become totally estranged from their fellow human beings.

'Out of estrangement comes a sense of individual entitlement without moral restraint to impose your own ego on others,' he said. 'We have become habituated to... a gush of blood from an innocent body on the screen. If you gaze on these things in isolation... with no bonds of family or friends, you come to think this is a human norm.'

the *Guardian*, 14 March 1996

evidence is often quoted by politicians. Additionally, you may have commented how a major tragedy can provoke an immediate knee-jerk response on the subject of totally unrelated media violence. You may also have questioned why the piece was subtitled 'TV violence' when the article was about a film.

The question of audiences being influenced by violence portrayed by the media (television in particular) is the most common of the debates on audience behaviour. Many of the arguments in this debate are based on the models you have studied, especially that of the hypodermic needle theory. These debates exist on a variety of levels – in magazines, in both the **tabloid** and **broadsheet** press, in the home, as well as in debates in Parliament. On another level they are discussed in media studies classes and by academics. In these latter cases they are based on reliable data which can be examined and evaluated.

Activity

In your investigations into models of audience behaviour, you have already become aware that for every theory there is an alternative. In groups discuss the different debates that exist and make a list of them. Note the range of contexts – academic, tabloid press, etc. – where these debates take place. Think, too, of the different organisations, pressure groups and individuals who frequently question the relationship between the media and their audiences. Then share the information until you have one definitive list. Make notes on your discussion and keep them in your portfolio.

Not all the relationships between media and their audiences are negative, however. There are also continuing discussions on how audiences respond to film and certain television programmes as well as to poetry, literature and music, and how these media enrich the lives of audiences.

You will have listed many of the academic debates – those between active and passive models, for example – and perhaps noted that positions which relate to new theories often seem more plausible than those relating to old ones. You will also have noted that audiences themselves debate the way they approach media texts. You should also have commented on how the tabloid press and politicians frequently present facts about media influence without adequate research.

Assignment: Part 2

Write a report about the debates on the influence of the media on audiences. Use a variety of sources to illustrate the range of debates that take place on this subject. Use the notes you have from previous activities and information given in this section to assist you in your research.

Assignment: Part 3

Conduct the following two small-scale audience research studies:

1 a **In groups choose different media products, for example, an extract from a soap, newspaper or magazine article, etc.**
   b **Prepare a short questionnaire to obtain audience response, including a few questions which will identify your audience – the class – in terms of age, gender, etc.**
   c **Present your media product to the rest of the class and ask them to fill in your questionnaire.**
   d **Video the class as they watch/read/listen to it and compare their actual behaviour – they laugh, they look bored, for example – with their responses to the questionnaire.**
   e **Analyse the results of your research and, individually, write down your descriptions of the audience's responses, adding any conclusions that can be drawn.**

2 a **Decide on a particular aspect of audience behaviour that you want to investigate. You may wish to use one of the models of audience behaviour as a basis for creating a questionnaire to obtain audience response.**
   b **Ask a member of your family or a friend to watch/read/listen to a media text and to reply to your questions.**
   c **Make notes on their answers and then add your own conclusions. Make a note of the methodology you employ and, finally, evaluate the results of your research.**

3

Analysis of published data

We live in a world that is often described as media-saturated and we consume media products as a regular part of daily living. The amount we consume – and the reasons why – are researched by many different organisations, as you have seen in the earlier sections of this study unit. Each of these organisations produces evidence to support its findings and it is this published data which you will be analysing in this section.

It is easy to feel overwhelmed by data. Tables of statistics can seem incomprehensible until you learn how to read and organise the information they contain. In this section of the study unit you will acquire tools to enable you to understand the basic elements common to all published audience research data. You will also learn how to evaluate the data and how to use it to detect trends of consumption in the media.

You will be dealing with published data, the majority of which is secondary. The difference between **primary data** and **secondary data** is shown below.

Primary data	Secondary data
Raw data that has been collected but not evaluated from:	Data that has been evaluated and published in some form. It may include:
• observation • questionnaires • researchers' notes.	• survey results • survey analyses • other research findings.
	This data can be 'internal' – i.e. within the organisation being researched, or 'external' – belonging to an independent research organisation or published.

All published material, whether it is in magazines, books, computer print-outs or annual company reports, is secondary data.

Primary data can be understood as undigested information which has not yet been analysed. It can be useful to go back to primary data if you need to check the validity of secondary data (to verify figures, for example). You will be collecting primary data and producing secondary data later on when you carry out your own research projects. In this section, you will only be working from secondary data.

Sources of published data on media products

Before undertaking any research, you need to identify a clear focus for your investigations. You should therefore decide which product you are interested in and exactly what it is you want to find out about it, and then formulate a **research question**. For example, you might wish to know about the Western movie and whether the genre is still as popular as it was, say, 20 years ago. Or you might want to find out about the growth of access to the Internet in your region. Published data exists to enable you to answer such questions and to identify trends in market consumption.

Activity

Choose a media product and find out how many people read/watched/listened to it over the period of one year. Try to make sure that this information is the most up-to-date available.

In your research you will have discovered that comprehensive annual figures for media consumption can be found through the joint bodies which you identified in Section 1. You may also have found that there are a number of trade magazines which routinely publish such data.

Activity

Working individually, research and make lists of possible sources of published data on the consumption of media products under the headings of different media. Combine your lists in class until you have a single list.

In your lists you should have included trade magazines, books and the joint bodies for each of the media. You may also have included as useful sources companies' annual reports, research organisations and libraries, particularly those of colleges and universities that teach media studies. You may also have discovered that there is a great deal of data available on the Internet. Modify your list and keep it in your portfolio.

Analyse and interpret published data

When you begin to analyse data, you may find it helpful to ask the following questions:

Details of all of these sources can be found in *The Media Guide*, published annually by Guardian Newspapers/Fourth Estate.

Libraries, while they are an invaluable source of material, may not always be convenient and the books you need may well be out on loan. You may therefore prefer to try to find sources of data which can be kept in class for general access. A directory which includes detailed information on newspapers and magazines, television, radio and the cinema is *BRAD* (British Rate and Data). This directory is revised each month and therefore a local advertising agency may be willing to let you have an old copy. Agencies need to know about every slight change in media consumption, but even a three-month-old *BRAD* will be able to provide you with sufficiently up-to-date information.

Background:	Who carried out the research?
	Who commissioned the research (for example, the media organisation or an independent agency)?
Data collection:	How was the data collected?
	How were those questioned chosen?
Methodology:	What methods were used to carry out the research?
Accuracy of conclusion:	Having examined how the research was carried out, do you feel that the conclusions were justified?

For example, if you intended to analyse the consumption of your local newspaper, you might start by asking whether the circulation of the paper had risen or fallen over the past year and why. You might begin to answer these questions using data on circulation figures provided by the newspaper for potential advertisers. (You might have looked up these figures in *BRAD* – see above.) You would begin to analyse them by looking at the background. The figures would have been provided by the Audit Bureau of Circulations on behalf of the newspaper.

See Section 1 for more information on the Audit Bureau of Circulations.

The ABC observes rigorous standards of checking before allowing data to be released as official ABC figures which can be quoted by any publication. Its methodology is entirely quantitative. It can therefore only provide average numbers of copies sold. To find the reason why the paper's circulation had risen or fallen, you would need access to qualitative data.

Activity

Imagine that you are commissioning a piece of research to find out how many people watched the soap *Home and Away* over the past month. Write guideline notes to give to your researchers, suggesting useful sources of data and indicating ways of analysing them.

Your guideline notes will be useful when you come to do your own research in the final part of this study unit.

To understand trends in media consumption fully, however, you need to know more than just the numbers of consumers. You may want to know how the audience was composed. This means dividing the audience up according to a variety of demographics and lifestyle categories. To present such material clearly, it is often useful to use tables or pie charts, as in the following example:

Viewers of some popular quiz shows: by social class groups – audience (in millions)

Programme	AB	C1	C2	DE
Have I Got News For You?	0.94	0.89	0.73	0.46
Fifteen-to-One	0.32	0.55	0.76	1.40
The Crystal Maze	0.33	0.58	0.60	0.68

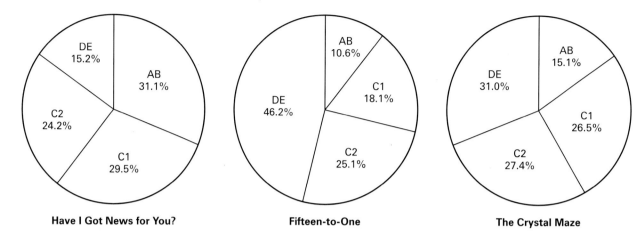

Fig. 6.12
Viewing figures (on the
previous page) expressed
as percentages

Activity

**Turn the figures in the following table into percentages, and then
present the results as diagrams such as pie charts or graphs.**

Viewers of some
popular quiz shows: by
age groups – audience
(in millions)

Programme	18–24	25–34	35–44	45–54	55–64	65+
Have I Got News For You?	0.32	0.57	0.73	0.44	0.42	0.53
Fifteen-to-One	0.15	0.18	0.19	0.32	0.56	1.62
The Crystal Maze	0.37	0.45	0.51	0.24	0.26	0.36

The bar chart on the next page summarises the results of research
conducted on musical tastes by MORI for the *Independent on Sunday*.
MORI interviewed a representative **quota sample** of 1,017 people aged
16–54 at 73 **sampling points** throughout Great Britain. The interviews
were conducted face to face, in the home, on 19–20 December 1995.

Some of the results of this research may not be very surprising – for
example, the fact that classical, easy listening and folk are considerably
more popular among the 35–54 age range than indie, techno and hip
hop/rap. There are other results, however, which may be more interesting:
jazz and rock 'n' roll, for example, can be seen to appeal across the board
and despite changes in musical fashion, chart pop remains the most
generally popular type of music.

Trends in media consumption

Activity

**Discuss the data presented in the bar chart and comment on
further aspects of music consumption that it demonstrates.
Drawing on the data and on your own knowledge of the music
scene, suggest possible inferences that can be drawn from the
data in relation to audience share.**

Fig. 6.13
Independent on Sunday/MORI pop survey

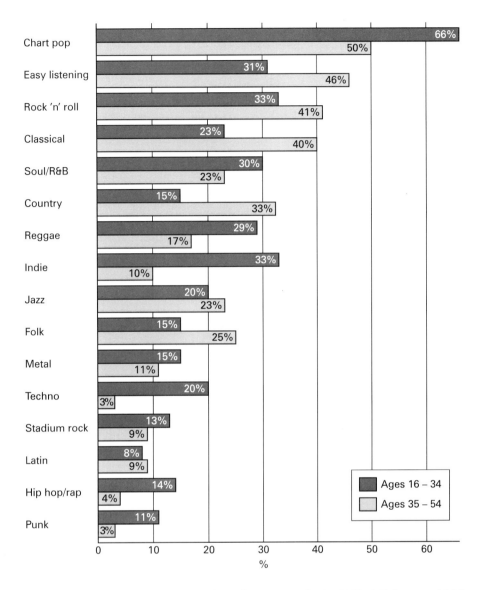

Independent on Sunday/MORI, 4 February 1996

The changing audience profile is reflected in the age and continuing popularity of some well-known performers, such as Lou Reed and the Rolling Stones. Many of the press reports of the last Rolling Stones tour drew attention to the fact that the age of the audiences ranged from 15 to 50. Younger fans are attracted by new releases and join the ranks of those who have been fans for many years.

One of the inferences that can be drawn from these figures is the way in which the audience for certain types of popular music, specifically chart pop and rock 'n' roll, cannot be considered as appealing solely to the youth market. This was not the case 30 years ago, when these types of music first evolved. What has happened is that the market segment has changed its profile: the audience has aged along with the medium itself.

Activity

Discuss other examples of media products which have changed the shape or profile of their market segment – one example would be the sudden widespread popularity of music tracks used in jeans commercials. Make notes of your discussion for your portfolio.

Further examples might include minority TV programmes, such as *The X-Files* transferring to mainstream TV channels or the re-release of films which have won Academy Awards.

You may have considered other products which have benefited from cross-media marketing, such as adaptations of classic novels which have been marketed as film/TV '**tie-ins**'.

The activity above focused on changes in the size and composition of audiences for media products. Trends can also be observed in the changing objects of media consumption.

They're only here for the peer

SIX YEARS ago, the youth beer market was rocked by the arrival of a Mexican bottled lager which was bizarrely bought with a segment of lime shoved in the top of the bottle. Pubs, clubs and wine bars rushed to stock the new beer and the sales graph for limes shot through the roof. The low budget advertising campaign for Sol won awards for helping achieve its phenomenal success.

Today the brand is struggling in the saturated imported lager market and a new report into the youth market published this week reveals the brand as the least desirable bottled beer among 18 to 24 year olds.

In sharp contrast, the study reveals an explosive demand for premium cider and alcoholic 'soft' drinks. Cider has come from virtually nowhere in the youth market a few years ago and alcoholic lemonade and cola are also making huge inroads.

The new research is published on Thursday by ROAR (a collection of seven media groups:

EMAP, Guardian Media Group, Channel 4, Mills & Allen, Kiss FM, Cinema Media and BMP/DDB Needham). The research panel includes 1,000 young people between the ages of 15 and 24, whose views, habits and tastes will be constantly monitored.

The wide-ranging research covers media habits, leisure activities, changes in behaviour and attitudes. The most important part of the research for advertisers is the need to explain why young people are more prone to switch brands and buy new brands than older consumers.

The study explains advertising's lack of influence by claiming that peer group pressure, the style and music media and a natural distrust in sales messages dilute advertiser influence. Young people are more sceptical than previous generations. Brands need to be style leaders among peer groups to establish legitimacy.

The youth market is highly saturated . There are thousands of variants and new products can

be easily copied by rivals. Any genuine innovation in the youth market, such as alcoholic soft drinks, often involves pushing the regulatory boundaries. To make matters more difficult for advertisers, reaching young people is harder. The explosion in media means that advertisers need to compete more vigorously for their attention.

According to the research, there is little good news here for advertisers. Top Of The Pops remains the most popular TV programme among this age group, with 50 per cent of all respondents claiming to always try to watch it. It is just 1 per cent ahead of *The X-Files* in the loyalty stakes and 17 per cent bigger than the third most popular programme, Casualty. Advertisers who believe that their commercial messages are most effective when they appear next to programmes that attract active and involved viewers, will take cold comfort from knowing that all three programmes appear on the advertising-free BBC.

Sean Brierley, the *Guardian*

The *Guardian* article examines the youth market and argues that peer group pressure is a more important factor than advertising in changing the tastes and habits of young people. Changing fashions are one reason for shifts in patterns of consumption of media products; other reasons are technological, economic and social.

Activity

Find examples to illustrate changes in consumption of media products resulting from each of the following:

- introduction of new technology
- economic factors (such as cost of product, effects of recession, etc.)
- changing patterns of audience lifestyle.

New technology not only produces changes through creating new products, but also has a profound influence on existing products. Examples of this include the effect on cinema audiences of the advent of television or the flexibility created by new printing processes, which enables newspapers to target specific markets with special supplements. Economic factors are the principal determinants in the development of many media products.

You may also have thought about how trends in the consumption of media products are directly influenced by the amounts spent on marketing

Study Unit 7 considers how price plays a vital rôle in the marketing of all media products.

those products. How we live also affects trends in media consumption and you may have noted aspects of changing lifestyles in the 1990s, such as increased leisure time, producing a large number of specialist magazines devoted to a wealth of hobbies and leisure activities.

To evaluate data to enable you to discover trends, you will first need to obtain your data and you may wish to do this from a variety of sources. For example, you might want to find out which music magazines are the most popular. You could begin by analysing your own choices and those of your friends. You could then write a short questionnaire and give it to the class. Finally, you might decide to contact the publication and ask them for their **circulation** figures.

When you come to evaluate these sets of data, you might decide that the notes about your own consumption and that of your friends are interesting, but not necessarily representative. The circulation figures, on the other hand, provide you with real data, but only give you a broad statistic. They do not tell you what different age groups bought the magazines or why. But by combining the questionnaire with the circulation figures, you can add qualitative research to the quantitative research and get a fuller picture.

Activity

Undertake a short research project to ascertain trends in watching video films.

- Begin by noting anecdotal evidence – how many films you and your friends have watched over the past month and which ones you liked best.
- Add to this (possibly unrepresentative) information by creating a questionnaire to ask similar questions of your friends, making sure that the questionnaire includes questions to gauge demographics.
- Interview your local video shop manager and compare the shop's best-seller lists with national figures which you research from trade magazines.
- Finally, evaluate your evidence and note any differences between the national figures and your **anecdotal evidence**. Divide the activity among the class, making notes on your own participation for your portfolio.

In carrying out this activity, you may have discovered that there are inferences which can be drawn regarding the different appeal to different age groups of certain films, the popularity of certain genres and how often the films which reach the best-seller lists are those which have been most heavily promoted.

Through thorough analysis of published data, trends in media consumption can be measured. This research – and the trends it highlights – is used by media marketing departments, both to market existing products and to develop new products. At its most basic this results in the replication of successful films, such as *Rocky V*, made according to a formula which has proved to be successful. At a more complex level, such research will indicate, say, a trend in the consumption of health and fitness magazines or a trend of listening to the radio while travelling to and from work. Commercial research companies research trends in media consumption in detail, down to specific hours of the day.

Preparing for your assignment

In your assignment you will analyse data in order to identify trends in the consumption of a media product and explain some of the reasons for such changes.

In carrying out your assignment you will find it helpful to begin with a general question which will determine what data you need to research. Such a question might be: How have patterns of cinema attendance changed and why?

The following procedure shows one way in which you can identify trends through the analysis of published data. It is not the only possible method and you may wish to approach your assignment in a different way, but you will find that by setting out your research procedure in clear sub-headings, you will find it easier both to handle and present your material.

Aim

To ascertain how patterns of cinema attendance have changed and why.

Range of survey

Ten years.

Possible sources of information

Anecdotal: Informal evidence based on your own and your friends' cinema-going habits.

Internal: Data on attendances from a local independent cinema, including results from questionnaires giving a demographic break-down of attendance. (Cinemas which are part of national chains are less likely to be able to provide such data.)

External: Published data – in this case the latest copy of the *BFI Film and Television Handbook*. Also reference books published by the Policy Studies Institute, for example, *Cultural Trends* and *Facts About the Arts*.

Information analysed: stage 1

Procedure

Choose period of survey: The latest available figures are for 1993, so the period of analysis will be 1983 to 1993.

Assess data according to background, methodology, and reliability:

The figures in the tables and the graph are quantitative. They have been produced by independent research agencies and based on the box office figures provided by the cinema distributors to these bodies. They are the industry standard and are a reliable record of annual attendance. They do not include any demographic breakdown or qualitative analysis.

Fig. 6.14
Cinema admissions, 1983–93

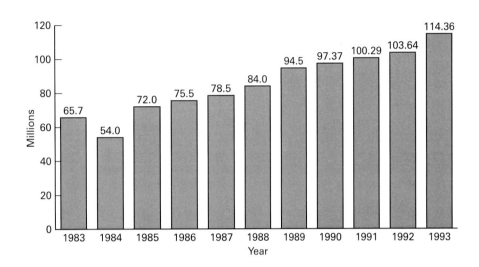

Screen Digest/CAA/BFI in *BFI Film and Television Handbook 1995*, British Film Institute

Fig. 6.15
UK consumer spending on feature films, 1982–93

Year	UK box office (£m)	Video rental (£m)	Video sell-through (£m)	Movie channel subscription (£m)	Total spending (£m)
1982	207	–	–	–	207
1983	125	310	–	–	435
1984	103	425	40	–	568
1985	123	300	50	–	473
1986	142	375	70	–	587
1987	169	410	100	–	679
1988	193	470	175	–	838
1989	227	555	320	–	1,102
1990	273	550	365	47	1,235
1991	295	540	444	121	1,400
1992	291	511	400	283	1,485
1993	319	528	643	350	1,840

BVA/*Screen Digest*/EDI/*Screen Finance* in *BFI Film and Television Handbook 1995*, British Film Institute

Fig. 6.16
Types of release for UK films, 1983–92

Proportions of titles produced in the UK per year which achieved:

(a) a wide release (b) limited release or were (c) unreleased(%)

Year	(a)	(b)	(c)
1983	51.3	46.2	2.5
1984	50.0	44.0	6.0
1985	52.8	35.9	11.3
1986	55.8	41.9	2.3
1987	36.0	60.0	4.0
1988	29.5	61.2	9.3
1989	33.3	38.9	27.8
1990	29.4	47.1	23.5
1991	32.2	37.3	30.5
1992	38.3	29.8	31.9

BFI/*Screen International/Screen Finance* in *BFI Film and Television Handbook 1995*, British Film Institute

Fig. 6.17
UK sites and screens, 1983–93

Year	Sites	Screens
1983	707	1,304
1984	660	1,271
1985	663	1,251
1986	660	1,249
1987	648	1,215
1988	699	1,416
1989	719	1,559
1990	737	1,685
1991	724	1,789
1992	735	1,845
1993	723	1,890

BFI Film and Television Handbook 1995, British Film Institute

Further information required: stage 2

Market by segment: Attendance figures for one recent year according to age and social group.

Analytical information: Historical analysis of patterns of cinema attendance with reasons.

Sources for Stage 2

Recent data produced by CAVIAR. Information from film books and magazines on audience attendance from library sources – BFI Handbooks, *Sight and Sound*, *Screen International*, Raymond Kent *Measuring Media Audiences* (Routledge 1994).

Information provided

Fig. 6.18
Percentage of people attending cinemas* by age, UK

Age	1984	1986	1988	1989	1990
7–14	73	87	84	85	85
15–24	59	82	81	86	87
25–34	49	65	64	72	79
35–44	45	60	61	67	70
45+	13	25	34	35	41
All persons aged 7+	38	53	56	60	64

* Percentage attending at least once in any given year.

HMSO, 1992

Fig. 6.19
Audience composition
for 1991

	Percentage of average audience	Percentage of population
Male	51	48
Female	49	52
Age		
15–17	15	5
18–24	40	13
25–34	26	19
35+	19	63
Social class		
AB	26	18
C1	32	24
C2	22	27
DE	20	31

Source; CAA/NRS, 1991

Fig. 6.20
Cinemas: screens, seats,
admissions and box
office receipts

	1955	1970	1975	1980	1981	1982	1983	1984
No. of cinema complexes	4,483	1,493	1,100	942	877	803	707	660
No. of screens in complexes with:								
one screen	4,483	1,461	848	584	506	441	370	334
two screens	nil	52	198	284	298	284	266	260
three screens	nil	16	484	694	710	707	657	632
Total number of screens	4,483	1,529	1,530	1,562	1,514	1,432	1,293	1,226
Seating capacity (thousands)	4,087	1,466	879	688	622	568	505	459
Estimated annual admissions (millions)	1,182	193	116	96	84	60	63	53
Average admission price (pence)	9.0	30.5	61.2	141.3	162.4	177.4	189.9	194.3
Estimated percentage of capacity filled	–	21	19	20	19	16	18	15
Estimated gross box office takings during year (£ million)	105	59	71	136	136	107	120	102

Business Monitor MA2, Department of Trade annual cinemas enquiry;
Screen Digest, October 1984, in John Myerscough, *Facts About the Arts*,
Policy Studies Institute, 1986

Conclusions

From analysis of data in stage 1, the pattern of cinema consumption shows
a steady increase. Trends in cinema consumption from 1983 to 1993 show
that consumer spending has more than doubled despite the advent of
video rentals and sales. Nor have the amounts spent on movie channel
subscription halted the increase. The number of sites, however, has gone

down, although the number of screens has risen dramatically. The total number of admissions shown was at an all-time low in 1984, but has continued to rise since then.

Additional conclusions can be drawn by going outside the study period and comparing attendance figures with the data shown in the table of screens, seats, admissions and box office receipts. These figures show that while attendance rose from 1983 to 1993, they do not come close to matching the high figures for cinema attendance in 1955 and that the seating capacity in 1984 was nearly ten times smaller than that in 1955.

Inferences that can be drawn from this data are that audiences are continuing to attend the cinema despite additional sources of films on alternative media. The growth of video created a new market for films, but did not stop people going to see films in cinemas. However, bearing in mind the data from 1955, it is clear that this was not always the case. The introduction of television to Britain drastically affected the pattern of attendance of cinema audiences. Trends do not indicate any possibility that either cinema attendances or the number of cinemas will ever rise to their pre-television levels.

From the demographic figures, while there has been a 26 per cent increase in cinema attendance over the survey period, among the 25–34 age group this has been a 30 per cent increase, while for the 7–14 age group the rise has only been 12 per cent. The group that most often attends the cinema, however, is now the 15–24 age group and not the 7–14 age group which attended most frequently in 1984. Additional analysis of attendance by market segment can be made from the internal and anecdotal evidence.

From information collected from articles and commentaries

Additional background reading to support the evidence analysed offers a number of reasons for the rise in cinema attendances. These were, noted R. Chilton and P. Butler, 'fuelled by quality film products and an unprecedented level of investment in new and refurbished cinemas. Probably the most significant change in the last few years has been the growth in purpose-built multiplex sites, which offer up to 14 different screens, comfortable seating, quality sound and projection, food, drink and parking.'

Much of this activity came about as a result of research into cinema audiences, which revealed that audiences found cinemas to be uncomfortable, unwelcoming and poor value for money. Cinemas continued to use research to build a picture of what cinema audiences wanted. At the same time, film distributors decided to maximise their marketing drive by showing one or two blockbusters each season and by targeting audiences more precisely by age – for example, by putting on a popular Disney film during school half-terms and holidays. For the first time in the UK, they also advertised films on television.

Additional research shows that the results of the trend as seen through age groups should not be taken to represent a general trend in every respect. It tends to reflect the attendance of one or two blockbuster films each year.

From Raymond Kent (ed.) *Measuring Media Audience*, Routledge, 1994

In 1984 the top film happened to be *The Jungle Book* with an audience of 6.4 million. In 1990 it was *Ghost*. The popularity of one such film can therefore have a disproportionate effect on attendance figures – see the table of weekly cinema admissions which shows how audiences rose during the weeks when *Ghost* was on release.

Fig. 6.21
Weekly cinema
admissions (in millions)

	1989	1990	1991
Sept.	1.58	1.45	1.49
	1.78	1.35	1.58
	1.53	1.49	1.42
	1.52	1.43	1.47
Oct.	1.47	2.01*	1.32
	1.64	2.21*	1.35
	2.08	2.98*	1.92
	1.72	2.49*	1.91

*_Ghost_ on release

R. Chilton and P. Butler as
above

Use this list when you are
working on your assignment to
help you identify the reasons
for the trends which you have
analysed.

Summing up

In the 1980s, cinemas in Britain realised that they had to work hard to attract their audience if they were not to lose them completely. They addressed this problem through market research, by improving their product and through the marketing of blockbuster American films. Multiplexes, providing multi-entertainment centres, proved that audiences could be lured back to the cinema. The habit of cinema-going was re-established and withstood the growing popularity of video. Future predictions would therefore indicate that this pattern would continue, with more multiplex sites and longer runs of fewer big American films.

In order to draw inferences from analysis of data, you need to be able to research and understand the reasons for changes in consumer behaviour. In the above example the reasons for changes in cinema attendance were:

- _product_ – the cinemas were made more comfortable with better facilities
- _price_ – cinema had to prove that compared with cheaper viewing of films on video they offered value for money
- _marketing_ – distributors improved their marketing of blockbuster films and targeted audiences using data from market research.

Activity

The above categories are the most common causes for changes in consumer behaviour, but there are other reasons which you have already noted earlier in this section. In order to interrogate your data more efficiently, make one list to include all the major reasons.

To product, price and marketing, you may have added peer-group activity, fashions and reasons arising from technological, economic and social factors.

Assignment

Choose two media products, one from the print and graphics sector (i.e. a newspaper, magazine or comic) and one audio-visual product and write a report identifying trends in the consumption of those products. Support your arguments with examples of published data. Give step-by-step analysis of your procedure, indicating the sources for your data and how you have analysed the information.

Write down the inferences that can be drawn from your research and any possible future predictions that can be suggested from your conclusions.

4 Research projects

In this section you will put into practice the information you have acquired on research into media products by carrying out two research projects of your own. You will plan, carry out and evaluate the research. One piece of research will investigate consumption of a media product, using the information you have gathered in Sections 1 and 3, and the other research project will enable you to draw on your understanding of the theories of audience behaviour which you studied in Section 2. One of these pieces of research will be into one of the media products that you yourself developed in earlier units and the other piece of research will be into a media product which is widely available.

Whatever your research project, it needs to be planned in a proper sequence. In the marketing research industry there are five stages of research, which are discussed below. You will also use these five basic stages.

Fig. 6.22
The five stages of
marketing research

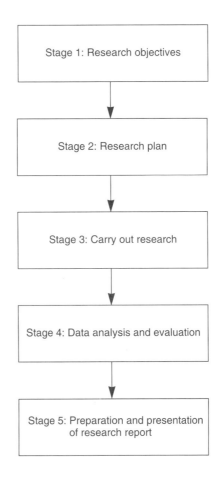

Adapted from Peter Chisnall, *Marketing Research*, McGraw-Hill, 1992

Stage 1: Research objectives

Your ability to set clear and well-defined objectives will determine the success of your research project. In addition, your objectives need to be achievable within the constraints of your resources (time, people, finance, etc).

Activity

Write a short summary of the objectives you might have for a research project for a media product. This can be for a research project into either consumer or audience behaviour. In pairs evaluate each other's summaries and check that they are clear, well focused and achievable.

In your summaries you will have identified the media product and the information on consumer or audience behaviour that you want to discover, such as the potential market among 15–18 year olds for a new music magazine or the amount people remember from one evening's news bulletin. You will have included the scope of the research – the period of the research project and the target market being analysed.

It is important to know the range of your objectives, because research will only give you the information it is designed to obtain – a piece of research that was intended to show how many people read chat magazines will not be able to tell you why these magazines were bought, for example. If that was what you had actually intended to research, then you would need to include it in your summary of objectives, so that you adopted the appropriate research methods.

Stage 2: Research plan

In marketing and audience research, no work is ever begun until a plan has been written and approved. It is at the planning stage that any problems can be identified and dealt with. In your research projects planning is just as important. It is at this stage that you can work out precisely *how* you are going to carry out your research, *what* research tools you are going to use – questionnaires, interviews, etc. – and *who* you are going to question, or as researchers would put it, what sample of your market you will be testing. You will also assess your plan in terms of the resources you have at your disposal.

Before you begin your project, you therefore need to write your plan. This can be in note form, but it should show how you have arrived at each decision. Your plan can be presented under the following headings: methodologies, research tools, audience sample and resources.

Methodologies

Which methodologies you choose will depend on the nature of your research project. You will need to decide whether it is quantitative, qualitative or a combination of the two. You will find it useful to make a list of all the factors you hope the research will elicit; then go back to all the different methods which you described in Sections 1 and 2 and compare their capabilities with your requirements. As you carry out your research (stage 3), you may realise in the course of testing out your methodologies, that other methods of research will be more effective. In this case, make the necessary changes and write notes on why you have done this. It is quite valid for you to make such changes, since only experience can finally prove which is the best methodology, taking into account your particular objectives and the resources available to you.

Research tools

Peter Chisnall, *Marketing Research*, McGraw-Hill, 1992

Much of the above on methodologies is also relevant when it comes to planning which research instruments you will use. By now, you will be aware of the many factors which influence the consumption of media products and the way that audiences behave. As Peter Chisnall comments in his guide to marketing research: 'Because buying behaviour is complex and is affected by many variables – economic, psychological, sociological, cultural and demographic – the approach by marketing researchers should be subtle and well designed.' The same is true of all forms of audience research. When you choose your tools, you need to remember that there are a wide range of possible responses and design your research instruments accordingly. You may find the chart opposite showing the complexity of buying influences useful in focusing your tools to obtain the most useful responses. Do not be concerned if, at planning stage, you write in one or two options. As you carry out your tests on research tools and continue to check them against your resources, you may well need to make changes. In your plan, therefore, you can make a note such as: 'qualitative research using in-depth interviews or telephone interviews, depending on resources'.

Activity

Discuss what research tools would be appropriate for your research projects, bearing in mind the resources available to you. You might wish to combine your resources and carry out some of the research in groups. Offer alternative suggestions for different kinds of research projects. Make notes of your discussion and of any conclusions that you reach.

Fig. 6.23
The complexity of
buying influences

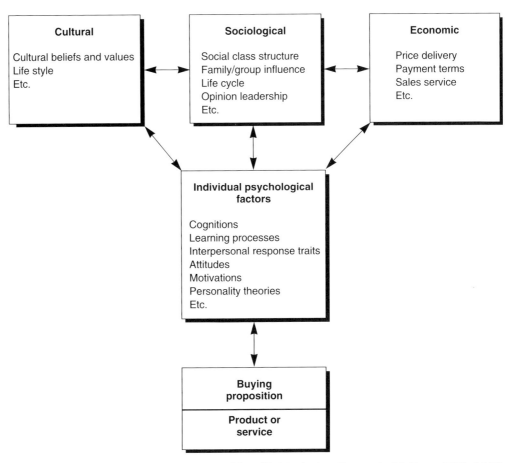

Peter Chisnall, *Marketing Research*, McGraw-Hill, 1992

Audience sample

You are not going to be in a position to imitate a research organisation like
MORI and use a representative sample of the population, although you
may find it helpful to understand the nature of sampling, so that you can
ensure that your chosen sample is as representative as possible. Your
sample will need to relate to the product – for example, it would not be
productive to ask your friends about their attitudes to BBC Radio 3 if you
know that they mostly listen to Virgin Radio and BBC Radio 1. Your
chosen sample will also influence your methodologies and research tools.
For this reason it should be selected at the planning stage.

There are many forms of sampling, which is one of the basic techniques
employed in market research. The two main forms are *random sampling*
and *quota sampling*.

Random sampling is used by major research bodies and is based on the
theory of the relationship between the population as a whole and random
percentage samples drawn from the population. In practice this is a fixed
number of respondents picked at random from electoral registers and
other national lists. It is also sometimes known as probability sampling
because it is based on the concept that since the choice is random, there is
a fixed probability of any member of the public being chosen.

Fig. 6.24
A good example of quota control divided demographically

Sample

Age	M	F	Total
Socio-economic group AB			
16–24	1	1	2
25–34	–	–	–
35–44	–	1	1
45–64	–	–	–
65+	–	–	–
Socio-economic group C			
16–24	1	–	1
25–34	–	1	1
35–44	1	–	1
45–64	1	2	3
65+	–	1	1
Socio-economic group DE			
16–24	–	1	1
25–34	3	–	3
35–44	2	1	3
45–64	2	4	6
65+	1	3	4
Total	12	15	27

Peter Chisnall, *Marketing Research*, McGraw-Hill, 1992

No sampling methods work unless they are well designed and painstakingly carried out and analysed. Also, always remember that the design of your sample will depend on your resources.

Quota (or non-probability) sampling simply means that the sample is no longer totally random, but that a specific group has been chosen as a basis for the sample. Non-probability sampling also includes haphazard and **convenience sampling**. For example, if you found it easier just to ask a few friends, there is no statistical likelihood of anyone else being chosen. But then neither could your results be said to mirror the entire population of the UK! In quota sampling researchers are required to find a number of respondents under each social group and age in order to fill their quota. So that they do not just interview one specific age and class, they are given a quota control like that shown left. This is a highly effective method and the results can be analysed without the need for complex statistical analysis.

The methods outlined above are those used primarily in the collection of quantitative data, but they are also valid in qualitative research. Since you are unlikely to have the resources to carry out random sampling that is representative of the population as a whole, you need to ensure that your research objectives make allowances for the scale of the research that you can carry out. For example, it would be difficult for you to carry out significant research into whether there is a gap in the market for a new comic, but you could effectively set up a test to be carried out by a junior class to find out what kind of features they enjoy in the comics they read.

Resources

You will need to consider resources at every stage of your project – from the moment you consider your objectives, throughout the planning stage and while you are carrying out the research. You will need to be aware of the cost of the project in terms of your time, the time other people can allot to it, any financial costs involved and any special material needed. This might include paper for questionnaires, time on computers, access to tape and videos, etc. You need to make notes on how you have assessed your project in terms of the available resources.

Stage 3: Carry out research

Designing research tools

Having decided whether your research is to be quantitative or qualitative and having chosen your methodology accordingly, you need to begin to design the research tools that will enable you to gain the most comprehensive answers to the questions you have posed.

You may have decided to use a questionnaire with tick box questions. This tool is only as good as the questions which you include in it. Opposite are some questions about the *Radio Times* from a readers' survey designed for the magazine by NOP Research. Note that the questions do not simply focus on which elements of the magazine are enjoyed by the respondents,

The inducement of a prize draw, if your resources will allow it, is known to boost the numbers of those who reply. Remember it does not need to be a material object – an offer to wash a car would appeal to many adults. Be creative.

In commercial market research, a variety of methods are used with focus groups, many of which are based on psychological research. The aim is to probe beyond the conscious decision to try to establish what other factors are involved. You might wish to try out some of these techniques to produce a uses and gratifications survey.

but the questionnaire also includes a number of questions which will reveal the buying behaviour of the consumer: who decides to buy the magazine, how they purchase it, whether they consider it to be value for money. The answers to these questions will reveal the consumer's perception of the magazine. Note also that there is a prize draw for those filling in the questionnaire.

A questionnaire is the tool you will probably think of first, but if you have a more subtle objective than that of mere consumer actions and preferences, then you will need to use a more subtle approach. You might give out media diaries for your respondents to fill in or you could tape or video an informal discussion about a media product. You might also devise questions for in-depth interviews or panel discussions – also called 'focus groups'.

The best method is to combine a number of different techniques, such as word association, filling in speech balloons or sentence completion. Each of these techniques is designed to elicit immediate responses, which will act as a check on the responses obtained through more open discussion, where there is always the risk that some participants will be influenced by others. The techniques, therefore, should be used in conjunction with

Fig. 6.25

open discussion to identify how participants *really* feel about a given media product. They will only work, however, if they are well designed.

Word association is a technique you may know as a game. You have a list of unrelated words. You say a word and ask someone to say the first word that comes into their head. You then write down that word. In a focus group you would add some 'test' words in among the 'neutral' words. For example, you might begin with the words 'hot' and 'big', to which the responses are often 'cold' and 'small', and continue with a variety of other neutral words such as 'tree' and 'table'. You would then insert the 'test' words, which would depend on the media product you wanted to investigate.

Filling in speech balloons uses cartoons – you do not need to be an artist, stick characters will do – to set up scenes that you want your respondents to comment on. For example, you may place your characters in front of a television screen and write the name of a programme on the screen. You could show the characters as being different ages and different sexes and give each of them a separate speech balloon.

Sentence completion is more complicated and requires thinking of a variety of responses that your focus group might make. Begin with short sentences that are easy for them to complete and work up to the harder ones. This technique is considered to be one of the most effective in getting people to write down their inner feelings.

Activity

You are running a focus group on the subject of soap operas. Form paired groups. Each group should choose one of the above psychological techniques (so that each one is tested in class) to design and then test on the other group. Discuss the tests in class and evaluate them according to which ones worked best – i.e. whether they produced information that offered insights into audience behaviour. Then analyse why you think they were (not) effective.

As you carry out your research, you need to make sure that the tests you have set up are being properly administered. If you have designed your research tools well, then you should find that the results they provide are meaningful. It is worth bearing in mind, however, that it is people you are researching and people are not reliable.

In any research project record-keeping is very important: keep a log of what you do, together with reasons for any choices you make. Even if things go wrong, you should note them down and any additional actions you took to remedy the situation. This will prove useful for any future research you undertake.

An example of sentence completion:

My favourite soap character is…

Soaps are popular because…

The best soap opera is…

The characters in soap operas are…

People who watch soap operas are…

The lifestyles of soap opera characters are…

- 'People will tell you what they think you want to hear.
- People will lie – they won't tell you what they actually think.
- People won't know what they think and will just give you some answers to get rid of you.
- People will tell you what they actually think, but they may not have any information and what they think might not be very useful.'

A. A. Berger, *Media Research Techniques*, Sage, 1991

Stage 4: Data analysis and evaluation

However thorough your research has been, it will be of no use unless you keep a log of all your findings and evaluate the data you collect. Write down all the information you collect, so that you can analyse it later.

When you begin to analyse the information, you should bear in mind your objectives and use them as a point of reference. If your research is quantitative, you should carry out some simple statistical analysis, such as making percentages of the results against the total numbers questioned. If your research includes frequency counts, for example, how often the consumer watches/listens to/reads the product, then you might wish to analyse your results against published data.

In analysing qualitative data you should examine your research against existing models of audience behaviour, against other published data, etc.

It is only after the raw data has been analysed that you can begin to understand the patterns of consumer behaviour that you are looking for. It is at this stage that you can break down your information according to gender, age and other demographics. You can judge to what degree these groups have responded differently. Make sure that the results are not biased because only certain groups were approached and not others. Bias can occur even in professional market research. Analysis depends on the reliability of the research and if you feel that for any reason your results may not be reliable, then you should note this in your analysis.

Evaluate all your data in terms of how successfully it has fulfilled its objectives. You should also evaluate its potential usefulness, noting the extent of your research and how representative you feel it is.

Stage 5: Preparation and presentation of research report

The final success of your research project will depend on how well you present your findings. Turn your statistical information into clear diagrams, so that they can be more readily understood.

The easiest way to present your projects is to follow the stages listed above. Under each stage heading insert the necessary information, adding any notes that you have made from class activities.

Make sure that your conclusions have a real grounding in the evidence you supply and are not simply guesses loosely based on the research. If in doubt, check and double-check your results until you are satisfied.

You may find it helpful to exchange your findings and report with another member of the class so that you can evaluate each other's work and then amend it before presenting the final research version.

Assignment

Carry out two pieces of audience research, following the five stages of research presented above. The research should include:

- one investigation into the consumption of a media product, using a product which has been generated by your class
- one investigation into audience attitudes and behaviour, testing the theories of audience behaviour with real audiences.

You should:

- clearly indicate your research objectives, your notes on the methodologies and research tools you have chosen (including the reasons for your choice) and notes on how you have decided to sample the audience and why you decided to use that particular sample
- include notes on how you evaluated your research in terms of the available resources and a log of how you carried out your research
- include the results and analysis of your findings, together with your conclusions and an explanation of how you justify them.

Summary

In this unit you have been concerned with the uses of both quantitative and qualitative research to investigate and interrogate audiences.

In Section 1 you looked at some of the principal ways in which audience research is carried out and obtained information about official research bodies, as well as independent research agencies.

Section 2 gave you some insight into the complex debates about how audiences receive media products and you investigated the competing claims of passive and active models of audience behaviour.

In Section 3 you examined published data and considered ways in which such data are analysed and evaluated. Finally, in Section 4, you carried out your own audience research to assess responses to two media products.

Glossary

anecdotal evidence evidence which consists of informal personal responses

audience fragmentation division of an audience into smaller, sometimes specialist, groups

audience panels 'a representative sample of individuals, households or organisations that have agreed to record, or permit the recording of, their activities or opinions in respect of an agreed range of products, services or media-use behaviour on a continuous or regular basis' (Raymond Kent, *Measuring Media Audiences*, Routledge, 1994)

broadsheet an A1-size newspaper, such as *The Times*

circulation figures the number of copies sold of any print product

convenience sampling a method in which convenient groups, such as a class of students or members of a social club, are contacted for sampling purposes

couch potato a slang phrase to describe someone who watches many hours of TV

demographic relating to physical and socio-economic factors, such as age, geographical location, income, etc.

focus group a group discussion in which group members have the opportunity to express their views and react to the views of others

hegemony the power of ideas exercised by a dominant or privileged social group over subordinate social groups

independent cinemas cinemas which are not part of either of the major national circuits

knocking copy from advertising – describes the kind of text which attacks a rival product

lifestyle profile a way of categorising consumers according to their habits of consumption

lobbying organisations pressure groups which try to influence Members of Parliament to bring about or to resist changes in the law

moral panic 'A condition, episode, person or group of persons emerges to become defined as a threat to societal values and interests' (S Cohen, *Folk Devils and Moral Panics*, MacGibbon & Kee, 1972)

persona the character which a person presents or which is addressed by a media text

positional theories describes the way in which audiences are 'represented' by being put in particular positions in relation to media texts

primary data data acquired from first-hand sources

product launch the first time that a new product is made available to the public

quota sample a sampling method which uses a minimum from each specified sub-group in the population

random survey a survey in which opinions are elicited from a haphazardly chosen group of respondents

ratings lists showing the relative popularity of radio and TV programmes

research question the objective of a piece of research formulated as a question

sample a group of people selected to respond to a survey

sampling point a place where survey questions are put to members of the public

secondary data data acquired from published sources

tabloid a newspaper whose pages are A3

tie-in a book published (or reprinted) to coincide with the release of a film or the transmission of a TV programme

video nasties a journalistic label given to particularly gruesome horror films on video (often not released in the cinema)

Marketing the media

**G
N
V
Q**

Contents

LONGMAN

Introduction

The media industries, like other industries, have to market their products. These products have to reach their audiences, both consumers and advertisers. The marketplace in which the media operate is highly competitive and all the media industries devote considerable resources to ensuring that they maintain their share of readers, listeners and viewers.

In this study unit you will gain some understanding of the principles behind effective marketing. You will acquire practical insights into the processes involved in:

- carrying out market research
- planning a media marketing campaign
- designing appropriate advertisements for **media products**
- making a marketing presentation for a media product.

In Section 1 you will investigate the main marketing activities carried out by the media industries. You will look particularly at the variety of activities employed in promotion and at typical ways in which audiences are identified and categorised.

In Section 2 you will develop your own media marketing plan, according to a principled and practical action framework. In Section 3 you will prepare drafts and treatments for advertisements for media products. Finally, in Section 4, you will present your drafts and treatments to client audiences and receive feedback on your presentations.

Throughout the unit, you will be concerned with ways of evaluating the effectiveness of your marketing ideas.

1 How the media are marketed

The principles and practice of marketing in the media are similar in many ways to those in other industries. You should bear in mind, however, that not all media products are purchased or consumed in quite the same way as other manufactured products.

In this section, you will explore the aims of marketing in the media and consider the principal approaches employed. You will compare marketing approaches and analyse the effects of marketing on media products.

The aims of marketing

Marketing in the media has a number of different aims. Perhaps the most obvious is to generate income or profit, but equally important aims are to anticipate audience needs and to satisfy audience expectations. The Chartered Institute of Marketing defines marketing as 'the management process which identifies, anticipates and supplies customer requirements efficiently and profitably'. This, however, only highlights the rôle of marketing in maximising benefit to an organisation. Another broader definition given by the Institute is 'the ability to attract and retain customers'. This captures the balance between a company's short-term need for profit and the longer-term need to build and keep an audience, so as to ensure continuing profitability and growth.

What is marketing?

Many people think that marketing is simply **promotion**, but most marketeers work on the basis of the '4 Ps': Product, Price, Place and Promotion. Together the 4 Ps form the **marketing mix** and can be sub-divided as shown in the chart on the next page. It is up to the marketing director to decide at the planning stage how much emphasis to place on each element.

Product	Price	Place	Promotion
brand	setting the price	locality	**public relations**
packaging	comparative pricing	regionalisation	**direct marketing**
reliability	special offers	delivery and stocks	**sales promotions**
special features	discounts and subscriptions	display	**corporate image**
			marketing research
			advertising

Adapted from S. Majaro, *Essence of Marketing*, Prentice Hall 1993

The first three Ps – Product, Price and Place – are more important in selling products such as toothpaste or washing powder than they are in promoting media products. However, they do need to be taken into consideration.

Product

'People don't buy products, they buy brands.' L. Light
How to Survive Lifestyle
Channel 4 1988

A key aspect of establishing a brand is building up **brand loyalty**. This is extremely important when it comes to the purchase of newspapers and millions of pounds are spent every year in creating special features and packaging to make magazines stand out from their competitors. Special features, such as free CDs, computer disks and fold-out posters, are often designed to appeal as much to advertisers as to consumers, since many media products rely on advertising as their major source of revenue. Packaging is a vital element in the sales of media products – for example, the way a video looks on the shelf can be a decisive factor in persuading the customer to rent or purchase it. Packaging is also a highly effective way of drawing attention to the identity of a brand and thus reinforcing brand loyalty. Well-known examples of videos which highlight the identity of their product in this way include MGM musicals and Disney cartoons.

Activity

Working in small groups, discuss the following questions:

- What are your media brand loyalties?
- Which newspapers/magazines do you regularly buy (or read)?
- Do you automatically buy the latest release by your favourite pop group?
- Do you listen to/watch a particular radio station/TV channel or are you loyal to certain programmes?

Reliability does not simply mean that a product functions properly (for example, compatibility problems with computer software; failure to receive satellite signals) but also that expectations of quality are maintained. For example, **readership** and listening/viewing figures can be affected by the departure of key writers or presenters. The decline in the Radio 1 audience in the early 1990s provides an example of this. The special feature or **unique selling point (USP)** of *Radio Times* and *TV Times* prior to 1991 was that they had a monopoly on printing weekly radio and TV listings. When this restriction was lifted and newspapers and other magazines were allowed to print the schedules, the **circulation** of the two listings magazines dropped immediately and they have never succeeded in regaining the same volume of sales. These examples illustrate very well how marketing has to respond to the effects of change and competition – another key marketing aim.

In cases where media products are financed principally through advertising, the development of the product itself can be influenced by that advertising. For example, a large amount of property or recruitment advertising may lead newspapers to create special supplements on topics which relate to these advertisements.

Activity

Discuss what kinds of pressure advertisers might place on media products and how these pressures can affect the product.

In your discussion you will have covered the manner in which advertisers control media content by only advertising in successful programmes/magazines/newspapers. This puts pressure on editorial departments to make their product widely appealing and thus neglect issues of interest to minority groups. You may have noted that editorial departments have to produce features to link with advertising supplements such as travel, computers or recruitment. You may have wondered whether editorial departments are given lists of regular advertisers and told not to run stories that are critical of them. For example, some women's magazines agree not to publish positive editorial material about the competitor(s) of any major advertiser in an issue where that advertiser has a large advertising supplement.

'Lots of glossy magazine editors see their product as wrapping paper for advertising.'
R. Malan *Independent on Sunday* 3 March 1996

Make notes from your discussion and keep them in your portfolio. They will form part of the evidence indicators for this unit.

Price

Setting the price of a media product will depend on a wide range of factors. **Pricing policy** will take into account aspects such as the relationship between price and cost, **psychological price barriers** and the consumer's perception of a fair price. Pricing policy will also depend on the nature and size of the **target market**. Consumers pay lower prices for a

'This is an advertisement that should never have run! Buy *The Independent* this Saturday and you can get *The Independent on Sunday* for just 10p. The other newspapers started a price war, but we believe a newspaper should be judged by the depth of its coverage, not by the depth of its pockets. We think you'll agree that *The Independent on Sunday* is worth a lot more than just 10p.'

Transcript of ad broadcast on Classic FM for the *Independent on Sunday* 27 May 1995

product which enjoys bulk sales to a mass market, while they expect to pay higher prices for a quality product which may have more limited sales. In the case of new media, such as CD-ROMs, prices are often set high for a number of reasons. These include the development costs of the new product, the cost of researching and building the new audience and the cost of advertising the nature of the new product. Consumers will normally expect prices to go down as new technologies become more widespread. For example, films which were priced at between £80 and £100 when they first became available on video in the early 1980s can now be purchased for £10–£15. Sometimes prices are set artificially high. This has been the case with CDs and there has been a great deal of media and consumer pressure to persuade record companies to lower their prices.

Every marketing manager will be acutely aware of how much his/her competitors are charging for a similar product. Sometimes comparative pricing will lead to a price war, such as the one waged in the 1990s by national newspapers facing declining circulations. This is a good example of marketing policy putting the long-term benefits of building an audience before the short-term benefits of immediate profit. It is, however, a risky tactic, which in the past has led to the death of at least one newspaper.

It is worth bearing in mind who controls pricing policy. Until the recent demise of the Net Book Agreement, it was the publisher who determined the price of a book. Now this is controlled by the bookshop, supermarket or other retail sales outlet. When the consumer pays to watch a film, the price of a cinema ticket is not controlled by the film producer: it is set by the owner of the cinema chain and the film-maker has no control over this.

Activity

Discussion

What do *you* think are fair prices for the following media products?

- a cinema ticket
- your local newspaper
- a new interactive computer game
- a new film on video
- the BBC licence fee
- a football fanzine.

Place

The delivery of a newspaper to your door might not seem to be an obvious preoccupation of the **media marketeer**, but the transport of stock to ensure reliable delivery is vital. A three-day strike can lead to the permanent loss of a major section of readership. Equally, if there is not enough stock available to meet intensive demand, the result will be disappointment and probable loss of future sales. Adequate stocks are therefore essential.

The successful relationship of a local media product to its community or locality is what enables it to win out over national competition. This is particularly evident at times when there are local problems, such as major rail delays or severe snowfalls and, in these cases, the audience for local radio will show spectacular gains. A vivid example of this was during the great storm of 1987 when power cuts blacked out most television sets: car radios and battery-operated transistors provided an invaluable source of information.

Regionalisation is a bonus in marketing. It means that a specific market can be targeted – for example, Anglia Television has sub-divided its regional news coverage into smaller areas with the slogan 'Nearer to Home'. Display plays an essential rôle in the selling of media products, particularly newspapers, magazines and videos. On the newsagents' and supermarket shelves these products face massive competition. In order to attract the **impulse buyer**, designers of media products are increasingly conscious of the need to make their product stand out through the use of arresting covers, distinctive **spine messages**, free gifts and **point-of-sale (POS)** display materials.

Activity

Answer the following questions on your own and then discuss your answers in groups, bearing in mind that the answers will vary according to the product.

1 **If you wanted to buy a particular media product (for example, a video or a magazine) and your local stockist had sold out, would you:**
   a place an order with the stockist?
   b look for the product elsewhere?
   c buy an alternative product?

2 **Which of the following things might attract you to buy a magazine that you do not normally read?**
   a the visual impact of the cover
   b a cover photograph
   c details of articles/special features
   d free gifts or special offers.

Promotion

The major activity of media marketeers, however, is promotion. This covers a diverse range of activities and some of these can themselves be sub-divided. Public relations (**PR**), for example, involves community relations. **Sponsorship, media sponsorship** and education and sales promotions can include special incentives and merchandising. Promotion, in fact, comprises a whole range of marketing activities.

Public relations

The aim of public relations is to send out a clear and carefully planned message about the company or product to its various audiences and to ensure the company's or product's good reputation. Public relations involves dealing not only with the public (community relations), but also with the media. A community relations department will deal with complaints and reply to enquiries, as well as handling promotional customer relations. This could involve taking the product out into the community, for example, the Radio 1 *Roadshow*.

Media relations can be reactive or pro-active. The reactive side involves answering questions and dealing with media attacks on controversial issues. Typical examples might be the censorship of a programme, the high salary of a director or the leaking of information about in-house squabbles. Pro-active work means going out to promote the company or product. Media marketeers often make use of other media to publicise their products. Common examples are personal stories of stars, released to coincide with the launch of a new film or television programme, and interviews with authors just before the newspaper serialisation of a new book. As well as this, the PR department will create news stories to give exposure to their product. One of the most successful examples of this was the media coverage of the trial of Mandy and Beth Jordache for the murder of their abusive husband/father in the television drama serial *Brookside*. The trial generated as much news coverage as any actual trial, as well as countless column inches of media discussion.

Activity

Discussion

Think of a recent storyline in a popular soap/drama serial, which raised important social or moral issues.

- Did you talk about the story at school/college? At home? With friends?
- Did you discuss the issues raised?
- Did you know anyone who had not previously watched the programme, but who subsequently became a regular viewer?

The PR department may also handle education and sponsorship. By making education packs available to schools and colleges, the product is given high visibility to potential future customers. Sponsorship also works through presenting the product in association with other highly visible – and successful – fields: the arts, sport or a television programme. Sponsorship offers additional media coverage and the perception that the product is giving something back to the community.

Further information about the rôle of public relations can be obtained from The Institute of Public Relations, 15 Northburgh Street, London EC1V 0PR

'Central fosters and nurtures arts activity through a mixture of funding and practical support aimed at enriching the cultural life of the local community across its transmission region.'
Central Independent Television PLC in *Association for Business Sponsorship of the Arts Annual Report* 1991

Direct marketing

Direct marketing is generally considered to be one of the most effective forms of marketing and a large number of specialist marketing companies have been set up to work uniquely in this area. Direct marketing includes telemarketing, mail order, direct response marketing with advertisements in print and on radio and television, direct selling and direct mail. Telemarketing is selling from telephone contacts and is widely used for classified advertisements, job recruitment advertisements, etc. Mail order is not so common for media products, but is widely used by charities and the fashion industry. It is used, however, for the actual sale of books, CDs and videos through book clubs and music clubs. Direct response marketing includes any advertisement with a telephone, fax or e-mail number which requires an immediate response from the consumer to obtain further information about the product. Direct selling uses advertising to sell directly to the consumer. Good examples of this are the *Encyclopaedia Britannica* and the Time-Life video series, such as *Predators of the Wild*. Direct mail is the most widely used means of direct marketing. However, direct mail is only effective when it is targeted – otherwise it becomes junk mail. The success of direct mail is dependent on effective and appropriate print. Print has to be written and designed with the target market in mind. The media do not use direct mail as frequently as companies with a personal message to sell, such as charities and finance companies. Exceptions are magazines which are only sold on subscription. *Reader's Digest* and the consumer magazine *Which?*, for example, use direct mail competitions as one of their main marketing activities.

Further information can be obtained from The Direct Marketing Association, Haymarket House, 1 Oxendon Street, London SW1Y 4YZ

Sales promotions

Further information about sales promotions can be obtained from The Institute of Sales Promotion, Arena House, 66–68 Pentonville Road, Islington, London N1 9HS

Sales promotions are used to attract new customers and to persuade existing customers to spend more. Promotions can take the form of incentives (encouragement to buy) such as discounts on the product itself or special offers for other products.

Merchandising stamps the identity of the media producer or of a specific product on to other consumer products. In the case of a film, for example, it is useful in building up advance interest, whereas with a video it can extend the life of the product long after its launch. Merchandising is often implemented through the sale of the product name, logo or image to a **licensing house**. Merchandising is therefore one area of marketing that is a source of revenue rather than expenditure.

'Batman took the United States by storm in the spring and summer of 1989. Tee-shirts, posters, key chains, jewellery, buttons, books, watches, magazines, trading cards, audio-taped books, video games, records, cups and numerous other items flooded malls across the United States with images of Batman, his new logo, and his old enemy, the Joker. Presaged by a much-pirated trailer, Batman the film drew unprecedented crowds to theatre chains, of which the two largest distributed four to five million brochures for mail order Bat-materials. ... Film clips were packaged as advertisements and free promotional materials [were provided] for the interview and movie review circuits on both broadcast and cable television.'

E. R. Meehan, *The Many Lives of the Batman*
Routledge, Chapman & Hall 1991

Fig. 7.1
Batman merchandise

Activity

In groups, discuss:

- the kind of marketing activities used in the Batman campaign
- what other marketing activities could have been used
- how promotional items such as those in Figure 7.1 help to create awareness of the product.

Think of recent examples of similar promotional campaigns.

You will certainly have discussed the variety of merchandising items. You may also have mentioned the importance of the **logo** in this particular campaign. The logo is like the tip of an iceberg. It is the visible expression of corporate identity and plays a vital rôle in making a large audience aware of a product. Newspapers and magazines reinforce their identity with a distinctive style of **masthead** (see Figure 7.2).

Corporate identity

Corporate identity, at its most basic, defines who you are:

'Corporate identity is at the heart of the expression of corporate vision. The way in which you manage your identity, the way in which you make your identity accessible to everyone, has to be done through design.'

J. Sorrell, Chairman of Newell & Sorrell
(International Identity Consultancy)

Case study: The *Guardian*

In February 1988 the *Guardian* underwent the most radical reorganisation and redesign of a quality newspaper ever carried out in Britain. Market research had identified two goals.

- The first was to reassure existing readers that the new-look paper would retain all its traditional strengths, such as the quality of the writing, the breadth and depth of its coverage.
- The second was to persuade as many casual readers as possible that the paper would be worth buying on a more regular basis.

The re-launch was publicised across a wide range of media during a four-week build-up: there were advertisements and articles within the paper itself; an advertisement in the *Observer*, two weeks before the re-launch, which did not comment on the new design; billboard posters appeared just before the launch date, but again gave nothing away about the new look; a series of television commercials ran for two weeks before the launch and the soundtrack was also used on commercial radio. PR activities included special news features on television and radio and in the local and national press, as well as extended features on BBC2's *Newsnight* and on *Channel 4 News*. The *Guardian* also targeted its advertisers with advertisements in the trade press for the three weeks leading up to the launch. The paper's sales figures rose by 9 per cent in the first month.

Activity

In groups, discuss the logos and mastheads shown in Figure 7.2. How do you think they are meant to appeal to different target audiences? If you were asked to design a logo for the following products, what kind of impression would you want your logo to make?

- a children's comic
- a record label
- a computer magazine
- a local radio company.

Fig. 7.2
A selection of logos

Marketing research

You have covered many of the objectives and methods of market research in Study Unit 6 and you have learned about the importance of audience research in media marketing. However, it is worth pointing out here that marketing research includes market research, media research, product research and consumer research. Market research examines the potential sales of a product before it is put on the market and evaluates its sales after the launch. Media research studies a target audience to try to improve an organisation's promotional activities. Product research looks at the competition and the potential market for a product, and consumer research investigates why consumers buy products and what products they want to buy. The combination of all these types of research provides the data which enable marketing departments to plan their strategy and choose which marketing activities to use, and where best to employ them.

Further information about marketing research can be obtained from The Market Research Society, 15 Northburgh Street, London EC1V 0AH

Advertising

Advertising is the most expensive form of marketing, but also the most visible. It is promotion that is directly paid for, for example, commercials, poster sites and print advertising. Advertising can be **blanket advertising** or **targeted advertising**. Anyone can walk by a poster site: this is blanket advertising. But the placing of advertising can also be highly targeted. For example, commercials are scheduled before, after and during programmes that share the same target market as the advertiser. Another example is when advertising is placed in specialist magazines which will be read by the target market (such as videos of foreign films being advertised in specialist film magazines). The people responsible for placing advertising are called **media buyers**. They have a clear idea of their market and can judge which media products will enable them to reach that market.

Promotion of a media product in trade journals is important to attract both **display** and **classified advertising**. Advertising can account for over 50 per cent of the income of some newspapers and magazines, and constitutes 100 per cent of the income of **freesheets**. How a product is advertised to potential advertisers is therefore just as important as how it is advertised to readers, listeners or viewers.

For a range of materials about all aspects of advertising, contact The Advertising Association, Abford House, 15 Wilton Road, London SW1V 1NJ

Fig. 7.3
Advertisement with Internet address

Visit *The Green Mile* on the Internet

Where you can catch up with Stephen King and enter a fabulous competition to win *The Green Mile* memorabilia

www.penguin.co.uk

Activity

The advertisement (left) illustrates a piece of advertising which is utilising technological developments (one of the aims of effective marketing) by referring potential customers to the provider's entry on the Internet. Working in small groups, use the range of marketing activities outlined earlier in this section of the study unit to decide on examples of activities which you think would be best suited to each of the following aims:

- anticipating audience needs
- satisfying audience expectations
- generating income or profit
- maximising benefit to an organisation
- managing the effects of competition
- enhancing audience perception.

In your discussion, you will probably have come to the conclusion that good marketing depends on a combination of activities which will enable you to achieve different aims. For example, while blanket advertising can enhance audience perception, it may not be the most cost-effective way of generating profit or of maximising benefit to the organisation. Carefully targeted TV commercials, combined with an attractive sales promotion, might be a more productive use of your marketing budget. Such decisions will depend to a large extent on the analysis of your marketing research, which you will be examining more closely in the next section.

Effectivenes of marketing

It is essential to assess the effectiveness of media marketing. Effectiveness may be measured in terms of direct sales, box office returns or listening and viewing figures. For example, when the television companies release their Christmas schedules, there is fierce competition for media audiences. Media products need to appeal to their audiences, but also (with a few notable exceptions) to the advertisers. Figures 7.4 and 7.5 draw on listening figures for two sectors of sound broadcasting – one which is concerned with the drift of listeners between two BBC network radio stations and the other which is designed to attract advertisers to the expanding field of commercial radio.

'Radio 2 is poised to outstrip Radio 1 FM for the first time in its share of listening. ... Official figures for the second quarter of 1994 revealed that those who tune in to Radio 2 listen for longer than those who select any other station – an average of 12 hours 10 minutes a week.'

A. Culf 'Waves of Affection', the *Guardian* 24 October 1994

Fig. 7.4
Rajar table of average weekly listening figures, the *Guardian* 24 October 1994

Radio 2 on top

Average weekly listening to each network

Radio 1 FM:	9 hours 12 minutes
Radio 2:	12 hours 10 minutes
Radio 3:	3 hours 32 minutes
Radio 4:	10 hours 19 minutes
Radio 5 Live:	4 hours 9 minutes
BBC regional:	9 hours 6 minutes
Classic FM:	5 hours 9 minutes
Virgin 1215:	7 hours 54 minutes

Source: Rajar/RSL

Fig. 7.5
Commercial Radio full-page ad, the *Guardian* 4 February 1995

Over 75% of business people listen to Commercial Radio.

Commercial Radio reaches more than 75% of all business people every month. That's around 900,000 of them. More than the daily business readership of all national broadsheet newspapers put together.
Commercial Radio. Its time has come.

Assignment: Part 1

This is the first part of an assignment which will enable you to provide evidence for your portfolio. The second part appears at the end of this section.

As a group:

1 **Make a list of marketing activities, using the examples you have already studied (i.e. Batman and the *Guardian*).**

2 **Add to your list other activities which came up in discussion.**

Individually:

1 **Choose one media industry and make notes on its principal marketing activities and how these are evaluated.**

2 **Share your results with the rest of the group.**

3 **Write a report on the range of marketing activities carried out by different media industries. Analyse each of these activities in terms of the marketing aims which you have stored in your portfolio.**

Identifying the market

'Most magazine publishing is concerned with reaching specifically targeted audiences, who must be either sufficiently large or wealthy to generate [enough] advertising to render them profitable.'
 M. Alvarado, *et al. Learning the Media* Macmillan 1987

'One example is "The Lively Lady". She's buying brands that offer glamour and exoticism. They may be witty and clever and fun ... the *Daily Mail* is her paper.'
 C. Restall 'McCann Erickson Woman Study 1985', L. Light *How to Survive Lifestyle*, Channel 4, 1988

When a marketing director wants to plan a campaign for a product, he/she needs to identify the target market. This is to enable the marketeer to sell the product not only to the consumer, but also to potential advertisers. Identifying the market for a particular product is done by breaking it down into areas – this is known as **market segmentation**. Marketeers have found that the most useful ways of classifying the market are through **demographics**: this characterises the population in terms of age, sex, occupation, location, education, ethnicity and socio-economic class.

As you have seen in Study Unit 6, the other most common approach is through an analysis of **lifestyles**. Every advertising agency has its own set of lifestyle definitions which characterise the consumer in terms of aspirations, tastes and spending habits. The purpose of this, as Larry Light, President of BSB International, explains in *How to Survive Lifestyle* is 'to get a deeper understanding of the customers and what really moves them.' He identifies five lifestyle types: *Strivers, Achievers, Traditionals, Adapters* and *the Pressured*.

While they find lifestyle profiles useful, however, marketeers realise that they can be arbitrary and subject to swings in fashion. They therefore rely more often on ACORN classifications – segmentation according to types of housing. In Figure 7.6, you can see an ACORN household profile applied to the HTV viewing region (1984).

Fig. 7.6
ACORN household
profile applied to HTV
viewing region (1984)

HTV's segmentation by demographics/residential area
Living Standards: ACORN Household Profile

		Households			
			HTV	*GB*	*HTV*
		No.	*%*	*%*	*Index*
G24	Council estates with overcrowding	407	0.0	1.4	1
G25	Council estates with worst poverty	625	0.0	0.5	6
H26	Multi-occupied terraces, poor Asians	0	0.0	0.3	0
H27	Owner-occupied terraces with Asians	1 315	0.1	0.9	7
H28	Multi-let housing with Afro-Caribbeans	2 303	0.1	0.7	17
H29	Better-off multi-ethnic areas	2 353	0.1	1.6	7
I30	High status areas, few children	48 268	2.3	2.3	102
I31	Multi-let big old houses and flats	28 114	1.4	1.8	75
I32	Furnished flats, mostly single people	9 254	0.4	0.7	62
J33	Inter-war semis, white collar workers	88 826	4.3	6.1	71
J34	Spacious inter-war semis, big gardens	111 935	5.4	4.9	110
J35	Villages with wealthy older commuters	76 217	3.7	2.8	131
J36	Detached houses, exclusive suburbs	39 097	1.9	2.1	90
K37	Private houses, well-off elderly	63 269	3.1	2.7	112
K38	Private flats with single pensioners	19 023	0.9	2.0	45
U39	Unclassified	683	0.0	0.0	81
Area Total		2 065 800	100.0	100.0	

Source: 1984 estimates based on 1981 Census, CACI Market Analysis Division
(Courtesy of TVMM) taken from S. Price, *Media Studies* Pitman 1993

The other most common form of segmentation is based on social grade
classifications which define the population according to social status and
occupation (see Figure 7.7).

These classifications enable the marketing department to form a profile
of the kinds of people who form their audience. Marketing can thus be
targeted directly to appeal to those within these groups.

Fig. 7.7
JICNARS social grade
definitions and
population profile

JICNARS SOCIAL GRADE DEFINITIONS

Social Grade	Social Status	Occupation
A	Upper middle class	Higher managerial, administrative or professional
B	Middle class	Intermediate managerial, administrative or professional
C1	Lower middle class	Supervisory or clerical, and junior managerial, administrative or professional
C2	Skilled working class	Skilled manual workers
D	Working class	Semi and unskilled manual workers
E	Those at lowest level of subsistence	State pensioners or widows (no other earner), casual or lowest-grade workers.

POPULATION PROFILE

Social Grade	All Adults Over 15%	Men %	Women %	Housewives* (Female)%
A	2.6	2.8	2.3	2.4
B	13.9	14.9	12.9	13.3
C1	25.8	22.1	29.3	27.9
C2	24.7	29.3	20.4	20.8
D	19.4	20.5	18.4	17.5
E	13.6	10.4	16.6	18.1

Total of adults over 15 = 45,099,100 (Table based on all informants.)

* A housewife, who may be male or female, is defined as a member of a private household who is primarily responsible for or shares such household duties as shopping or cooking. In some instances there could be more than one housewife in a household. The social grade of a housewife is based on the occupation of the head of the household.

	'000	%
Female housewives	20,255	82.06
Male housewives	4,428	17.94
All housewives	24,683	100.0

These are the standard social grade classifications using definitions agreed between Research Services Ltd., and JICNARS. They are described in a JICNARS publication *Social Grading on the National Readership Survey*.

Activity

For each of the media products listed below, identify the audience in terms of ACORN lifestyle types and JICNAR social grades.

- Walt Disney's *The Jungle Book*
- ITN *News at Ten*
- *Marie-Claire*
- Your local daily newspaper
- *The Sun*
- *The Spectator*
- *Brookside*
- Classic FM

You should have come to the conclusion that some products appeal across a range of different social groups and lifestyles, whereas others need to be targeted towards a much narrower sample. You will have discovered that sometimes the differences are social and sometimes they are due to age or other factors.

Assignment: Part 2

This is the second part of the assignment for this section of the study unit.

1 Individually, choose a media product to research. Find a partner in the class who has chosen a different type of product.

2 Find out what marketing activities are used by the media producer you have chosen.

3 Exchange the notes showing the results of your research with your partner.

4 Individually, write a report on the marketing activities employed by the two media producers, analysing and comparing these activities in terms of their aims and effectiveness.

2 Planning a campaign

The success of any marketing campaign depends to a great extent on obtaining accurate research data and using it to develop a realistic and timetabled plan. In this section, you will obtain market research data for selected media products and check your data to ensure that it is sufficient, up-to-date and accurate. You will prepare a product forecast, develop a marketing plan for your product and justify the development of your product in terms of this marketing plan.

To determine your marketing objectives, you need strategic research on the market, product, customers, prices, distribution, competitors and past marketing activities. This research will enable you to establish the position of your product in the market, the customers to be targeted, how their needs will be satisfied and how your product will work in the competitive marketplace.

Any marketing campaign, whether for an existing product or a new one, begins by carrying out and analysing a wide range of market research. The data produced by this research will tell you everything you need to know about your potential customers – their behaviour, their buying patterns and their preferences. It will tell you how well or badly your competitors are performing in the market and give you information on the demand for the product itself – sales trends and changes in market share.

Customer behaviour

In considering customer behaviour you need to form a picture of the lifestyle of your potential audience. This can be done in terms of the kind of classifications which you looked at in Section 1 (ACORN, JICNAR, etc.). This kind of categorisation enables media marketeers to build up a profile of their potential audience in terms of where they live, what they do, their gender, their age, their income and their leisure interests.

Buying patterns

In evaluating buying patterns, make sure that your research covers not only what people buy, but where, when and how much they buy. Remember, too, that buying patterns do not remain constant and that it will be important to find out how patterns of consumption have changed and may be continuing to change.

Customer preferences

If you are conducting research into the performance of an existing product, it is essential to find out about customer preferences in relation to competing products. If you are launching a new product, information about customer preferences will enable you to make the best possible forecast about how the product will perform.

Competitor activities

Remember that you should not view your product in isolation, but in the context of a busy marketplace. You can estimate how successful your product will be by studying the performance of your competitors: what they are doing, how they have performed in the past, what they are planning for the future and how they are reacting to new technologies. (Do not forget that new technologies themselves may be a source of competition.)

Sales trends

It is not enough simply to get a 'snapshot' of current sales figures. You need a longer-term view of sales in relation to underlying market performance. Individual sales or audience figures can be distorted by a whole range of factors, such as seasonal variations or special events. (It would not be sensible, for example, to base an analysis of viewing figures for BBC TV's *Panorama* in 1996 on the audience figures recorded for the interview with the Princess of Wales.)

Changes in market share

The total number of consumers for an existing type of media product is likely to remain relatively stable. It is therefore important for media producers to have not only information on sales trends, but also an up-to-date awareness of how their product is performing in relation to its competitors. They need to know what proportion of the total population of consumers for a particular product they are continuing to attract. Dramatic changes in market share can be produced by the entry of new products and new technologies into the marketplace. Conversely, the disappearance of a product will inevitably increase its competitors' market share.

Activity

'In the early 1980s, attendance at this cinema had slumped to an all-time low. Nobody really enjoyed coming here: the floor was littered with cigarette ends and the seats were uncomfortable. We started to assess why people went to the cinema and what we were competing with. We realised that we had to sell the whole experience of an evening out against competition from eating out at a local restaurant or watching a video at home. We created two smaller, but more comfortable screens and installed a café-restaurant. The foyer was carpeted and the admission prices went up. We also made it possible for people to make advance credit card bookings. Last year, as in the previous five years, our admissions rose by 10 per cent and we aim to continue developing our audience growth.'

John, independent cinema manager

Read carefully through the above text. Using the information you already have on market research, make notes on how each of the changes carried out by the cinema management has been informed by market research. Keep these notes in your portfolio.

The starting point for your notes about the decisions taken should have been the management's objectives – i.e. to find out what it was that audiences wanted and to what extent the cinema was succeeding in satisfying their needs or failing to do so. The cinema will have drawn on qualitative research regarding audience behaviour patterns and preferences, as well as quantitative research on attendances and sales trends. You may have considered the various economic, social and technological developments which have had a significant influence on leisure habits – for example, the expansion of medium-price and low-price restaurants or the rapid growth of the home video market. Cinemas have been forced to take account of such changes in consumer behaviour – to adapt or die!

Preparing a product forecast

Activity

Discussion

You are marketing a media product and you have therefore commissioned some market research. Before you act on the data, you must be sure that it gives you the information you need. What points do you need to consider in order to evaluate the data?

In your discussion, you will probably have mentioned that research data should give you a reliable picture of the actual or potential market for your product. When checking the validity of any market research, you need to ask yourself the questions on the following page.

- Is the scope of the research *sufficient*? Does it give enough information about the market and about the customers? Have the researchers interviewed enough people?
- Is the research *up-to-date*? Is it based on the latest available figures? Have arrangements been made for the research to be kept up to date?
- Is the research *accurate*? Has it been cross-checked against similar previous research? Have any sample checks been done (for example, re-interviewing)? Are there any factors which may have distorted the results (for example, only one age group interviewed)?

Using these questions and any further points which may have arisen in your discussion, draw up a checklist for your portfolio. You will need to evaluate the market research data which you will be collecting later in this section of the study unit.

'It's extremely expensive now to start a national paper and although it's possible, as the case of the *Independent* has shown, certain parts of the market, like the popular end, are extremely difficult to penetrate. You not only need a lot of money to start up a paper, you need a lot of money to keep it in play while you build an audience.'

G. Murdock in A. Hart *Understanding the Media*, Routledge 1991

'By taking advantage of new technology ... the *Independent* was able to produce a paper at a fraction of the cost of its nearest rivals. In 1985 the *Daily Telegraph* needed around 4,000 people to produce their paper. The *Independent* carries out a similar process with just over 500, successfully targeting a young up-market audience.'

A. Hart, ibid.

These quotations show how in starting a new national paper the management had to think about getting capital to cover cashflow, who their audience were in relation to potential sales and how to set their budgets. All of this would have been put into a detailed product forecast.

Activity

Individually, make a list of the factors you need to consider in a product forecast. Pool your ideas in groups. Then compare your list with those produced by other groups in the class and make notes for your portfolio.

Product forecasts enable media organisations to assess alternative courses of action, to set targets and monitor performance. In your discussion you should have mentioned predicted or projected sales/audience figures, budgets and cashflow. A product forecast can be an A4 sheet of paper or the length of a small book, depending on the size of the product. If your product is a major blockbuster movie, costing many millions of dollars, your expenditure will cover hundreds of individual costs and your estimate of potential sales will depend on a wide range of sources of income, including international sales, video sales and revenue from merchandising. Film companies often have teams of accountants working to produce product forecasts. However, there are a few basic elements that form part of every forecast and you should bear these in mind when you do your own forecast as part of your assignment at the end of this section.

For example, if you were intending to launch a 'What's On' magazine in your locality, you would:

- first undertake market research to assess the need for such a publication
- then prepare a product forecast, beginning with a month-by-month sales prediction for the first year of publication
- arrive at an estimate of potential sales from market research
- possibly send out questionnaires along with the mail-shots from local venues, to find out how many of their audiences would consider purchasing your magazine
- research sales of similar magazines in towns with roughly the same size of population and similar audience profiles.

Your sales estimate would determine your initial **print run**. It would then be necessary to cost the magazine on the basis of this print run. This would give you an income target to aim for. If, for example, your research had revealed that potential sales were 500 copies per month and that the average price for such a magazine was 50p, you would already have a potential monthly income of £250. If the cost of producing 500 issues was £500, you would then have to find an additional £250 of advertising. In this way you would be able to work out the price per page, half-page, quarter-page and so on of advertising, again researching what local advertisers regarded as a reasonable price to pay.

Do not forget that you should be able to make use of the audience profiles of the venues featured in your magazine to attract potential advertisers. You would be able to target different advertisers to different sections of the magazine, for example, up-market retailers and local accountants opposite classical music listings, and record and video shops in the rock music section.

Budget

By now you should have adequate data to set an annual budget, using your monthly sales and income projections. You should have allowed for a gradual growth in sales and a possible falling-off in advertising after an initial surge of interest. You should have taken into account the costs of marketing the magazine, such as posters, advertising, direct mail, etc.

Cashflow

You should now be in a position to set out monthly cashflow figures to check whether you have enough funds to cover your expenditure. Writers, illustrators, photographers and printers all have to be paid on time, though your income might take much longer to come in. It can take up to six months, for example, for advertisers to settle their accounts and if you have decided to distribute through a national distributor, you might discover that they settle on a quarterly basis. You will therefore need substantial capital to cover your cashflow during the first year of publication, as you have seen from the example of the *Independent*. Newly launched magazines and newspapers often fail after a few months due to two key factors: lack of adequate research and insufficient capital.

The marketing plan

Remember that your product forecast is only that: a forecast. Sometimes it is necessary to make changes along the way. You may decide that it is more cost-effective to have a much larger print run, which is distributed free of charge at key venues, and to generate all your income through advertising. In this case, you would need to readjust your targets and revise your budget accordingly. Above all, constantly monitor the performance of your product against your targets and take action whenever and wherever you feel it is necessary.

Marketing is a costly process and for a campaign to be as effective as possible, careful planning is essential. Figure 7.8 describes the principal stages involved in any marketing campaign, starting with the product analysis.

Fig. 7.8
The marketing cycle

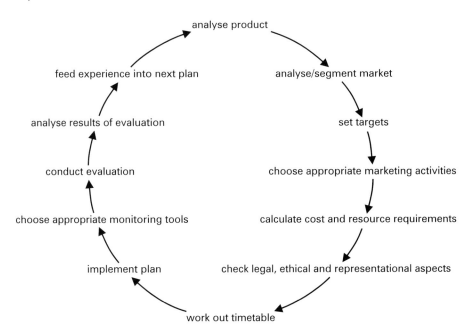

Activity

Match the diary entries below to various stages of the marketing cycle.

Fig. 7.9

20 MON
am: Debrief with Monica on last month's lifestyle survey
pm: Meeting on 5th floor with Finance Dept. re print quotes for summer poster campaign – <u>can we afford bus sides this autumn?</u>

21 TUES
am: Team meeting on preparations for this summer's agricultural show. <u>NB size & position of stand,</u> print requirements, merchandising – <u>can we cut down on last year?</u>
pm: Discussion with editors on last year's coverage – <u>any chance of increasing ad sales to ensure larger</u> supplement? – timetables – brief ad sales teams

22 WEDS
9 am – John: run through advertising campaign re Equal Ops (<u>Better ethnic mix in new photo shoot</u>)
pm – Weekly staff meeting. <u>Where can we cut costs this month? Can we drop autumn sponsorship plans?</u>
6 pm Chamber of Commerce Retailers' Group: discuss ways we can get titles promoted in shop windows, present new plan for streamlining ad sales

23 THURS
am: – Julian from City Playhouse to discuss special offers for next season for Loyalty Cardholders
Lunch: George (Royal Bookshop) – talk thru next week's literary lunch
pm – Brief Julie on setting up **sample group** for poster campaign lunch
eve – Attend opening exhibition of Artists Unlimited (NB make sure our **signage** went out this morning)

24 FRI
am – Newsagents' monthly meeting – check that delivery times have improved!

1   **Which stages are included in the diary extract?**

2   **Which are missing? (Note: some stages may be repeated and some diary entries may include more than one stage.)**

Discuss the reasons behind each day's activities.

You will have discovered that there is a certain amount of overlap in the planning stages and that some activities are useful in both planning and evaluation. In drawing up your plan, it is useful to ask yourself certain questions. You may find it useful to remind yourself of all the key marketing activities you studied in Section 1.

1   *Analyse product.* What are you selling? Is the product good enough to justify its marketing? Is the price realistic in the current market? Does the packaging convey the message you need to communicate to your audience? Is the brand clearly identified?

2 *Analyse/segment market.* Who are you selling to? How do you define your market segment? How are you targeting your marketing?

3 *Set targets.* What are your targets? Are they realistic? Are they achievable?

4 *Choose appropriate marketing activities.* Are they the best marketing activities to achieve your objectives? For example, will your target market respond better to discounts or to a poster campaign?

5 *Calculate cost and resource requirements.* How much will your marketing campaign cost? Are there sufficient staff to carry it out efficiently? If not, have you costed in additional staff requirements?

6 *Check legal, ethical and representational aspects.* Does the campaign reflect a fair policy regarding equal opportunities/ethnic minorities? Is there any aspect of the plan that needs to be checked out on legal grounds?

7 *Work out timetable.* Are you ready to plan your timetable? Have you agreed your timetable with the other members of the team? Is it realistic in terms of resources?

8 *Implement plan.* Is there anything else you need to consider before you 'green light' your plan?

9 *Choose appropriate monitoring tools.* Have you set up a market research team to monitor your plan? Will they be able to provide you with adequate feedback?

10 *Conduct evaluation.* Have you checked that your data is sufficient, up-to-date and accurate?

11 *Analyse results of evaluation.* How well did your campaign work? Did you achieve your target sales/desired increase in listening or viewing figures? Did it reach the right market? Did it stay within your budget? Were you able to carry it out according to your timetable?

12 *Feed experience into next plan.* What can you learn from the experience? Is there anything that can be improved or needs to be changed? Does the product need to be modified in any way? (This is an extremely important phase of the marketing cycle. All the information you have gained from preparing your marketing plan should be used to assess the development of the product in terms of brand, packaging, reliability and any special features.)

Assignment

1 Draw up a marketing plan for a media product to cover the period of the next 12 months. You could use a media product of your own or an existing product.

2 When organising your plan, you may find it helpful to use headings from the marketing cycle on page 352. Bear in mind the following points:

- The plan should be based on your own market research data and include a detailed product forecast.
- It should be supported by a written record (which may be in note form) showing how you checked the validity of your market research data and how you prepared your product forecast.
- Draw on the notes you have kept in your portfolio on using and evaluating market research and making a product forecast.

3 When you have completed your marketing plan, you will be able to use it to evaluate the product itself in terms of brand, packaging, reliability and any special features. Your portfolio should include notes on how you justify any innovations or modifications you may decide to make.

3 Creating advertisements

'Advertising could achieve better results if more people who create it would take the trouble to learn which techniques are most likely to work.'

D. Ogilvy, *Harvard Business Review* July/August 1982

When you were drawing up your marketing plan in Section 2, you decided what were the most appropriate marketing activities, assessed in terms of audience, cost, timescale, etc. In this section you are going to take this on to the next stage and prepare drafts and treatments for the kind of advertising you would need. Advertising is one of the most visible marketing tools and can also be one of the most expensive. You will consider the factors which influence decisions about advertising. You will evaluate your ideas, prepare a realistic schedule and assess your drafts and treatments against various content issues.

Refer back constantly to your marketing plan to ensure that you do not lose sight of your objectives.

What type of advertising?

Fig. 7.10

Activity

1 Who do you think the advertisement in Figure 7.10 was aimed at?

2 Was this a form of blanket advertising or was it aimed at a particular segment of the market? If the latter, what do you think is the age/social group being targeted?

In groups, create the profile of the person(s) you think this advertisement was aimed at. Discuss your ideas with the rest of the class and think of other ways in which the same product could be sold to the same audience.

You will probably have discussed poster campaigns, print advertising and radio commercials. You may have considered many other examples of sales promotion, such as point-of-sale displays, on-pack offers, trailers and indirect forms of marketing, such as sponsorship.

Back in the Sixties, what mattered was being seen to be creative. These days that just isn't enough. There are still a few creative people who think the ad is more important than the product, but for most of us it's the effectiveness of advertising that counts – how well it sells the product. Methods of evaluation are improving all the time – we have area tests, statistical and non-statistical analysis, direct response and consumer reaction. Every ad that we produce has to prove that it's just as effective as any other type of marketing. Generally, an advertising campaign needs to function across a whole variety of media, so you get the same image and the same message on your screens, in print and in a poster campaign.

Kim, Creative Director

How do I choose which media? Well, first of all, I have to look at what has been successful up to now, but these days the bottom line is always cost. If you just look at the figures, though, you might think I'd never buy anything except poster space. But that would be crazy. Poster sites have their uses, but generally only to back up other forms of advertising. They're blanket advertising – not targeted. The cinema network is the most expensive, but if I want to hit the 18–25 market, it makes a lot of sense. Regional papers are the best for local campaigns and **test marketing** and national papers are great when you can tie the ads into a feature. At the moment we're researching the potential for advertising on the Internet. There's obviously tremendous potential here, as yet largely untapped, but a great deal of research needs to be done on its effectiveness in terms of sales. I must admit that the growth of cable and satellite TV channels, the explosion in magazine publishing and the success of multi-section newspaper titles means that audiences are more fragmented than ever before. As a result media buyers like myself are constantly having to look at new ways to reach your target market. Look at those Oliver and Claire cartoons for Mercury at the beginning of '96. They bought up every single ad space in the broadsheet sections of the *Guardian*, the *Independent* and several other papers. At the end of the day, that had to be a gamble.

Brian, Media Buyer

My job is selling space to advertisers, so I'm competing with a wide variety of other media. It's up to me to convince advertisers not just that we're better than anyone else, but that our ads really shift their products. Obviously, being part of a successful organisation helps, but it's much more than that – everything we do is very carefully targeted, so we can direct advertisers to the most appropriate niche. It's much more creative than just simply selling.

Julie, Advertising Sales Manager

Activity

In groups, choose two promotions from the list below and decide

a) **what form(s) of advertising you would use to sell these products**

b) **where you would place your advertising:**

- launch issue of CD-ROM history of rock music
- summer issue of 'home/garden' magazine with special feature on conservatories
- wedding week promotion in popular TV soap
- re-launch of early evening TV news
- video release of latest Hollywood action movie
- special edition of local newspaper to coincide with move to new high-tech business park
- launch of new late-night phone-in programme.

Example

If you were selling a new football highlights video, you might decide that your target audience was primarily C1, C2 and D males of all ages. You might therefore choose print as your advertising medium and concentrate your adspend on tabloid newspapers.

In choosing which types of advertising would be most effective, you should have thought carefully in each case about what market segments you were targeting. You may have found that some products cover more than one age group and/or social grouping, whereas others are aimed at a much smaller market. These factors will be reflected in the type of advertising you have chosen and where you have placed it. You will have considered the most cost-effective use of advertising resources.

The content of advertisements

Activity

You may feel that the kind of advertisement in Figure 7.11 is not acceptable today. Discuss the following questions:

- Why should advertisers not employ this approach today?
- What considerations do contemporary advertisers have to keep in mind?
- What laws are there to control advertising? Are they effective?

Fig. 7.11
Ad for IPC young
women's magazines
from *Campaign* 1985

You may find it useful to obtain
information from some of these
organisations: The Advertising
Standards Authority (ASA),
Broadcasting Complaints
Commission, Broadcasting
Standards Council (IBA)
Independent Television
Commission (ITC), Press
Complaints Commission (PCC)
and The Radio Authority.
Addresses, telephone numbers
and other useful information
can be found in *The Media
Guide* (published annually by
Guardian Books/Fourth Estate).

In your discussion, you will almost certainly have touched on questions of race and gender. You may have considered other issues such as ageism, the use and portrayal of children in advertisements and the various areas of legislation covering advertising. You may find it useful to contact government and media bodies who can provide information on such issues. For example, the Advertising Standards Authority observes the British Code of Advertising and Sales Promotion Practice by ensuring that print, poster and cinema ads are 'legal, decent, honest and truthful, ... prepared with a sense of responsibility to the consumer, ... [and] conform to the principles of fair competition as generally accepted in business ...' The Authority is independent of both government and the media industries and is financed by a levy on advertising space. The Independent Television Commission (ITC) has a similar code of advertising standards and practice and ensures that independent radio and television advertising is limited to six minutes per hour (averaged over any twenty-four hour period). Your local radio, television and newspaper companies will also be able to tell you how they monitor their own advertising.

Figure 7.12 shows the structure of an American advertising agency account group. This particular model assumes that all aspects of the campaign are being handled by the agency. Often, however, some of the advertising functions are carried out by an in-house marketing team and other specific functions are delegated to the agency. In smaller agencies the task of creating the actual advertisement is again undertaken by outside specialists. This is particularly true in the case of making television commercials. In a typical advertising team the tasks are divided between the in-house marketing team and the advertising agency.

Fig. 7.12
The hierarchical
structure of an
advertising agency

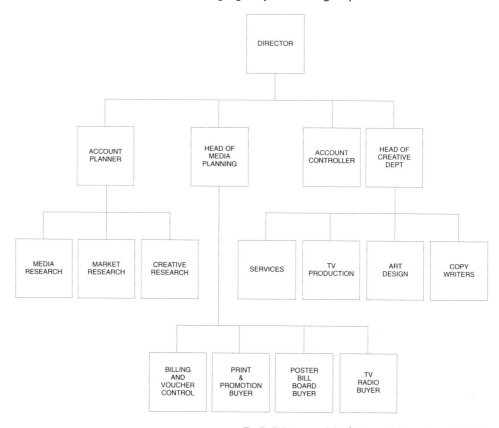

Advertising agency account group

R. J. Watson, *Marketing* (Chambers 1988)

Effective advertising

Each year the advertising industry gives a wide range of awards for outstanding achievements. It is significant that since the early 1980s effectiveness has been a much more important basis for such awards than creativity for creativity's sake. The quotation below explains how *Encyclopedia Britannica* won an advertising award.

> 'Selling a 32 volume set of encyclopaedias off the page is no mean feat. Yet despite the recession and CD-ROM competitors *Encyclopaedia Britannica* has continued to use direct selling methods successfully.
>
> The target market was wide; broadly characterised as BC1, but more importantly defined by attitude. Prospective customers want to help their children in education and want to give them a good start.
>
> This campaign gave parents confidence and comfort with the product, plus enough information to get them interested to respond so that the sales force could then do the actual selling.
>
> The ads were placed in the national Sunday press, *Sunday Magazine* and *You* magazine. Three per cent of leads from *Sunday Magazine* and 10 per cent of leads from *You* magazine were converted into sales.'

Marketing supplement,
'DMA Royal Mail Direct
Marketing Awards 1994'

Activity

Create your own advertising effectiveness award scheme. Choose one advertisement from any medium which you think is particularly effective, for example, radio, TV, newspaper, magazine or poster site. Write notes on the advertisement, referring to the checklist below. Present your case to the class, explaining why you think your advertisement should win the award.

- Are the ideas original/interesting/amusing?
- Do the illustrations/graphics grab your attention?
- Is the advertisement successful in getting its ideas across?
- Does it include sufficient information about the product?
- Is it targeted in terms of a well-defined market?
- Is it effective in promoting product awareness, for example, brand name, product identity, packaging?
- Is it legal, decent, honest and truthful?
- Could it cause any offence?
- Does the advertisement fulfil its objectives?

In considering the advertisements nominated for your class award, you will have realised that there are a range of factors which contribute to advertising effectiveness and which can be considered in terms of content, style and impact.

Assignment: Part 1

This is the first part of a three-part assignment which will enable you to provide evidence for your portfolio. Further parts appear later in this section.

You are going to develop advertisements for the product which was the subject of your marketing plan in Section 2. Draw up a schedule, along the lines of the example in Figure 7.13 (overleaf) for your own advertising campaign. The schedule should illustrate your choice of advertising media and the timing and frequency of your advertising.

Creating successful advertising

To make your advertising as effective as possible, you may find it helpful to consider the following points.

Preparing to write

Who are you communicating with? Is your style suitable for target age group, gender, etc.? What are you trying to communicate? Organise your information. It is often useful to do this under the headings *What? Where? When? Why?* and *How?*

Fig. 7.13
Memo to all heads
of department re
launch of 'US'
Magazine

MEMO

To: All Departments
From: Head of Media Buying, UK

REFERENCE: Launch of US Magazine. Glossy lifestyle magazine for both sexes.

	Promotions	TV and Radio	Print
JANUARY	Finalise advertising schedule. Begin advertising research. Start work on product dummy.	Finalise TV and radio booking. Exchange contracts	Finalise print schedule and exchange print and poster contracts
FEBRUARY	Evaluate advertising research. Set up potential advertiser database.		
MARCH	Use positive research results for sales brochure with product forecast and estimate of circulation. Design brochure and send to printer.		
APRIL	Start selling advertising to prospective advertisers.		Ads in trade journals
MAY			Ads in trade journals
JUNE			Ads in trade journals
JULY	Begin PR campaign. Profile of editor in trade press etc.		Ads in trade journals
AUGUST	Prepare for launch. Create list of media to invite to launch.	Classic FM sponsored daily programme and ads begin	Teaser poster campaign opens nationally on bus shelters for one month. Ads in trade journals
SEPTEMBER	**MAGAZINE LAUNCH**	Classic FM continues Channel 4 TV ads for one week from launch day	Launch poster campaign on bus sides and bus shelters. Ads in trade journals
OCTOBER		Classic FM continues Channel 4 TV ads for 3 days from publication date	Ads in trade journals
NOVEMBER		Classic FM continues Channel 4 TV ads for 3 days from publication date	
DECEMBER		Classic FM continues Channel 4 TV ads for 3 days from publication date	

Above is draft advertising schedule for 'US'. This has been prepared bearing in mind that the initial print run is 150,000 and we are looking for a "settle-down" circulation of 50,000.

Target audience: ABC1s nationwide. Limited budget (£75,000) has meant that Channel 4 TV ads have been restricted to initial launch date and short burst around publication date. We have chosen slots before current European film season (subtitled films) as these have been discounted despite good peak viewing period and they fit our audience profile. Programme sponsorship and heavy dependence on Classic FM has been chosen because it currently reaches 3 million ABC1s and has a good record for effectiveness in the print market. The programme combines with drive-home information for peak listening period. The poster campaign will instigate brand awareness and this will be reinforced by display materials with newsagent incentive offers. Trade advertising in *Campaign/Marketing Week* building to launch and weekly thereafter to include circulation figures if they match or exceed our estimates.

Style

Keep it simple. Use short words and sentences. Keep to one idea per sentence. Use active verbs (for example, 'Buy now!' rather than 'This product can be bought now!') Make it personal. Keep in mind who you are aiming to communicate with and address them directly. Use design and layout to make your copy exciting, but also easy to read. Make sure the design is relevant and appropriate. Avoid clutter. One strong image is better than several small ones.

Content

Check all your facts for accuracy. Make sure that your advertisement will be acceptable to the public and does not break any laws or codes of practice in relation to race, gender or minority groups. Don't make extravagant claims. Avoid empty adjectives such as 'a *unique* film'. All films are unique: you should say what is distinctive about your film. Marketeers often make use of a framework, such as AIDA:

Attention	Grab attention using a punchy headline and/or strong images.
Interest	Explain the headline and amplify it to add any other essential information.
Desire	Build on the initial interest and make the reader/listener/viewer decide that he/she wants your product.
Action	Show how the reader/listener/viewer can obtain what you are offering. Make responding as easy as possible.

Assignment: Part 2

This is the second part of the assignment for this section of the study unit.

You are going to prepare treatments and drafts for the advertisements which you scheduled in the first part of the assignment.

1   Before you start to design your advertising, you need to prepare a treatment. This is an outline plan which should take into account the marketing plan and all your subsequent discussions. Use the notes you made for the product forecast in terms of market position and competition, target audience, current marketing strategy and future marketing objectives. You should also include a brief record of discussion of any relevant content issues (i.e. legal and ethical questions). If you are planning to produce radio or TV/film commercials, you should also include ideas about casting, locations, music, etc. where appropriate. These must be realistic in terms of available budget and resources.

'To be effective, advertising must pick out the special characteristics of a product and emphasise them. In this way the product is differentiated from its competitors because it embraces something unique. It is not always easy to create that specialness, but failure to do so means that advertising works at product rather than brand level and any expenditure by one firm may help competitors as well.'

P. Tinniswood *Marketing Decisions* Longman 1981

2 **Produce two or three draft advertisements to meet the requirements specified in the marketing plan. Each draft should consist of headline, body copy and rough sketches. If your drafts are for radio or TV commercials, you should include a rough-sketch storyboard.**

Activity

1 Make notes in the margins of the drafts which you produced in the first part of the assignment.

2 Exchange your revised draft with a partner for evaluation. The evaluation should include consideration of any relevant legal, ethical or representational issues.

You will probably have discussed the importance of concise headlines, striking illustrations and informative copy. You may also have considered the relationship between these elements and the impact of memorable slogans (catchphrases) and variations in design and layout.

Assignment: Part 3

This is the final part of the assignment for this section of the study unit.

1 **Check your draft advertisements and make any further modifications which you feel are necessary.**

2 **Expand the notes which you made in the margins of your drafts to produce full treatments, explaining the approaches you have taken.**

Making a presentation

Before the marketeer places advertising in the marketplace, he/she has to sell the idea to colleagues and to the client. In this final section, you will concentrate on what makes an effective presentation. You will then prepare and deliver a presentation which describes a media product and the drafts and treatments for advertising which you prepared in the previous section.

'As Marketing Director of a major media conglomerate, I'm responsible for the marketing of a wide range of media products. Our current holdings include book publishing, cable channels, song publishing, recorded music, television production, film production, television stations and magazine and comics publishing. I suppose I'm on the receiving end of around 20 presentations a month – and that's apart from **pitches** from agencies who'd like to handle our accounts. Anyone making a presentation to me has to follow some basic ground rules. They need to show me that they:

- understand the product
- know the target market
- have absorbed all the relevant market research
- have identified the USP
- can create advertising with worldwide appeal
- can present their approach simply and effectively.

Effective presentation means getting the message across concisely and clearly, with uncluttered graphics and charts. For me, time is money. I simply don't have the time to listen to a whole lot of statistics – if a presentation doesn't sell itself to me within the first five minutes, it won't work.'

Alex, Managing Director

Activity

Consider the following list of presentation tools. Which do you regard as most appropriate to present the product and draft/treatment that your group has been working on? Bear in mind the resources and time available to you.

1 *Storyboard*: drawings or photographs arranged in sequence which show the visual continuity of a commercial, with copy adjacent to each picture describing the video action and the accompanying sound track.

2 *Posters/overhead projector*: can be used to show development of advertisements from initial sketches to final artwork.

3 *Flipchart*: can be combined with other presentation tools to demonstrate the rationale behind each successive stage of the creative process, for example:

- We rewrote the headline to make it stronger.
- We enlarged the illustration.
- We cut the body copy by 50 per cent.

4 *Audio and video tapes*: market research interviews (including **vox pop**); extracts showing development of radio and film/TV commercials from **first take** to final version.

5 *Collages*: comparative display of other advertisements (print or audio/visual) in the same field.

6 *Handouts*: background or supplementary information on product and/or advertising strategy.

7 *Demonstration*: may be live (i.e. a dramatic presentation) or a 'demo tape' (audio or video) to give your audience a rough idea of how the proposed advertisement(s) will work on screen or on the air.

Activity

When you listen to someone giving a talk (at school/college or on television), what gets your attention and what holds your interest? In groups, make lists of dos and don'ts for speakers. Exchange ideas with other groups and decide what are the most important things to remember when you are making a presentation.

You will probably have discussed the way that a speaker organises and presents information, as well as his/her use of voice and body language. You may also have considered the importance of thorough preparation. Below are some guidelines on both preparation and delivery.

Preparing your presentation

1 *Planning*. Thorough planning will help you to be more confident and will ensure that your presentation is properly focused.

2 *Audience*. Think carefully about your audience. What do they already know? What do you need to tell them? What kind of approach will be the most appropriate?

3 *Organisation*. Your presentation should have a clear structure and cover your main points in a logical order. Help your audience by giving 'signposts': start with an outline of the structure of your presentation and conclude with a summary of the main points you have made.

4 *Visual aids*. In presenting ideas for advertising, visual aids are indispensable. Charts, diagrams, graphs, etc., add interest and variety, help your audience to focus and can convey statistical information clearly and economically. But make sure that your visual aids are *appropriate*, *clear* and above all, *necessary*.

5 *Rehearsal*. You may find it useful to try out your presentation on the other members of your group. This will enable you to identify any potential problems and anticipate the reactions of an audience.

Delivering your presentation

1 *Notes/script*. Notes (on paper or a series of cards) should provide you with a framework of key points to cover. You can then expand these points during the presentation. Alternatively, you may prefer to write out a full presentation script and read from it. However, in this case, rehearsal should have made you familiar enough with your script to feel able to depart from it from time to time to expand on a point or give a further example.

2 *First impressions*. When making a pitch, first impressions are crucial. Think about the best way of getting your audience's attention. If you are thoroughly prepared, you should feel much more confident.

3 *Rapport*. Establish a positive rapport with your audience. If you are speaking from notes, make sure that you look up frequently and establish eye contact. Be as positive as you can. An audience will respond to your enthusiasm – or lack of it. Watch out for non-verbal signals (i.e. posture, facial expressions) which might tell you how people are reacting.

4 *Clarity and style of delivery*. Speak clearly and give your audience time to absorb what you are saying. It is vital for you to sound interested – break up your delivery and vary the tone as much as you can for different sections of your presentation (for example, explaining, giving examples, summarising conclusions, etc.).

5 *Signalling*. Remember that your audience is hearing your presentation for the first time. Help them to see the direction of the presentation by giving verbal signals (for example, first, next, then, etc.).

6 *Body language*. Think about ways in which non-verbal behaviour can help you to relax and make your presentation more natural. Maintain eye contact with your audience and don't be afraid to move or use your hands when it feels natural to do so.

7 *Visual aids*. Allow your audience enough time to take in information from visual aids – and make sure that they can be seen!

8 *Audience reaction*. Be prepared to respond to questions – or say you will deal with them at the end.

Activity

1 Individually, prepare a five-minute talk on a topic which interests you and which you know something about.

2 In small groups, deliver your talks, taking it in turns to act as audience and observers. Use the guidelines above to evaluate each other's talks, making notes on successful features as well as things which could be improved.

> 'I think the main secret is enthusiasm. If you've got enthusiasm …, then the people who are listening to you will have enthusiasm. Keep it pertinent, always keep it pertinent. You can wander off, so it's important that you do your research, that you know what you're talking about, and keep … to the objective you've set yourself.'
>
> Alan Wroxley, Sales Manager, Brother Electronics

Assignment: Part 1

This is the first part of a two-part assignment which will enable you to provide evidence for your portfolio.

This assignment involves making presentations of the drafts and treatments for advertising a media product which you prepared in Section 3. The audience of 'clients' for your initial presentation will be the other members of your class.

You may find it helpful to use the following headings to organise your presentation:

- relevance to product
- relevance to target audience
- content issues
- style
- resources (human, material, financial)
- choice of advertising media
- timing and frequency.

Prepare and deliver your presentation to the rest of the class. Receive informal, verbal feedback from your audience on the effectiveness of your presentation.

Activity

1 In groups, discuss the ways in which you will need to adapt your style of presentation for an audience who are familiar with your product, but who have not been involved in your assignment.

2 Design a draft questionnaire to elicit more formal feedback from such an audience.

When planning a presentation, perhaps the most significant consideration is how much your audience knows and how much you need to tell them. If you spend a lot of time telling them things they already know, they are likely to lose interest before you get to your main point. On the other hand, if you assume too much background knowledge, they may not appreciate the logic of your arguments. If you are unsure about the extent of their familiarity with your subject, the best solution is probably to begin your presentation by summarising as *concisely as possible* the background which you think they need.

Ongoing evaluation is an important part of all kinds of marketing activities. In designing your feedback questionnaire, you should aim for a balance of 'hard' and 'soft' data, i.e. objective, quantitative responses to specific questions and more open, subjective assessment. Remember that collating and analysing responses to questionnaires can be extremely time-consuming, so make sure that your questions are:

- focused (asking for the right information)
- unambiguous (clearly expressed)
- unbiased (neutral and open).

In order to obtain data which can be reliably analysed, responses are best collected in a form which will produce percentage answers, for example, using a scale to measure responses. This kind of 'hard' data can be supplemented by means of spaces on your questionnaire which allow scope for personal reactions from your audience.

Assignment: Part 2

This is the final part of the assignment for this section.

The audience for your second presentation should be someone who is able to give you more specialised feedback. This could be an advertising or marketing person, a local media producer, or your tutor acting as the 'client'.

1 Prepare and deliver your presentation. Your objectives are to inform your audience about the product and to describe/demonstrate how your advertisements would work. Make full use of the resources available to you to make your presentation as persuasive as possible. The presentation should:

- describe the product and its target audience
- identify and justify the main objectives of the advertising
- outline and justify your advertising strategy
- explain your approach (including the rationale for slogan/logo)
- illustrate your ideas for advertisements as graphically as possible.

2 **Get feedback on your presentation, employing your questionnaire. Analyse the feedback information you have received to evaluate your presentation. Make notes summarising this evaluation.**

Summary

In this unit you have been concerned with the principles and practice of marketing in the media.

In Section 1 you looked at definitions of marketing in general and identified the particular aims of marketing in the media. You examined in detail the range of approaches employed by media marketeers, comparing the effectiveness of these approaches and analysing their effects on media products.

Section 2 emphasised the importance of planning and forecasting based on reliable research data. You planned your own marketing campaign, including a detailed product forecast, ensuring that the research data supporting your plan was sufficient, up-to-date and accurate. You also included notes to demonstrate how you had checked the validity of your research and to justify the way in which the marketing plan may have affected the development of your product.

In Section 3 you considered the factors which influence decisions about advertising before going on to develop and evaluate your own treatments and drafts for advertising a media product.

Finally, in Section 4, you prepared and delivered presentations of your marketing plan and the treatments and drafts for advertising, obtaining feedback on the effectiveness of your final presentation by means of a questionnaire and evaluating the results.

Glossary

adspend the amount spent by a company on its advertising

advertising the commercial promotion of a product

blanket advertising advertising aimed at the widest possible market, sometimes known as the 'scatter gun approach'

body copy the main part of the text of an advertisement

brand a specific make or mark of a product which can be recognised by its design

brand loyalty the inclination of the consumer to continue buying the same brand

circulation the total number of people who buy a particular publication

classified advertising text-based, small advertisements for recruitment or personal sales or services, for example, motor cars and holidays

corporate image the image projected by a company including its logo

demographics the division of a market into segments according to age, sex, income, etc.

direct marketing marketing a product through direct channels of communication with the consumer

display advertising advertising in a publication which stands out from other advertisements and editorial material by having its own typeface, border, illustration, etc.

first take the first in a series of uninterrupted camera shots which make up a film

freesheet a newspaper distributed free to people's homes, the production of which is paid for by the advertisements in it

impulse buyer someone who buys a product without prior intention

licensing house a firm which acquires the rights to merchandise a named product in other forms

lifestyle a non-scientific segmentation of the population according to aspiration, personality and perceived values

logo the design or particular use of graphics for a company name which is used to identify that company

market segmentation how the market breaks down into categories according to the consumer's buying habits

marketing mix the combination of marketing tools selected for any particular campaign

masthead the title of a newspaper or magazine as it appears on the front cover, ie. in a distinctive typeface

media buyer the person responsible for placing advertisements in the media on behalf of an organisation

media marketeer person whose job it is to market media products

media products types of material published or broadcast by media industries

media sponsorship the identification of a television or radio programme with a company, which is paid for by that company

pitch (sales pitch) content of a sales presentation which endeavours to sell a product or a service

point of sale (POS) the place where the product is sold, for example, newsagents

psychological price barrier the highest price a consumer is prepared to pay for a particular product

pricing policy the setting of an appropriate price for a product being offered to the consumer

print run the number of copies printed of any publication

promotion the combined means of delivering the message about a product through publicity, sales campaigns, advertising, etc.

public relations (PR) the means of ensuring good relations between a company and the public, including the media and the press

readership the total number of people who read a particular publication

sales promotions promotional and sales techniques aimed at short-term increases in sales, such as discounts and free gifts

sample group a representative group of consumers questioned to identify the reactions of a much larger group

signage an umbrella term covering signs, banners and other promotional display material that highlights a company's corporate identity

spinc message slogan or message printed on the spine of a magazine, aimed at attracting the consumer

sponsorship planned expenditure by business on sport, the arts or other activities for mutual benefit

target audience/target market
specific, defined group of
consumers at whom a marketing
campaign is targeted

targeted advertising advertising
which is directed at a specific
market segment

test marketing marketing to a
segment of the community in
order that new products or
marketing strategies can be tried
out prior to a full launch

unique selling point (USP) the one
distinctive feature of a product
which sets it apart from its
competitors

vox pop (*vox populi*, **i.e. voice of
the people**) the opinions of the
population at large as seen from a
random sampling

Investigating media industries

G
N
V
Q

Contents

Introduction

The media play an increasingly important rôle in people's lives. In order to understand fully how they affect our view of the world, it is important to understand the context in which the media operate. This means that you need to know:

- who the owners of the media industries are and how the media relate to each other
- what controls there are over what we read, watch and listen to, and what official bodies are responsible for regulating the media
- how technological changes and economic factors are changing the media
- what opportunities exist for training and employment in the media.

In Section 1 you will investigate the main media producers in the UK. Who are they? What are their products? How are they related? Where does their money come from and how do they spend it?

You will then consider the media in their social context in Section 2. How do the media see their rôle in society? In what ways are they controlled by Parliament and by the law? How do different media industries regulate themselves? How far should the media be allowed to go 'in the public interest'?

In Section 3 you will explore the development of the media industries. How are new technologies changing the media? To what extent do economic factors and changes in our lifestyles influence the media industries?

Finally in Section 4 you will examine employment in the media industries. What jobs do people do? How have patterns of employment changed? What kind of training is available for jobs in the media?

1 Ownership and control of the media

> 'The government has decided that there is a need to liberalise the existing ownership regulations both within and across different media sectors.'
>
> Department of National Heritage, 1995

The concept of ownership in the media is complex. If you buy a book, you assume that you own it. But how far does that ownership extend? Does it extend to your being able to sell it? Could you reprint pages of it in a book of your own? The answers are clearly no. Your consumer rights do not give you ownership of the text – the copyright of which belongs to the author or to the publisher – or the right to sell it (except as a second-hand book). In more complex media products such as television and film there are layers of ownership: the screenplay is the copyright of the writer, the director may claim the rights to how it is finally cut (and prevent any other version from being screened), the **distribution rights** may belong to one or several companies, covering the world, and so on.

In this section you will peel away the layers of media ownership and investigate who controls the media. You will also examine expenditure and funding of the media in relation to questions of control and discover how media products and consumers are affected by these factors.

Principal UK producers

> 'A **monopoly** is a bad thing until you have one.'
>
> Rupert Murdoch

It is very easy to consume media products without being aware of the producers. If you were asked to name the producers of all the media products you regularly consume, you might come up with the names of a few publishers of course books, since they are often referred to by their publishers rather than by their titles – for example, *Chambers* for the dictionary published by that company. From repeated viewings you might remember that *Neighbours* is produced by The Grundy Television Corporation. But how many others do you know? Do you know who owns the daily newspaper your family reads, the local television company or the distribution rights to the last film you saw?

Useful sources of information on media producers are the *Guardian Media Guide* (published annually by Guardian Newspapers/Fourth Estate), the *BFI Film and Television Handbook* (published annually by the British Film Institute) and *BRAD*, the monthly directory of all the media, back copies of which should be obtainable from any advertising agency. (See Section 3 in Study Unit 6 for further information about *BRAD*.)

Activity

Make a media diary over the period of a week, writing down the name of the producer for each media product that you watch, listen to or read, together with the name of the product. You may find that there are credits for more than one producer, for example the film *Four Weddings and a Funeral* was a Polygram/Channel 4/Working Title production. In this case, write down the names of all the producers involved.

Combine your lists with other members of the class until you have one final list of producers and their products. At this stage your knowledge about these producers may be fairly sketchy, but add as much as you can to each name, indicating whether the producer is a local, national or international company, and whether they are print, audio, audio-visual or new media such as the Internet or CD-ROM. (You may wish to make use of icons to identify these different features.)

One fact that will have emerged already is that almost every major film and video is American. Look at the tables showing the top 20 films at the UK box office in 1993 and the top ten video rental titles in 1993. From these, you will see that all the top box-office successes in the cinema and the top rented videos were made and distributed by American companies.

Fig. 8.1
Top 20 films at the UK box office, 1993

Rank	Title	Country	Distributor	Box office (£)
1	*Jurassic Park*	US	UIP	46,564,080
2	*The Bodyguard*	US	Warner Bros	14,665,069
3	*The Fugitive*	US	Warner Bros	14,002,047
4	*Indecent Proposal*	US	UIP	11,885,752
5	*Bram Stoker's Dracula*	US	Columbia	11,548,429
6	*Sleepless in Seattle*	US	Columbia	9,417,608
7	*Cliffhanger*	US	Guild	9,219,405
8	*A Few Good Men*	US	Columbia	8,416,625
9	*Aladdin*	US	Buena Vista	8,167,165
10	*The Jungle Book* (re-released)	US	Buena Vista	7,415,989
11	*In the Line of Fire*	US	Columbia	6,817,821
12	*The Firm*	US	UIP	6,816,581
13	*Forever Young*	US	Warner Bros	6,787,327
14	*Sommersby*	US	Warner Bros	6,668,012
15	*Home Alone 2: Lost in New York*	US	Fox	5,663,186
16	*Demolition Man*	US	Warner Bros	5,628,613
17	*Under Siege*	US	Warner Bros	5,422,549
18	*Much Ado About Nothing*	UK	Entertainment	5,133,502
19	*Groundhog Day*	US	Columbia	5,098,267
20	*Made in America*	US	Warner Bros	4,999,057

EDI, in the *British Film Institute Film and Television Handbook*, 1995

Fig. 8.2
Top ten video rental
titles, 1993

Rank	Title	Company	Country
1	Sister Act	Buena Vista	US
2	The Bodyguard	Warner	US
3	Under Siege	Warner	US
4	The Universal Soldier	Guild	US
5	Lethal Weapon 3	Warner	US
6	Single White Female	Columbia TriStar	US
7	Home Alone 2: Lost in New York	FoxVideo	US
8	Patriot Games	CIC	US
9	A Few Good Men	Columbia TriStar	US
10	The Last of the Mohicans	Warner	US

BVA/MRIB, in the *British Film Institute Film and Television Handbook*, 1995

Another thing you will discover as you progress through this study unit is that while the number of media products is constantly increasing, ownership is contracting.

Fig. 8.3
Market share of top five
companies in various
media sectors, 1991

	%
ITV programmes (transmissions)	45.5
National daily newspapers (circulation)	95
National Sunday newspapers (circulation)	92
National and regional daily newspapers (circulation)	75
Books (sales)	40
Single records (sales)	58
LPs, cassettes and CDs	60
Video rentals	66

Sources *IBA Annual Report and Accounts* (1985–6); *32nd Annual Report of the Press Council* 1985 (1986); *Jordan's Review of Marketing and Publishing Data* (1984); *British Phonograph Yearbook* (1986); British Videogram Association
*Gallup, (1986)
Curran and Seaton 1991

Activity

As you can see from the market share table, at the time that this table was compiled 95 per cent of the national press was owned by the top five companies. At the time of writing, there are eight companies which between them own the national press.
Research the total current ownership of national newspapers and see whether there have been any changes. (You can find details in the *Guardian Media Guide.*) Write a brief profile of each of the eight companies, listing the papers they own, together with their annual circulation figures and their percentage share of the market.

Types of media organisation

'We're a really small office – there's only the two of us and a telephone and a fax line, but we take on extra staff when we're actually in production. We sold one documentary series to the BBC last year and we're currently developing two series which we're trying to sell to Channel 4. In both cases we need additional sources of funding – for our wildlife series we'd like to bring in an Australian TV company – and for the series we're producing on small railways around the world we're looking at getting a sponsorship deal from one of the new railway companies. We're not like a big film studio – if an idea doesn't work, at least we won't have invested hundreds of thousands developing it. And when it does work, you do get very healthy returns – our last series paid off the mortgage!'

Alison, independent producer

'We are a small animation cooperative and very little of our work ever gets seen on television. Mostly we produce material on health and safety, which is used in training videos. Occasionally one of our films is accepted by a film festival and then we can enjoy the rare pleasure of it being seen by a live audience. We are funded mostly through local government and grants from our Regional Arts Board, with occasional **development funding** from the BFI.'

Jude, Workers Animation Co-op

'You may think it's difficult trying to please everyone all the time, but in my job that's what I have to do. I have to maximise profits to keep the shareholders happy, produce high-rating programmes to please the public and attract the advertisers, and at the same time I have to produce quality television to fulfil our obligations under the **franchise agreement**. As you know, we have been extremely successful in achieving all of these aims, but we can't afford to be complacent. One very important development over the last few years has been **cooperation**: production costs these days are so expensive that if we are going to undertake a major new production, we will always look for partners. One recent example was Yorkshire TV's tie-in with Atlantic Video and Mills and Boon. I'm currently working on setting up a similar package, though obviously I can't release any details yet.'

Chief executive, independent television company

'What marks out our company is that we maximise our income by controlling a product at every stage of its life. We own companies at the source of production and at all stages of the production process – such as our recent acquisition of film processing laboratories in north London – and we also own the **distribution companies**. To be frank, I can't see the point in making anyone else richer: if I find that any of our companies is spending money buying in materials, then I want to know why. Take newspapers, for example: the cost of paper has rocketed recently, so I'm looking very keenly at the possibility of buying up Russian paper mills.'

Head of media conglomerate

'When I first started working here at the Television Centre, I got lost all the time – it is such a huge building. Now, of course, I'm well aware that Network Television is just one of 14 BBC Directorates, each one with its own personnel, training, finance and press and PR functions. Our Directorate covers both BBC1 and BBC2 and is divided into eight separate units. I work in Factual Programmes and we're scattered all over the place, not just in this building. Factual Programming is really an umbrella covering music and the arts – all those Prom concerts and operas on BBC2 – features, documentaries, science programmes and community and disability programmes. So, as you can gather, we are rather a diverse family and by no means equally funded. Since **producer choice** came in, we now have to bid against each other for every pot of gold and the atmosphere has become much more aggressive.'

'Peter', BBC Television Centre

The BBC's policy of 'producer choice' is examined below in Media ownership patterns.

These case studies provide 'snapshots' of several different types of media organisation. You will see that they range from small independent producers to vast global empires. In between, there are private companies, such as those which own regional newspapers and magazines, and public service organisations such as the BBC. In order to gain a fuller picture of these types of organisation, it is helpful to see how they are categorised and to learn some of the basic terms which apply to their structure.

Activity

Research and write short definitions of the terms overleaf, including at least one clear example of each. You might note how the Yorkshire tie-in with Atlantic Video and Mills and Boon, mentioned above, provides an example of the concept of cooperation.

Fig. 8.4
UK media top ten quoted companies

	£bn
Reuters Holdings	10.4
Thorn EMI	7.3
BSkyB	6.7
Reed International	5.6
Granada Group	4.2
Pearson	3.8
United News & Media/MAI	3.1
Carlton Communications	2.4
News International	2.1
Daily Mail & Gen Trust	1.5

Datastream in *Marketing*, 15 February 1996

Reuters, the international news agency, appears in the No. 1 position here, as News International is the newspaper division of the much larger News Corporation conglomerate.

- Media conglomerate
- Monopoly
- Multinational organisation
- Diversification
- Independent production company
- Demerger
- Public service organisation
- Production workshop
- Voluntary sector arts organisation

In writing your definitions, you may have come to realise that a number of the above terms may fit the same organisation. It is important to grasp how these terms are used, so that you can use them yourself when investigating media organisations in this study unit.

Media ownership patterns

If you read the financial pages of national newspapers, you will find that mergers and takeovers of media companies take place regularly. Whereas a few years ago there was little shared ownership between the print, film and television industries, today the reverse is true. Not only are they all interrelated, but the pattern of relationships is constantly shifting. Look, for example, at the various British media interests of the Pearson Group.

Fig. 8.5
British media interests of the Pearson Group

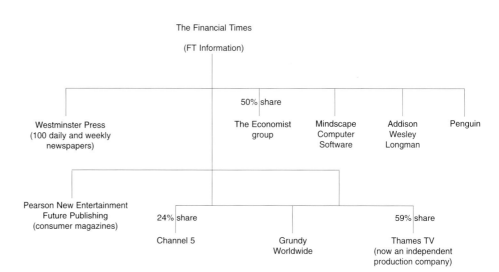

Note: Percentages indicate that the Group owns that percentage of the company. When other titles are added to the chart many of them will also own percentages of these companies.

Activity

Using the Pearson Group as a starting point, make a large wall plan charting the ownership of the major UK media companies. Begin with the eight companies that control the national press, which you profiled earlier, and add to them EMAP, which owns 70 regional newspapers nationwide, as well as over 150 consumer and business magazines, and Reed International, which owns a range of regional newspapers and also controls IPC Magazines. You might like to start with national newspapers as your top line, with regional newspapers underneath, then magazines and publishing houses, followed by terrestrial television companies and finally satellite and cable television and new media. The bottom line could be local radio.

Divide the research among the class with different areas allocated to different groups. Think carefully about the design of the chart: since the companies are linked together in so many ways, you will need to find a clear way of representing these relationships.

Write a short account of the process of building up the chart, describing how it develops, recording what you learn from doing it and noting your own contribution. Keep this in your portfolio.

In researching and designing this chart, you should have discovered how even local companies are linked with larger companies that are themselves, in turn, owned in part by vast multimedia conglomerates.

You should be aware that while the chart you have produced provides a picture of the principal owners of the media in the UK, there are also many small independent companies, although they operate principally as producers – small publishers, independent television production companies, indie record labels, for example. When it comes to the distribution and broadcasting of their products, these small companies very often have to use a major company or chain. This is particularly true of film distribution, since over half of all takings in the UK are for **multiplex** screens and 61 per cent of these screens belong to MGM, Odeon, UCI, Warner Bros and Showcase. All of these companies are linked to major distribution companies and all but one are American, although the British company Virgin has now bought some of MGM's screens.

Activity

Discuss the implications of media ownership. What advantages do you think there are in media companies owning other media companies? What advantages or disadvantages are there for the producer and the consumer?

In your discussion you may have covered some of the following points:

- **Penetration** of worldwide markets.
- Virtual monopoly of some products and consequent limitations on consumer choice.
- Cross-media promotion – for example the use of News International newspapers, such as *The Times* and the *Sun*, in establishing an audience for BSkyB.
- Benefits of size with regard to pricing policy – for example the ability to slash the price of a product and sustain the consequent loss of revenue, boosting circulation at the expense of rival products.
- Benefits of size with regard to investment in new technologies – for example News Corporation's acquisition in 1993 of the Delphi Internet service.

Fig. 8.6
British TV merger potential, the *Guardian*, 16 February 1996

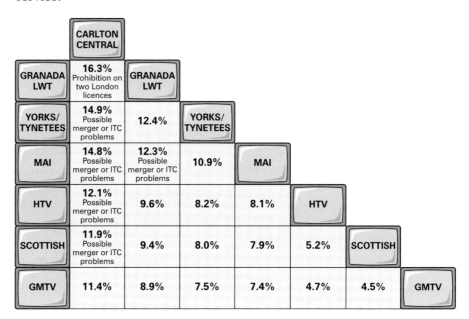

	CARLTON CENTRAL						
GRANADA LWT	**16.3%** Prohibition on two London licences	**GRANADA LWT**					
YORKS/ TYNETEES	**14.9%** Possible merger or ITC problems	12.4%	**YORKS/ TYNETEES**				
MAI	**14.8%** Possible merger or ITC problems	**12.3%** Possible merger or ITC problems	10.9%	**MAI**			
HTV	**12.1%** Possible merger or ITC problems	9.6%	8.2%	8.1%	**HTV**		
SCOTTISH	**11.9%** Possible merger or ITC problems	9.4%	8.0%	7.9%	5.2%	**SCOTTISH**	
GMTV	11.4%	8.9%	7.5%	7.4%	4.7%	4.5%	**GMTV**

You will see how mergers enable television companies – and other media companies such as newspapers – to capture a larger proportion of audience share. This makes their advertising space more attractive to advertisers, enabling them to earn additional revenue.

Activity

- In small groups, find current examples of a media product which exists in at least three different formats, such as film + video + book. (Video cases often show these details.)
- List the names of the companies involved (producers, distributors, retailers, etc.). Are they part of the same multimedia conglomerate? Is each one part of a different multimedia conglomerate? Or are they separate independent companies? (The reference book *Who Owns Whom* in your local library will be a useful source of information.)
- Compare your results with those produced by other groups in the class and identify those companies which appear most frequently.

One of the most important ways in which a media conglomerate can increase its revenue is through multimedia packages, a process known as multimarketing. These packages are created and sold by different companies within the group, for example a film which is made by one of the group's production companies, promoted in the group's newspapers and magazines, released worldwide by the group's distribution company, shown worldwide on the group's various satellite and cable channels and released worldwide on video by the group's video company. There may also be other possible spin-offs, such as a soundtrack album released on one of the group's record labels, a **novelisation** published by one of the group's publishing divisions, a computer game distributed by the group's software division or merchandising sold through the group's retail outlets. An example of this is *Batman Forever*, which is a Warner Bros production, a Warner Home Video with a novelisation published by Warner Books, Little Brown and the soundtrack on Atlantic Records, which is also part of the Time Warner Entertainment Group.

Assignment: Part 1

This is part one of an assignment which will enable you to provide evidence for your portfolio. Further parts appear later in this section of the study unit.

1 **Work in groups. Each group should choose *one* of the following (so that all of them are covered):**

- a magazine publisher
- a radio station
- a terrestrial commercial TV channel or a cable TV company
- a recording company.

2 **Contact the organisation you have chosen and find out:**

a who owns the organisation
b whether the owner company's range is local, national or international
c what its other media interests are
d whether it has connections with other media producers
e whether it has non-media interests.

3 **Present your findings to the class. Group presentations should include a question-and-answer session.**

4 **Individually, write a report based on the group presentations, including any useful additional points which may have arisen in discussion. Keep this in your portfolio.**

'The *Independent* really reflects the views of me, the editor, and my colleagues working together as a team, trying to decide every day what we think the readers want now. As far as the daily management of the news and the editorial coverage is concerned, the shareholders have never expressed any comments on it, either good or bad. The shareholders are keenly interested to see that their investment pays off and they're much more likely to comment on a lack of financial control, say, than they would be on a particular angle of a news story.'

Andreas Whittam Smith, former editor of the *Independent*, quoted in Andrew Hart, *Understanding the Media*, Routledge, 1991

'The BBC's status as a public corporation has, in the past, obscured its identity as a creature of the state. If anyone doubts the reality of this legal dependence, let them examine Clause 13.4 of the BBC's licence, which was used by Douglas Hurd when enforcing the Northern Ireland ban. "The Secretary of State may from time to time by notice in writing, require the Corporation to refrain at any specific time or at all times from sending any matter or matters of any class specified in such a notice."'

Nicholas Fraser, 'Broadcasting battle of conscience' in *Broadcast*, 17 March 1989

'The *Telegraph*, the national newspaper group headed by Conrad Black, has been hit hard by rising newsprint costs and the price circulation war. Profits for 1995 fell by almost £10 million to £35.5 million... Overall newsprint costs rose £12 million. The rises came as newspapers remained locked in a price war unleashed by Rupert Murdoch's News International titles in 1993. However, the *Daily Telegraph* increased its cover price by 10p last year to its current 40p.'

The *Guardian*, 28 February, 1996

Fig. 8.7

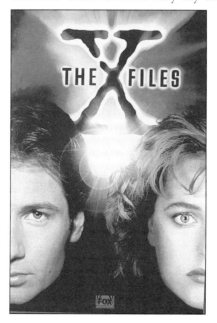

Activity

You have studied the ownership patterns of commercial companies. Now discuss whether some of these same patterns might relate to public service and state-controlled sections of the media.

In your discussion you have probably considered the various divisions of the BBC and how they work in the same manner as multimedia conglomerates to promote and support other divisions within the Corporation. You may have mentioned magazines such as the *Radio Times* or *BBC Food and Drink* which carries recipes featured in the BBC programme *Food and Drink* and is advertised immediately after the programme. You may have compared this with the manner in which News International newspapers promote forthcoming programmes on BSkyB, which is owned by News International. You may also have considered how the size of the BBC, like that of a conglomerate, enables it to compete in the world market.

Up to now, in studying the patterns of ownership of media products, you have concentrated on the effects in terms of revenue, ability to compete in the market, etc. These are the issues that would be highlighted by media producers themselves – and by the government, whose legislation made recent changes in ownership possible. But patterns of ownership also have far-reaching effects on the products, on those who work in the industries and on the consumer. Some changes, such as the newspaper price war bringing down the cost of a national newspaper, may be beneficial to the consumer, while others may be adverse. Consider the arguments about sport or new films being shown on television and how some programmes may only be available via additional subscription (Pay-TV). Consider, too, how popular American series appear on satellite before they reach terrestrial television and the consequent pressure on consumers to acquire satellite TV. This happened with the third series of the *X-Files* In addition, however much owners may say that they do not exert direct influence on their media products, there are bound to be some restrictions. Journalists, editors and producers have to take into account the interests of the owner. This form of control has important implications for the independence of the media, for media products and for the integrity of those who work in the media industries.

The battle for independence may also have its casualties. The BBC made immense efforts to placate the government, so as to ensure that when its **Charter** was renewed in 1996, advertising and sponsorship were not imposed on it. The Corporation achieved this by introducing tough cost-cutting measures, including staff cuts of 7,000 between 1986 and 1990. It also introduced the concept of producer choice, which makes every programme an independent entity bidding for funding against other programmes and buying its resources from within the BBC or from the external market (this area will be studied in more depth in Section 3). The radical measures imposed by BBC management were extremely unpopular with BBC staff at the time, but have been justified by management by the BBC's success in fighting off changes in its funding. Its ability to show that it is delivering value for money, is more accountable and cost-effective, has convinced the government to allow it to continue to be funded by the licence fee.

New technologies are generating new ownership patterns and the technology of the Internet means that users are increasingly dependent on the products and services provided by a handful of large corporations such as Microsoft's computer software and BT's telephone lines.

Assignment: Part 2

Part 2 of the assignment will enable you to provide evidence for your portfolio of ways in which specific products and groups of consumers are affected by patterns of ownership in the media.

Prepare an outline for an investigative consumer programme, such as *Watchdog*, on the battle between terrestrial and satellite television for the rights to broadcast sports programmes. You may choose to plan this either as an audio programme or using video.

1 Decide on the extent of your investigations, what questions you would need to ask and who you would approach.

2 Work out a realistic timetable for making the programme, including adequate time for planning and research.

3 Divide the different tasks among small groups, making full use of all available skills.

4 Research how in February 1996 the government legislated to prevent BSkyB or other subscription companies from obtaining the rights to broadcast eight major UK sporting events, including the FA Cup Final and the Grand National. Investigate how the situation has developed since then. (Note that the government did not bring in the legislation which the House of Lords had requested for terrestrial television to be permitted to screen highlights of sports events shown on satellite and cable. Note, too, the controversy that surrounded the Pay-TV extra charge for the Tyson-Bruno boxing match in March 1996.)

5 Contact the sports editor of your local newspaper and look up back issues to find out what the paper said.

6 Use all this information to plan the questions you would ask. Decide who you would interview – for example, the chairman of the local football team, spokespersons from the local commercial television company and from BBC local radio, etc. You might also consider whether you would want to include some *vox pop* interviews with members of the public.

7 Make notes on how you would introduce and close the programme.

8 Finally, write notes on your personal contribution to the project and put these in your portfolio.

The influence of funding sources

You will now explore the legal and other regulations that control the media. However, the overriding controls on the media are the economic factors, the hard economic realities which determine the success or failure of every media product. These **economic determinants** can be found at every stage of the production, distribution, dissemination and consumption of a media product.

Activity

Select three media products that you are familiar with, including print, audio-visual and new media. Make a list of the sources of funding for these products. Extend your list to include any other media products that you can think of. How do you think any of these products might be affected by the nature of their funding?

You will almost certainly have included the purchase price of a product (for example, video, CD, CD-ROM, newspapers and magazines) and the sale of advertising and subscriptions (satellite and cable television). If you have included a film product, you may also have considered sources of revenue such as **box-office receipts**, national and international television sales (terrestrial, cable and satellite), **video rights** and possibly income from **merchandising**. In considering a record company, you may have also included income from the sale of promotional videos to television.

In considering film companies, remembering the work you have done in Study Unit 7 on marketing the media, you may also have noted that it is only when distributors are able to spend very large sums on marketing that they can benefit from such vast sales and, in most cases, sales of this size are confined to big-budget American '**blockbusters**'. In the case of a small, independent production – for example a film that has been co-funded by

The film *Four Weddings and a Funeral*, co-funded by Channel 4, was one of the very few examples of a low-budget British production to achieve worldwide box-office success without the advantage of massive expenditure on marketing by its distributors.

Channel 4 or the BBC – it may only be screened in one London cinema and subsequently in smaller regional independent cinemas before it is shown on television. There is no additional funding from its television transmission, since it was co-funded by a television company.

You will have seen how the activities of the consumer – the person buying the end product – have a direct effect on the income of the media company. Thus, what the company produces is dictated by consumer choice.

'In the highly competitive women's weekly [magazine] market a half-million circulation figure is accepted as a prerequisite and ailing titles face the axe.'

Marketing, 15 December 1995

- The BBC's domestic services are mainly financed from the sale of TV licences (£89.50 for colour; £30 for black and white).
- In March 1996, licence income amounted to well over £1.8 billion. This figure represented over 21 million current licences – approximately 20.5 million for households with colour TV.
- Since May 1988 the licence fee has risen annually in line with inflation except for 1991-2 when the level of the licence fee was reduced in real terms by 3%. The government's intention is to encourage the BBC to develop other sources of income.
- Licence income is supplemented by profits from trading activities, such as exports of TV programmes, video sales, publications, hire and sale of educational films, film library sales and exhibitions based on programmes.
- The BBC is prohibited by its Royal charter from gaining any revenue via advertising.
- The BBC World Service is funded by a Grant in Aid from the Foreign Office (£180.6 million in 1995/96).
- The Open University broadcasts are funded from the Open University.
- BBC Worldwide is a totally commercial operation. None of its activities is subsidised from the licence fee or Grant In aid, and the BBC has strict rules to ensure that fair trading principles are observed.

Fig. 8.8
BBC income, 1995/96

Adapted from *Britain 1995: an Official Handbook*, HMSO, 1994

Fig. 8.9
The BBC licence fee costs around 24p a day

Write a short account of the relationship of the funding of media products to consumer choice. Include a chart showing a number of media products, noting whether the consumer choice is direct (for example, buying a cassette or paying the subscription to a movie channel) or indirect (for example, increasing viewing figures and encouraging more advertising). Use the details above of BBC funding to enable you to include the BBC in your study. Refer to a wide variety of media products including new technologies.

You might wish to extend your notes to consider the following questions.

- Can the need for a large audience – and maximum profits – have a damaging effect on the product?
- If there is no direct consumer choice, are the views of the consumer taken into account by the media producer?
- Does the drive for profit prevent the voices of minority groups from being heard in the media?
- Apart from choosing whether they buy, watch or listen to a particular media product, what influence can consumers have over the media?

You may have noted that while media producers will spend millions of pounds in promoting their products to the consumer, consumers themselves have very limited access to the media and can only exert control by their choice of what they watch, listen to and buy. This choice is, however, extremely powerful and programmes are specifically manufactured to attract the largest possible audience. You may have mentioned the battle of the ratings (see Study Unit 6) and how this leads away from minority interest programmes and towards more light entertainment.

The BBC licence fee

It is also worth analysing actual programme content in this context. Consider how pilot programmes are used to test consumer reaction and how their reception can influence not simply whether the full series is commissioned, but even which actors are cast in lead rôles. Think of how film stars are described as '**bankable**': the Hollywood stars on the so-called A-list are those who can 'open a movie'. This means that any film starring one of these actors is guaranteed to generate massive box office returns throughout the USA on its opening weekend.

The implications for funding through the public sector can be seen by studying the BBC. You saw earlier how the introduction of producer choice enabled the BBC management to change the entire way in which programmes were funded. The Corporation was forced to make itself more cost-effective and thus prevented the government from undermining the

Requests for repeats are welcome and can be made by writing to BBC Viewer and Listener Information, 201 Wood Lane, White City, London W12 7TS, or by telephoning the Information Office on 0181–743 8000. There is little advance warning about when a programme will be repeated; however details are usually available in the *Radio Times*. BBC Staff Guide

Stars such as Harrison Ford and John Travolta can now secure fees of around $20 million a picture.

independence which it has traditionally enjoyed as a result of being funded by the licence fee. This will be explored more fully in the next section.

As you have seen, until a few years ago the BBC was relatively free of financial constraints, but now is subject to the same pressures as other media producers to ensure that each programme it makes earns as much as it can.

There are several other ways in which the media are controlled by funding bodies. Some of these are direct and some are indirect.

Activity

Contact a local film company or regional cinema and find out how it is funded. If it has to fill in forms to obtain this funding, ask for copies and study them. Write a summary of what information the organisation has to provide to satisfy the funding bodies and what reasons there may be for having to provide it.

You will have discovered that small independent film-makers who get grants from Regional Arts Boards or from the Arts Council have to fulfil a range of criteria to obtain that funding. This will include proving that their project is of high quality and innovative, and also that they are able to obtain other funding and can market themselves adequately. Independent cinemas which are funded by the British Film Institute and local authorities and the British Film Institute itself also have to fulfil quality control criteria, as well as showing that they are run efficiently. You may also have noted that all these government bodies which fund the arts receive their funds from the Department of National Heritage and have to prove that the organisations they fund are accountable to the public and deliver value for money. You may well have noted that the pressure on small independent organisations is just as intense as in the BBC.

Investors and advertisers

The late Peter Cook, who owned the satirical magazine *Private Eye*, was unique in that he never interfered with the content of the magazine, but simply wrote cheques whenever they were needed. He was greatly mourned. Most investors are not so detached.

Other sources of funds include investors and advertisers. Investors generally do not try to control the media they help to fund. However, their aim is to obtain a good return on their investment and this means that they want healthy profits. This puts pressure on the media producer to aim for a wider audience and tends to discourage experimental work which may attract fewer people.

Some film-makers have said that Academy Awards should be given for funding rather than for the content of the film, since getting the funding is much the hardest part! A survey of every British film made in 1981 found that producers had to cast their nets wide. There was a 35 per cent proportion of non industry backers which included banks, the National Coal Board Pension Fund and a record company.

'"When I started trying to raise money for films," producer Timothy Burrill said, "There were only eight or nine sources, including the UK and American majors. Now there are unlimited doors to knock on, private financiers etc. This of course has made our lives easier and harder."'

From Antoinette Moses, 'British film production 1981' in *Sight and Sound*, British Film Institute, Autumn 1982

'Elizabeth Taylor is to take walk-on parts in a string of US sitcoms to plug a new perfume for Elizabeth Arden... Enough product placement, certainly, to give our own [Independent Television Commission] a heart attack.'

The *Independent*, 20 February 1996

Newspapers, magazines and commercial television could not exist without advertising and the influences exerted by advertisers are considerable.

Companies, politicians and celebrities alike will try to use the media to promote themselves and their products or services. The media are subject to increasingly complex attempts at **news management** and **disinformation**, as well as a whole range of marketing techniques. **Product placement** is not allowed to be too obvious, but even a small degree of product placement in the right programme is worth a great deal of money to the company. Airlines, in particular, often do product placement deals with film and television companies. This usually means a quite unnecessary shot of a plane taking off or landing, which shows the airline name or logo quite clearly. Interestingly, the restrictions placed on companies sponsoring a television programme usually prevent any product placement by the sponsoring company.

All journalists are constantly pressured by public relations (PR) companies and in-house public relations people working for business, government or individuals, who offer a variety of inducements in order to get a favourable mention of their product, or person. Travel companies are an excellent example of this and while journalists try to remain impartial, they may note in an article that they were a guest of a particular company, and it is companies which can afford such '**freebies**' which often get the most coverage. A more disturbing issue is that of medical journalists subjected to pressure by drug companies.

Another form of advertising is the **advertorial**. This often appears to be editorial, but always includes the words 'Advertiser Promotion' in small letters at the top of the page. Advertorials also appear in **freesheets**, where there is paid editorial together with advertising. But while advertorials are usually clearly advertising, there is now a major campaign backed by the National Union of Journalists (NUJ), the Institute of Public Relations (IPR) and the Institute of Practitioners in Advertising (IPA) to stamp out the practice of magazines and newspapers demanding payment for stories taken

Fig. 8.10
Advertisement feature which appeared in *Radio Times* 20 – 26 April 1996

directly from press releases. This is often linked to a new trend of asking for payment for the cost of printing photographs which have been provided by PR companies. The danger of this practice is that, especially in the trade press, it would lead to paid-for publications and the implications for companies who cannot pay are obvious.

Expenditure in context

The close relationship of income and expenditure is a self-evident factor of economic life. You cannot spend more than you have. Expenditure on media products is therefore determined by the level of funding. There are several aspects of media expenditure, however, that are worth studying in the context of media control, the most important of which is where the money is spent and why.

Fig. 8.11
The *Sunday Times*: what each copy costs to produce. Note how expenditure is divided among production, newsprint, the distributor, editorial and overheads

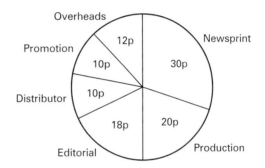

Graeme Burton,
More Than Meets the Eye, Edward Arnold, 1990

Local recording studios and newspaper offices may be able to provide information on expenditure for the production of CDs and magazines. An excellent source for imformation about TV drama budgets is the case study on the production of *Vanity Fair* in R. Giddings et al, *Screening the Novel* (Macmillan, 1990).

Activity

Research the budgets for:

- a 60-minute television drama
- a CD
- a magazine

in terms of how the expenditure is divided between production, distribution, marketing, artists' fees and overheads. Compare the total cost per product against its price.

You may have found some of these figures surprising. For example, in costing a CD the dealer's profit represents a considerably higher percentage of the cost than the royalty paid to the artist. The cost of **newsprint** – which has risen dramatically in recent years – is a major part of the cost of a newspaper.

Now look at the table on the next page showing the number and range of new British programmes that Channel 4 claimed it could have provided for UK viewers in 1995 if it had not been required to subsidise ITV.

Fig. 8.12
How Channel 4 could
have spent its money

		Hours	Cost per hour £000	Total £m
Drama				
3	Drama series (e.g. *Rector's Wife*, *GBH*)	15	700	10.5
12	Film on Four	20	500	10.0
2	Teenage drama series	100	80	8.0
1	Multicultural film (e.g. *Bandit Queen*)	2	500	1.0
3	Low budget films	3	333	1.0
3	New film-makers scheme	6	250	1.5
1	Drama series	10	600	6.0
	Total additional drama	156		38.0
Factual				
5	Documentary series (e.g. *Beyond the Clouds*)	20	125	3.0
6	Education series (e.g. *Time Team*)	21	120	3.0
3	Current affairs specials/mini-series (e.g. *Power and The People*, *Falklands War*)	12	167	2.0
2	Schools series	13	100	1.3
3	Experimental series	15	100	1.0
3	Regional series	18	85	1.5
2	Religious series (e.g. *Witness*)	10	100	1.0
1	Early evening science series	4	125	0.5
2	Science documentary series	8	125	1.0
3	Science specials	3	166	0.5
1	Youth documentary series (e.g. *Moss Side*)	4	125	0.5
1	Disability strand	5	100	0.5
3	All Night Zones	100	25	2.5
	Total additional factual	233		18.3
Arts and entertainment				
1	Multicultural arts series	12	85	1.0
1	Multicultural factual series	6	85	0.5
2	Late night discussion series (e.g. *After Dark*)	20	50	1.0
4	Children's series (e.g. *Wise Up*)	27	75	2.0
4	Comedy series (e.g. *Drop the Dead Donkey*)	24	166	4.0
3	Music and Arts series	18	85	1.5
4	Arts events (e.g. *Glyndebourne*)	6	333	2.0
1	Christmas animation (e.g. *The Snowman*)	1	700	0.7
4	Daytime series	125	35	4.3
2	Youth sport/activity series	7	70	0.5
1	Saturday morning sport enhancement	(–)	(–)	0.2
	Total additional arts and entertainment	246		17.7
	TOTAL ADDITIONAL PRODUCTION	635	117	74.0

The *Guardian*, 18 December 1995

Activity

Discuss the costs of television in the light of this table and the budgets you have analysed and consider the following questions:

- Why does drama cost so much per hour? Why does a modern TV drama usually take the form of a series or a serial rather than a single play?
- How often are major drama series scheduled, compared with comedy series and sport?
- If television companies are pressured to make more profit, which programmes do you think will be cut first?

- Channel 4 has a special responsibility to provide minority-interest programmes. Do you think other television channels offer the same range of programming? (Compare the programmes scheduled by Channel 4 and BBC2 for one week to check your opinion.)

When funding is limited, the constraints on spending are increased and every item of expenditure is assessed in terms of value for money. Increased productivity is demanded in all media industries as staff are cut and budgets pruned back. Typical effects of these cuts are that the sums paid per hour by television companies to independent producers are reduced, the number of specialist writers commissioned to write features is cut down, marketing budgets are reduced and companies merge – with further cuts in staff.

Another potential result of such cuts is that newspapers and magazines rely increasingly on ready-made features provided by public relations companies and, as you have seen above, this has serious implications for editorial independence. News stories from abroad, which are shared between papers and originate from a single source, often a news agency, will not provide the depth and variety that is obtained from having several independent, knowledgeable foreign news correspondents in place. Such factors affect both the consumer – who will not receive such a full picture as before – and the quality of the product itself.

Assignment: Part 3

Write a report on the influences of funding and expenditure relating to ownership. Drawing on the information that you have gathered in this section of the study unit, show how both products and consumer are affected by these influences.

Assignment: Part 4

Use all the information that you have collected so far in this section of the study unit to prepare the following case studies.

- With a partner, choose six producers of media products to study in depth (three each).
- You should ensure that you each include one example of a producer which is local, one which operates nationally within the UK and one which is an international organisation. The six should also include one audio-visual producer (film, TV, radio), one audio (for example, music, audio-books), one print (newspapers, magazines, comics, books) and one new media producer (CD-ROM, etc.). You may wish to use the same companies which you researched in Part 1 of this assignment.
- Also make sure that you cover a range of size of organisations, so, for example, one producer may be a small independent television or animation company, while another may be a major institution such as the BBC.
- Exchange your three reports with your partner. Evaluate each other's reports and then amend/extend your own reports accordingly.

2 Regulation of media industries

The purpose of this section is to enable you to understand how the media industries are regulated. You will investigate the concept of regulation and the legal framework in which it operates and identify the official bodies which impose regulations on the media industries. You will also analyse the means through which the media regulate themselves through organisations, codes of practice and the media's own concept of professionalism. In addition, you will study the wider issues regarding media regulation, including access to the media, freedom of expression, access to information, censorship, tolerance and propaganda.

Activity

Read the statements below. Consider who the speakers might have been and decide whether you agree or disagree. Then, in a small group, discuss the statements. When you have finished, be prepared to share your views with the rest of the class.

'The content and conduct of the press and media are carefully regulated. We are a civilised country with laws and regulations to ensure health and safety and to protect the public. Just as we have regulations to ensure that the restaurants we visit are clean and healthy, so too, we have laws and organisations to regulate the media. Just think about the laws of slander and libel and laws to protect the naming of child victims of crime. If it wasn't for the various Broadcasting Acts, the Cable and Wireless Act and the Official Secrets Act, there would be anarchy. It's in the **public interest** to have these regulations. In a war situation, for example, you can't say what you like because that is tantamount to telling the enemy what you are doing. I sleep better knowing that our media are tightly controlled.'

'It's all very well for the media to demand more self-regulation, but when the public are offended, they want an official body to complain to. Without the Monopolies and Mergers Commission we might end up with all the media in the hands of one individual. And just think what children might watch if films and videos did not have to be vetted by the British Board of Film Classification.'

'Self-regulation is the key. The last thing the media needs is more laws. Journalists, editors, TV producers – they all know what is acceptable to the public. Anyway, if we're in any doubt, we have our own codes of practice and in-house guidelines on things like racial and sexual equality to make sure we don't overshoot the mark.'

'Personally I think we should let the public have more information about what goes on in the rest of the world. But it's not the **house style**. Soap stars, sleaze and royal scandals, that's what sells the paper. So who am I to rock the boat? At least I always double-check all my facts to make sure that what I write isn't just gossip or innuendo.'

'We have a free press in Britain – it's not like it is in other countries where the government own it all and decide what you are going to read or hear. Anyone can publish a newspaper here provided they don't break the law. It's the people who decide what they want to read and that can only happen in a democratic, free market environment.'

'It's all very well for the media to demand freedom of information, but it isn't their children at risk. What we need is more censorship to control sex and violence on our screens. If *Child's Play 3* had been banned, then little Jamie Bulger might be alive today.'

'The "Video Diaries" created by the BBC's Community Programmes Unit have been a tremendous success. Giving video cameras to members of the public and getting them to make programmes about their lives has produced some of the most powerful documentaries we have seen in the last few years. It's about time the public had real access to the media.'

Your discussion should have identified some of the central areas of public debate about media regulation. Here are some points that you may have noticed:

- There are many laws covering different aspects of media activity.
- There are a number of regulatory bodies in the UK which specifically cover the media, in addition to laws which everyone has to uphold.
- Many people working in the media believe that self-regulation and individual media codes of practice are the best way to regulate the industry.
- The 'house style' of a media company may exert control over content, while professionalism brings with it a degree of self-regulation.
- Freedom of information, access to the media and the nature of censorship are issues which arouse passionate feelings and which are the subjects of constant debate.

The legal framework

In addition to the legislation which is covered below, there are also other laws which affect the media. These include the Obscene Publications Act, the Cinemas Act, the Cinematograph [Animals] Act 1937, the Video Recordings Act 1984 and the Protection of Children Act 1978, as well as laws relating to contempt of court and blasphemy.

In addition to the laws which everyone in the UK is bound by, there are several pieces of legislation relating to the media which have been passed by successive governments. These cover several areas of media activity such as media ownership, how the media are run and what they broadcast or publish. While anyone is free to publish a book, magazine or newspaper, no one may make an audio or audio-visual broadcast without a government licence. The BBC is one licence-holder while the Independent Television Commission (ITC) has been set up to award licences in the independent television sector. Those who broadcast illegally are called 'pirates' and it is illegal to listen to them. In the 1960s it was the success of the pirate radio broadcasters, broadcasting pop music from off-shore boats, which forced the BBC to rethink its own pop music programming and led to the birth of Radio 1.

All laws are subject to change. Sometimes it is public opinion which brings about these changes, while sometimes MPs initiate legislation – one example is the Private Member's Bill put forward in February 1996 by Tory MP Peter Luff, the Periodicals (Protection of Children) Bill, which would require magazines to carry a warning on the cover page about articles thought to be unsuitable for readers below a certain age. In times of war, governments often pass additional laws to control the media. It is also through legislation that regulatory bodies are set up by government to ensure that the media industries observe the law and these bodies may be changed – or disbanded – by subsequent legislation.

New media are posing many problems for governments throughout the world because of the difficulty (at the time of writing) of subjecting them to any form of regulation or censorship. For example, in 1989 Chinese students involved in mass protests against their government made use of fax machines to inform the rest of the world how the protests were being brutally suppressed. In 1996 the Saudi dissident, Mohammed al-Mas'ari, who was fighting extradition from Britain, had been using faxes as a means of political propaganda in Saudi Arabia. The Chinese government has announced that it would like to prevent its population from receiving information on the Internet.

Deregulation

The 1990 Broadcasting Act paved the way for a loosening of control over the media, so as to allow for more competitive bidding for television and radio franchises. It gave the ITC the power to award television broadcasting licences to those companies who submitted the highest bids, subject to their also meeting the requirements of a '**quality threshold**'. The independent television companies now had to compete for positions within a free market economy where they had to decide how much to bid. The new franchises created a situation in which the companies that had been forced

You saw in the last section how the economic and organisational benefits of size make such takeovers and mergers attractive to management and investors.

by competition to make very high bids suffered financially, while other companies retained their franchises with much lower bids. For example, compare Central Television's unopposed bid of £2,000 with that of Yorkshire TV at £37 million – see the map. This led to a financial climate in which takeovers and mergers between companies became inevitable.

Fig. 8.13
Who won the franchise battle?

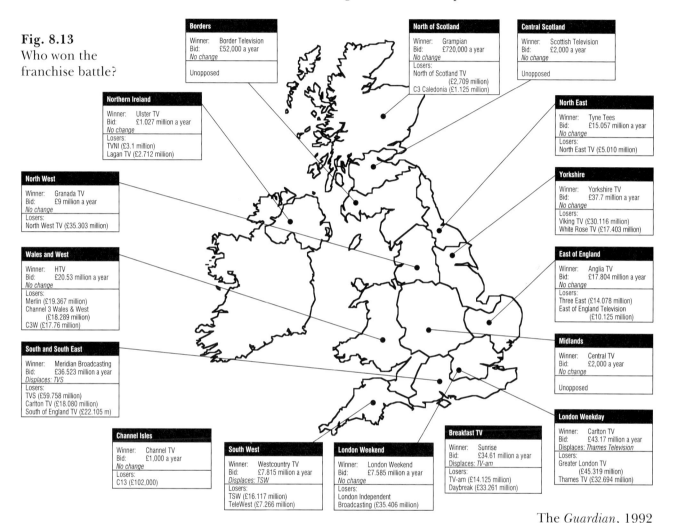

The *Guardian*, 1992

In 1993 LBC from London, Devon Air and Sunset Radio from Manchester all failed to have their licences renewed.

Deregulation had a similar effect upon independent radio. In 1993 and 1994, for example, the Radio Authority readvertised 129 licences. In most cases, the original licence-holding station managed to have its licence renewed, but not in every case. In some cases competition was especially high: for example, June 1993 saw 48 applications for six FM frequencies and two new AM frequencies in London.

In Sections 3 and 4 you will have the opportunity to study the possible future effects of deregulation on the media in terms of future ownership patterns, the financing of the media and training and employment.

The 1996 Broadcasting Bill will further loosen control on cross-ownership between newspaper groups, TV companies and radio companies, although it continues to enforce the regulation that press groups with more than 20 per cent of the market cannot control ITV franchises. However, TV companies can buy newspapers with up to 20 per cent of total UK circulation and newspaper companies can control up to 15 per cent of the total UK television audience.

Read the text above and the following quotes. Then write a short summary on deregulation noting both the arguments for and against.

'The Broadcasting Act 1990 was an important liberalising measure... [It] was designed to allow the companies to compete more successfully in the international marketplace.' Department of National Heritage, 1995

'We welcome the opportunity to build our media businesses.' Lord Clive Hollick, proprietor of MAI, which bought Anglia Television and announced a merger with United News & Media.

'What we've seen over the last six years is the government bit-by-bit dismantling a strong and wisely governed system to be slowly replaced by a commercial free-for-all.' Anthony Smith, former director of the British Film Institute

In your notes you may have concluded that deregulation enables television companies to be large enough to make and buy more expensive programmes. On the other hand, you may have argued that it has led to lower quality broadcasting and the cutting of many media jobs. You may have expressed concerns about the loss of regional voices when ITV companies merge and production is removed from its former local base. You may have noticed that the number of companies on the map at the time the franchises were awarded has already shrunk considerably and that deregulation has resulted in much of the media falling into the hands of a small number of companies.

Cable regulations

Cable television is not new, but because of the massive cost of laying cable across the UK, its development was initially slow. The economics of cable made it unprofitable until it was agreed (in the 1990 Broadcasting Act) that cable operators would be allowed to offer telephone-linked services. Following that decision, the development of cable showed a major increase. In 1993, cable was available to 700,000 homes and this leapt to over a million in 1994. Forecasters believe that the 1993 figure of 21 per cent – see the table showing cable and satellite penetration – will have doubled by the end of the decade. The original 11 cable franchises were granted by the Department of Trade and Industry (DTI) but the DTI's rôle was superseded by the Cable Authority, though this body was itself taken over by the ITC in January 1991.

The Act empowered the ITC to grant two licences to each cable operator, one for the system and one for the programmes. Only one set of licences is issued to each area, licences which are awarded on the basis of an annual cash bid, in addition to a range of conditions being met.

'Cable will do more than change television. It will change our lives.' *Sunday Times*, 7 December 1980

Fig. 8.14
Cable and satellite penetration 1986–93 (%)

Year	Cable	Satellite
1986	12.2	–
1987	13.3	–
1988	14.3	0.1
1989	14.5	2.3
1990	16.6	5.9
1991	19.1	7.9
1992	21.5	10.2
1993	21.1	12.1

Cable Television Association, in the *British Film Institute Film and Television Handbook*, 1995

Activity

Imagine that you are a new cable operator putting in a bid for the franchise for your local area. In order to produce an effective bid, you will need to carry out some preliminary research into the kind of information required by the ITC and the regulations you will need to abide by.

- Divide your research among different groups. One group might contact your local cable operator, while another might contact the ITC. Another group might prepare a case history of a local cable operator as an example.
- Jointly present your evidence to the class. You might wish to invite a representative from your local cable company to hear your findings and evaluate your report.

In carrying out this research you will have learned about the basic regulations required by the 1984 Cable and Broadcasting Act and how they apply both to the running of the system and to the content of the programmes broadcast.

National security

The Official Secrets Act (originally passed in 1911 and updated in 1988) and the Prevention of Terrorism Act (extended in 1988) are the two Acts which limit the activities of the media in the interests of national security.

Activity

In recent years there have been several key events which have shaped the way in which the media are currently controlled through the Official Secrets and Prevention of Terrorism Acts.

- In small groups, research one of the following or any other recent example which you think is appropriate:
  - the cases of civil servants Sarah Tisdall and Clive Ponting
  - the banning of the Duncan Campbell programme on the Zircon satellite spy system
  - the Carrickmore affair
  - the screening of Thames Television's *Death on the Rock* in the light of the previous news coverage of the event.
- Write a brief summary of the example you have chosen and note down your opinion on whether the government was right in its actions.
- Report your findings to the whole class and compare the ways in which legal restrictions operated in the various cases.

You may find the following
sources useful:
- *Teaching the Media* by Len
  Masterman Routledge, 1994
- *Death on the Rock* by Roger
  Bolton W. H. Allen, 1990
- the work of the Glasgow
  Media Group
- various issues of *Index on
  Censorship* (Writers and
  Scholars International).

'Truth is the first casualty of
war.'

Bear in mind that it was the cases of Clive Ponting and Sarah Tisdall that
caused the government to extend the provisions of the Official Secrets Act,
so as to prevent civil servants from making public any abuses or
mismanagement in their departments, even when such disclosures could
fairly be considered to be in the public interest.

Activity

**In times of war, regulations regarding media coverage change.
Read the following Ministry of Defence (MoD) guidelines for the
Gulf War and study the *Daily Mail* report.**

Fourteen categories (covering 32 subjects) of information cannot be published or broadcast without talking to the Ministry of Defence.
These include:

- Numbers of troops, ships, aircraft and other equipment: specific locations of British or Allied military units; future military plans.
- Photographs showing locations of military forces. Photographs of wounded soldiers.
- Information about casualties should not be broadcast until next of kin contacted.
- Specific information on British ships and planes which have been hit.
- Information on how intelligence is collected.

The *Guardian* 29 January 1991

Fig. 8.15

Geoffrey Levy, *Daily Mail*, 25 February 1991

Discuss the MoD guidelines, bearing in mind the following questions:

- Do you feel that the guidelines were necessary? Or that they were too extensive?
- Do you feel that public opinion is controlled by such restrictions?
- What controls would you expect if Britain went to war again?
- Do you think that the *Daily Mail* report was propaganda and if so, was it necessary?
- Bearing in mind the MoD restrictions, could the story have been presented in any other manner?
- Do you feel that you are getting the whole truth from such a story? Should you get the whole truth in times of war?

Make notes from your discussion and keep them in your portfolio. You may find that you will want to use them, together with other notes you have made on national security, for the debate on censorship which forms the final part of the assignment in this section of the study unit.

Your discussion could also have considered the widely held view that it was the media coverage of the Vietnam War in the late 1960s and early 1970s, causing the war 'to be fought in the living rooms of America', which led to public outrage about the USA's involvement in Vietnam and its eventual withdrawal. Do you feel that this has caused governments to be more or less restrictive in their wartime regulations?

Copyright

Activity

Research and answer the questions below. You may find that in some cases there is more than one possible answer. In these instances note down the different arguments.

1. **The following statement has been printed as part of copyright details in all books published since 1993: 'The author asserts the moral right to be identified as the author of this work.' What do you think it means?**

2. **What is an ISBN number?**

3. **If you download information from the Internet, are you entitled to put it into a student magazine without getting anyone's permission?**

4. **What laws are there to prevent unauthorised copying and showing of commercial videos?**

5. **Is it possible to copyright an idea for a book?**

6. **Who do you think should own the copyright on a film – the writer, the producer or the director?**

'When the Marx Brothers were about to make a movie called *A Night in Casablanca*, there were threats of legal action from Warner Brothers, who, five years before, had made the film *Casablanca*. Groucho Marx, in his letter to Warner Brothers, wrote: "... I had no idea that the city of Casablanca belonged exclusively to Warner Brothers... I just don't understand your attitude... You claim you own Casablanca... What about Warner Brothers? Do you own that, too? You probably have the right to use the name Warner, but what about Brothers?"'

Groucho Marx: The Groucho Letters, Sphere Books, 1967

Defamation

Most people's knowledge of the law of libel comes from reports of vast damages awarded to politicians and pop stars who have won cases about untrue comments made about them in the media. The law of libel exists to protect the reputation of individuals from false accusations which have been recorded in permanent form.

Libel law has always favoured the wealthy. For example, it was used frequently and indiscriminately by businessman Robert Maxwell to gag any possible criticism of his actions. *Private Eye*, the satirical magazine which has often dared to publish when others have been frightened off, has been nearly bankrupted on numerous occasions by the loss of a libel case, or simply by the huge legal costs involved in fighting such cases.

Slander covers the same principles for the spoken word.

Activity

Research two examples of libel cases where the media are involved. Write a short summary on who brought the cases and why. Did they win or lose the actions? Do you feel that the media defendants were being taken to court unfairly and that the cases were an unnecessary form of media control? Or do you feel that the media had broken their own guidelines and deserved to be found guilty of libel? Do you feel that the damages were fair considering the nature of the libel? Do you feel that the people libelled would have been able to bring such actions if they had been poor?

Contempt

Under the British laws of contempt the media are forbidden to publish or broadcast anything that might prejudice a fair trial. This includes cases in both the criminal and civil courts. The concept of 'trial by media' is generally disliked and the importance of a fair trial agreed upon. Comparison between the British system and the mass media coverage of the O J Simpson trial in the USA has further endorsed this belief. However, in civil cases the issues are less clear cut. The *Sunday Times* was prevented for many years from publishing the full details of the Thalidomide case (where babies were born deformed after their mothers had taken the Thalidomide drug during pregnancy) because of outstanding writs issued by Distillers, the manufacturers of the drug.

Individual journalists can also be charged with contempt – and imprisoned – for refusing to reveal their sources to the courts under Section 10 of the 1981 Contempt of Court Act.

Regulatory bodies

A leader in *Media Week* in 1994, commenting on the ruling by the *Monopolies and Mergers Commission* that Northcliffe Newspapers could not acquire the *Nottingham Evening Post* unless it fulfilled certain editorial conditions, said that this would be welcomed by many advertisers and readers. The writer noted that an obvious temptation for Northcliffe would be to increase profitability by cutting staff and sharing editorial and research across the group. The Commission's ruling would prevent this and ensure that news coverage was local to Nottingham and not imported from Derby or Leicester.

The *Radio Authority* awarded radio licences to two rock formats, Virgin FM and Crystal FM, in October 1994.

'The Labour Party has confirmed it is planning to scrap the Radio Authority if it wins the next general election... Labour's media spokesman said that the functions of the Authority could be split between Labour's proposed new regulatory body, OFCOM (a revamped OFTEL) and a new-style *Independent Television Commission*... The Radio Authority was set up on 1 January 1991 by the 1990 Broadcasting Act, taking over the radio duties of the former IBA [Independent Broadcasting Authority]. It was born out of a belief that radio and television were such separate entities that they could not be served by a single regulator.'

Report in *Broadcast*, 9 February 1996

Asked what practical assistance the *Department of National Heritage* could give to the UK film industry, Virginia Bottomley, Secretary of State for National Heritage, said that 'Film and television production and facilities are already benefiting from National Lottery funds. Over the next five years the Lottery will provide some £100m. Digital broadcasting will create new opportunities and, through Pay-TV, new sources of funding for British film-makers. To free funds for investment in digital services, the government will not levy [tax] the new digital multiplexes for the first 12-year licence period'

Report in the *Guardian*, February 1996

'The *British Board of Film Classification [BBFC]* was established in 1912 by the film industry as the British Board of Film Censorship when local authorities started to impose their own, widely varying censorship on films under legislation originally designed only to give them control over safety standards in cinemas. By the mid-20s it had become general practice for local authorities to accept the decisions of the Board, which had already become entirely independent of the industry. In 1984 Parliament passed the Video Recordings Act and the following year, the chief officers of the Board were designated as the body to implement the Act by classifying videos for sale, rent or loan. At this point the Board's title was changed to reflect the fact that classification plays a far larger part in the Board's work than censorship.'

A Student's Guide to Film Classification and Censorship in Britain, British Board of Film Classification

'The Video Recordings Act (1984) made video regulation statutory and replaced the voluntary schemes which had been initiated between the BBFC and the video industry from 1982 onwards. (Only in the first two years of video's emergence as a popular medium in the early 80s was it unregulated and it still fell under... the Obscene Publications Act.) ... Finally, in 1994, the VRA was amended by the Criminal Justice Act, which placed new **statutory obligations** on the BBFC in its treatment of videos.'

'Forbidden cinema' in *Sight and Sound*, British Film Institute, 1995

'The year 1994 saw the first test of the clause in the 1990 Broadcasting Act requiring commercial TV to report impartially on matters of major public interest. The Conservative Party chairman Sir Norman Fowler had alleged political bias in a *World in Action* programme called "Tory Tax Bombshell". The Independent Television Commission rejected the complaint, saying that a TV current affairs programme has a right to examine an issue such as the imposition of new taxes.'

Adapted from *The Media Guide 1995*, Fourth Estate, 1994

Assignment: Part 1

This is part one of an assignment which will enable you to provide evidence for your portfolio. Further parts appear later in this section of the study unit.

Make a list of existing regulatory bodies from those mentioned in the above reports. Divide into groups. Each group should research one regulatory body and produce one case history showing how that body operates. The groups should then present their findings (which may be videoed) to the class.

The research findings should also be put into a general class file which can be presented as a booklet on media regulatory bodies in Britain. You should also copy into your portfolio all the work that you yourself have put into the research, together with notes on the process and copies of any letters written during the research.

The ethical framework

Refer to Study Unit 2 for the Press Complaints Commission Code of Practice.

You will have seen that there are laws and regulatory bodies to control many aspects of the media. But there are other areas where media industries police themselves through voluntary codes of practice, designed to prevent unacceptable standards of production or irresponsible behaviour. There are also a number of bodies which are responsible for implementing this kind of self-regulation. These include the Press Complaints Commission, the Broadcasting Commission, the Broadcasting Standards Council, the Advertising Standards Authority and the BBC Programme Complaints Unit.

The BBC and the Independent Television, cable and satellite companies have a range of self-regulatory guidelines and codes of practice. The ITC has in its licence conditions a range of content requirements, which include consumer protection measures covering taste, decency, accuracy, impartiality of news and current affairs.

The BBC publishes *Guidelines for Factual Programming*, which covers some 86 topics. No BBC producer can allow a sensitive news story to be broadcast without reference to these guidelines and, in cases of particular sensitivity, without seeking further guidance from superiors and legal advisers. This form of self-regulation is particularly important to ensure that what the BBC calls 'the four fundamentals' – fairness, independence, reliability and sensitivity – are maintained and to preserve an appropriate balance between news coverage that is in the public interest and respect for the privacy of individuals.

D-notices are issued to prevent publication of something which is considered to be a sensitive defence issue; editors and producers obey them on a voluntary basis. They are not legally binding, although some of the information might at the same time be covered by the Officials Secrets Act or the Prevention of Terrorism Act.

The question of self-censorship was widely debated during the Rosemary West murder trial in 1995, when newspapers and radio and TV news editors differed considerably over the degree of detail which they thought it right to publish/ broadcast.

Voluntary media controls

In addition to the formal guidelines outlined above, there are a number of ways in which the media regulate themselves through voluntary controls. These include self-censorship which is created by D-notices and the threat of possible legal sanctions. The media employ teams of lawyers to prevent their products from infringing any laws, but it is often the case that these lawyers create much more stringent in-house regulations than those of the laws themselves. 'Press lawyers are inevitably more repressive than press laws,' the barrister Geoffrey Robertson has written, 'because they will always err on the safe side where they cannot be proved wrong.'

The media also exercise self-censorship in cases where they feel that viewers, listeners or readers may be unduly shocked or offended. Despite the availability on video of films in their original cinema versions, you will find that an increasing number of films transmitted by the terrestrial TV channels have been 'edited for language/violence/sexual content' – (see the film listings each week in the *Radio Times*).

Economic controls

Economic issues regulate the media just as much as actual legislation, if not more so. You should consider here the work you did in Section 1 on the manner in which the media are controlled. These economic factors are themselves a form of voluntary control for media industries.

Activity

Research the codes of practice set out by the ITC and BBC with regard to factual programming. Then, in class, watch or listen to a news or current affairs programme and make notes on the following questions:

- Do you feel that the programme kept strictly within the BBC or ITC guidelines?
- Do you consider that the programme presented a biased opinion or were all shades of opinion represented equally?
- Do you think that all the participants were treated fairly?

Now watch or listen to a programme such as *Feedback* on BBC Radio 4 or *Right to Reply* on Channel 4, in which the listener/viewer is allowed limited access to make a complaint. Choose one example to summarise and decide whether, from what you have heard or seen, the original programme was unfair. Do you think that the complainant's views were given sufficient weight? Write down your conclusions.

The Advertising Standards Authority

Advertising is a cross-media activity regulated by the Advertising Standards Authority (**ASA**), which exists to promote and enforce high standards in all non-broadcast advertisements. It ensures that the British Code of Advertising Practice and the British Code of Sales Promotion Practice are observed throughout, so that advertisements are 'legal, decent, honest and truthful'. The authority is funded by a tax on advertising space and so it remains quite independent of the government and the industry.

Activity

Contact the ASA to ask for a copy of its Code of Practice. Use this Code of Practice to test a number of advertisements in the press. You may wish to create a reconstruction with one person/group arguing on behalf of the advertiser and the other using the guidelines of the ASA to adjudicate.

Professionalism

The notion of quality control is easy to understand in the production of a chocolate bar or any other commodity which never changes. You have the prototype and you reproduce it, making sure that the original quality of the product is constantly maintained. In the changing world of the media, quality control is a more difficult concept to describe, yet there are ways in which it is exerted throughout the media and many of these methods can usefully be grouped together under the broad heading of professionalism.

Except in the case of very small media companies, such as books created by desktop publishing, there is a division of labour in media industries. In a national newspaper, for example, there are specialist journalists and editors for different departments such as foreign news, the financial section, sports coverage, etc. There are also a variety of different professions concerned with production, marketing and managing the paper. Many of these professions have their own members' organisations.

Activity

- Individually, note down as many members' organisations as you can think of. Form groups to pool your lists and finally exchange lists with other groups until you have one list for the whole class.
- Extend your list by researching members' organisations in media directories and make a final list of all the various associations, guilds, federations and unions.

- Then divide up the list so that everyone in the class writes to a different organisation to ask them for a document which sets out its aims.
- Write a summary of these aims and then, in class, add them all to a large poster. You may find that some are similar and can be grouped together. Reading the poster as a whole, you will be able to see how each individual profession has its own form of quality control which its members' organisation helps to maintain.

You will probably have considered unions such as the National Union of Journalists (NUJ) and Equity (the actors' union) and you may have considered associations like the Association of British Editors and the Association of British Illustrators. You may also have listed the Directors' Guild and the Writers' Guild.

Section 4 looks at how training is used to create a sense of professionalism.

You may also have discovered that these organisations exert quality control not only through peer approval and by maintaining a standard for their members, but also by hosting awards ceremonies.

House style

The BBC maintains that its programming provides 'journalism of impartiality and authority' and 'authoritative and creative coverage of sport'. This ethos of the BBC – how it sees itself and presents itself to the public – can be described as its 'house style'. The collective way it carries out its work creates a form of professional practice which can be used as an argument against the imposition of any changes. Thus, in *Extending Choice*, a document published by the BBC prior to the renewal of its Charter in 1996, the Corporation stated that a single BBC brings, in addition to other benefits:

- 'Concentrated investment in specialist skills and expertise at a level which could not be duplicated by a number of smaller organisations'
- 'The extended use of that specialist expertise across all of the BBC's radio and television channels to deliver the best possible programming to each audience'.

This form of quality control is frequently described in the stated aims of an organisation. In *Extending Choice* the BBC set out its aims to deliver 'value for money', 'accountability' and in regard to programming it said:

> 'The BBC will therefore focus its activities on four key rôles, aiming to set standards in each of these programme areas. It will offer:
> - A wide range of news, current affairs and information programming
> - Fresh and innovative entertainment and a showcase for both traditional and contemporary British culture
> - Specialist and general programmes that help to educate their audience
> - Programmes and services which communicate between the UK and the rest of the world.'

Summarised from *Extending Choice*, BBC, 1992

When Channel 4 was set up in 1982, it aimed to break new ground and seek new professional standards in British television. Its structure was not the hierarchical, monolithic organisation of the BBC, but a body of – often young – heads of programming who were open to ideas from anyone. In December 1995 John Willis, Channel 4's head of programmes, wrote a feature in the *Guardian* on how Channel 4 had remained true to its aims. He commented that the ITC, in its 1993 Annual Review, had praised 'high standards of quality innovation and distinctiveness in many programme areas' and that in 1995 the ITC had said that 'C4 has also remained impressively true to its **remit**'.

In this way stated aims can create a house style that extends beyond the influence of one or more individuals. The stated aims of Channel 4 and the BBC regulate the quality of their programme content and act as a form of quality control.

Fig. 8.16
Two examples of Channel 4's broadcasting: Brookside and The Girlie Show

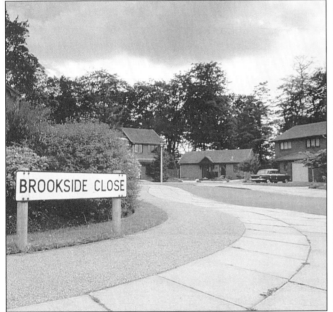

Activity

Useful sources of information would be the ITC, which has taken over the rôle of the IBA, or the British Film Institute Library.

Research the original remit that the (then) IBA imposed on Channel 4.

- Check what its stated aims were and summarise them.
- Read a week's listings for Channel 4 and decide whether you agree that the company is 'true to its remit' or do you agree with its critics that it has neglected its aims in the search for higher ratings?

House style is not always a positive attribute. It can institutionalise a set of values which can curb creativity as well as nurture it. It can embody the views and beliefs of editors and producers to such an extent that other individual voices in the organisation cannot be heard. Since the majority of all such editors and producers are white, middle-class males, this is bound to create a certain imbalance of points of view.

The views embodied in a house style may also be influenced by the media proprietor, especially when the proprietor has control over the appointment of the editor and producer. The BBC, being such a large organisation, may mostly escape such direct influence, though it suffers from its extremely hierarchical structure and an excess of bureaucracy. But the controls exerted by the BBC Governors are noticeable whenever there is a hint that material to be broadcast may prove to be controversial. The Governors are appointed from the ranks of the 'good and the great' and the chairman is a government appointment.

Such controls represented by a house style can lead to bias in reporting. This can be seen in a recent historical perspective when reviewing the reporting of such events as the police actions taken during the 1980s against union pickets during the miners' strike and the print workers' strike at Wapping. Certain groups may also always be represented in a positive or negative light – the Queen Mother, new age travellers, animal rights demonstrators, etc. Until the 1960s all forms of authority, including the police, the judiciary and the royal family, would have been portrayed in a positive light in almost all of the national media. You may find it interesting to research how this has changed and with what results.

Editors often have an agenda of their own which they feel accords with their readers'/viewers'/listeners' attitudes and opinions. They will censor reports of accidents and other incidents which they feel might shock. This can be observed by comparing UK news coverage with that in other European countries which gives fuller and franker details and uses much more explicit pictures. Editors may 'spike' – not publish – stories which do not fit in with the current editorial line that they wish to pursue. For example an editor of a tabloid newspaper wanted a photograph of an 'elitist' audience coming out of a London opera house to illustrate a feature on lottery funding, but when the photographer found that the audience on that occasion was, in fact, largely young and multi-ethnic, the pictures were not used.

Although the media are controlled by laws on racial and sexual equality, the degree to which they exert voluntary controls over such material differs between tabloid and broadsheet newspapers.

Activity

Discuss whether you feel that there is enough control over the use of racist and sexist terms in the media or do you think that anyone should be free to say what they like? Make notes of your discussion.

The term 'house style' can also include the style of reporting itself – broadsheet versus tabloid. The emphasis given to a piece of news reporting can be shifted and a completely different interpretation can be given, even when the content of the story is virtually the same.

In February 1996 the *Independent on Sunday* announced itself as republican and its house style is now strictly anti-monarchist.

What's wrong with being called short or fat, reciting Baa Baa Black Sheep, or being called a chairman?
- Do you mind any of these terms?
- Have Politically Correct lobbyists gone too far or do they have a vital rôle to play?

An ad by a BBC researcher prior to a current affairs programme (the *Guardian*, February 1996)

Watch or listen to two news broadcasts with different house styles on the same day such as *Channel 4 News* and ITN's *News at Ten* or BBC Radio 1 and BBC Radio 4. Make notes about the treatment of one specific piece of news. What do you feel are the main points to emerge from each broadcast? Are the facts the same? Is the emphasis the same?

In your comparisons you will have found that even identical stories can be given a different emphasis through the manner in which they are reported. By only reporting some of the information, a news feature may only tell part of the story.

Assignment: Part 2

Using all the information that you have gathered so far (including your notes for the first part of the assignment), write a report summarising how the media are regulated, including both the legal and ethical frameworks. Your report should also deal with the influence that the ethos of professionalism can exert over media products.

Freedom of information, public interest and censorship

> 'I regard [censorship] as meaning the denial, or interdiction of information by decree (usually Order in Council, occasionally by Statute) when applied by government... In my view this is justifiable in two categories only and they should be drawn as narrowly as possible... National Security [see above] and "commercial confidentiality".'
>
> Alan Clark in *Index on Censorship*, 2/1995

> 'The classic liberal position – that both individual and collective freedoms are best secured by rights enshrined in laws, all of which have necessary limitations and restraints to ensure a balance between protective freedom and abusive licence – is being dismantled... We must create a new framework of rights, adding some, such as the freedom of information.'
>
> Mark Fisher in *Index on Censorship*, 2/1995

Fig. 8.17
'Dieu et mon right-to-know' by Posy Simmons from *Index on Censorship* 2/1995

411

Assignment: Part 3

Hold a class debate in the style of BBC TV's *Question Time*, with a chairperson, a panel of guest speakers and contributions from the 'studio audience' (the members of the class). The debate will focus on questions concerning freedom of information, public interest and censorship.

- Invite guests to be the panel of experts and ensure that they represent a wide range of views. For example, they could include a local businessperson or politician with very traditional views about control of the press in the interests of national security and the preservation of social values, an artist whose work has been censored, a member of the Campaign for Press and Broadcasting Freedom, a representative from the National Viewers and Listeners Association, a representative from the British Board of Film Classification. If you cannot get actual guests, you should choose members of the class to play their rôles.

- As a class decide on the range of the debate. Individually, write down questions for the speakers. Pool your questions and select those which you think will provoke the most useful discussion. What are the topics you want to debate? What would be good questions to lead into these topics and to ensure that they are covered in depth? (As well as controlling the debate, the chairperson should ensure that the debate covers the appropriate topics in sufficient depth.)

- The questions could refer to recent examples of censorship or freedom of information issues. Make sure that the debate covers the whole issue and does not just generate an agree/disagree reply. For example, the Tory MP Peter Luff banned his 11-year-old daughter from reading magazines such as *19*, *More!*, *Sugar* and *Mizz* because of their features on sexual matters. A question relating to this story would cover not only whether he was right, but whether there should be legislation or voluntary controls to protect younger children from reading teenage magazines.

- Every member of the class should prepare a question that the chairperson can use.

- Everyone in the class should make at least one contribution to the debate. You should indicate in advance the area you wish to comment on and research that area prior to the debate.

- Video or audio-record the debate.

- Watch the video and discuss it. Did it cover the points you had hoped it would? Make notes on the debate to summarise the different attitudes expressed on the issues and put these notes into your portfolio.

- Consider whether your own attitudes to issues of censorship were influenced by the debate. Make notes and add them to your portfolio.

3 Development of the media industries

This section will help you to understand changes taking place in the media industries and how recent technological advances together with economic factors are influencing this process of change. You will also need to consider how these changes are having their effect in terms of how we consume the media and how changes in our lifestyles also influence media production.

Activity

Fig. 8.18

In a small group, use the headings and questions below to focus more closely on the recent and emerging technologies in the media industries and how they are influencing your patterns of media consumption. Take notes of your discussion.

- When your parents were 17 (date)
- Today (date)
- When your children will be 17 (date)

Which of the following technologies are/were/will be in common use?

Typewriters; word processors; computerised typesetting; desktop publishing; records; audio-tapes; CDs; CD-ROM; on-line services; modems; the Internet; 16 mm film; video (VHS, Pneumatic, Betamax); **linear audio and video editing**; digital audio and video recording; digital audio tape; satellite receivers for audio and television; **satellite uplink** transmitters for mobile telephone; video and other digital communications; computer animation; high-definition television; NICAM and all-around stereo TV sound; **interactive television**.

Which of the following comments best describes the patterns of media consumption for each age group?

a 'We simply have the choice of a few television stations and a few local and national radio stations. There are some good pirate radio stations too.'

b 'I think we have too much choice nowadays. I'm going to get one of those new "ME-TV" boxes to monitor and then programme my viewing. It will get to know my preferences and then offer me the programmes that I like to watch.'

c 'I'm looking forward to the time when one box will do it all. At the moment I've got a sound system, a video, a television, a personal computer, a modem, a telephone, and then there's the kids' stuff and all of their computer games and wires going all over the house. We seem to go to different parts of the house at different times for different media experiences.'

Think about the predictions each generation makes about the future. What do you think each generation could expect from the next ten years in terms of technological advance and how the media is consumed?

Emerging technologies

You will have understood how the last 20 years have witnessed technological advance which is quite unprecedented. Recent changes in the way that information can be recorded digitally and then transmitted via satellite, cable or telephone wire have meant that so much information has never been so readily available at such low cost. We are living through a period of time that historians may come to refer to as the 'information revolution' . The pioneering work of the satellite links transmitting the pictures of man's first steps on the moon were, at the time, incredibly expensive. Now, satellites, fax communications and wide area computer networks (the Internet) can be used to bounce back images at a fraction of the cost.

The pace of technological advance is so rapid and the ease with which society and individuals embrace and accept technological change is such that these advances are hardly noticed. The article from *The Observer* on the next page draws some attention to technological advance as it impacts upon the consumer end of the telecommunications industry.

In 1987, the IBA magazine *Airwaves* records for winter 1987/8 noted that only 78 per cent of households had a video-cassette recorder, 2 per cent of households had cable TV and only 0.5 per cent of households had satellite television.

Activity

Discuss the implications of the article from *The Observer* and list the way that new technology is influencing our consumer habits in the household. You should consider:

- the multiple uses of television and media convergence
- how the viewer has increasing control and choice for flexible viewing beyond the controls of the programme schedulers
- the potential for interactive, computer-based shopping
- the effect upon the advertising industry
- the effect upon traditional print-based media
- the influence of CD-ROM and on-line communications for information retrieval
- the potential influence on our traditional 'single voices' of authority such as the BBC.

How wired will we be in the year 2000?

J Walter Thompson advertising agency's estimates for growth in digital television between now and the end of the decade point to 40 per cent of homes having some kind of access to more than the bog standard five TV channels as well as 40 per cent having personal computers and a further 40 per cent having some sort of game. Of course it could always be that these are the same 40 per cent of homes that are rich techies. The rest of us will have to get by with quill and parchment.

The other question about this tantalising glimpse into the future is just who is going to pay for all this? If advertisers are reluctant to back new media, it will be to the detriment of the punter.

% households with:

	1995	2000
Television	99	99
Video cassette recorder	78	85
Personal computer (PC)	18	40
PC/modem/on-line subscribers	2	26
Games/CD-console/PC CD-ROM+	24	40
Digital terrestrial TV (set top box)	0	19
Any satellite/cable (incl. set top box)	22	36
Video on demand ADSL telephone link	0	21
Any digital or analogue multimedia	22	40

Source: J Walter Thompson/Graphic News

Fig. 8.19

Emily Bell, *The Observer*, 28 January 1996

Factors affecting the development of the industry

Above all, the 1990s is the decade of unprecedented change for the media industries. In addition to the broad technological and consumer trends outlined above, there are other important trends that have contributed to the development of the industries.

Deregulation

For a full discussion of the 1990 Broadcasting Act and deregulation see Section 2.

Deregulation forced the commercialisation of the media industries which suddenly became more aware of business practices and market principles. Bidding too little might mean losing the contract, while bidding too much might mean having to withdraw funds from the expensive business of television and radio production and so lowering the quality of broadcasting. Another effect of the 1990 Broadcasting Act was to ensure that 25 per cent of independent television programme production was to be carried out by independent producers. This meant that the large television companies began a process of slimming down and cutting costs by reducing numbers of staff on full-time permanent contracts while becoming increasingly cautious about expenditure on high-cost news, sports, film and serial productions.

Producer choice

Similar pressures have led to dramatic rethinking of the principles of production that operate within Britain's public-sector broadcasting company, the BBC. Reorganisation of the BBC into a number of costed resource bases has meant that BBC producers can now make use of independent services and facilities when they are more cost-effective than those in-house. It has also encouraged producers to think more in terms of bi-media productions so that the same material can be used by both radio and television. This is particularly true of news broadcasting.

Consumer choice and subscription

As post-industrial societies develop in the information age, the individual spends less and less time engaged in full-time employment. People stay in education longer, retire earlier and generally are living longer than ever before. These broad changes are affecting all the media industries. Twenty years ago, for example, people regularly bought evening papers on their way home from work. As lifestyles change, with more people commuting to work by car or working from home, the place of the evening paper is disappearing.

Today people are able to choose media and consumer experiences to suit their personal lifestyle using the technology that is available. Dialling into electronic newsgroups for information and computer or television shopping are examples.

Recent trends highlight the increasing commercialisation of the media. Subscription to various satellite channels is now commonplace and the consumer is used to paying for the subscription by credit card. The next stage will be 'pay-as-you-view' television (Pay-TV) where viewers give the satellite company their credit card numbers so that their accounts can be debited automatically for the programmes that they watch. This took place for the first time in Britain in 1996 when BSkyB offered pay-as-you-view access to the Bruno-Tyson boxing match. What is true for satellite will also be true for cable-based media provision and is true for many on-line services that can be accessed via the Internet. All of this raises important political questions and you should be able to consider how far access to information is a right, and how far it is a commodity to be purchased.

Sponsorship

The potential of the media for promotion and marketing activities of other non-media organisations has always been understood, with commercial producers drawing significant portions of their income from advertising. Recent trends have witnessed more indirect forms of promotion taking place through sponsorship deals such as the ITV network weather forecasting being partially funded by the nuclear power company Powergen. In Britain, television sponsorship is in its infancy with tight ITC regulation controlling the potential for abuse through devices such as product placement.

Global media economies: media convergence and media imperialism

Finally, you need to recognise the trend towards increasing multinational ownership of the media and the potential for reselling a given product to new audiences in other markets. While the global concerns of Rupert Murdoch's News Corporation is often cited as a case study, similar trends towards corporate ownership are taking place across the media industries. This book, for example, is published by Addison Wesley Longman, a company owned by the Pearson Group which has worldwide involvements across the range of media industries.

Activity

Scan through the listings of Pearson's principal, subsidiary and associated undertakings (Figure 8.5) and consider the transnational and multimedia nature of this global media corporation. Make your own lists outlining what you consider to be the economic, political and social advantages and disadvantages of this phenomenon. You may wish to consider these advantages/disadvantages from the point of view of society, the consumer, the shareholder, the employee and other media producers.

The impact of technological change

As more and more media ownership is in the hands of large organisations which often subcontract to smaller production companies, there is increasing pressure for business efficiency and the maximisation of profits. This has led to media convergence where companies understand the multimedia potentials of their products and can repackage their products in different forms. Large groups such as Pearson and News Corporation understand the overlapping nature of global markets for information, education and entertainment and the interrelated nature of media consumption. In the introduction to Pearson's annual report for 1994, the chairman writes: 'Our newspapers can entertain as they inform, our classical fiction can educate as it entertains. Just as important, more and more "new media" products and services, such as computer games for young children that teach as they entertain, carry much of their appeal where the main markets overlap.'

As you have already discovered, there is a growing trend for cross-national ownership of the media. Most of Britain's magazines are owned by a few large companies. Reed Elsevier plc (with its subsidiary IPC magazines), an Anglo-Dutch operation, and EMAP are among the largest with over 160 mainstream titles between them. In June 1994 EMAP bought into a group of French magazine companies making it France's third largest publisher. This trend has implications for the advertising industry and the companies that commission it as advertising campaigns are structured and costed to be delivered across a wider range of media outlets.

There are also political considerations to be considered and you will need to understand the ways in which international media flows tend to be originated from within the relatively restricted centres of the advanced commercial states in Europe and North America, via international corporations, to world markets. This has clear implications for the spread of ideological values of consumer capitalism and democracy across the world.

Although the debate extends beyond the bounds of this course, you may wish to consider how far western-based media exert their ideological influence and, indeed, how far western governments support the expansion into world markets. The USA, for example, has diplomatic and trade links with Turkey which obligates Turkey to purchase and transmit a set quota of programmes made by American television networks. In contrast, more radical Islamic states, such as Iran, have been careful to limit their purchases of western-based television and to censor its content.

Fig. 8.20
McDonalds in Moscow

Activity

In June 1994, the *Guardian* devoted its media supplement to a review of the decade. It published a series of interviews where specialists from within the British media industries reflected upon the developments that they could foresee within the next decade. Read what the specialists had to say and then write down your own predictions to share with the rest of the class.

Fig. 8.21

Looking ahead to 2004

SIR DAVID ENGLISH
Chairman, Associated Newspapers

NATIONAL newspapers will be only slightly less powerful but probably fewer in number by at least two. The Mail group will dominate the middle market, the Express will have new owners but still be failing, the Guardian will protect its niche and the Times will have increased its price and lost some sales.

The electronic superhighway will not be completed and many of the multi-media electronic forecasts will prove false. Cable will have established its superiority over satellite. Internet will be commonplace and thus less fashionable. The biggest developments will be in wireless.

ANDREW NEIL
Executive editor, on Assignment (Fox TV); editor, Sunday Times

MULTI-SECTION newspapers are here to stay but there will be fewer papers. Tabloids will struggle because of competition from tabloid TV, satellite, cable; there will still be a broadsheet market because of the quality of writing and design.

There will be electronic delivery of information. People will be able to get everything on a specialist subject downloaded into their fax machine overnight but sensible people will still take a newspaper.

In TV there will still be room for the big networks. It is wrong to think about 500 channels in Britain – in terms of information retrieval, there will be an infinite number. You will be able to use your TV screen to call up the latest book or magazine. It will empower people rather than editors or producers.

MICHAEL JACKSON
Controller, BBC2

CLEARLY there will be a lot of channels but in a curious way that might help the established networks. People will view the networks, plus two or three extras, perhaps Discovery, MTV or sports. With a great profusion of choice, people tend to latch on to what they know. I don't think the explosion of 500 channels and video on demand will come as quickly as some suggest, although if I had shares in video rental shops I might sell them.

BBC2 absolutely will have a role in providing a mix of programmes opposite the thematic channels. The key parts of the network's architecture like series drama and nightly news will still be there.

RICHARD BRANSON
Chairman, Virgin group

WE will have digital audio broadcasting (DAB), so people who'd like to listen to Virgin 1215 on quality better than AM will finally be able to do so. Even more will listen on satellite than at the moment. Our listening figures will be similar to R1's. Virgin will take live broadcasts into planes. Businessmen will be able to keep in touch with the stock market and there will be phones and faxes on every plane.

MICHAEL GRADE
Chief Executive, C4

SEVERAL certainties: there will be more government inquiries, green and white papers and legislation. The BBC will be accused of political bias by whoever is in power. Sky will have Wimbledon, the Cup Final, the World Cup, and the Olympics exclusive. Lord Rupert Murdoch will be a British

subject. The *Sunday Times,* on the anniversary of Death On The Rock, will run a feature on how TV got it wrong. I will still be at C4 waiting for a reply from the BBC on our 1994 offer of cooperation. The BBC will be in the midst of another strategy review. (Dear Ed, as promised, I haven't worked in the C4 funding formula!)

LIZ FORGAN
Managing director, BBC network radio

TV, except the licence-funded BBC, will be struggling to raise budgets for serious original production. Radio will be having a new Golden Age as low costs meet new technology to make it the place for creative talent.

DAB will reach most of Britain, bringing CD quality and an end to quarrelling over scarce bits of spectrum. Test Match Special shall lie down with the Afternoon Play, each on its own frequency.

DAVID GLENCROSS
Chief executive, Independent TV Commission

TEN years ago we were threatened or promised wall-to-wall Dallas. It hasn't happened yet and I don't think it will be by 2004. The ITC will then be giving glowing end-of-term reports to GMTV and Carlton and conceivably may be digesting its new responsibilities for the BBC given by Parliament in 2002.

TIM DELANEY
Creative director, Leagas Delaney

TECHNOLOGY will change the way we talk to each other – will I need a whole group of people in Kuala Lumpur when I can communicate through fibre optics from one office?

There will be greater pressure on the BBC because of the continuing downward audience share to around 30 per cent. The Labour government will decide the BBC's cultural worth and give it a mandate for 25 years.

JOYCE TAYLOR
Chief executive officer, United Artists Programming

MULTI-MEDIA will not develop as fast as all the publicity suggests. BT and others have hyped video-on-demand and other advances, but what products will the technology carry?

For multi-channels the future is bright: their attraction will be enhanced as they grow and increase. They will need programming, some from secondary markets but some too, happily, from new production. New alliances and funding arrangements will emerge to secure it. Subscription will become the key ingredient.

JOHN PERRISS
Chairman, Zenith Media Worldwide

TEN years is when the 'digital superhighway' concept will begin to come alive. TV will still take about a third of total adspend but that will have become more fragmented as over 50 per cent of homes will be connected to cable or satellite. Papers will still be a strong force and radio will have grown more. Magazines in the broader market segments will continue to decline.

Media planning and buying will have almost universally unbundled from the provision of creative services, which will be a specialist sector. Media agencies will be offering strategic media consultancy remunerated by fees and implementation services paid by commission.

Interviews by Andrew Culf, the *Guardian,* 20 June 1994

Assignment

Prepare three case studies describing recent and emerging technological trends in the media industries and how they are affecting the industry and its consumers. The case studies should be presented in the form of poster displays with short oral presentations to the rest of the class.

1 Decide on three companies across the range of industries that you would like to contact. Give your reasons.

2 Prepare a set of questions to cover these areas:
   a the particular *technological changes* and how they have affected the processes of production
   b the *background to the technological changes* and how they were introduced
   c the *financial, organisational and employment implications* of the changes
   d the *sociocultural impact* of the changes on the consumer
   e the *political, economic and social impact* of the changes.

3 Arrange to interview someone in each of the three companies and, if possible, carry out your investigation within the context of a work-shadowing experience.

4 Think about how you can check the validity of the information you have obtained. Read around the subject.

5 Try to collect as much hard data in the form of company reports and other documentation as possible.

6 Prepare your information in a form that can be easily received by the rest of the class.

7 Evaluate each presentation and then carry out a whole-class discussion to summarise the general trends across the range of media industries.

4

Employment and training in UK media

The purpose of this section is to help you understand more about work opportunities within the media industries. You will consider the main functions carried out in the industries and how employment trends are changing. You will also investigate methods of training in the industries, the nature and rôle of employer and employee organisations and something of the legislation that covers issues of employment, health and safety, and equal opportunities.

Fig. 8.22
A media professional.
Michael Urban of
Reuters transmitting his
digital pictures from
behind the goal,
Euro 96

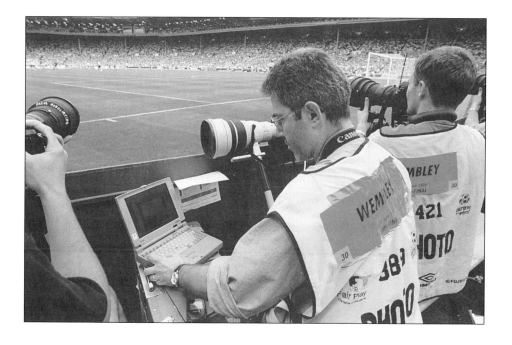

Jobs and functions in the media industries

Activity

On the next page there is a list of key words taken from a range of advertisements for positions in the media industries. Use these to make your own word groupings. In a small group, discuss the jobs involved. For example:

Designer/Mac literate/QuarkXpress/Freehand/Illustrator: Someone who carries out design work using desktop publishing skills. The person is probably trained, with an art school background.

Book fairs	Library
Books	Mac literate
Broadcast	Magazine
Cataloguer	Market researcher
Circulation/advertising figures	Methodically accurate
Designer	Operate and maintain
Editor	Pre-press printing and
Engineer	finishing processes
Equipment and systems	Press officer
Exhibitions	Production controller
Fast and accurate reports	Publisher
Features editor	QuarkXpress
Freehand	Reporter
Freelance writer	Reports
Good proofreading skills	Research assistant
HTML	Statistics
Illustrator	Subeditors
Internal and external relations	Web servers
Journalist	WorldWide Web editor

In your discussions you may have concluded that:

- there is an overlap between different jobs. The same title may be applied to different media – editors, for example, are found in publishing and broadcasting.
- there may be other jobs that have not been listed (make your own lists now).
- some of the jobs may be full-time and others may be freelance.
- some of the jobs are very specialised professions and others are more managerial and administrative.
- there are particular skills – interpersonal, managerial, technical, academic – associated with each job.

Fig. 8.23

Try to get more information about particular jobs by responding to advertisements in the trade press and the media supplement of the *Guardian*.

You may have thought about the place of each job in relation to the flow of media production.

Each of these 'main functions' of the media absorbs hundreds of thousands of people with a wide range of professional skills: technical, creative, managerial, communicative, analytical, information gathering and processing. Each industry – publishing, radio, audio-visual and the new media – have their own particular job titles, training schemes and expectations of your qualifications, background and experience when you are applying for a job. Sometimes the skills of an individual are transferable – for example a BBC radio producer is equipped to apply for a post in television production – and sometimes they are not – for example, a graphic designer for a magazine may have difficulty qualifying for a job as a set designer in a film company.

Origination

Origination includes all of the activity pre-production. This is the process of planning and researching, budgeting, allocating rôles of responsibility and commissioning freelance staff, preparing the production schedule, preparing treatments, storyboarding (in the audio-visual industries) and scripting. At this stage the marketing research and audience research work are also carried out.

Audience research is discussed fully in Study Unit 6.

Production

Production patterns vary according to the particular industry, but this is a crucial creative stage where the media artefact is produced. Production here also includes the post-production phases of cutting and editing, and adding the titles and credits in audio-visual and visual productions.

Distribution

Distribution involves the processes of ensuring that the media product reaches its audience and, again, the patterns vary according to the industry. Each industry has its own complex web of organisation, agencies and forums to present the produced media to its audiences. Here too, the function of marketing overlaps and interfaces with that of distribution. Any discussion of distribution will consider:

- national distributors – broadcasting networks, newspaper conglomerates, theatres, concert halls and cinema chains, magazine, book and software wholesalers
- local distributors – local newspapers, theatres, cinemas, radio and television stations, and the retailers of magazines, books and computer software, and points of access to the Internet.

Transmission

Transmission is the area where the technical and commercial specialists work to ensure that the media product reaches its audience. It includes the technical and engineering staff involved in the broadcast of terrestrial, satellite and cable television and radio; computer network (local area network – LAN – and wide area network – WAN) managers and so on.

Marketing

Marketing is essential to the successful operation of any media business. It is closely linked with the functions of origination, distribution and transmission to ensure that audiences consume the product in order to finance more productions.

For a full discussion of marketing see Study Unit 7.

Activity

Look at the list of jobs found in the origination and production phases of the audio-visual and audio media industries in the UK. Add to the list by including the names of jobs found in the transmission, distribution and marketing phases. When you have finished, decide which of the jobs are likely to be full time or part-time and which are likely to be carried out by permanent staff and which by freelances.

Fig. 8.24

Production/Studio Production

Producer	Production Coordinator
Director	Assistant Director
Producer/Director	Production Assistant: Studio
Production Supervisor/Manager	Production Assistant: Film/Tape
Production Secretary	Floor Manager
Associate Producer	Vision Mixer
Script Supervisor	Continuity

Post Production

Tape Editor/Assistant Editor	TeleCine Operator
Film Editor/Assistant Editor	Sound Operator: Film/Tape
Picture Editor	Graphics
VT Operator	Neg Cutter
Caption Generator Operator	Dubbing Mixer: Film/Tape
Electronic Graphics, i.e. Harry Operators	

Sound

Sound Mixer/Recordist	
Boom Operator	Sound Assistant
Sound Maintenance	Sound (all grades) Tape/Film
	Sound Director

Camera/Lighting

Director of Photography	
Lighting Director	Gaffer/Lighting Chargehand
Lighting Camera Operator	Electrician
Camera Operator: Film/Tape	Lighting Console Operator
Focus Puller	Grip
Clapper Loader	Camera Operator: Film/Tape
	Camera Assistant: Film/Tape

Research/Writer/Script Editors
Art Department

Design Assistant	
Production Designer	Art Director
Props/Prop Buyer	Graphic Designer
Animator	Costume Designer
Set Designer	Cell Painter

Set of Scenic Crafts

Scenic Artists	
Carpenters	Plasterers
Painters	Prop makers
Stagehands	Drapes
	Craft Labourer

Make-up/Hair/Costume/Wardrobe

Make-up Supervisor	
Make-up Artist	
Make-up Assistant	Costume Supervisor
Wig maker	Costume Assistants
	Dressmaker

Skillset questionnaire, in *Employment Patterns and Training Needs 1993/4,*

Skillset

Look at the cycle that illustrates the rôle of music videos in generating the demand to justify investment in the production of new records, CDs and tapes. Identify the distribution, transmission, and marketing functions within the cycle and explain the nature of the work that is being carried out. Estimate the numbers of people involved, and the nature of their work.

Fig. 8.25

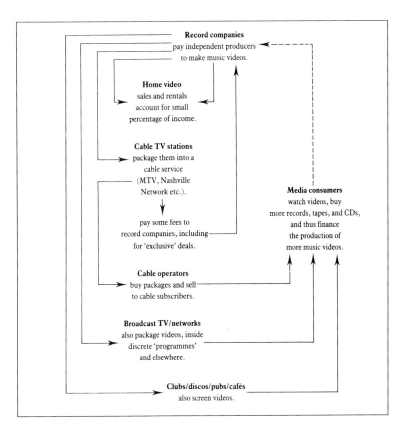

Freelance work

Deregulation of the media during the 1990s together with the prevailing employment trends – resulting from economic restructuring and the impact of new technology – has meant that media production is increasingly dependent upon freelances.

Freelances take on short-term work which is often salaried by single-payment contracts rather than fixed monthly incomes. Skillset is the industry training organisation for broadcasting, film and video. In 1994 it published a report on the employment patterns and training needs for the broadcasting industry which recorded the following information:

> 'The industry relies on a wide range of highly skilled, specialised occupations working in production, technical and post-production areas. Many of these skills are unique to the television, film and video industry: no other industry requires the same skills.

A significant proportion of this specialised workforce works on a freelance basis. Of an estimated 28,000 people working in production, technical and post-production areas:

- 13,000 are employed as permanent staff or on contracts of one year or more by companies across the industry.
- 15,000 work on a freelance or short contract (less than one year) basis.
- The industry's reliance on freelance labour has increased in the past five years. In 1989, the IMS Skill Search study estimated that freelances comprised 39 per cent of the specialised labour force. The 1993/94 Skillset survey suggests an increase to 54 per cent.

The freelance sector is diverse, not a homogenous, uniform pool. People with different skills experience the industry in different ways in terms of where they work in the industry, their propensity to be fully employed, their income.

Two-fifths of freelances had worked in more than one sector of the industry during the previous year. Multi-sector working was a characteristic of those working in camera/lights and sound.

Two-thirds of freelances are based in London or South-east England for work and living purposes, representing a slight increase in the proportion working outside those areas since 1989.'

Fig. 8.26
Distribution of the workforce, 1989 and 1994

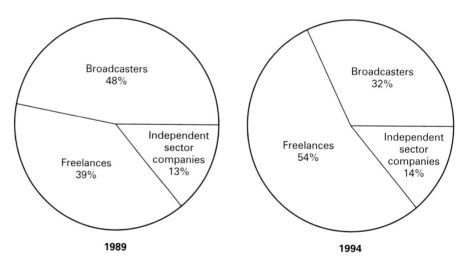

1989

1994

Skillset Report, 1994

Sections 1 and 2 describe more fully the impact of new technology as it has influenced patterns of production and distribution in all sectors.

Similar trends are apparent in the print-based media industries and the new media where new technology has changed the patterns of employment and the organisation of the media industries.

As it has become easier and easier to output media products to a wide range of audiences, there has been an increasing awareness of the segmented nature of media markets which has led to a more sensitive understanding of the need for training and education.

Activity

Discuss the following statements and decide which best reflects the nature of your GNVQ course and your understanding of career opportunities within the media.

'The whole of the industry is crying out for competent skilled people who have a practical understanding of the media industry that they want to work in. This means that they should be up to date with the technology and production processes and can organise their time.'

'What the industry needs is good communicators who are flexible and can turn their hand to changing circumstances, use their initiative and work in a team.'

'Narrow vocationalism is a dead-end road. As soon as someone thinks that they are trained, their career is over. Training must be a continuous process and what the industry needs is people who are bright and creative, not people who are equipped with a limited set of technical competences.'

'Like everything else, it isn't just what you know but that magic combination of who you know and being there at the right time. It is very difficult to describe and prescribe clear career paths within the media but I do think that the new entrant needs to show a broad range of work experience.'

'Most graduates are recruited for their general abilities rather than their subject specialisms. A profound theoretical understanding of ideology and the processes of representation is very interesting but the question is, can the candidate do the job? We expect to have to train most new entrants, often at high cost to the company, and then after two or three years they will be applying for new jobs again.'

'If you want to be a journalist, I'm not sure how far I would recommend a degree in Media Studies ... degrees in English, Politics, History and Economics are probably more important if coupled to an enquiring mind and good interpersonal skills as an interviewer.'

Education and training

The 1990s have witnessed the dramatic growth of media studies as a subject in mainstream education. It is acknowledged within the National Curriculum Guidelines for English which begins in primary school, extends into postgraduate work and is an ongoing part of a media professional's working experience. Schools and colleges are running more and more courses in A level Media Studies, Film Studies, Photography and, more importantly, GNVQs in Media and Communication. Higher Education degrees and HND programmes are mushrooming. Close scrutiny of higher education reveals that many linked courses and course options are often bundled under the heading of 'Media Studies'.

The 1990s have also seen increasing cooperation between the media industries and education. This has continued with the understanding that education must provide the industry with individuals who are flexible, with transferable skills, high levels of technological competence and communication skills. The National Council for Vocational Qualifications (NCVQ) works in the development of media-related training programmes, which is coordinated by Skillset. This is seen as being the industry-led body whose rôle includes describing detailed statements of areas of competence that need to be achieved by NVQ trainees. In the area of audio and audio-visual production, competence areas of interest are grouped at different levels under the headings of: sound, research, journalism and factual writing, production, coordination and production management. Unlike more traditional educational programmes, NVQs are assessed in the workplace and can continue during full- or part-time employment. To gain an NVQ in sound, for example, trainees have to demonstrate competence in a number of clearly defined areas: being able to identify and use different types of microphone, adjust sound levels, record, edit, playback, work effectively with colleagues, evaluate their own performance and so on.

Outside the area of media production, other programmes, including NVQs, are also relevant to work in the media industries. The individual seeking a career in the media should be clear about their chosen career direction, depending upon their interests, and carry out further research into training opportunities in the fields of Art and Design, Stagecraft, Business Studies, Information Technology, Printing and Publishing (especially desktop publishing), Telecommunications, Management Studies.

Although there are no hard and fast rules to govern the choice of course and qualification for career progression within the media, the following observations may be made:

Skillset: Tel. 0171-306 8585

- Advice on opportunities for **broadcast training** can be obtained from Skillset, which was established in 1992 as the government-recognised industry training organisation with the specific aim 'to promote and develop training for our changing industry in order that we can maintain and enhance our reputation for quality skills'. Skillset is funded and supported by the Advertising, Film and Videotape Producers Association (AFVPA), the BBC, Channel 4, the Federation of Entertainment Unions (FEU including BECTU), the Independent Television Association (ITVA), the Independent Visual Communications Association (IVCA) and the Producers Alliance for Cinema and Television (PACT). Further specialised training schemes exist within established organisations such as the British Film Institute (BFI) and smaller independent training organisations. The most useful starting point for further enquiry is the *Guardian Media Guide*.

- **Newspaper journalist training** is closely linked to NVQ training, and the long-established National Council for the Training of Journalists (NCTJ) can give more information about courses and career opportunities. Further advice may be obtained from the Newspaper Society and the National Union of Journalists (NUJ). Most larger local newspapers also carry out their own training programmes which are respected by the profession.

- **Magazine journalist training** is covered by the Periodicals Training Council (PTC). The PTC has been active in the promotion of NVQs and can advise on training opportunities.

- **Training for working in the new media** is less clear cut. One suggestion might be to request information from journalists working in the computer-related press. Future Publishing might be a useful starting point.

BFI: Tel. 0171-255 1444

NCTJ: Tel. 01279 430009

Newspaper Society: Tel. 0171-636 7014

NUJ: Tel. 0171-278 7916

PTC: Tel. 0171-404 4168

Future Publishing: Tel. (01225) 442244

Industry organisations

Any media professional who is serious about getting the most from his/her job joins a union or professional association. There are many employee organisations that are funded by membership subscriptions in order to inform and advise across a range of services. At the forefront of their work, these employee organisations are concerned with the following services:

- defending members' interests by negotiating over pay, pensions, working hours, grading and holidays
- campaigning in public, to Parliament and the European Parliament and Commission so that media professionals are adequately represented
- giving free preliminary legal advice and fighting for employee rights in the case of disputes over many issues including redundancy and unfair dismissal
- pursuing compensation claims on behalf of employees who have sustained injuries at work
- offering preferential loan schemes and insurance, discounts on some goods and services and financial advice
- advice on taxation and pensions

429

- providing information packs on training opportunities and a regular journal for members
- campaigning for equal opportunities, equal pay and pensions, racial and sexual equality, enhanced maternity and paternity rights, shorter working hours and access to work for the disabled
- providing information about employment opportunities.

The largest media trade union is the Broadcasting, Entertainment, Cinematograph and Theatre Union (BECTU) and there are many others catering for different professional groups within the media industries. Particularly important are: the NUJ, the Writer's Guild, Equity (the actors' union), the Musicians' Union, the AEEU (the electrical, electronic, telecommunications and plumbing union) the Telecommunications union and the Advertising, Film and Videotape Producers' Association.

In addition to employee organisations, there are a few employer organisations and many professional bodies. With the growth of freelancing there are several new employer organisations such as the Producers Alliance for Cinema and TV (PACT) which can advise employers as they enter into commercial contracts and take on staff. Professional and trade bodies include organisations such as Skillset, the Publisher's Association and the Newspaper Society.

Activity

Imagine you hold the positions listed below. What professional organisations, trade unions and other associations would you want to join? What would you expect from them? Why would you need them? Consider the different needs for information, advice, broader understanding of national trends, access to training opportunities, legal aid, help in case of accident, injury, dismissal and redundancy, financial assistance, information about insurance, and health and safety, etc.

- A young journalist working full-time as a trainee on a local newspaper.
- A video film director who has just set up a new company with two other directors, all of whom have extensive experience making television advertisements.
- A sound engineer in a local independent radio station.
- An actor with some experience of working in television situation comedies.
- A freelance animator.
- A producer on a permanent management contract with the BBC.
- The director/owner of a medium-sized advertising agency.

Legislation

Anyone who is working or who employs others to work for them is subject to the labour laws of the UK together with laws governing libel and slander, equal opportunities and health and safety. As a member of the European Union, Britain is obliged to observe the treaties and directives issued by the European Commission and the judgements of the European Court of Justice. In effect, this means that all member states are working towards the same set of principles which includes a commitment to equal pay for equal work wherever an individual is working within the Union, and a citizen of a member state is entitled to seek work anywhere in the union. This umbrella system has meant that in some areas, such as rights to pensions, the illegality of discrimination on grounds of sex and the outlawing of setting limits to compensation agreements, there is uniformity across the Union.

As regards pay and conditions, however, there is no actual uniformity, but rather the agreement that member states should work towards the principal of uniformity. This issue was highlighted in the much-publicised decision of the British government in 1992 to opt out of the Social Chapter of the Maastricht agreement. The Social Chapter had included proposals to introduce further directives in the area of employment law such as increasing employee involvement in company decisions, allowing for paternity leave and paid time away from work for family reasons, harmonisation of employee rights in the case of dismissal, the length of the working week and the working day.

Assignment

Prepare a multimedia report to serve as a guide to students wishing to find jobs in the media industries.

• As a class, identify particular companies from the range of media industries – publishing, radio, television, film and the new media – then decide which you would like to use for your case study about one media industry.

• Plan your information gathering and interviewing to find out about:
  – the particular functions of a selected company within that industry and how it works with other related companies (for example a magazine would link up with a particular distributor)
  – the employee structure of the company, with job descriptions
  – an overview of changes forced by new technology and a description of employment trends
  – the pattern of education and training both for entry and within the company
  – the use of employee and employer organisations
  – issues regarding legislation.

431

- Use the particular example of your case study and relate it to the industry at large.
- Decide on the best way to present your findings to the rest of the class using video data, printed matter and audio recordings where possible.

Summary

In this unit you investigated the scope and nature of the media industries.

In Section 1 you identified the principal UK media producers and explored the complex patterns of interrelated ownership across the media. You also examined the nature of funding sources and patterns of expenditure and assessed the influence of ownership and economic factors on products and consumers.

Section 2 focused on the legal and ethical frameworks within which the media operate. You identified the regulatory bodies relevant to media in the UK and explained their rôles and functions. You looked at ways in which the media are often self-regulatory, paying particular attention to the balance between freedom of information in the public interest and the need for censorship to protect the individual. You also considered the concept of professionalism within media institutions and its effect on media products.

In Section 3 you explored the development of the media industries and the extent to which new technologies are changing the nature of the media. You also considered the influence on the media industries of economic factors and changes in contemporary lifestyles.

Finally, in Section 4, you looked at training and employment in the UK media industries. You investigated methods of training, changes in the nature of media jobs and the nature and rôle of industry organisations. You also identified the employment legislation relevant to the media industries.

Glossary

advertorial text in a newspaper or magazine which is paid for as advertising, but is designed to look like editorial

bankable an adjective used to describe film stars whose presence in a film guarantees large box office returns

blockbuster a book or film that is outstandingly successful in a mass market

box-office receipts the income generated from ticket sales at a box office

Charter (BBC) the legal document (renewed in 1996) which incorporates the BBC's constitution and guarantees the Corporation's political and economic independence

cooperation the sharing of resources by two or more media companies for mutual benefit

development funding funding – generally from government agencies – for the early stages of a media project, such as the development of a film script

disinformation false information given deliberately to hide the truth

distribution companies companies which control the dissemination of films nationally and internationally and are also responsible for the marketing of these films

distribution rights the authority to market a media product and to receive income from doing so

economic determinants the economic factors which influence all aspects of the production and consumption of media products

franchise agreement the contract by which areas of UK radio and television broadcasting were sold to independent operators

freebie a free gift often given as an incentive to journalists – free air travel, for example

freesheet a newspaper or magazine which generates all its income from advertising and is distributed free of charge to its readers

high definition television picture with enhanced picture quality for more detailed images

house style the distinctive presentation, both of language and graphics, which creates the distinctive identity of a media product

HTML (hypertext markup language) a coding language which is used among other applications in writing World Wide Web pages and setting up links to other sites on the Internet

interactive television TV that the viewer can respond to and control, for example when watching a football match, the viewer would be able to choose which camera angle to watch the match from

local area network (LAN) a network of computers used by an organisation on one site

linear audio and video editing editing video, audio or film when the recording has taken place on a continuous line of tape (compare with digital recording). There is no digital pulse to indicate where the recording starts and stops, the tape has to be wound through to come to the position required

merchandising toys, clothes and other products, using images from popular films and television programmes, which are licensed for sale to manufacturers and provide an additional source of income

monopoly the control of most or all of a business activity by one company in such a way as to dominate the market

multiplex a large cinema with a number of separate screens

news management attempts by individuals or companies to influence how the news is reported

newsprint the low-cost paper used for printing newspapers

NICAM 'near instantaneous compounding multiplex' – a stereo sound system

novelisation the adaptation of a film or television programme into the form of a novel

on-line services information and other services that can be dialled up by the computer

penetration (of market) the extent to which a company or conglomerate has control over a specific market

producer choice the system introduced in 1993 as part of an efficiency drive within the BBC, whereby in-house resource departments compete with outside suppliers in terms of efficiency and cost-effectiveness

product placement the use of a product in a media text (particularly film and television) so that it is visible, although not actually advertised

public interest information which is broadcast or printed for the benefit of the community at large

public service used to describe a media organisation which publishes or broadcasts for the benefit of the public and not to generate income for shareholders

quality threshold the requirement set by the ITC that companies bidding for radio and television franchises should demonstrate a certain level of quality in their programming – for example, guaranteed provision of local news coverage and/or original drama

remit the responsibility imposed on a media company to fulfil a range of set criteria

satellite uplink sending information up to a satellite orbiting Earth to be forwarded to a receiver

state-controlled controlled and/or funded by the government

statutory obligations duties which are fixed or controlled by law

terrestrial television television which is broadcast from the earth rather than from satellites

video rights the authority to market a film or television programme in the form of a video

wide area network (WAN) computers networked across a range of sites – for example, electronic banking is feasible because of WAN within a bank

World Wide Web editor a person who sets up and writes World Wide Web pages for the World Wide Web

Glossary

The following terms are used in the mandatory units for Intermediate and Advanced Media: Communication & Production GNVQ.

Aesthetics
the principles for deciding what is attractive to the senses in art.

The term refers here to the product specifications, primarily in terms of production rather than content, for example:
- clarity of page layout
- effective and appropriate use of colour
- framing, composition and clarity of photographic images
- effective combination of adjacent shots in a video sequence
- sound effects enhancing meaning in a radio programme
- notions of unity and variety.

Audience
i) the complex mass of people who receive media products by reading, listening and watching. The tendency to regard audiences as homogeneous should be avoided. They can be differentiated in terms of age, gender, class, race and lifestyle, for example. Audiences can be seen as a public to serve or a market to be sold to.

ii) the small group of people who attend a student's presentation.

Genre
a style or category of a media form with its own characteristics. Television and radio programmes can be classified into these genres; news, drama, quiz and game shows, soap operas, situation comedies, documentaries. (There are others.)

Often genres can be further divided so that situation comedies could be classified as domestic, anarchic and occupational, for example.

Magazines could be classified as: hobbies, music, female interest, sex, sport, regional, satirical, political, humorous and so on.

The concept is less appropriate for newspapers, but distinction could be made between different kinds of publication:

eg broadsheets and tabloids, or even red masthead tabloids (The Sun, Daily Mirror and Daily Star) and middle-market tabloids (Daily Mail and Daily Express); paid-for papers and freesheets; local and national; evening, morning, weekly.

There can be genres within publications: features and news, leaders and sports reports, for example.

It is important to realise that the definitions of genres are not fixed and that genre characteristics develop and change.

Media codes
codes are a critical description of the rules about ways of communicating in specific media. For example: montage – the putting together of different shots of a film – is a code unique to films. It has its 'rules' such as, in Hollywood-style montage, always starting with an establishing shot, using reverse-angle shots in dialogue, using jump cuts to compress dead time, and using flashbacks and flash-forwards for digression and forecasts.

Codes in journalism would be about the use of headlines, lead paragraphs and lead stories, the use of short paragraphs, the inclusion of direct speech in stories, the use of semi-colloquial English in some tabloid newspapers and so on.

Media conventions
established practices which have often become so familiar that they appear natural. For example: on-screen newsreaders facing the camera, voice-overs in documentaries, interviewees talking to interviewers and being seen in three-quarter shot,

435

news stories having headlines, pop music radio programmes have DJs to introduce records. Often synonymous with media codes.

Narrative structure

narrative is story-telling and stories have structures, from the simplest such as beginning, middle and ending to the more complex such as those identified by Vladimir Propp in his analysis of folk tales; initial situation, dispatch, departure, consent to counteraction, qualifying tests, failure, main test, results of test, unrecognised arrival of hero, glorifying test, return and transfiguration. Structure involves both the chronological sequencing of events and the way those events are narrated:

- the narrator's intervention between raw information and the text, for example advising the reader how to interpret something
- the ways in which characters are introduced and presented
- the points of view from which events are related.

Narrative techniques are not confined to fiction, but are used in factual texts such as news and documentaries.

Paper edit

written, detailed decisions (made from a comprehensive list of recorded material) about what to include in or exclude from an audio-visual production.

Production handbook

a reference book for students on production research that would contain as a minimum:

- details on sources of information, including addresses and contact lists
- guidance on research methods
- research on target audiences
- key legal and ethical considerations
- information on: finding locations; obtaining permission to film, to use other people's copy or pictures; obtaining props; transportation; the criteria for assessing risk.

Proposal

a summary of the content of a production along with an indication of the style of presentation, indicating the need for commentary, music, archive material etc. In a commercial setting proposals are often used as the basis for a commission of work so the proposal would also include information about who the programme is aimed at and the technical requirements and resources.

Representation

literally re-presenting something. Representation is about how and why the media portray people, events, ideas and issues by selecting from a range of possibilities. The media have the power to re-present reality and it matters profoundly how that power is used. It is partly a matter of selection – who is portrayed, who is ignored – and partly a matter of how the portrayal is done – are new-age travellers always presented as troublemakers, for example? how often do they speak for themselves and in what circumstances?

Synopsis

as used here this means a brief summary of the plot or content of a film, video, radio broadcast or audio-visual presentation (see Treatment).

Treatment

a summary of the content of an audio-visual production along with an indication of the style of presentation (humorous, satirical, serious, aggressive and critical and so on). It should also indicate whether there is a need for commentary, incidental music and sound effects (see Synopsis).

Index

This book is part of the **Longman Media: Communication & Production** GNVQ series

Advanced Media authors   **Chris Newbold**
                                Antoinette Moses
                                John Coulter
                                Richard Horsman
                                Philip Holmes
                                Alan Pulverness
                                Matthew Farthing

Series consultants   Patrick Brereton,   *Lecturer, Northampton College*
                        Dr Andrew Crisell BA M. Lit   *Senior Lecturer in Media Studies,*
                                                      University of Sunderland
                        Chris Newbold,   *Lecturer in Mass Communications,*
                                                      University or Leicester

Addison Wesley Longman Ltd
Edinburgh Gate, Edinburgh Way, Harlow, Essex, CM20 2JE
England and Associated Companies throughout the world.

Text © Addison Wesley Longman Ltd 1996

The rights of Chris Newbold, Antoinette Moses, John Coulter, Richard Horsman, Philip Holmes, Alan Pulverness and Matthew Farthing to be identified as authors of this work have been asserted by them in accordance with the Copyright, Design and Patents Act 1988.

First published 1996
ISBN 0582 277949

Design: Gecko Ltd
Set in New Baskerville $10^1/_2$ / $14^1/_2$ pt
Printed in Great Britain by Pindar plc, Scarborough

The publisher's policy is to use paper manufactured from sustainable forests.

Acknowledgements

We are grateful to the following for permission to reproduce text, photos and other copyright material:

Page 6AL	Popperfoto
Page 6AR	Popperfoto
Page 6BL	Telegraph Colour Library
Page 6BC	Telegraph Colour Library
Page 6BR	Telegraph Colour Library
Page 9	© Crown Copyright, reproduced with the permission of the controller of HMSO
Page 10R	Peugeot
Page 10L	Porsche Cars
Page 13	The Kobal Collection
Page 30	BARB
Page 31	Ronald Grant Archive
Page 32	Ronald Grant Archive
Page 38	The British Board of Film Classification
Page 58	Mam, Red Flannel Films, 1988
Page 60	National Readership Survey (NRS Ltd)
Page 65	by permission of The Press Standards Board of Finance Ltd
Page 66	Comedia Consultancy Ltd
Page 67	City of Phoenix, Film Office
Page 68	Central Film Facilities
Page 71	Musicians' Union
Page 72A	Harper Collins Publishers Ltd
Page 72B	Copyright © Guinness Publishing Ltd 1996
Page 75	M8 Magazine
Page 77	John Coulter
Page 80B	Brookhall Historical Farm
Page 82	BBC Radio 4, Atlantic 252
Page 86	Transperience
Page 87	Pulse Productions
Page 113	Down Democrat 29.9.93
Page 124	Trevor Clifford
Page 125	The *Guardian*, *Daily Express*
Page 126	The *Guardian* 1.4.96/Clare Dyer
Page 140	The *Sun* 5.4.96/Photo of Mike Antonucci © John Bushell
Page 165	Jonathan Taylor/Cloud Nine Photographers
Page 169	Pulse Productions
Page 174	Pulse Productions
Page 175–6	Pulse Productions
Page 184	Jonathan Taylor/Cloud Nine Photographers
Page 190	Trevor Clifford
Page 191	Trevor Clifford
Page 209	Jonathan Taylor/Cloud Nine Photographers
Page 279	Trevor Clifford
Page 281	*Broadcast*/BARB
Page 282	Trevor Clifford
Page 287	Audit Bureau of Circulations Ltd
Page 289	Nationional Readership Survey (NRS Ltd)
Page 292	Steve Bell
Page 293	*Radio Times*
Page 295A	Ford Motor Co Ltd
Page 295B	Lever Brothers Ltd
Page 296A	Highland Spring
Page 296B	Health & Safety Executive/MAP plc
Page 302	Leeds Postcards
Page 303	The *Guardian* 14.3.1996
Page 309	*Independent on Sunday* 4.2.96
Page 313	British Film Institute
Page 314A	British Film Institute
Page 314B	HMSO, 1992
Page 315A	CAA/NRS
Page 315B	Policy Studies Institute, 1986
Page 317	Raymond Kent, *Measuring Media Audiences*, Routledge, 1994
Page 318	Peter Chisnall, *Marketing Research*, McGraw-Hill 1992
Page 321	Peter Chisnall, *Marketing Research*, McGraw-Hill 1992
Page 322	Peter Chisnall, *Marketing Research*, McGraw-Hill 1992
Page 323	*Radio Times*
Page 332	S. Marjaro, *Essence of Marketing*, Prentice Hall 1993
Page 338	Gareth Boden
Page 340	Express Newspapers plc, *Private Eye*, Classic FM, *Classic Bike, Kerrang!*
Page 341	Penguin Books Ltd
Page 342A	The *Guardian*, 24.10.94
Page 342B	Radio Advertising Bureau
Page 345	National Readership Surveys (NRS Ltd)
Page 356	Admiral Insurance Services Ltd
Page 360A	R.J Watson, Marketing, Chambers, 1988
Page 376	British Film Institute
Page 377A	British Film Institute
Page 380A	Datastream
Page 382	The *Guardian* 16.2.96
Page 384	Ronald Grant Archive
Page 387	BBC
Page 390	*Radio Times*
Page 391	© *Times* Newspapers Ltd, 1996
Page 392	The *Guardian* 18.12.95
Page 397	The *Guardian*, 1992
Page 398	The Cable Communications Association
Page 400A	The *Guardian* 29.1.91
Page 400B	*Daily Mail*, 25.2.92/Solo Syndication
Page 409	Channel Four Television, Brookside Productions Ltd
Page 411	Posy Simmonds/Index on Censorship
Page 413	Telegraph Colour Library
Page 415L	Telegraph Colour Library
Page 415R	The *Observer*, 28.1.96
Page 418	Tony Stone Images
Page 419	The *Guardian* 20.6.94
Page 421	Popperfoto
Page 424	Skillset

We were unable to trace the copyright holders of the following and would be grateful for any information that would enable us to do so.
Pages 58, 61, 80A, 307/8, 334, 359,377B, 425
Picture researcher: Louise Edgeworth